Science &Ideology in the Policy Sciences

Paul Diesing

ALDINE PUBLISHING COMPANY
ALDINE NEW YORK

ACKNOWLEDGMENTS

Portions of the following work have been presented at seminars and colloquia at Buffalo (sociology), M.I.T. (International relations) and Notre Dame (economics) and the comments made on those occasions have broadened my understanding of the subject. Clark Murdock's extensive comments and discussions have been most helpful. Mark Huddleston, Ian Mitroff, Richard Tobin, and Paul Zarembka have read and commented on all or part of some draft.

H
51
D53

First published 1982
Aldine Publishing Company
200 Saw Mill River Road
Hawthorne, New York 10532

ISBN 0-202-30301-2 cloth; 0-202-30302-6 paper

Library of Congress Catalog Number 81-71341

Printed in the United States of America
10 9 8 7 6 5 4 3 2 1

CONTENTS

Dedicated to Daniel Ellsberg
Heroic benefactor of the social sciences

In my view . . . everything depends on grasping and expressing the ultimate truth not only as Substance but as Subject as well.

The embodiments which a culture seems to have left behind it, it still possesses in the depths of its present. . . .

Hegel (and Freud)

All that Hegelian stuff and nonsense.

Robinson

One Social Studies of Science

I. The Study of Science

In the fall of 1975, about the time I was beginning work on this book, a new professional society was formed. It was called "the Society for Social Studies of Science," and Robert Merton was its first president. This society institutionalized an attitude that had been developing for well over ten years, and that underlies the present volume. The attitude is that science is a human activity and therefore is a proper subject matter for social studies. Science is one of the things that people do, and therefore it can be studied in the same way that other human activities are studied.

   Membership in the society is open to any student of science in any of the social sciences, history, or philosophy. This rule institutionalizes the recognition that all branches of social science have something to contribute to the study of science, just as they all contribute to the study of man in general. First, science is a cognitive activity, so cognitive psychologists are uniquely qualified to study it. Second, it is also a goal-directed activity, aiming at objective truth, so the philosopher's clarification of goals, methods, and norms and his evaluation of specific practices are also relevant. Scientific activity always occurs in a context of personality-in-role, so personality psychologists and social psychologists have a contribution to make. Science is a social activity, occurring most directly in small groups but also in

1

larger associational networks and institutions, which are the subject matter of sociologists. As with all social activities, decisions must be made about resource allocations and allocation policies ("science policy"), and these are political and economic decisions, made in accordance with power and influence distributions and on the basis of information flow through communication networks. The goals, norms, and technical understandings on which science policy decisions are based are part of the culture of science. Finally, historians help us understand the social system and culture of science by tracing its development from the past into the present; they also present science systems and cultures from other times and places, for comparative understanding of our own system. Note that the comparative understanding of man and its attendant sense of cultural relativity that has ordinarily been provided by anthropologists is provided in this case by historians of science.

To include all these specialists in a single organization suggests that they each have something to learn from the others. It also suggests the possibility of combining several specialized disciplines in a single study of science; or rather it recognizes the fact that such interdisciplinary studies are already common—for example sociological-psychological-philosophical (Mitroff, 1974), historical-sociological (Merton, 1949), anthropological-philosophical (Maruyama, 1978), philosophical-historical (Toulmin, 1961; Feyerabend, 1975).

Social studies of science also make explicit something that is only implicit in social science generally. When social scientists study social science, *we are studying ourselves*. The object of study and the studying subject are identical. When we investigate the history of social science over the last several decades, as the present work does, we investigate our own collective past; *we write autobiography*. The purpose of such writing is not that of the memoir writer, namely to report previously unknown facts in such a selective way as to justify one's career for others; it is rather that of the therapy patient, to deepen self-understanding by seeing how we have come to be what we now are. By re-examining familiar events from the distance of a decade or more we can perhaps see more clearly what we were then doing and becoming; and by tracing old struggles and compromises into the present we are sensitized to their present, disguised influence on us.

In a more general way all social science is self-study, since we are all part of mankind. However, "mankind" is such a vague abstraction that it does not capture much of our identities or self-definitions, so it is easy to distinguish ourselves as scientists from those nonscientists we study. The scientist/society or self/other distinction runs all through the social sciences, though it varies in sharpness. The distinction is sharpest in the experimental method, where the experimenter treats his S's very differently from the way he treats himself. It is weakest in participant observation, where the scientist becomes a member of the group she is studying and studies herself along with the others; but even here a certain detachment or otherness necessarily remains.

In experimentation, where the self/other distinction is very sharp, self-study may even increase the sharpness of the distinction. Specifically, the experimental study of experimenters, pioneered by Rosenthal (1966), can be used by experimenters to become more self-conscious and sophisticated in their research tactics; but if the S's are continued as naive as before, the E/S difference will have become even greater. There is a fundamental error here. The S's may not be as naive as the E thinks (Wax, 1975) and experimentation then becomes a game of mutual deception and trickery. The S's pretend to be as naive as they are supposed to be, while trying to guess the real purpose of the experiment; the E tries to guess whether the S's have seen through his deception, while also trying to control his unintended influences on the S's and avoid self-deception. Is that science?

The advantage of explicitly studying ourselves, as in participant observation and social studies of social science, is that both internal and external avenues of investigation are open to us. We can treat ourselves as subjects, noting our reactions, perceptions, and strategies; and we can treat ourselves as objects ("those other scientists"), counting citations, constructing sociometric nets, and content-analyzing our writings. Each avenue can supplement the other: we know what citations mean because we ourselves have cited others in our works, and the objective meaning of strategies appears in their objectifications, the works of science.

II. The Study of Ideology

The purpose of the present work is to examine how ideology operates in the policy sciences. By "policy sciences" I mean economics, political science, and sociology, plus occasional fragments of other fields. By "operates" I mean the way in which ideologies influence the conduct of inquiry.

I use "ideology" in Schumpeter's sense to include both values and cognitive categories. The cognitive component for Schumpeter consisted of a preliminary "vision" of a set of phenomena to be studied

(Schumpeter, "Science and Ideology", 1949; *History of Economic Analysis*, 1954, Part I, Chapter 4). Keynes' vision, for example, was of Britain as an advanced capitalist society with declining investment opportunities and excessive thriftiness, whose economy tended to stagnate because of deficient consumer demand and investment (1954, Part V, Chapter 5). This account of Keynes' vision is itself shaped by Schumpeter's own vision; Schumpeter interpreted Keynes as failing to include the all-important entrepreneur in his vision of society. For Schumpeter society without the entrepreneur is *Hamlet* without the Prince of Denmark; such a society inevitably stagnates, as Keynes saw.

Ideologies derive in some fashion from the scientist's relation to the dominant classes in society: they "are likely to glorify the interests and activities of the classes that are in a position to assert themselves" (Schumpeter, 1954, p. 35). "The public mind reflects more or less treacherously . . . the class structure of the corresponding society and the group minds or attitudes that form in it" (1954, p. 38). Schumpeter does not develop this point, which he derives from Marx, and I shall try to work it out more carefully than he does.

Ideologies have cognitive, cathectic, and moral components. The cognitive component is the vision, bringing out certain phenomena for study and providing the categories for studying them. The cathectic component is our pro or con attitude toward these phenomena. This component is a powerful source of ideological distortion in science: "love distorts indeed, but hate distorts still more" (1954, p. 43). The moral component is the one that locates problems to be studied and provides the criteria for solution.

Many policy scientists emphasize almost exclusively the cathectic and moral components of ideology and accordingly regard the effect of ideological bias on science as altogether negative. Strong feelings for or against a phenomenon necessarily interfere with objective study; and valuations, inevitable for human beings, also distort and ought to be separated from one's scientific work to some extent. There is disagreement on the issue of how much value neutrality is possible or desirable, and I shall take up this issue in succeeding chapters. But mainly I wish to study the cognitive component, the vision that focuses on certain phenomena and the categories that control the study of those phenomena.

My interest is descriptive, evaluative, and prescriptive. I intend to locate the main ideologies that now occur in the policy sciences and describe the effects of each ideology on scientific work. I shall show 1) how each ideology produces a preference for certain problems, methods, and hypotheses; 2) how it sensitizes scientists to certain phenomena and suggests certain interpretations of those phenomena; and 3) conversely, how it closes off other phenomena and concepts from investigation and testing. I shall also show how ideologies produce distorted communication, allowing some concepts to be communicated but blocking or distorting others.

Accordingly, Part I is descriptive and evaluative. It takes up each current ideology in its historical order of occurrence during the period 1930-1975. The ideology will be located in the work of a prominent practitioner or school, and then the effects of that ideology will be traced in the work of the school. Then there will be a tentative evaluation of the way in which its ideology limits and facilitates the work of the school. Chapter 11 summarizes the historical findings of Part I, and Table 11.1 provides a guide listing the ideologies to be discussed.

Part II attempts to develop the policy implications of Part I. Since ideologies make both positive and negative contributions to science, it should be possible to devise a policy to increase their positive and decrease their negative contributions. To find such a policy, I first attempt to clarify the goal of the policy sciences—truth—during the period since 1930. Then I examine several policies proposed by others and end with my own proposal. The policy will deal with the organization of our own research, or, in Churchman's terminology, with the design of our inquiring system.

A study of the effects of ideology on science must distinguish ideology from all the other components of inquiring systems that may have similar effects. This is where social studies of science are so important, since these other components must themselves have been studied with some precision. The present work therefore builds on other social studies of science, and is defective (among other reasons) because many aspects of science have not yet been adequately studied.

Several examples will illustrate the problem of distinguishing ideology from other components of science, a problem that runs throughout this book.

First, both ideology and scientific activity are affected by personality in role to some extent. I use the expression "personality in role" to remind the reader that personality is always composed of a repertoire of roles and identifications—son, daughter, sister—and thus is social from the start. This means that the effects of ideology on science are included in the more general effects of personality on science. But those specific effects due to ideology will then be quite similar to the other effects due more directly to personality. And since the effects of personality on science have only recently begun to be studied (Fisch,

1977; Mitroff, 1974; Mitroff and Kilman, 1978) they are imperfectly understood as yet and can easily be included in ideological effects by mistake.

As an example of personality factors, Mitroff and Ong have discussed and illustrated the macho-masculine syndrome common in science and scholarship (Mitroff, 1974, pp. 130–131, 140–142 summarizing a David McClelland article, 144–145, 264–265, etc.; Ong, 1974). In Ong's older tradition, the Talmudic scholar using standard pilpul techniques on a sacred passage to defend his interpretations and to attack other interpretations, or the PhD candidate defending his thesis in Latin against all comers, is proving his masculinity. In Mitroff's interview data the physical scientists exhibit the "masculine" attributes of hard-driving, aggressive, critical, domineering attack on others' theories and defense of their own theories. They treat science as a game against Nature—and against other scientists—which they try to win by breaking down or outflanking the opponents' defenses and by devising their own impregnable theory. Underlying this attitude toward science is a sense of oneself as distinct, even isolated, from others and potentially open to attack. In an aggressive society it is necessary to have one's verbal defenses always ready to meet an attack, and to discourage attacks by gaining a reputation for quick belligerence. Comradeship is possible only between men who have proved their masculinity in repeated encounters of this sort.

The "generational revolt" theme of Schumpeter and Feuer is another aspect of this masculinity syndrome (Schumpeter, 1954, p. 46; Feuer, 1975, Chapter 3). The pervading ideology is emphatically taught to the new generation as the only respectable way to think, and those who refuse to think that way are rejected as screwballs or incompetents. That is, the previous generation, the fathers, believe they already possess the truth and are not willing to yield its custody to their successors. The new generation must establish its masculinity, its worthiness to possess the truth, by defeating the fathers' theory and asserting a new one in its place—and the fathers must resist. Consequently, new ideologies break into science suddenly rather than taking shape gradually.

The psychological studies of Mitroff, Roe, McClelland, and others were primarily of natural scientists; when I consider social scientists I find a very important "feminine" component, and in fact a broad distribution from strongly masculine natural science types through various mixtures to strongly feminine types. The "feminine" component includes empathy for others' feelings and ideas, acceptance of the state of affairs one is studying and inclusion of oneself in it, the search for response from a significant other or community, and acceptance of others into that community. The feminine component produces a different kind of science from that produced by Mitroff's macho scientists, and the various mixtures produce still further differences. The difference in personality distribution is in fact the most important distinction between the natural and social sciences known to me, though of course this difference must necessarily express itself in a number of other ways.[1]

The most obvious expression of personality differences is in one's choice of method. The "masculine" scientist, with his sense of separateness from potentially hostile others, tends to feel most at home with an experimental method. Experimentation makes a sharp distinction between the active experimenter and the passive subject, and its manifold controls provide a bastion behind which the experimenter can conceal himself and control the world. The "feminine" scientist gravitates to some type of participant observation, in which the empathetic scientist learns to participate in the subject's activity and comes to understand it from the inside. Statistical surveys and interviews, with their varying combinations of empathy, receptiveness, and statistical controls, are emotionally appropriate to mixed personalities.

Methodological preferences can thus be interpreted as an expression of personality factors. However, some ideologies also imply preferences for particular methods. Now, suppose we are studying a school of scientists who use causal modeling and multivariate analysis, who aggressively assert the scientific superiority of their method and their theory, and who in particular lose no opportunity to expose the inadequacies of earlier theories. Are we observing primarily the expression of masculine assertiveness, or of ideology, or indeed of group loyalty and ethnocentrism? An easy answer is that personality and group loyalty provide the emotional drive and ideology provides the cognitive categories. However, this distinction tends to evaporate in practice, since drives express themselves through the use of cognitive and logical categories. A more careful answer would require the systematic application of analytic techniques to writings and life histories to locate the dominant personality factors. Until such studies are done we cannot reliably distinguish ideology from personality.

Second, cognitive factors such as wishful thinking and cognitive balance are continually operative in scientific thought, as in all human thought, and produce distortions that might mistakenly be attributed to ideology. Two examples will illustrate. Lewis Feuer, in his bitter tirade against the New Left (1975), has occasion to refer to

Georg Lukacs. He has Lukacs asserting that even if all of Marxism's empirical predictions were invalidated he would still believe in the truth of Marxism, and Feuer comments: "In other words, the higher 'truth' of Marxism transcends all commonplace scientific verifications" (1975, p. 105). In reality, Lukacs' words present an entirely different assertion:

> Let us assume that recent research had proved once and for all that every one of Marx's individual theses was false. Even if this were to be proved every serious "orthodox" Marxist would still be able to accept all such modern conclusions without reservation and hence dismiss every single one of Marx's theses—without being compelled for a single minute to renounce his orthodoxy. Orthodox Marxism, therefore, does not imply the uncritical acceptance of the results of Marx's investigations. It is not the belief in this or that thesis, not the exegesis of a "sacred" book. On the contrary, orthodoxy refers exclusively to *method* (Lukacs, 1971, pp. xxv–xxvi).

Lukacs is asserting that Marxism is a research program which submits all of its hypotheses to criticism and scientific test and holds no proposition immune to empirical falsification. Feuer has twisted this antidogmatic statement into its exact opposite. To see Lukacs' meaning, substitute "survey research" for "Marxism" or "Marx."

The cognitive process here is a common one. Feuer believes that all Marxists are dogmatic antiscientific ideologists; Lukacs is a Marxist so he must be antiscientific; and sure enough, here is an example of Lukacs' dogmatism.

Another example comes from an article of mine on objectivity (1972). I reported that at SUNY-Buffalo clinical interviews are taped and replayed immediately afterward, so that the therapist and patient can together explore their interaction. I was mistaken. The replay is for the therapist and his teacher; thus the therapist rather than the patient gains in self-awareness.

These are examples of wishful thinking in which one sees what he wishes to see or expects to see. It may be that ideology in some cases provides the wish that distorts perception, but the distortion itself is a common cognitive process. It can be corrected without changing the ideology (or other source of the wish), which then expresses itself in some other fashion. Consequently, examples of cognitive error or distortion, if they are correctable, need not be listed as effects of ideology. They are accidental effects, since ideology is neither necessary nor sufficient to produce them. However, they can sometimes be clues to the nature of one's ideology, as in the above examples.

Next, ideology always operates in a social context and so must be distinguished from other shared understandings and traditions—shared problems, shared mentors and opponents, shared methods and techniques, and so on. For example, I shall argue later that Keynes' *General Theory* (1936) represents a shift of ideology as compared with his neoclassical contemporaries like Lionel Robbins, Henry Simons, and Wassily Leontief. However, a good deal of Keynes' differences with his contemporaries derive from his membership in the "Cambridge school" along with Joan Robinson, Roy Harrod, R.F. Kahn, and Piero Sraffa. This school derived from Alfred Marshall and carried over some of his important ideas and preferences: a preference for the empirical over the formal in the economist's empirical-formal dilemma; a consequent preference for empirically correct assumptions even at the cost of theoretical looseness and confusion and loss of generality; a willingness to include psychological and even moral elements in one's model of economic man; and an interest in the short run and short-run dynamics and a skepticism about the usefulness of long-run equilibrium models. (I am following Parsons' interpretation of Marshall here, not Friedman's.) In addition, Keynes' long and close association with the British Treasury and deep interest in money and banking distinguished him from the other Cambridge economists and relate him to neoclassical monetarists like Milton Friedman. Somehow the ideological elements in Keynes' thought must be distinguished from those other shared understandings and interests. The basic solution is controlled comparison: see what Keynes shared with non-Cambridge, nonmonetarist, formalist Keynesians like Domar and Kalecki; see what distinguishes Keynes, Robinson, etc., from non-Keynesian students of Marshall such as Pigou. In general, sociological factors such as citations, collaborations, and shared teachers define schools and suggest shared ideology, but conceptual analysis locates actual ideological similarity or difference.

Another distinction to keep in mind is the one between ideology and truth. To show that certain ideas have an ideological origin does not imply anything about their truth or falsity. The question of truth is settled by cooperative processes of empirical testing and criticism of tests, not by tracing origins. The same ideology may produce some theories that stand up to empirical tests and others that do not stand up. I agree entirely with Schumpeter's argument on this point (1954, p. 43). To be sure, the process of testing is also strongly contaminated and distorted by ideology; here I disagree with Schumpeter. Perhaps the most important reason for studying ideology in science is to locate its effects on the testing process, the process of finding facts and comparing them with theories, so we can improve awareness and control of ideological influences.

A final difficulty in the study of ideology is its negative emotional connotation for many people. Ideology is seen as bad. It is something that other people may be cursed with, but not I. To locate ideological elements in someone's thinking is to make an accusation and to provoke an angry denial. It's a quick way to make enemies, and who needs enemies? Besides, the strong emotions that are activated interfere with conceptual clarity.

To avoid this problem I shall drop the concept "ideology" and replace it with the concepts of standpoint and perspective as Mannheim (1936) has developed them. These concepts include everything Schumpeter and others have meant by "ideology" without, I hope, the negative emotions. In what follows, terms such as "ideological" and "ideologue" will appear only as they occur in the theories being analyzed in these chapters. They will appear as represented in others' theories but not in mine. In addition the word "ideology" will reappear in Chapter Twelve as part of Mannheim's "ideology/utopia" pair, but those are different concepts.

III. The Study of Standpoints and Perspectives

We conceive the scientist or school of scientists as identifying with or relating to a certain location in society and as viewing society spread out around that location. This location I call the standpoint. The location is where "we" or people like ourselves are. Like ourselves, the people there are active; they plan, make decisions, and act; they are selves or subjects. The surrounding world is the object to be acted upon, the other, the system. The object takes on certain characteristics from the fact that it is Object, the to-be-acted-on; it takes on other characteristics from the fact that it is studied from a certain standpoint; and it takes on yet other characteristics from its degree of sameness or difference with the Subject.

For example, for many specialists in international politics (such as George and Smoke, 1974), the Subject is the US Government and more particularly the President and the State Department. The Other, the International System, is the set of governments of the other major powers. Some of these, such as Britain, are similar to the US; others, such as the Soviet Union, are very different. Congress is also part of the Other, the to-be-acted-upon. George and Smoke's problem is "How well has US deterrence worked in the last few decades?" The US executive is the actor, practicing a deterrence strategy well or poorly; George and Smoke wish to evaluate the actor's performance in order to improve it. Other governments are actors too—from this standpoint the Self/Other relation is rather close—but they are different sorts of actors. They may, for one thing, be aggressive—otherwise there would be nothing to deter and no reason to write the book—but the US by definition cannot be aggressive. "I" cannot be an aggressor. Consequently, others cannot practice deterrence; they practice counterdeterrence, a response to US deterrence strategy. Also their strategies are not as well known as ours; their strategies must be estimated or pieced together and may not be known at all. It is difficult to estimate the other's strategy because other governments may practice deception as part of that strategy, employing their scientists and historians for that purpose also. The US government may also practice deception on others and even on Congress, but we do not of course deceive ourselves so our strategy is known by definition.

The scientist need not always locate himself personally at the standpoint from which he views society, but he must necessarily have some close relation to that standpoint. If he were distant from it—the Soviet government for a conservative US political scientist—he could not effectively conceive it as Self, as Subject. In the George and Smoke case the relation is that of advisor to the US State Department. The purpose of the knowledge provided in the George and Smoke book is to enable the US Executive to practice deterrence more effectively.

The Perspective is the angle of vision from the standpoint; it is the way the world looks from that location. Perspectives are always embodied in a set of categories that distinguish the main features of society. One feature that is almost always prominent is the Subject, the part of the world that is here where we are. Another feature is the world out there, the Object or System. The System in turn is usually divided into several interacting parts. The Subject, the part that is here, may be a prominent interacting part of the System or it may be more sharply distinguished from the System as its opposite. Finally, there must be a category that locates the scientist and relates him or her to both Subject and Object.

The perspective or set of categories must be distinguished from the theories developed by use of the categories. The latter, the theories, are the results of scientific research, while the categories are the underlying presuppositions of research. For some people the concept "ideology" includes both categories and theories, and becomes synonymous with "system of beliefs." The main difficulty with this usage is that a variety of theories can be constructed on the same categorial foundation, so that the study of ideology becomes rather broad. The present work focuses on basic categories, though a few familiar theories are discussed to illustrate the use of categories.

Each set of categories is a way of thinking about society. It brings certain aspects of society into focus and structures them in a certain way. At the most fundamental level, some perspectives focus attention on the Subject and others on the Object. In the former case science is the study of subjectivity, of free, creative, rational human action and its consequences; in the latter case science is a study of the causes, correlations, and dynamics of an external reality.

Conversely, each set of categories leaves some aspects of society out of focus and makes it difficult or even impossible to study them. For instance, a science of causes and correlations tends to have an awkward time dealing with creativity or intentionality, and a science of free human action tends to have trouble studying the unconscious determinants of action. The difficulties tend to be rationalized or explained away by arguments that deny the existence of such things, or arguments that such things are inherently beyond the scope of science, or arguments that such things ought not be studied.

The strengths of a perspective consist of its ability to bring certain aspects of society into clear focus, thereby making their empirical study possible; the weaknesses of a perspective consist of the way it distorts or hides other aspects of society.

The question of the strengths and weaknesses of particular perspectives is a major concern of the present work. We shall be concerned, first with locating these strengths and weaknesses and second with suggesting what organization of perspectives in science will maximize the strengths and minimize the weaknesses.

Each standpoint and perspective also includes a set of values; these will be taken up in Chapter Thirteen, while Part I concentrates on cognitive factors.

The concepts of standpoint and perspective are my suggested answer to several puzzles that have long concerned me and others. One is the existence of interminable and highly emotional controversies among social scientists: controversies between neoclassicists, Keynesians, and institutionalists; between exchange theorists, functionalists, and ethnomethodologists; between pluralists and elitists, world system theorists and national development theorists, growth and no-growth advocates. Very little intelligent discussion occurs in these controversies. Typically a polemicist constructs an absurd distortion of the opposing theory, conclusively refutes it, and thereafter ignores it except for occasional expressions of contempt and further refutation.

The opponents in turn reject the characterization of their theory, the method, the data, and the refutation, and respond with their own refutation and distortions. Sometimes there are debates, in which the two sides talk past each other. The pluralists and elitists both long ago concluded that their opponents' theories had been conclusively refuted; monetarists are convinced that all the evidence confirms their theory, and their opponents are equally convinced of the opposite; and so on.

I formerly believed that these controversies resulted from differences of method, which made the method and data of one school seem unscientific to the other (Diesing, 1971, Chapter 1). I called for a more tolerant appreciation of different methods and for the different kinds of theory that result. Unfortunately in some cases such as the pluralists and elitists there are no substantial differences of method to account for the misunderstanding and the animosity. I now believe that differences of method are one expression of more fundamental differences of standpoint and perspective. It is differences of perspective plus their associated value differences that prevent tolerance, understanding, and communication. Each school must translate the doctrines of an opposing school into the concepts of its own perspective to understand them, and the result is some kind of distortion and moral outrage; and similarly with the reply.

Here personality factors come in and confuse the issue. Interminable controversies continue in part because many scientists like to fight with words. They come alive emotionally in an attack and defense atmosphere; their creativity is activated in conflict. These people do not want to resolve controversies, so they keep them going. I suggest that this form of the masculinity drive can provide the motivation for a controversy while perspectives provide the cognitive weapons used in argument.

Another puzzle is the failure of some theories to develop for a decade or more, after which they suddenly leap ahead. For example, George and Smoke (1974, p. 504) observe that deterrence theory has never developed beyond its initial starting point, and then proceed to develop it (see also George, Hall, and Simons, 1971). Now, Alex George is a brilliant political scientist, but his predecessors in deterrence theory were not stupid by any means; why could they not imagine the additions he has made? Another example is the theory of the firm, long stagnant until Herbert Simon and associates produced their tremendous new ideas in the 1950's. I suggest that in these cases the dominant perspective set limits to innovations, limits that were transcended by a shift of perspective.

I now illustrate the standpoint-perspective concepts with a brief impressionistic treatment of two marginal standpoints.

A standpoint that scarcely occurs in economics but is present in sociology and political science, especially international politics, is one that may be called "traditionalist conservatism" or "traditionalism." Exemplars are Robert Nisbet, Leo Strauss and his numerous disciples, Eric Voegelin, Dante Germino, Carl Friedrich, F.G. Wilson. Their standpoint is the Wise Man: Plato and Aristotle . . . Adam Smith, Tocqueville and Marx, J.S. Mill . . . Weber. The Wise Man has seen deeper into the abiding structure of social reality than ordinary men. He has gotten beyond transient superficialities and confusing appearances, the shadows on the cave wall, and has grasped some part of the eternal truths. Collectively, these men have produced the great ideas that lie at the foundation of social science, whose details remain to be worked out by lesser men. A few of them—Aristotle as against Plato for Leo Strauss, Marx as against Tocqueville for Nisbet (1966, p. viii)—may have grasped an essentially negative or perverse or opposite side of reality; but these false truths are just as important as the others, both for completeness and because the tension they create has stimulated the other wise men to make their greatest discoveries.

The traditionalist conservatives themselves are the Interpreters of the Wise Men. The task of the interpreter is to make the ideas of the Wise Men intelligible to ordinary people, and also to correct the erroneous interpretations that have built up over the centuries. Since ordinary men are not wise enough to see through appearances to the eternal realities, they also are not wise enough to understand these truths fully when they read them in the Great Books. Thus the truths get corrupted, and transient fads or old errors are read into the great books as truths. In addition, Leo Strauss has emphasized that most of the Wise Men lived under tyrannical governments and had to speak in parables to avoid censorship. A comparison of Hegel's recently published notes for his lectures on the Philosophy of Right with the more conservative version that passed the Prussian censor (which has been regarded as authentic Hegel ever since) confirms this thesis. The Interpreters must then interpret the parables and add the hidden meaning to bring out the full doctrine of the great books.

The Object to be known from this standpoint is the set of eternal truths about human nature and society, the laws of motion of society, the Ideas, Nisbet's fundamental concepts—Community, Authority, Hierarchy, the Sacred, Alienation—the nature of Justice and the Good, and so on. This object exists behind or beyond the confused and changing appearances that captivate ordinary attention, and makes these appearances intelligible insofar as they are worth noticing at all.

If we examine the Subject/Object relation we see that the Object clearly dominates the Subject in this case. The Object, the system of laws or truths, is unchanging, complete, perfect; subjects, those who know, are short-lived, imperfect, and continually changing. Indeed, the goal of science is to assimilate the Subject into the Object—to live in that heavenly city, as Plato would say. Wise men come closest to this ideal, because they have most nearly purged their thinking of error and thereby raised themselves to the level of comprehending theoretically the truth as a whole. Lesser men are a greater distance from the Object and more preoccupied with the petty and changing details of daily life.

A striking example of the dominance of the Object over the Subject is Popper's assertion that objective knowledge does not need a subject to exist; "Knowledge in the objective sense is *knowledge without a knower:* it *is knowledge without a knowing subject*" (1972, p. 109). Knowledge for Popper exists in Plato's timeless world of Being or logical truth, which Popper calls the Third World. Wise Men can apprehend portions of this world, study them and discover other portions of the truth thereby, but if men all died or turned their attention elsewhere the truth would still be there. Truth does not vanish when we stop thinking about it. Popper's traditionalist standpoint explains his intense animosity toward social studies of science, which study the knowing subject (for example, Popper, 1970, pp. 57–58). For Popper the study of the Subject is the path away from the truth into the changing world of appearance, fashion, non-being, the Second World.

Hegel is the Wise Man who has emphasized the negative or perverse or opposite side of traditionalist doctrine. Instead of extolling the Third World of eternal, objective truth he has argued that the Subject, man, creates the system of truths and indeed society as his own objectification, thereby indirectly making himself. For Hegel the goal of science is the return from the Object to the Subject, the use of our objectifications to know ourselves. All social science for Hegel is self-knowledge, study of the Subject. This perverse, opposite idea of Hegel's has not sat well with the Interpreters, who have pointed out that the Subject/Object distinction is a temporary appearance only and vanishes in the Absolute (Schelling's absolute, not Hegel's); so Hegel must have meant that man should contemplate the Absolute, the perfect system of eternal truths. So it goes.

The proper organization of science for traditionalist conservatives is hierarchical. At the top are the Wise Men; but they are all dead, and only their collected works remain as the ultimate source of truth. Next come the great interpreters—Jacques Maritain, Leo Strauss, Ernest Barker, Walter Kaufmann, and so on down through lesser interpreters. Next come the teachers, who have sat at the feet of some interpreter and read the others; and finally the students. Natural movement is up the hierarchy as one's wisdom increases. Most students carry their received wisdom into public life and move no further up the ladder, but a few of the wisest students become teachers. A very few of the teachers become interpreters, finally publishing their book on Locke or Weber after having studied all the other interpreters and written commentaries on a few of them. Once in a generation a Great Interpreter appears, opening new insights into the whole great tra- dition. And who knows, it is not impossible that even in this century a new Wise Man might appear, synthesizing the tradition anew.

The Object visible from this standpoint is the Great Ideas. Two areas are obviously invisible. One is historical novelty in society, as distinguished from new instances of old truths. There may in fact not have been any historical novelty recently; but if some were to occur the traditionalist would be constrained to interpret it either as a new instance of familiar phenomena, or as a passing trifle unworthy of serious attention. History necessarily becomes the moving image of eternity. See, for example, Nisbet's comments in Alberston, 1975: there is nothing new about student demonstrators of the 1960's.

His perspective constrains the traditionalist to make these interpre- tations. If he is to rise to the rank of Interpreter he must continually train himself to see the eternal in the passing, to concentrate on essentials and ignore trivia.

The second area blocked from observation is the interpreter's position in his own social situation, also his own personality, his own cognitive processes. Interpreters must lose themselves in the ideas of the Wise Men to transmit these ideas as faithfully as possible. Any additions that they themselves make, other than an application of the ideas to our time, are either a sign of intellectual inadequacy or a sign that they themselves are claiming to be new Wise Men. One interpreter may point out another interpreter's personal contributions and suggest that these are caused by the interpreter's personality and social situation, but this is always a criticism, not a scientific investigation. The scientific question always is, Have the ideas, the truths, the laws, been interpreted properly?

But how have the Wise Men been selected? By the Interpreters, of course, but on what principle? How did Tocqueville get onto Nisbet's list, and why was he selected as the positive to Marx's negative? Here an important contribution has been made by the Interpreter, the Subject, which cannot be studied by the traditionalist. The actual position is the reverse of the official one: the Wise Men are dependent on the Interpreters for their status, not vice versa; Interpreters, not Wise Men, select the positive and negative eternal truths, and read their own ideas into the great books.

A minor standpoint, found at the fringes of economics in the work of such economists as E.C. Harwood, can be called the hoarding consciousness. It is that of the man who has managed to accumulate some savings through decades of hard work and abstinence. His reward consists in seeing his pile grow year after year, and in the knowledge that his old age is now secure against financial misfortune. This consciousness merges into Keynes's "rentier" consciousness, the standpoint of the man who treats his pile as capital and expects to live off its dividends.

The object of knowledge for this standpoint is the financial system which determines and sustains the value of money; the focus of attention is the value of money and particularly the value of one's hoard. Savings have the highest reality; they represent real labor and real abstinence and promise security against life's uncertainties. Savings are mine and they are my protection against the world. But savings are not safe; their value depends on the value of money, and this is constantly under attack by all sorts of speculators, businessmen, labor leaders, and misguided economists with an influence on government. The value of money is in fact constantly falling, so that the value of one's savings shrinks even as its dollar value grows; and the constant danger is that this moderate, controlled inflation may break loose into hyperinflation, destroying the value of money entirely. The villains here are businessmen and labor leaders who collusively raise wages and prices, knowing that in the ensuing inflationary scramble they will come out ahead of those Boulding calls "the less active members of society" (1953, p. 64); government deficits induced by all sorts of special interests getting favors from government; and worst of all the Keynesian economists, who have encouraged deficit spending and attacked the habit of thrift, the very foundation of Western civilization (Röpke, 1937).

There is a solution to inflation: gold. For the hoarding consciousness gold is real money with real value, while paper money is only a promise to pay real money or goods, an IOU (Harry Schultz, 1970, Chapter 1). And today even this promise to pay is meaningful only in Switzerland, where paper money is still backed by gold at a ratio of

130 gold to 100 paper. When paper is not backed by gold, and inflation and devaluation are regular phenomena, paper money becomes an "IOU nothing," in Harwood's words.

The ideal solution to inflation and Keynesian mischief is a return to the gold standard at 100% backing; this would make even paper money proof against any economic catastrophe and would guarantee the value of savings. But as this is not to be expected, the next best solution is for the prudent investor to put his savings into gold or Swiss banks (Schultz, 1970).

The proper organization of science from this perspective is the free market. The gold economists offer their advice and their teaching on the market in the form of books and monthly bulletins; the prudent investor buys their advice in the hope of profiting from it. The wisest advice will eventually attract the most customers, and the foolish advice will be forced out of the market.

I need not detail all the shortcomings of the hoarding perspective, as it is a marginal phenomenon today. Nor have I been able to collect and analyze the most recent pronouncements (1981). Obviously the focus on monetary stability makes it difficult to analyze the economy as a productive system, producing real values rather than merely dividends. However, nothing in the perspective prevents the economist from attending to productive processes if he chooses to; he merely wishes to focus on something else. Similarly, it would not be impossible for him to analyze the role of British financial domination in maintaining the gold standard before 1914, and estimating the political and financial foundations needed for such a system today. The focus on gold provides no concepts for making such a study, so the concepts would have to be borrowed from some other perspective.

In contrast, what is really invisible from this perspective is the possibility that gold itself has no more intrinsic value than paper. A neoclassicist would say that gold has value because of the speculative demand for it, not because dentists use it to fill teeth. Its value, including its value in jewelry and household adornment, comes from opinion, from taste, as does the value of paper money, although a different opinion is involved. The symbolic value of gold relates especially to insecurity, because gold has in the past been immune to the fluctuations in value that characterized other kinds of money. In the 1970's this has no longer been the case, and the gold market has had the same speculative fluctuations as a nervous stock market.

But if the value of gold did depend on speculative opinion, the gold standard would provide no automatic stability and might be quite destabilizing, as speculative gold flowed in and out of a country. This topic would have to be investigated with the concepts of some other perspective.

The fundamental emotion underlying the hoarding standpoint, financial insecurity, is likely to disturb people moving toward the fringes of the productive system—those approaching retirement, those whose productive skills have become obsolete, those who are living on inherited wealth and have no confidence in their own productivity. Fromm (1947) has developed this latter theme in more detail. Thus the hoarding standpoint itself gets its appeal and its following from certain fringe characteristics of our economy. The fact that financial insecurity, the value of gold, and the hoarding standpoint are a product of economic fluctuations is necessarily invisible from the hoarding or rentier perspective. The hoarder sees society as stealing from him, not as creating and sustaining him. Its corollary is also invisible: a return to gold would not be a shift from imaginary to real money, but purely a shift of productive resources from one portion of society to another portion.

The final topic of this chapter is how standpoints are discovered. I have found that the most direct way is to see how a school or tradition distributes its freedom and its determinism. As Kant argued, we necessarily think of ourselves as free and the Object of science as determined. Freedom is a necessary characteristic of an actor, a Subject, either ourselves or someone similar to us with whom we empathize. Freedom in turn brings other characteristics with it. A free person or class or occupation or official can be offered advice, can be held responsible or blamed, and can have its conduct evaluated for effectiveness. We do not advise, blame, or evaluate Objects, only Subjects. Consequently when we find out where a school of writers directs its advice, to whom it attributes responsibility, whose policy or strategy it evaluates, we have located its standpoint.

Once we have located a standpoint we can discern some of its characteristics by seeing what "freedom" means for it. In traditionalist conservatism, for instance, the Wise Man is free, and freedom consists in living beyond the chains of illusion, beyond preoccupation with the petty tribulations of the passing scene. He is free because he knows the truth and lives in it.

The characteristics of the actor and of his freedom also determine the subject/object relation, especially the distance between subject and object. If the Wise Man is free because he knows the truth, then freedom is distributed in gradations through society corresponding to the "degrees of knowledge" (Maritain) and may expand or contract. A small portion of human society may pass over to the status of Subject by learning the truth. And conversely the freedom of the subject consists in losing himself in contemplation of the object in its eternal aspect. Thus the subject/object relation is close and the boundary is permeable in both directions. On the other hand, if the Federal Reserve Board is free, the target of advice, because it controls interest rates and the supply of money, then the object, the system of monetary flows and aggregates, is not at all free and is sharply distinct from the subject. It is also subordinate, under the control of the subject. If all men (though not women) are free, then the object of knowledge is the products of human actions, which necessarily bear traces of their makers' freedom. In this case the scope of freedom cannot be expanded, as with traditionalism, but it may possibly be contracted by depriving some men of freedom.

The kind or degree of determinism attributed to the object also depends on the subject/object relation and especially the distance between the two. In general, the greater the distance, the higher the degree of determinism attributed to the object. Kant's sharp and static distinction between subject and object, freedom and determinism, is quite misleading here; the social sciences do not work that way. They recognize several degrees or kinds of determinism, not just one (Wright, 1978, Chapter 1).

The standpoints and perspectives to be analyzed in the following chapters will all be described from the inside, as they appear to their adherents. That is, when I describe a standpoint, I will describe it from its own perspective at first. When I contrast two perspectives I will shift back and forth between the two perspectives. When I evaluate a perspective I will shift to a contrasting perspective. In each case I will attempt to specify the perspective from which a statement is made, unless the perspective is clear from the context. However, the reader must remember that all statements in the following chapters are being made from a perspective, that the perspectives shift, and that he or she must locate the perspective to understand the statement.

Part I

TWO Neoclassical Economics

I. The Neoclassical Perspective

The beginning of the neoclassical period is conventionally located in 1870 with the appearance of marginal utility analysis. The neoclassicists regard marginal analysis as the tool which enabled them to refine and systematize the basic truths of the classical economists while avoiding various classical errors, such as the labor theory of value and the theory of rent as a residual payment. By 1930, when the present study begins, the neoclassicists had long been established as the dominant economic tradition with several branches.

The heart of neoclassical economics is the theory of the firm. Assuming supply and demand functions that specify prices of resources and products at any given quantity, and assuming a production function that specifies the marginal contribution of resources to output, it is deduced that the firm at equilibrium will use those techniques and resource mixes that maximize the balance of returns minus costs, and will produce that quantity at which marginal cost equals marginal revenue. The household can also be treated as a firm that produces labor and supplies it up to the point at which the marginal return from labor equals the marginal return from leisure.

There is also the theory of the industry, with several branches depending on the shapes of the demand and supply curves for individual firms in the industry. The simplest case is perfect competition, in which all supply curves for the individual firm are vertical and all demand curves are horizontal, that is, all prices remain the same no matter how much is demanded or offered. In this case it is deduced that at equilibrium all factors of production are compensated in proportion to the marginal value of their contribution to production, and the price of a product equals its marginal cost. In all other cases, ranging from imperfect competition to monopoly and monopsony, one or more curves are slanted or curved; that is, price varies depending on the quantity demanded or offered for sale. Given curved demand or supply functions, it is deduced that some factor receives a disproportionate compensation (quasi-rent, etc.).

There is also a theory of a whole economy composed of a number of industries. It is deduced that at equilibrium under perfect competition each factor of production including labor is employed in that industry and at that ratio to other factors that maximizes its marginal value product. No factor is unemployed and each receives the compensation it deserves. This is also substantially true in imperfect competition; but oligopolistic or monopolistic industry will receive disproportionate compensation. Next, the whole economy grows when some production function changes due to a new invention. This results in lower costs of production and a drawing of resources into the affected industry; when the whole economy reaches a new equilibrium the benefits of the invention have been distributed throughout the economy and everyone is better off.

Underlying the theories of the firm, industry, and economy is the postulate of individual rationality, which assumes that the individual has likes and dislikes, that is that he values various goods in some order. In addition, each individual controls a collection of resources, including his own labor and knowledge. Given his knowledge of the various possible ways to use his resources, he allocates them to the various uses in such a way that the last unit of resources yields an equal increment of utility no matter how it is used. In this fashion he maximizes his expected utility from given resources, just as the firm maximizes its expected returns from its resources.

Let us examine some characteristics of this theory in order to locate its standpoint and perspective. It is a theory of long-run equilibrium; that is, it assumes opposing forces with constant, unchanging characteristics. These forces are inner-directed; their characteristics are not dependent on characteristics of the opposing force. With such forces, their opposition will necessarily work itself out to a system state in which all forces are evenly balanced and no more change occurs. This is long-run equilibrium. With forces whose nature changes depending on their opposition or their own history no such evenly-balanced state can ever occur, because the balance of forces changes itself over time. Thus, the theory is static in two respects: it is a theory of static equilibrium, and the forces whose opposition ends in equilibrium are themselves unchanging in their inner characteristics.

Dynamics are studied in the neighborhood of equilibrium, where the pattern of opposed forces is worked out to see whether they move toward or away from the equilibrium state. Dynamics are also studied in the neighborhood of a disturbance, when some external change upsets an equilibrium, to determine the manner of movement toward the new equilibrium.

The forces that determine both dynamics and equilibrium are forces of individual rationality. Usually the two opposed forces are a set of buyers and a set of sellers; the buyers prefer a lower price and the sellers prefer a higher price, so the outcome is a middle price. If there are more buyers than sellers in a given price range the least interested buyers will find themselves outbid by more eager buyers and will shift to some other product; so also with sellers. Thus individuals shift their resources around at the margin, by exchange and by production, seeking a package of resources that makes them happier; and this activity continues until everyone is as happy as he can be and therefore seeks no more changes. This state is long-run equilibrium.

Human nature is fixed; it is eternally the case that individuals have preferences and knowledge, that they are rational, and that they seek to maximize expected utility. Knowledge and preferences do change, but the theory gives no account of these changes; they are exogenous. A theory of how preferences change would be a psychological or sociological theory, not an economic theory. A theory of information processing and testing, of uncertainty reduction through feedback and filters, would be a cognitive theory, not an economic theory.

Since system dynamics are based on the forces of individual rationality, neoclassical theory is primarily microtheory. At its foundation is the theory of individual choice, which Robbins even declared to be the defining characteristic of economics (1935). The theory of the firm is the next best developed, then the theory of various sorts of industry; the Walrasian theory of general equilibrium, a macrotheory, is the most elaborate, cumbersome, and abstract construct of all. One moves in the macro direction by aggregating: all individuals, all firms, all products, and so on. That is, the system is a collection, a totality of individuals and resources. There is no inherent limit to the number of units; more can be added merely by jostling the others around a bit.

Accordingly, from the neoclassical perspective the horizon of the

System, the Object, stretches out from the individual to infinity with no sharp boundaries visible anywhere. There is an infinity of possible investment opportunities, for example in Hayek's business cycle theory (Klein, 1947, pp. 52-53). One must merely add a curve of diminishing returns from investment; the theory then states that investment will occur up to the point at which the cost of capital (interest) equals its expected return. There is an infinity of possible employment opportunities, with diminishing returns; this explains why structural unemployment and surplus labor necessarily are due to wage floors or fixed wages (analogous to interest rates). There is an infinity and insatiability of human wants, and therefore no limit to the desirability of economic growth, which continues to infinity in principle. There is an infinity of demand if prices are low enough, so long-run overproduction is impossible. There is an infinity of resources waiting to be discovered, though with rising or sharply rising cost curves, so that rationing or price control always leads to shortages by discouraging prospecting for resources.

The above considerations suggest that the neoclassical standpoint is the rational individual. Society is spread out around the individual in all directions, offering limitless opportunities for exchange. Society is entirely an aggregate of individuals; there are no group minds. Consequently individual decisions are the ultimate cause for all social changes. Individuals are the active element in society; all social outputs—GNP, growth rate, quantity of money, resource allocations—are the consequence of myriads of individual decisions.

For example: "Holders of money . . . can make the real amount of M anything that in the aggregate they want to. If they want to hold a relatively small quantity of money, they will individually seek to reduce their nominal cash balances by increasing expenditures. This will not alter the nominal stock of money to be held . . . but it will raise the flow of expenditures and hence money income and prices and thereby reduce the real quantity of money to the desired level" (Friedman, 1959, p. 330; 1966 reprint, pp. 90-91).

We get further evidence that this is the neoclassical standpoint if we ask, "Who is free?" The answer is that all men are free in the sense that they are capable of rational choices which maximize expected utility. Socially, all men are free unless they are coerced by other men or by government (Hayek, 1960, Chapter 1; Friedman, 1962, Chapters 1, 2; Knight, 1947, Chapter 1). Government, an instrument of coercion, can increase freedom only by police power, which reduces the coercion of men by other men. Metaphysically, freedom means the ability to make rational choices; socially, it means the ability to act on those choices without hindrance from other men. The opposite of freedom is coercion.

Further evidence comes from the fact that numerous neoclassical economists have explicitly stated that their standpoint was individualism. The strong version of the statement is called "methodological individualism," the assertion that society is an aggregate of individuals plus the effects of individual actions, and that groups and group minds are fictitious entities. The weaker version is ethical individualism, a concern for individual freedom in these times of collectivism and totalitarianism.

If the neoclassical standpoint is the rational individual, the neoclassical perspective is how society looks from this standpoint. First, the Subject, the one who acts on society, is the individual. This is the generic individual, man in general. What the Subject sees in society is primarily other subjects like himself, subjects with resources and preferences, subjects making decisions, subjects engaging in exchange and production. Second, there are all the conditions in which individual decisions are made. These conditions include existing resources including money, existing technology, current prices, current contractual relations and power relations, current production and exchange in process, and current flows of money and products. These conditions constitute the Object to be known. They are all the consequence of many decisions stretching far into the past. Current flows and production are the consequence of previous production and exchange decisions, which in turn were based on previous prices and resources, and so on.

The knowable, then, is twofold: first the Subject, individual rational action; and second the Object, the system of exchange and production, resources and technology. Clearly the Subject dominates the Object in this perspective. The Object is a complex set of consequences which derive their existence and their intelligibility from the decisions embodied in them. Subjects are in principle more knowable than the consequences of their actions. Social science, the science of human rationality, is subjective; natural science, the science of things, is objective.

The Subject is known directly, from the inside, since each of us is a subject and knows himself as such. This means, however, that only the general process of rational choice, which all subjects have in common, is knowable; the particular preference schedules and resources that differentiate individuals are arbitrary, changeable, and external to us. We may estimate someone else's preferences from his actions, but then his preferences may change and our "knowledge" has vanished. There can be no science of how preferences change.

The neoclassicists give a number of different accounts of how the Subject is known. 1) Von Mises, writing in 1933, asserts that our knowledge is a kind of Kantian a priori: " . . . what we know about our action . . . is derived not from experience, but from reason. What we know about the fundamental categories of action—action, economizing, preferring, the relationship of means and ends . . .—is not derived from experience. We conceive all this from within, just as we conceive logical and mathematical truths, a priori, without reference to any experience." "Our thinking about men and their conduct . . . presupposes the category of action" (Mises, 1960, pp. 13-14). 2) Leontief, writing in 1948, asserts that our knowledge is empirical: "The truly fundamental postulates of the orthodox theory deal with the general nature of economic choice . . . in sinking its foundations deeper in the ground of experience than does the Keynesian analysis, the traditional theory is able to use a smaller number of separate assumptions . . ." (Leontief, 1966, p. 95). He means that the neoclassical models are founded on the empirical postulate that individuals act to maximize expected utility, a truth located deep in experience, while the Keynesian models postulate consumption functions, labor supply functions, and the like, whose shape depends on econometric data, that is, on the changing superficialities of a particular time period. 3) Machlup prefers Schutz's phenomenology as a foundation (1952a, pp. vii, 370; 1970) and lists still other approaches (1952a, p. 417).

By the 1940's the neoclassicists were very much on the defensive with regard to the postulate of individual rationality, and they retreated to new positions. 1) The postulate may be empirically unrealistic, but all science is built on unrealistic postulates and the crucial test is whether the models predict well (Friedman, 1953, Chapter 1; Machlup, 1946, 1952a, p. 408; Downs, 1957, p. 21). Note the ambiguity of "unrealistic." This becomes, in later versions, the statement that the postulate is arbitrary. 2) The postulate may be correct for only a few marginal firms or individuals, but that is enough to produce the predicted results (Machlup, 1952a, pp. 42, 47-50, 73; Riker, 1962, p. 20). 3) The postulate does not refer to individuals, but to the selective force of a market, which rewards individuals and firms who happen to act as if they were rational (Machlup, 1952b, p. 391; Friedman, 1953; Riker, 1962, p. 21; Alchian and Allen, 1964, pp. 16-17, 29-30). However, these various defensive positions are adopted merely for purposes of argument. Underneath, the neoclassicist *knows* that people are rational: "This marginalist way of thinking is so natural, so self-evident to anybody who thinks at all rationally . . ." (Machlup, 1952a, p. 32).

The Object is known by deduction from what we know about the Subject. The rationality postulate is fundamental to all models of the firm, industry, and economy. The remaining postulates of these models describe all the possible ways in which rational individuals can relate to one another (the various types of market), including the effects of varying distributions of land, labor, and capital. Many methodologists have discussed and justified the deductive method (Stigler, 1946, pp. 8-10, 16-20; Mises, 1960; Machlup, 1958; Robbins, 1935; J.N. Keynes, 1904). Long-run equilibrium never exists, but equilibrium models are used as baselines for more complex models, and for describing and studying deviations; they delineate the pattern of dynamics in a situation so we can predict the direction of change *ceteris paribus*; everyone thinks in terms of models, since the complexities of concrete reality are unknowable and knowledge necessarily involves abstraction from the concrete and therefore model-building. But underlying the numerous methodological discussions is the neoclassicist's belief that the rational individual is real and knowable, while the outward manifestations of rationality are complex, shifting, and indeterminate and therefore knowable only derivatively.

The proper organization of science for the neoclassicist is a special case of the proper organization of society in general. All human relations are exchange or gift relations of some sort, but exchange can be more or less unfair depending on the amount of coercion involved. The ideal relation among adults is the noncoercive or market relation in which exchange is freely entered into on both sides; and among the types of market the perfectly competitive one is the best. Science therefore should be organized on the free market principle in which knowledge is sold to students or other consumers at a mutually agreeable price, and produced to meet expected demand. Science policy then will be decided by the market, that is, by the consumer, since those teachers and researchers that produce and market knowledge in high demand will flourish, and others will not.

Continental universities were organized according to the market principle during the nineteenth century, when students paid their professor directly whatever they thought his lectures were worth. Today the gold economists, investment advisers, and various market and opinion researchers are organized in this fashion. Anyone can publish an investment newsletter, offer individualized investment advice, or offer to do market surveys; some practitioners do well, others not so well, according to customers' estimates of the worth of their services.

We turn now to the shortcomings of the neoclassical perspective.

The following is not a complete list, since some items require prior presentation of a different perspective to make them intelligible, and will be taken up in later chapters.

First, for those who believe that only individuals are real, system dynamics separate from and opposed to the purposes of individuals are difficult to conceive. Since production and exchange are a consequence of individual decisions, they should bear some intelligible relation to those decisions. Neoclassicists therefore explain system dynamics by relating them to the decisions of individuals. The depression of the 1930's must have been produced by someone's decisions. When money illusion occurs, it must have been produced by government attempts to fool people. Economic growth results from unpredictable individual inventiveness. Such an approach dissolves the system into a series of micro situations facing individuals with given preferences and resources.

The result again and again is a distorted interpretation of systemic phenomena, an interpretation which runs flatly against the facts and must be rescued by ad hoc assumptions.

Agricultural productivity is one example. T.W. Schultz (1945, Chapters 4, 5) argues that in the period 1900–1945 the productivity of labor in US agriculture depended directly on the rate of industrial unemployment rather than on any conditions internal to agriculture. Further, labor migration varied inversely with cyclical changes in productivity and wage levels: falling agricultural wage levels were followed by increased movement into agriculture, and the rising wage levels of the 1940's accompanied outmigration. Further, the rate of outmigration was greater in areas of higher wages and productivity than in lower-wage areas (Schultz, 1945, p. 206; D. G. Johnson, 1947, p. 208). These changes are the opposite from those deducible from neoclassical microtheory. Given individual rationality, falling wages and lower wages would lead to labor outmigration as individuals moved to higher-wage areas.

Schultz shows that the explanation is systemic rather than individual. During this period agriculture served as a reserve area or dumping ground for those unemployable in industry. The surplus labor and shortage of capital in the 1930's hindered technical improvements in agriculture, while the drawing off of this labor in the 1940's and early 1900's had the reverse effect.

Neoclassicists could easily account for such facts by arguing that the ceteris paribus clause did not hold. Falling agricultural wages will lead to outmigration ceteris paribus, but if industrial wages were falling even faster and at times effectively to zero, it was rational for the unemployed to move into agriculture. Further, all this additional agricultural labor would shift the labor supply curve along the production function and lower the productivity of labor. The productivity of capital would increase correspondingly; but if it was even higher in industry, it was rational for bankers to channel scarce credit out of agriculture. As for the differential outmigration of labor, perhaps there was either a differential level of information, or higher psychic transportation costs. Since long-run equilibrium was far away the standard predictions do not hold, and one must look for the particular disturbing factors which produce the unusual results.

But these ad hoc explanations dissolve the systemic relations between industry and agriculture into a series of arbitrary market situations facing individuals. Why were agricultural wages and productivity consistently lower than in industry during the period 1900–1945? The neoclassicist can invent many explanations: higher psychic income in agriculture, less human capital in agricultural workers, labor monopoly in industry, or employer preferences for white city dwellers. But if we ask why these facts happened to occur we move beyond the limits of neoclassic science. Why do employers have "a taste for discrimination" (Gary Becker, 1957)? There is no answer.

Tastes in general are out of bounds for the neoclassicist; they are part of the individual's freedom. If some workers prefer to live in the country that is simply a fact that science must accept. Marketing research, which attempts to estimate what consumers might decide to prefer, is compatible with freedom, but attempts to treat tastes as system phenomena are flatly rejected. Consumer sovereignty is a moral principle as well as an empirical hypothesis for the neoclassicist.

Yet the obvious regularities in tastes suggest that some systemic influences are at work. Consider the remarkable similarities in tastes among ethnic communities in the US and Canada. These people choose to speak the same language (not English), eat the same range of foods, believe in the same religion, despise or esteem the same other ethnic groups, vote for the same ethnic politicians, move into the same group of occupations. When their children break away they discard *all but one* of these similarities. Surely there is something regular here that scientists could study—and have, since Thomas and Znaniecki's *Polish Peasant in Europe and America* (1920).

The neoclassicist has no adequate way of dealing with the short run, since his is a long-run theory. Short-run phenomena can be treated as deviations from or approaches to long-run equilibrium, or as instances of individual irrationality or coercive interference with markets. That is, they are treated as empirical departures from equilibrium. Marshall in particular noted a variety of short-period phenomena, treating them as empirical qualifications of the received theory which show that life is richer and more complex than any theory. A systematic treatment of short-run phenomena, however, had to wait for two of Marshall's followers, Keynes and Parsons, neither of them neoclassicists.

Alternatively, short-run models can be constructed by adding more restrictive assumptions to the simpler equilibrium models. I am thinking of such standard models as the one-day models in which a perishable commodity is brought to market in the morning and must be sold to the specific buyers who happen to be there that day. These models run only under the assumption of individual rationality and perfect information, which themselves are long-run equilibrium phenomena according to the apologists for the rationality assumption mentioned earlier. And if one argues that this "day" occurs after a long run of days that have produced individual rationality, the same long run will have produced regular buyers with price expectations and other market imperfections that invalidate the model. Neoclassical short-run models are thus self-contradictory, useful only as mathematical exercises for students.

Uncertainty is a short-run phenomenon that neoclassicists have never been able to comprehend adequately (cf. Minsky, 1975, on this point).

The standard neoclassical treatment of uncertainty is Knight's *Risk, Uncertainty, and Profit* (1921). Knight distinguishes between risk, in which the probabilities of alternative outcomes are known, and uncertainty, in which no probability can be assigned. There is thus no rational way to make decisions under uncertainty. However, some people believe they have a gift for dealing with uncertain futures (or believe they have a gift for selecting people who can do so). If they act on this belief they become entrepreneurs, venturing their capital either directly or in the hands of their hired manager. If their belief is correct they are rewarded with profit; if their belief is mistaken they lose their capital. Profit is thus a reward for possession of a special gift or skill (pp. 310–312), and wealth is a sign that its owner has such a skill. However, this special gift is scarce, and the aggregate level of profit in an economy probably is zero or negative (Knight, 1921, pp. 362–366; 1947, p. 379).

My purpose is not to make haphazard charges of "ideological bias" but to examine categories and habits of thinking. Notice first that uncertainty is by definition unknowable, so nothing rational can be done about it, while risk, which can be estimated, is treated as devoid of uncertainty. The two categories are sharply distinguished. This makes uncertainty reduction logically impossible; that is, the theory does not deal with it. Uncertainty cannot be reduced, while risk is reducible to its certainty equivalent by statistics. The theory is static. Knight recognizes that in real life people reduce uncertainty, but that is not his topic. See also Shubik (1954) for a criticism of Knight.

According to Knight the standard way to deal with risk is by insurance (1921, Chapter 8). Insurance, however, is an anomaly for neoclassical theory because it does not maximize expected utility and thus is irrational. The insurance company can stay in business only by charging premiums whose value is greater than the expected value of the insurance policy. Friedman and Savage (1948) recognize this anomaly and save the theory by reinterpreting the phenomenon. They postulate a utility curve for money, and moreover a curve with a kink in it at precisely the levels at which insurance policies pay off. Thus the buyer of a policy is still by definition maximizing expected utility, though not expected money income. Friedman and Savage do not explain why there is a kink in the curve, however.

A third and more common way to deal with uncertainty is to treat information as a commodity with costs and expected returns; the rational maximizer then reduces uncertainty up to the point at which marginal costs equal marginal expected returns (Downs, 1957, pp. 214ff.). This approach is self-contradictory, as Shackle observes (1955, pp. 17–18). In order to form expectations about the value of information we do not yet have, we must know what that information is going to be like. But "Knowledge would not be bought if it were already possessed; and when we buy knowledge, we do not know what we are going to get." Consequently, it is impossible to form a rational expectation about the utility of knowledge.

A more recent expedient is to simply assume uncertainty away, along with all irrationality. This is the postulate of rational expectations, which says that individuals have perfect information which they use to make technically flawless predictions.

Missing from all these treatments of uncertainty are three closely related sets of concepts: 1) The whole set of cybernetic concepts, including information flow, feedback, filters, encoding and decoding, redundancy. These concepts make possible a theory of uncertainty reduction over time. 2) Concepts about how expectations are formed, tested, and modified through information flows. For example, D.G. Johnson observes, "Farmers are traditionally an important debtor group, and inflation, by breeding optimism, has invited rising land

Table 2.1. Price and production behavior in depression, 1929–1937.

	Drop (%), 1929–1932		Recovery (%), 1932–1937	
	prices	production	prices	production
Motor vehicles	12	74	2	64
Agricultural implements	14	84	9	84
Agricultural commodities	54	1	36	8

Source: National Resources Committee, 1939, p. 386, Table XXII. Cf. also Sherman, 1976, p. 165, Table 8.4.

and asset prices and increased debt, while deflation has resulted in foreclosure and bankruptcy" (1947, p. 10). Expectation concepts like optimism are an essential part of Keynes's theory, but for the neoclassicists optimism is a form of irrationality which is bound to disappear somehow. 3) Distinction between a security and an income goal. For example, Johnson (1947, pp. 39ff.), in his Keynesian-type treatment of agricultural decision-making under uncertainty, postulates two goals, income maximization and security against bankruptcy. (So also does Rothschild, 1947). The second goal is achieved by risk avoidance—crop insurance, diversification of crops, liquidity preference (pp. 42, 56), and change of the production mix as new information appears. Johnson's policy proposal, forward pricing (a type of indicative planning), also is designed to reduce uncertainty by adjusting the agricultural information system.

The security goal can also be expressed in game theoretic terms by saying that farmers are following a minimax strategy in a game against nature. Either way makes agricultural decision-making rational and intelligible, while Friedman and Savage's expedient saves the neoclassical theory by postulating an arbitrary fact, a kink in a postulated utility curve for money.

A more subtle distortion occurs when farmers and laborers are treated as economic men who maximize expected utility over the long run. If utility is maximized by equalizing the marginal returns from labor and leisure, an economic man will reduce his labor when wages go down and increase it when wages go up. The aggregate supply of labor will therefore increase when wages go up and decrease when they go down.

Farmers and workers, however, do the opposite. A farmer will work just as much or even more when agricultural prices decline (Schultz, 1945, p. 13). Thus in the period 1929–1932 when farm prices declined 54%, farm production declined 1% (see Table 2.1). Similarly, the laborer or his wife may take on an extra job when wages are low, reducing their work when wages rise. This negatively sloped labor supply curve looks irrational to the neoclassicist, who is skeptical even of its existence (Machlup, 1952b, pp. 43, 60). Farmers also use a variety of techniques other than overwork to maintain a steady income, such as varying the weight at which hogs are sent to market. Workers use trade unions to resist wage cuts, a practice that looks irrational or at least selfish and shortsighted to the neoclassicist.

A neoclassicist could explain away the anomaly of a negatively sloped labor supply curve by postulating a nearly vertical demand curve for money, if leisure is the price of money. Such a curve would imply that falling wages would induce an additional supply of labor. This ad hoc explanation, however, merely pushes the problem back a step. Why do some people's demand curves for money have that particular slope? This question the neoclassicist cannot answer, because preferences are ultimate for him.

What occurs here is an attempt by farmers and workers to maintain a standard of living or style of life, especially when they have a family to support and educate. Their goal is constant real income, not maximum expected utility. The neoclassicist's failure to appreciate the standard-of-living goal of farmers and workers suggests that his standpoint is not really that of the individual in the abstract. It is rather that of the businessman who maintains a balance sheet of costs and returns and who tries to maximize net return (or net value of the proprietary interest in the firm). A distortion results when the worker and farmer are treated as businessmen who "produce" and sell their own labor. They are, rather, family breadwinners whose role is to provide a steady consumption level for their family.

This recognition points to another topic that is difficult for the neoclassicist to deal with—the rearing of children. If one's theory describes society as a collection of individualists with arbitrary, individual preference schedules one must postulate that some people have an arbitrary preference for raising children, strong enough to ensure that their utility is maximized by a constant money income. Here is another kink in the imaginary utility curve for money. The regularities of family structure then become inexplicable, and the continuation of the family and with it the society seems to depend on an arbitrary occurrence, individual preferences for children. Some economists have recognized this problem and have excluded the family from the subject matter of economics (for example Knight, 1947, p. 383), asserting that the "individualist" standpoint is really "familist." Parent–child relations then do not have to be interpreted as cases of utility maximization.

The family in turn is one instance of another category that does not appear in the neoclassicist conceptual scheme—community.

From an individualistic perspective there can be no such thing as community in the sense of shared experience or common experience. Such concepts must always seem paradoxical and be treated as either metaphor or mysticism. An earlier example is the difficulties individualists had with Durkheim's concept of collective conscience. Durkheim was interpreted as asserting the existence of a group mind out there imposing itself on us; in other words, the collectivity was treated as another individual mind.

Yet the need for a concept of community has been evident. Families are needed to produce children and thereby reproduce the society, and some sort of loyalty is a necessary basis for the observed habit of law-abidingness that the neoclassicist recognizes is necessary for a successful free-enterprise economy. In addition political democracy, either in Knight's version of government by discussion or Schumpeter's version of government by two sets of rulers who compete for votes, requires a language in which political affairs can be discussed. But language, shared concepts, is the most basic form of community. When people share a language they have the same concepts, the same desires insofar as people conceptualize their wants to themselves, and therefore the same experiences. Here again the simplest solution is for the neoclassicist to exclude this topic from the scope of economics.

Finally, neoclassical theory is sexist. It takes a masculine perspective on human relations. This comes out in Vinacke's coalition experiments (1959; Bond and Vinacke, 1961) in which three or more subjects played a game against each other for money. The only way to win was to form a two-person coalition against the third, or three against two, etc., since the play of the game itself was mechanical. There were also games in which one person necessarily won because of his advantageous starting point and even a coalition against him necessarily lost. The experimental interest was in the preplay bargaining process in which two players agreed on a partnership against the third and also agreed on a division of their joint payoff.

Vinacke found that his subjects fell into two groups, which he called exploitative and accommodative. The exploitative group played as expected, forming two-person coalitions when and only when those coalitions would ensure a win, trying to break up an opposing coalition by large offers to one coalition member, and bargaining over relative payoffs. The accommodative people did not act this way. They would form three-person coalitions against nobody, dividing the payoff equally; or they would shift coalitions around in a regular way so there was no permanent loser; or an automatic winner would form a coalition with an automatic loser. The exploitatives were mainly men and the accommodatives were mainly women.

Vinacke's results were duplicated in coalition experiments of Laing and Olmstead (Ordeshook, 1978, pp. 253ff.). The experimental results fell into two distinct categories: 1) Competitive formation of a minimum winning coalition which took the whole payoff for itself. 2) Discussion by consensus which shared the payoff equally among all subjects. The competitive category included eight of eleven all-male groups; the even division category included six of eight mixed-sex groups.

Vinacke's exploitative men fit the pattern of the neoclassical theory of human nature: they maximized their long-run expected payoffs. The accommodative women did not fit this pattern. They suggest a human nature in which one is sensitive to people rather than to one's own utility. This sensitivity expresses itself in a pattern of equalized payoffs for all players, including compensation for natural inequalities, so that players are not competing. In terms of preferences, it consists of taking the other's preferences as one's own—induced preferences or interdependent preferences.

Induced preferences are entirely outside the neoclassic conceptual scheme; the neoclassical conception of human nature is a masculine conception.

The accommodative orientation is the basis for community in families and larger groupings. A community of interest occurs when people take their pattern of preferences from each other, so that they can act in common without bargaining over the payoffs.

The neoclassicist, faced with this empirical phenomenon, distorts it by calling it "altruism." There is a standard ritual disclaimer in the neoclassic texts: "This theory does not assert that human beings are necessarily egoistic. It applies to altruists as well as egoists, and to any pattern of preferences whatsoever." But the concept of altruism is a sexist distortion; it suggests a type of person who derives satisfaction from observing the satisfaction of another, a kind of charity or benevolent orientation. But the accommodative orientation consists of forming a joint preference schedule and sharing the payoff. It is not expressed by doing something to or for another in order to get one's own satisfaction.

In summary, I have argued that the neoclassical standpoint is not that of the individual in general, as neoclassicists have defined it for themselves. It is a masculine standpoint, and more particularly the small businessman's standpoint. It is alien not only to women but also to men whose primary orientation is toward a family. The system as seen from this standpoint is an aggregate of production and exchange relations among businessmen that results from their individual attempts to maximize their own expected utility. The system is intelligible either in terms of the long-run equilibrium toward which it tends or in terms of the individual decisions which set it in motion. Alien to this standpoint and difficult to perceive clearly are: systems whose dynamics are independent and opposed to individual preferences or which determine preferences and expectations as part of their dynamics; systems which do not tend toward any equilibrium but contain their own continual source of change; information systems in particular; and communities, including families and linguistic communities. Other concepts that get misinterpreted and distorted from the neoclassicist perspective will be taken up in subsequent chapters.

II. Oligopoly and Game Theory

We next take up a theoretical development within neoclassical economics that extended and partly transcended the neoclassic perspective. The empirical basis for this development was the expansion and merging of industrial firms, leading to the domination of whole industries by a few large firms. This process contradicted the Walrasian general equilibrium model by moving not toward competitive equilibrium but toward oligopoly; in addition the dynamics of an oligopolistic industry did not fit the perfect competition models, nor the monopoly model, nor anything in between. The early oligopoly models by Cournot, Bertrand, and Edgeworth were also inadequate (Machlup, 1952a, Chapter 12; Fellner, 1949, Chapter 2; Cross, 1965). For one thing, they assumed that each bargainer believes that the opponent's price is fixed, even after it has changed several times. This unrealistic postulate was necessary to assume away uncertainty and calculation about the opponent's future price, since the neoclassic models cannot model the process of uncertainty reduction. In short, the empirical behavior of oligopolistic industries was a problem for the neoclassicists.

Several solutions to this problem were developed in the 1930's and 1940's. The most direct solution was to develop new oligopoly models analogous to the perfect competition models. These models treat oligopoly as a type of market with a different shape of the demand curve and therefore a different long-run equilibrium position. For the industry one must also specify conditions of entry for new firms, thereby deriving a variety of price and production levels at equilibrium. However, these standard neoclassical models were also inadequate, both empirically (Rothschild, 1947; Triffin, 1940, Chapters 1, 2) and conceptually (Robinson, 1953; Shubik, 1959, pp. 148–150, 258, 332).

A typical Chicago school response was to retain the models and explain the empirical deviations as due to irrationality (Stigler, 1946, Chapters 11–15). The expansion of firms was explained by businessmen's irrational desires for power and prestige (Chapter 11). Why the taste for power should be irrational when all other tastes are simply given for the neoclassicist, Stigler does not say. In a more moderate version, Machlup suggests that a great variety of psychological factors, not necessarily irrational, are involved in oligopolistic industries (Machlup, 1952a, pp. 422ff.; cf. also Triffin, 1940). Why these same factors do not operate in other types of industry he does not say. In this solution the neoclassical models are treated as idealizations of reality; they describe the rational component of empirical reality, the intelligible component. The many deviations can then be described ad hoc as departures from this component. Their presence shows that empirical reality is richer than any theory, and that an economist needs intuition and rich experience as well as mathematical skill to do justice to it. Fellner's treatment of oligopoly (1949) is another example of this approach; he sees the oligopoly problem as explaining why there are deviations from joint maximization of profits (pp. 33ff.).

Another response, by institutionalists like Walton Hamilton, was to drop the neoclassical models (which they never were very fond of anyway) and concentrate on detailed case studies of oligopolistic industries.

The most adequate response was to shift perspective (Rothschild, 1947). The neoclassic rational firm responds passively to an impersonal market, including an oligopolistic market. It is given a set of supply and demand curves and calculates price and production levels accordingly. Rothschild suggests that one should instead begin from the analogy with military strategy or games such as chess. Rather than facing impersonal curves, the firm faces one or a few specific other firms in a struggle for survival and advantage. Thus there are two distinct goals: security or survival and profit maximization, the first dominating the second. This is the perspective of game theory, and game theory provides the definitive neoclassical solution to the oligopoly problem, by enabling one to model factors that previously were unknowable empirical deviations. The standpoint is still the individual exploitative businessman, but the Object has shifted from impersonal supply and demand curves to the personal opponent.

The explicit neoclassical basis of game theory is the rationality postulate. The players are assumed to have the goal of maximizing their own expected utility, the utilities of each player are assumed to be independent of all the others', and full knowledge of all preference schedules is assumed. The latter assumption is sometimes dropped.

The difference is that while neoclassical theory begins with a model of perfect competition and moves step by step toward a monopoly model, game theory moves in the opposite direction: it begins with a two-person zero-sum game and moves through more complex games toward the n-person variable sum game, the analog of perfect competition. This means that from the start the individual is faced with a particular opponent, rather than with impersonal supply and demand curves. Calculation immediately takes a different form: instead of estimating supply and demand curves one estimates the opponent's strategy, and instead of working out production mixes and levels one works out a strategy that will defeat the opponent's strategy. Moreover, the opponent's strategy is not impersonally produced by "the market" but is constructed as a response to one's own strategy. Games are symmetrical; each player's strategy responds to the other's response to his strategy.

In other words, competition is personal; it is rivalry. Frank Knight used to complain regularly that people did not understand the market economy; they confused competition with rivalry, while actually it was quite impersonal. But in game theory rivalry is the norm and impersonality is the ideal limit.

This perspective on business competition immediately enables one to see the importance of power, including market power and political power. If success in business consists of beating out one or more specific rivals, one's power relative to these rivals becomes a topic of the highest interest to the players. In game terms, the value of a game to a player depends on his power position relative to other players: the relative damage he can inflict on them in the DD cell of the game, the "fight" cell, and the relative advantages he can promise for cooperation (CC cell). Damages include such things as taking away customers and profits in a price war, controlling raw materials, inducing government regulations and specifications that favor one's products over the competitors'; the ability to inflict damage is also the ability to evade or to counter damage by the rival.

Once one is sensitized to power in the economy, and has concepts to deal with power, a whole new perspective on the economy opens up, quite different from the Walrasian perspective. The conceptual inability to deal with power in the economy is what makes the neoclassicist's models so unreal and misleading. The concept of market power enables one to explain the development of an industry from competition to oligopoly, a development that the older neoclassicist cannot understand and is forced to attribute to individual irrationality or government interference (Stigler, 1946, pp. 198–201, 211; Röpke, 1942, p. 117; Simons, 1948, pp. 34–35). If we assume an industry characterized by imperfect competition and not in long-run equilibrium some firms will have an advantage over others. The reasons may be very diverse, ranging from management skill through geographical advantages to fortunate relations to suppliers and customers. These advantages enable the firm to make a greater than average profit. But each such firm is a threat to neighboring firms, since it can take away their business sooner or later. To guard against this threat the others must strive to expand in their turn. Rothschild (1947) mentions a variety of defensive and expansionist tactics; the most obvious tactic for a game theorist is to combine forces with other equally threatened neighbors. N-person game theory, the theory of coalitions, explains this process and demonstrates, among other things, that the largest firm is not the most likely to survive, because it is the rational focus for opposing coalitions (cf. Riker, 1962, pp. 130–132, 138, Chapter 7). The threat of potential opposing coalitions, however, forces even the strongest firm to expand and/or seek allies for defensive purposes. As Robinson observes, "Anyone, by growing, is threatening the position of others, who retaliate by expanding their own capacity" (Robinson, 1971, p. 101). This process inevitably changes imperfect competition into oligopoly, at which point new dynamics take over.

The dynamics by which imperfect competition changes into oligopoly have been formalized by Shubik (1959, Chapter 10) as a set of games of survival. These games specify the variables involved in the development of oligopoly and the rate at which smaller firms are forced out or bought out. Variables include corporate assets, liquidation values, discount rates for future returns, ownership structure, production and inventory scheduling, advertising possibilities, and others. Note that some variables treated as incidental, or even noneconomic, in the neoclassical theory of the firm are shown to be relevant to the rate at which an industry becomes oligopolistic.

Shubik also describes the dynamics of a mature oligopolistic industry as games of stabilization (Chapter 11). As one or more firms in an industry become larger, they acquire both the incentive and the threat capability of regulating the price and output levels of the smaller firms; conversely, a coalition of smaller firms can regulate a larger one. These games do not explain why profit deviates from a hypothetical maximum;

in view of the inherent information problems (Shubik, 1959, Chapter 8) there is no way of estimating maximum profit and the concept of maximum becomes meaningless. They do explain price rigidity downward and upward and specify conditions under which price wars (games of survival) will occur.

The games also enable one to distinguish different kinds of dynamics that are confused in the earlier empirical-deviation treatments of oligopoly. For example, bilateral monopoly usually exhibits Chicken dynamics, while oligopoly and oligopsony are always n-person Prisoner's Dilemmas, and small coalitions exhibit Leader dynamics. Fellner's discussion (1949, pp. 3–33) confounds all three of these quite different dynamics.

The dynamics of competition and oligopoly, discussed above, are only one example of how the game-theoretic perspective has contributed to the advance of science. Let us now reflect on that perspective, to see what changes it has made in the neoclassical Subject and Object.

We begin with the Object. First, the neoclassical system was knowable only by reference to long-run equilibrium, including approaches to and deviations from equilibrium. Even individual rationality was primarily a long-run equilibrium characteristic; in the short run people are irrational. In game theory long-run equilibrium disappears. Games are all short-run processes; the long run can be brought in via the supergame with absorbing states (Amnon Rapoport, 1967; Snyder, 1971, pp. 93–102), but this is a recent development. The gaming experiments with 300 plays also suggest a long run (Rapoport and Chammah, 1965) but these experiments explicitly transcend the game-theoretic perspective. Second, some games do not have a determinate solution, but wander about indeterminately with continued play; there is no equilibrium at all. The indeterminateness of empirical oligopolistic industries was one of the characteristics that perplexed the neoclassicists and showed the irrelevance of their models, but for game theory indeterminacy can be easily explained. Third and most important, some games have paradoxical solutions which none of the players want but which they are powerless to avoid. The most famous example is Prisoner's Dilemma (Rapoport, 1964, Chapter 6; Luce and Raiffa, 1957, pp. 94–102). In two-person Prisoner's Dilemma, the simplest case, each player rationally prefers to cooperate with the other, but is forced by game dynamics and his own rationality into ruinous competition. Other examples are Hero and Leader, in which there are two opposed ways to cooperate, and the two players are forced in spite of themselves to struggle over these two ways, perhaps ending in mutual ruin (cf. Snyder and Diesing, 1977, pp. 42–43). Prisoner's Dilemma describes the dynamics of rivalry, while Leader describes the dynamics of coalitions and alliances.

Here we have a concept of a system, the Game, whose motive force comes from individual desires to maximize expected utility, but which becomes independent of its source and compels the players trapped in it. This phenomenon was noticed first in the 2 × 2 games but is even more noticeable in the expanded games such as expanded Chicken, a perfectly fiendish game (Hamburger, 1969; Snyder and Diesing, 1977, pp. 59–61). It also applies to the n-person games.

In particular, n-person Prisoner's Dilemma (Weil, 1966; Bonacich et al., 1976; Fox and Guyer, 1977) is a game-theoretic analog to perfect competition that brings out short-run characteristics that are invisible in the long-run equilibrium model. In n-person Prisoner's Dilemma any individual player can improve his position by playing competitively (D strategy) and will do so if he is rational. Up to a point the others are not damaged appreciably; but beyond that point the whole outcome set reverses and all lose. Three examples will illustrate.

1) Scitovsky argued that the perfect competition argument for free trade was mistaken, since any individual country could gain an advantage by restricting its monopolistic export supply and reducing its demand, thereby improving its terms of trade. But if more than a few countries did this, all would be forced to; then international trade would decline drastically, the terms of trade would return to their previous ratio, and all countries would lose (Scitovsky, 1942, cited in Robinson, 1971, p. x).

2) If all the merchants in a town have an understanding that they will remain closed on Sunday, all benefit. Any one merchant can benefit greatly by opening on Sunday, without appreciably damaging the others. As more merchants act rationally and open on Sunday, the benefits decline and the damage to the others becomes noticeable; beyond a certain point all must open and all lose.

3) In small-family agriculture an improvement in the corn/hog ratio induces the rational farmer to increase his hog production at great profit to himself. If more than a few farmers do this the declining hog price wipes out the initial benefits and forces all farmers to increase production to compensate for lower income; the hog price goes down steeply, and all farmers lose.

An example of n-person Hero (or Leader) appears in Keynes: ". . . since there is, as a rule, no means of securing a simultaneous and equal reduction of money-wages in all industries, it is in the interest of all workers to resist a reduction in their own particular case. In fact, a movement [to lower wages] will be much more strongly resisted than a gradual and automatic lowering of real wages as a result of rising prices" (1936, p. 264). In n-person Hero the first players to make a sacrificial move lose while others benefit; hence if players are rational no one moves first and all lose. The neoclassicist, who reasons directly from individual rational choice to the system via aggregation, cannot conceive such gamelike structures in the system, at least did not before Olson (1965). Consequently he is led to explain them as consequences of individual irrationality or union monopoly. And since the irrational is unknowable by neoclassical methods, such an explanation suggests that the perverse phenomenon is a temporary deviation of no scientific importance. Wage rigidity, for instance, has typically been attributed to "money illusion," a kind of forecasting error. However, game theory demonstrates that such gamelike structures are activated precisely by individual rationality, and that nonrational factors like conscience or group loyalty are necessary for an optimum solution.

In summary, a system based on personal rivalry or even on self-contained rational individuals has its own dynamics which are independent of and opposed to the purposes of the individuals in it. The dynamics are mainly Prisoner's Dilemma for competition and Leader for cooperation. The competitive system does not move toward long-run equilibrium, though short-run equilibrium (DD, for example all merchants open on Sunday) does occur. It moves rather through coalition dynamics to oligopoly: players are bankrupted or absorbed by coalitions that become leader dominated. Oligopoly stabilizes itself through responsible collusion of the larger players and punishment of the smaller players if they seek more than their allotted share (Shubik's K–R stability). Nor does the cooperative system move toward equilibrium; it exhibits rigidities, conflicts and other breakdowns.

This new conception of the System brings with it changes in the conception of the Subject. Game theory initially assumed the neoclassical Subject: the isolated individual with a self-generated preference schedule who examines all the alternatives open to him and selects the one that maximizes expected utility in the long run. However, in about a decade (Luce and Raiffa, 1957) this conception of the rational Subject had been destroyed; it had been demonstrated to be indeterminate, paradoxical to the point of absurdity, and presupposing nonrational components such as gambling propensities, conscience, and a sense of fairness or justice.

The argument begins with a definition (Luce and Raiffa, 1957, Chapter 2). What does "maximizing expected utility in the long run" mean? It means that the decision-maker must predict the consequences of alternative actions, then estimate and sum the utility of each action discounted by time, then compare the sums. But consequences occur in the future, and the future cannot be known with certainty. Consequences are therefore probable at best. But in the frequency theory of probability, "the probability of a single outcome" has no meaning; probability refers to a statistical distribution of outcomes. The probability of an outcome is the percentage of times it occurs in a large number of trials. Therefore, "expected utility" has meaning only in reference to a large set of similar actions. Given a large set, the expected utility of one instance is the midpoint of the distribution curve of utilities of the set. "Maximizing expected utility" therefore has meaning only when one is deciding on a policy to be carried out a large number of times (Borch, 1968, pp. 11-14). This point, incidentally, was already recognized by Knight (1921) in his discussion of the entrepreneur's ability to predict the future. The presence of such an ability, Knight argues, can be inferred only when there is a large ratio of successes in the long run, since the future is inherently probabilistic.

One can, however, make sense of "maximizing expected utility" in a single decision by calling the decision a bet, a gamble on the future. "The alternative that maximizes expected utility" becomes the "best bet." But what does "best bet" mean? By a parallel chain of reasoning, it is the bet a professional gambler would make as a matter of policy in order to maximize his actual returns. One way or another the long run is inherent in this conception of rationality. A short-run model, a single play of a game, cannot use the concept of maximization.

In game theory the above situation is conceptualized as a "game against Nature" (Milnor, 1954). The individual faces a world which he does not understand, and chooses a policy that will maximize his long-run returns. But this conceptualization immediately transforms the neoclassical conception of uncertainty and eliminates Knight's distinction between risk and uncertainty (Borch, 1968, pp. 77 ff.). Since we do not know Nature's strategy we must assume all outcomes to be equiprobable unless we have information to the contrary. This is an *a priori* probability that may or may not be reducible to frequency probability depending on which logician you wish to believe. In any case, a probability number can be assigned to all possible outcomes, based either on information or on the lack of information, and the need for Knight's "entrepreneur" disappears.

The situation is different in games against people, the normal oligopoly situation. Here the opponent is rational, so we know his strategy; it is the strategy we would choose if we were in his place.

Figure 2.1. Possible results in the game of matching pennies.
Numbers are payoffs to A.

		B	
		heads	tails
A	heads	1	-1
	tails	-1	1

Once the preferences of the players over the set of possible outcomes is estimated—and in a business situation this is not difficult—uncertainty disappears. All strategies are known and the value of the outcome for each player is therefore also known.

Here the conception of rationality changes again. Since the opponent is rational he will use his best strategy; and this is the worst one for us. Our best strategy, therefore, is the one which leads to the best of the worst outcomes. The rational player minimaxes rather than maximizes (cf. Luce and Raiffa, 1957, pp. 60–65). The above argument is based on the constant-sum game but can be extended to the variable-sum game.

In some games, those with a "saddle point," the minimax strategy is a specific one. However, there are games in which no one strategy is minimax. The simplest example is matching pennies, in which two players simultaneously display a coin, with either head or tail turned up. A wins if the coins match and B wins if they do not match. If A adopts a "heads" strategy, consistently turning up "heads" on his coin, B can play "tails" and win consistently; but if B plays "tails" consistently A should play "tails" and win. Similarly if A's strategy is to alternate heads and tails, B can win by alternating tails and heads. The minimax strategy is to play heads and tails at random with a probability of ½, for instance by flipping a coin. This destroys any unconscious patterns which the other player can discover and match to win. Thus the rational player will base his decisions on chance (Borch, 1968, pp. 111–115; Howard, 1971, pp. 42–43). Such strategies are called "mixed strategies" since they mix two pure strategies in a certain ratio.

Experimental evidence suggests that mixed strategies are beyond the calculating ability of most people (Lieberman, 1962), except in simple cases such as matching pennies. Braithwaite's " Matthew-Luke" game (Braithwaite, 1955; Luce and Raiffa, 1957, pp. 145–150) is an example in which a more complex mixed strategy is minimax rational.[2] This means that ordinarily one's opponent will not be completely minimax rational. But in that case one can do better by not minimaxing and by taking advantage of his deviations from the best strategy (Luce and Raiffa, 1957, pp. 77-85). The minimax rule is conservative; it minimizes losses against the best possible opponent, but sacrifices opportunities for gain against weaker opponents. Other decision rules are possible in such circumstances, and in fact three other rules were discussed in the early 1950's. Milnor, comparing and evaluating these rules in 1954, concludes, "It has become apparent that no possible criterion can have all of the properties that one would desire" (Milnor, 1954, p. 129; Luce and Raiffa, 1957, pp. 278-306; Ellsberg, 1956). In other words, there is no rational way to choose a rational decision rule. This means that even if the opponent is rational we cannot estimate his strategy with certainty, since he may be using any of the four decision rules. His choice will depend on nonrational propensities such as his attitude toward gambling.

The concept of maximizing expected utility has now evaporated. It cannot be stated with precision. (See Rapoport, 1964, Chapters 1-8, for a more detailed argument). Morgenstern is even more emphatic; speaking of game theory, he asserts, "The basic feature of the theory is to show that in economics one is not confronted with maximum problems . . . ; indeed the notion of a maximum has no meaning" (in Shubik, 1959, p. viii).

A similar fate overtook the concept of "maximizing general welfare" of neoclassical welfare economics. Arrow (1951) demonstrated that if one makes the neoclassical assumptions about individual rationality it is not necessarily possible to measure the level of general welfare. The concept is sometimes indeterminate. The crucial neoclassical assumption is the independence of individual preference schedules, which as we have seen is an essential part of the neoclassical standpoint, an essential part of "individual freedom." Arrow argued that it is necessary to have some nonrational, superindividual ordering of preferences to produce a determinate, measurable general welfare. In other words, a determinate general welfare can exist only in a community of shared preferences. The masculine-individualist standpoint presupposes a community maintained by "feminine" personalities and induced preferences.

The final absurdity revealed by game theory is the "paradoxes of rationality" (Rapoport, 1964, Chapter 6; Rapoport and Chammah, 1965, pp. 11-13, 24-29; Howard, 1971). In these cases the problem is not that "rationality" has no precise meaning; it is rather that whatever it may mean it leads to absurd results. In Prisoner's Dilemma played 300 times in succession the minimax-rational strategy yields a payoff so absurd that only a fool would act rationally, and no experimental subjects do (Rapoport and Chammah, 1965, p. 54). In Chicken "to choose a sure-thing strategy is to be a 'sucker' that capitulates entirely to the other side" (Howard, 1971, p. 181). A sure-thing strategy is one that maximizes expected utility no matter what the opponent does; it is a stupid strategy. But the opposite strategy, the one that deterrence theorists like Schelling advocate, can be even worse, leading to preference deterioration (Howard, 1971, p. 199) and mutual disaster. One cause of the deteriorating relations between France and Germany 1904–1914 was their successive "rational" strategy choices in a series of crisis games. A full exposition of the paradoxes of rationality would require a more technical discussion, so I omit it here.

In summary, the mathematical investigation of rational choice in game theory has demonstrated step by step that the neoclassical conception of rational choice has no clear meaning, and that whatever it means, "rational" choice can sometimes lead to absurd results. This applies primarily to oligopoly-type situations but can apply also to some competitive situations (n-person Prisoner's Dilemma). But the conception of rationality as the maximization of expected utility lies at the heart of the neoclassical perspective.

The two changes in the neoclassical perspective produced by game theory, changes in the Subject and in the Object, are two aspects of the same thing. Individual maximizing-rationality presupposes a certain sort of system, one that confronts the individual impersonally and passively as material for his activity. A system with its own dynamics that imposes itself on individuals contrary to their wishes though based on them is a system that is alien to maximizing-rationality (though not to other forms of rationality to be discussed in later chapters). The postulate of maximizing-rationality thus destroys itself by entailing a system within which it is alien, unintelligible, and produces absurd results.

Has this demonstration, which severely limits the usefulness of neoclassical individualism as a scientific standpoint, induced any neoclassicists to shift to a different standpoint? I know of no one who has shifted for this reason. Standpoints cannot be chosen or discarded in a rational fashion because they condition one's reasoning processes and thus are prior to individual rationality. Neoclassicists have not shifted to another standpoint because they cannot conceive of one. For example Stigler asserts, in discussing recent work on oligopolistic decision-making, that the assumption that monopolists do not maximize profits is an abandonment of all formal theory which we shall naturally refuse to accept until we are given a better theory. "Unless one is prepared to take the mighty methodological leap into the unknown that a nonmaximizing theory requires" (1976, p. 216), one had better stick to existing theory. Stigler's "unknown" apparently includes game theory. "To deny profit maximization, of course, is to deny our ability to make determinate statements about anything" (Haring and Smith, 1959, p. 582).

Instead, when confronted with the various paradoxes that make maximization a meaningless concept the neoclassicist typically assumes them away so he can get on with his model-building. For instance: "As a criterion for choosing among alternative courses of action, the concept of profit maximization is meaningless in an uncertain world. Therefore, in order to simplify the analysis, I shall assume a world of certainty" (Wenders, 1972, p. 66). Neoclassical welfare economists have ignored Arrow's theorem, which reduces their science to total absurdity (cf. E.K. Hunt, *The Ideal Foundations of Welfare Economics*, 1977).

What scientific value, if any, the neoclassical perspective still retains after 1957 is a question that shall concern us in several later chapters including Chapter Three. From the previous discussion we would expect to find such value in situations that resemble long-run perfect competition where community or alienation is no problem, rather than in oligopoly-type situations.

Three Extended
Applications of the
Neoclassical Perspective

The neoclassical economists of the 1930's limited their models to the economy, that is to the system of production and exchange mediated by money. They explicitly excluded politics, which they defined as the arena of rational deliberation about the legal framework of the economy. There were two kinds of rationality: economic, the allocation of one's own resources to one's own ends according to the marginal calculus; and political, the impartial discussion of the rules of social exchange. Government was the imperfect medium by which political discussion was transformed into laws and which enforced laws. The economy produced wealth and happiness; the political system produced justice, defined negatively as the minimization of force and fraud or positively as fairness (Hayek, 1960). An effective political system also depended on a nonrational habit of obedience to laws, since otherwise too much coercion would be needed to enforce laws.

Family life was also explicitly excluded from the marginal calculus. The household participated in the economy as a unit, and action within the family was based on love or other nonrational processes. Various arenas of irrationality were also excluded by one or another neoclassicist: insane people, defined as those who are ignorant of their own preferences; primitive cultures, governed by tradition rather than reason; people whose labor supply curve is negatively sloped; and people who live by impulse rather than foresight and calculation.

Beginning in the 1950's enterprising neoclassicists removed these limitations one by one and gradually extended the sphere of maximizing-rational calculation into the excluded areas. We shall examine several extensions in the present chapter and evaluate their contributions to science. In particular we shall ask whether these extensions have expanded the limits of the neoclassic perspective, whether they have overcome some of the formal difficulties discovered by game theorists, and whether they have produced empirical support for their models and concepts.

I. Politics

The extension to politics was sketched in Dahl and Lindblom's *Politics, Economics, and Welfare* (1951) but first worked out systematically in Downs' *An Economic Theory of Democracy* (1957). Downs discards the neoclassical dualism between impartial political deliberation and self-centered economic calculation by treating politics, too, as selfish. Politicians want to get elected to further their own ambitions; voters want policies adopted. The result is an exchange of policies for votes. Politicians promise and carry out those policies that will maximize votes; voters vote for the party that will maximize their policy preferences. Riker (1962) comments that a rational party will maximize, not votes, but the probability of getting elected, and this requires only slightly more than 50% of the votes. However, we need not pursue these details, as Banfield (1961) has provided a much more elaborate model of maximizing-rational politics. Downs limits himself to the exchange of votes and policies so he can develop a strict formal model with postulates and deductions, while Banfield constructs a looser model that enriches the rational core with a wide variety of empirical observations, insights, and generalizations.

According to Banfield, the big-city mayor and city politicians in general can be regarded as small businessmen (1961, Chapters 8, 11). The mayor sells a variety of commodities: jobs, personal favors, party posts, opportunity for graft; also administrative efficiency, honest government, city services, building projects, and blue-ribbon candidates. He is indifferent as to which of these he will provide, being interested only in providing whatever his customers will buy. His products are paid for with bits of "influence" (political power). The

Figure 3.1. The mayor as small businessman.

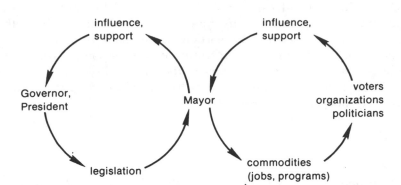

basic influence is votes, which keep him in office; derivative influence includes public support by newspapers, organizations, opinion leaders, and other politicians. Support in turn can be converted into votes and influence on other politicians.

The mayor's stock of influence constitutes his "working capital." This must be invested to replenish his stock of commodities. For instance, he can use his influence on the Governor, the Legislature, the County Board, or the City Council to promote legislation desired by his constituents–customers, or legislation which will give him a stock of jobs and favors to distribute. Or he can use his influence on other politicians to promote a national party ticket that will then supply him with favors from Washington.

The mayor operates under the imperative of maintaining and if possible increasing his stocks, both of commodities and of working capital (influence). Failure to do so means bankruptcy and exit from the political scene. The many other politician–businessmen in the urban political system all operate under the same imperative, and must therefore calculate costs and returns carefully in their constant business dealings with each other. The mark of success is a gradual increase in working capital, as the politician moves from ward politics to bloc or district leader to elective office to state and national power broker.

> In order to maintain itself and to accomplish its purposes, any organization must offer incentives of the kinds and amounts that are necessary to elicit the contributions of activity it requires. It must then use these contributions of activity so as to secure a renewed supply of resources from which further incentives may be provided . . . or else cease to exist (Meyerson and Banfield, 1955, p. 70).

Inequality is a normal characteristic of this political system. Politicians range in influence from the outlying precinct committeeman with only his personal friendship to distribute for a few votes, to the Mayor with 9000 patronage jobs in his pocket and 30–40 electoral votes deliverable to the right national politicians. Their customers range from the poorest voter who has only one vote, to the newspaper publisher or organization head whose support is worth hundreds of thousands of votes. The rich customer can buy a great deal—legislation, construction projects, efficient city services—while the poor voter gets very little for his one little vote. " . . . there were few rewards for the underlying population in Dawson's game" (Meyerson and Banfield, 1955, p. 79). The cause of the inequality is in part the Constitution (Banfield, 1961, p. 241), which distributes one vote to many people but larger amounts of influence to officials; in part it just seems to be given, and presumably results from differences of ability and enterprise.

The Downs and Banfield models clearly stay within the limits of the neoclassical perspective. The neoclassical economists assumed a political framework that would reduce force and fraud and allow markets to operate; Downs and Banfield make the same assumption. Both assume that a constitution already exists. Both assume that a loyal opposition party exists, that dissent is tolerated, that incumbent parties allow free elections and peacefully yield power if defeated. Downs assumes a habit of obedience to law (1957, pp. 12, 24, 30), though Banfield's more empirical model assumes this only for voters, not for politicians. Downs, following Dahl and Lindblom, assumes that every incumbent government automatically has enough power for its legitimate purposes (1957, p. 22), and Banfield avoids the issue of coercive power as distinct from influence.

For Downs political tastes are arbitrary, as for the neoclassical economists. Downs asserts that changes of political tastes are among the most important political events possible, but leaves the determinants of tastes outside his model (1957, p. 140). Banfield makes some empirical observations about probable sources of tastes but leaves the sources outside his model.

Downs' discussion of the Arrow paradox (1957, Chapter 4) shows that he, like the neoclassical economists, has no concept of community. Downs recognizes the paradox, in his assertion that without some nonrational ordering of voters' tastes, political rationality is impossible for both politicians and voters. In other words, maximizing-rational behavior presupposes a community that can be neither established nor maintained by individual rational choice. Downs asserts that the paradox is insoluble, and vaguely assumes that pervasive uncertainty about others' preferences permits politicians to make rational choices in spite of the paradox (1957, pp. 62–63). "This admitted dodge allows us to keep hold of the majority principle long enough to make some useful deductions from it" (p. 63).

The neoclassical economists dealt with the political-legal framework, though not the community framework, by assuming a second kind of rational thought that would establish and maintain it. Downs discards the second kind of rationality for the sake of consistency; but as a result the existence of a political-legal framework becomes unintelligible. Consequently the Downs model points beyond itself to the need for a different perspective to deal with the political-legal and community frameworks.

The same consequence appears empirically in Banfield's more empirical model. Banfield assumes the existence of a political-legal framework for machine politics and ignores the question of how this framework is maintained. However, Shefter's history of machine politics in New York City describes how each machine destroyed its own political framework and thereby destroyed itself (Shefter, 1976, 1977). New York machines exchanged material benefits for votes; but this sort of exchange induced a mentality of "rapacious individualism" in both politicians and voters, which in turn induced a political inflation cycle of more bribery, more graft, higher prices for support and votes, more visibility, and more opposition from nonparticipants until the system lost its legitimacy and collapsed. This was not simply an arbitrary change in voters' tastes, since the tastes were themselves induced by the system, and the successor system induced different tastes in some of the same voters as well as responding to other tastes ignored by the machine. Shefter's study of system maintenance problems is based on a broader perspective that includes at least part of the neoclassical perspective within it.

The Downs and Banfield models do not overcome any of the formal difficulties discovered by game theorists. Downs recognizes only one such difficulty, the Arrow Paradox, and declares that it is insoluble; Banfield of course does not deal with any of the difficulties. Actually

Banfield's vague model need not even assume maximizing-rationality for politicians and voters; it is compatible with bounded rationality and rules of thumb decisions.

Though the Downs and Banfield models do not transcend the limits of the neoclassic perspective, do they produce new empirical data? Downs does not; he ends with a list of testable hypotheses but no tests, and relies throughout his argument on everyday conventional facts about politics. Banfield does provide data, and the strength of his model is located in the six detailed case studies that accompany it, plus the excellent Meyerson–Banfield study (1955). Banfield has used his model as a case-study guide; it tells him to look for political exchanges, resources, prices, calculation, sources of supply, competitors, and long-term exchange relationships. The result is an enriched understanding of Chicago politics.

But how broadly useful is Banfield's case-study guide? Can it be used for case studies in all urban politics? According to Peterson and Greenstone, 1976, Banfield's model is one of three that are applicable to the politics of large US cities. The mayor's policy or conception of politics determines which model applies; Banfield's model applies when the mayor believes that urban politics ought to consist of pluralist bargaining among the major holders of political influence, with troublemakers and rabble-rousers excluded. In other words Banfield's model is a special case of a theory that also includes reference to beliefs about politics and to system-maintenance activities. The larger theory points to additional facts about system-maintenance that Banfield knows (Banfield, in Alcaly and Mermelstein, 1977, p. 8) but does not include in his case studies.

Downs' work and that of Duncan Black (1958) and Riker (1962) provided the impetus for several schools of "rational choice" theorists who have extended the maximizing-rationality postulates to politics. The great diversity of developments here cannot be adequately summarized in one chapter, so I shall select two overlapping currents of development for summary.

One is the Virginia school of Buchanan and Tullock, which derives from the Chicago school of neoclassical economics and in turn has its own offshoots all over the country, united around the journal *Public Choice*. This school applies neoclassic thinking to political topics, or more generally to "nonmarket decision-making." It argues that the political arena cannot be essentially different from the economy, because both are activated by individual decisions. The rational individual spends his money in the market and his votes in the political arena or nonmarket according to marginal calculation. The market aggregates spending decisions to produce, at equilibrium, a Pareto-optimum supply of private goods; the political arena aggregates votes to produce, at equilibrium, a Pareto-optimum supply of public goods (Buchanan and Tollison, 1972, Chapter 21). Public goods are goods that are either paid for or consumed collectively.

It appears that there are many types of public goods (Riker and Ordeshook, 1973, Chapter 9), and the classification of a good as private or public depends on tastes and is often arbitrary. Since most private production has external effects, one can focus on the externalities and call them public goods, or abstract from the externalities and call them private (Offe, 1972, pp. 53–55).

Unlike Downs, members of the public choice school typically treat government as a neutral medium of collective choice; they postulate "that politicians behave 'as if' they transmit the preferences of citizens into political outcomes" (Buchanan and Tollison, 1972, p. 39). Only if the results do not come out as predicted is it necessary to add postulates about interferences by politicians pursuing private goods.

Members of the Virginia school also write about constitutions, following the lead set by Buchanan and Tullock (1962). They define constitution as voting rules which determine how votes are aggregated into public choices. The ideal set of voting rules are those that far-sighted rational individuals would adopt unanimously to maximize their chance of maximally achieving future utility functions.

Buchanan and Tullock show that one can derive plausible voting rules from the assumption of individual maximizing-rationality, and that Knight's assumption of an impartial concern for the public interest is unnecessary. Voting rules, like game rules, are chosen for the long future, and individuals do not know what their specific wants will be far in the future. Consequently they must choose rules that will benefit them on the average, and such rules will be the same as those chosen by impartial statesmen. However, this extremely hypothetical argument brings out the limits of the neoclassical perspective more clearly than ever. The argument does not work in a society divided into classes or into racial, religious, or ethnic groupings (Buchanan and Tullock, 1962, p. 80) since in such a society individuals can predict their future status and choose voting rules accordingly. It also requires a consensus on fundamental values to work well (p. 116). In other words it does not apply to a complex multigroup society like the United States; such a society requires something other than rational self-interest to hold it together. I doubt that it applies to any existing society.

The authors themselves recognize and insist on the limits of their argument. Their model explains only one aspect of behavior, the maximizing-rational aspect (p. 21); since human beings are many-sided, they require other models to deal with other aspects of their behavior (pp. 30, 300). Elsewhere Tullock suggests that a minimum social science requires at least two branches: one dealing with the consequences of rational calculation, and one dealing with the molding or indoctrination of preferences, that is with socialization (Buchanan and Tollison, 1972, Chapter 23).

Buchanan and Tullock's treatment of voting rules is more complex than that of Downs and Banfield, who simply assume a constitution and a habit of obedience to it. However, the conclusion is the same: existing constitutions are not maintained by individual rational calculation. In politics as in the economy individual rationality requires a setting of community or value-consensus (coerced or voluntary) that it cannot itself maintain. To understand this setting requires a perspective different from the individualist neoclassical perspective.

The second trend of development may be called the "mathematical models of political choice" aproach, for example the *Mathematical Applications in Political Science* series and Niemi and Weisberg, 1972. This research community is unified primarily by their mathematical modeling method rather than by perspective and therefore is open to multiple perspectives. The assumption of rationality appears in many models, but different assumptions appear as well. In particular the influence of Coleman and McPhee is apparent in models of opinion formation, discussion, learning, and in stochastic response models (Niemi and Weisberg, 1972, passim.) Coleman and McPhee, students of Paul Lazarsfeld, have developed mathematical models of objectified social processes (Coleman, 1964; McPhee, 1962; McPhee and Glaser, 1962). Coleman, in turn, has picked up utility-maximization postulates in his later modeling work. For some of these mathematical modelers the rationality postulate is *a priori* true and alternatives are unthinkable; for others it is one of several convenient and fruitful postulates. Consequently the limits of the neoclassical perspective are transcended by including different perspectives.

The mathematical interest of these modelers has been mainly expressed in their game models of political processes—coalition building, committee decisions, voting, campaign strategies. All the paradoxes of rationality discovered by game theorists have been given political illustrations, and new paradoxes have been added to the list (Brams, *Paradoxes in Politics*, 1976). It is apparent that the institutional structure, the Game, within which individual decisions occur is an important determinant of the outcome. Even individual rationality takes different forms in different game settings: "The concept of rationality can be defined at various levels, depending on the environmental constraints assumed to be operative" (Brams, 1976, p. 27). A choice that is rational by one definition is irrational by another, and one can distinguish various degrees of "sophistication" in voting. The concept of maximizing expected utility is again shown to be indeterminate in politics as in oligopoly situations. The same indeterminacy appears at the level of voting rules, contrary to Buchanan and Tullock's arguments: different rules for aggregating preferences produce different outcomes, and no one rule seems intuitively preferable (Brams, 1976, Chapter 1). "The will of the people" or "majority will" can be just as indeterminate as "greatest good for the greatest number."

The Arrow paradox in particular has been discussed extensively and treated as an important key to understanding social structures. (Tullock, in contrast, has tried to argue Arrow's theorem away as a trivial puzzle: Tullock, 1967, Chapter 3). Arrow demonstrated that if individual preferences are randomly distributed and if other plausible conditions hold, then individual preferences do not necessarily sum to a determinate social maximum. However, in actual societies individual preferences are not random, but are organized by cultural conventions and ideals and by voting rules (Riker and Ordeshook, 1973, Chapter 4; Brams, 1976, Chapter 2). In other words, rational social choice is made possible by nonrational cultural factors which organize and structure individual preferences.

In summary, the "rational choice" models of political decision have blossomed out in all directions and produced many new insights into the individualist-rational aspect of politics. Game theory in particular has proved to be a fruitful tool for understanding many aspects of politics. At the same time, the need for a nonrational cultural or social framework for rational behavior has become inescapably evident. The rational choice theorists began by rejecting the neoclassical dualism between economic and political rationality, but arrived instead at a dualism between rational choice and a nonrational social setting for choice. The setting, whether described as arbitrary cultural conventions or the socialization of preferences, lies beyond the horizon of the neoclassical perspective and calls for a different perspective.

The dissolution and relativization of maximizing-rationality in gamelike situations has been confirmed and even extended.

The main weakness of these mathematical modelers and a priori deductive theorists is that they have been rather casual about empirical testing of their models. Mainly they have selected cases to illustrate their models and demonstrate empirical relevance. Or they have worked out postulates that would deductively "explain" some outcome known in advance. In some cases where the facts were obviously far from those predictable by a rational choice model, they have concentrated on explaining away the discrepancy (for example, Buchanan and Tullock, 1962, p. 192). The value of all such explanations and explainings-away must be estimated by comparing them with alternative explanations. But such a task calls for a perspective that can comprehend alternative explanations, a perspective broader than the neoclassical-individualist approach. When rational choice theorists can see only irrational, purposeless, unpredictable behavior beyond the scope of their models (for example Riker and Ordeshook, 1973, p. 10), they show the need for a perspective that can find regularity where they can see only chaos.

II. Interpersonal Relations

If men try to maximize expected utility in everything they do, we should be able to find evidence of rational choice in the trivial details of everyday life as well as the grand choices of politics. Every human interaction involves an exchange and/or production of some sort, and therefore costs and benefits for each participant. In a society of many potential interactors, a kind of market must appear in which the prices of exchanged goods are set by supply and demand; rational men will then choose those particular exchanges which maximize their benefit-cost ratio.

I. The attempt to treat interpersonal relations as rational exchanges was pioneered by Homans (1961, 1964a, 1967). In an earlier work (Homans and Schneider, 1955) Homans attempted to apply the postulate to one particular example of institutional behavior, unilateral cross-cousin marriage. However, this work is totally absurd, as Needham (1962) has shown in detail, so it need not be considered seriously.

Homans' reason for borrowing the postulate of maximizing-rationality is that he shares the neoclassical standpoint. He views society from the standpoint of the individual. This is made abundantly clear by his autobiographical remarks (1962), by his 1964 address "Bringing Men Back In," and by scattered statements elsewhere such as: "I think that what I have been saying is obvious in the extreme. The institutions, organizations, and societies that sociologists study can always be

analyzed, without residue, into the behavior of individual men"
(Homans, 1964b, p. 231). To this we need only add, as in the previous
chapter, that Homans' individual is a certain kind of man, one who
distinguishes himself from others and tries to maximize his own net
advantages. In Wildavsky's phrase, he is "Unable to conceive of
outside forces at work" on his preference function (1975a, p. 56).

Homans' work suffers from two severe methodological difficulties.
One difficulty is the confusion that results from transferring concepts
from the formalist tradition in economics to the empiricist tradition in
sociology. Formalists know the difference between a tautology, a
definition, and an empirical postulate, and are sensitive to the
deductive relations among mathematical or formal entities. They tend
to be casual about empirical exemplifications of models, and are more
sensitive to the abstract structures implicit in a situation than to the
particular empirical details. Empiricists like Homans, with his case
study background, are vague on the formal status of a concept, casual
about deduction, and uninterested or contemptuous of mathematical
models—Homans calls them "toys" and openly expresses his low
opinion of them (1961).

As a result Homans is vague on the logical status of his five basic
propositions (1961, Chapter 4). He presents them as empirical hypotheses and proposes to test them, but four of the five are tautologies
and therefore untestable.

> 1. If in the past the occurrence of a particular stimulus-situation has
> been the occasion on which a man's activity has been rewarded, then the
> more similar the present stimulus-situation is to the past one, the more
> likely he is to emit the activity, or some similar activity, now (1961,
> p. 53).

This proposition would be empirical if there were some measure of
the similarity of stimuli. Homans offers none, says the question is
exceedingly complicated, and asserts that he will not discuss the topic
further. But if the only evidence of similarity is the recurrence of
rewarded activity, the proposition is a tautology; it says that a
stimulus which elicits a response will elicit a response. That is, if an
apparently similar stimulus does not elicit the expected activity, one
can always find some difference of stimuli that will account for the
negative result.

> 4. The more often a man has in the recent past received a rewarding
> activity from another, the less valuable any further unit of that activity
> becomes to him. (1961, p. 55).

This proposition is true by definition. Homans proposes as a measure of value the inverse of the amount of a reward received in the recent past (p. 43). The greater the amount received the less the value. If we substitute this measure into 4, it becomes: The less valuable a rewarding activity is, the less valuable any further unit of that activity is to him.

Homans declares propositions 2 and 3 to be equivalent to the laws of supply and demand (p. 69): "2. The more valuable the reward gotten by an activity, the more often a man will emit it. . . . 3. The higher the cost incurred by an activity, the less often a man will emit it." Both are deducible, when carefully formulated in terms of costs and returns, from the proposition that men act to maximize net value or utility. That is, one must stipulate that costs are less than returns, that costs are constant for proposition 2 and returns constant for proposition 3, and that cost is measured by the value of foregone alternatives. But the basic proposition that men act to maximize net value is a tautology for Homans because the only evidence that men value something is the fact that they have pursued it in the past.

In short, propositions 2 and 3 are tautologies because they are deduced from a tautological version of the rationality principle. Proposition 4 is true by definition; proposition 1 is a tautology because it is deduced from the Skinnerian principle that rewarded activity is repeated. This principle is a tautology because the evidence that something is a reward, a reinforcer, is that it has in the past been followed by increased activity (Skinner, 1935, 1938, p. 62). The principle can therefore be stated as, "whatever has been found to reinforce a certain activity will reinforce it, *ceteris paribus*." This is a version of the consistency principle.

The second methodological difficulty is that in nonmonetary exchanges the goods exchanged, the quantity exchanged, and the "price," are difficult to discover empirically. This is not a situation suitable for quantitative econometric data; it calls for empathy and creative imagination. For this reason formalist economists like Pigou have avoided nonmonetary exchanges in their theorizing; but Homans the empiricist meets the challenge magnificently. He locates one good after another: approval, conformity to norms, fairness, status congruence, sociability, hurting someone who hurts you, pride, self-respect, altruism, aggression, and so on. Discrepant data, in which apparently rewarding activities are not chosen, are used to locate new kinds of goods that are chosen (for example, pp. 173–177). Or they are interpreted as evidence that the unchosen or low-ranked activities are not so valuable after all (p. 151 bottom). As for price, Homans evades the issue by assuming that all exchanges are of equal value.

The result, in spite of Homans' misconception that he is testing something, is an imaginative interpretation of small-group data as a process of rational exchange. His five propositions tell him to look for exchanges, rewards, and costs, and to relate changes or differences in rates of activity to these rewards and costs. His work parallels Banfield's interpretation of Chicago politics as small business activity. In both cases the very considerable achievement consists of systematic, empathetic interpretation of a great many empirical studies. Homans' achievement in turn has sensitized his followers to exchanges, rewards, and costs in small groups, as Gergen has observed (Hamblin and Kunkel, 1977, pp. 102-104). His followers have also been empiricists and therefore unconcerned with the logical characteristics of Homans' five propositions; to them any such propositions are an invitation to devise a measure and design an experiment.

Homans' followers have extended his ideas in a variety of directions (Hamblin and Kunkel, 1977). The dominant direction has been to treat rewards as reinforcers which can be used to control behavior. If a rewarded behavior is repeated (by definition of "reward") then a planned schedule of rewards can be used to modify behavior in any desired fashion. This sort of theorizing derives from Skinner, via Homans' incorporation of Skinner's principles, rather than from the Homans propositions discussed above. It is about as far from its neoclassical origins as possible: this is an objective, experimental, short run science which ignores rational calculation and which treats men as determined rather than as free. Yet it, too, derives from Bentham's utilitarianism. As Parsons (1937, Chapters 2, 3) and others have observed, utilitarian theory has tended to develop in two opposite directions, a subjective direction of free, rational calculation and an objective direction of control by reward and punishment.

Other followers of Homans such as Richard Emerson have located exchanges within networks of social relations (Hamblin and Kunkel, 1977, Chapter 4). One's position (role) in an interpersonal network determines which partners are available for exchanges and also determines one's relative power and thereby the terms of the exchange. Different types of networks distribute power differently and thereby produce different patterns of exchange. Concern therefore is with the structural characteristics of networks, using the theorems of graph theory and building on the work of Alex Bavelas and others (Cartwright and Zander, 1953, Chapter 33).

This sort of work plainly is no longer situated within the neoclassical perspective. It is objective, experimental, empirical, concerned with structural characteristics of networks as determinants of individual choice. Individuals calculate and try to maximize expected utility, but the roles they play determine the range of possible calculation and the stability of the exchange relationship. Neoclassic categories such as cost, opportunity cost (Thibaut and Kelley's CL_{alt}), and profit are combined with the sociological categories of roles and relations (Hamblin and Kunkel, 1977, p. 122) and the structural categories of graph theory like balance, centrality, positive and negative.

II. The most elaborate attempt to extend the neoclassic categories to the whole of human life is Alfred Kuhn's *Logic of Social Systems* (1974). Kuhn offers us a deductive system based on the postulate of maximizing–rationality and a large set of definitions, containing over a thousand deduced propositions by his count. These propositions extend Homans' conception of social behavior as exchange of utilities into the area of social institutions and organizations, including national government.

This enormous effort is remarkable for what is missing from it: this is vintage 1930 social science. The only economic organization considered is perfect competition; oligopoly theory, with its problems and insights, is missing. All the rest of macroeconomics, including both cyclical and secular growth phenomena, is missing. The system is in fact static and by Kuhn's own admission does not deal with any kind of change. Bargaining is treated at the level of Zeuthen (1930); the insights and paradoxes of game theory are omitted, including the game-theoretic work on uncertainty. Walton and McKersie (1965) is cited, but their category of integrative bargaining is omitted (Kuhn, p. 176), as well as their treatment of attitude structuring. The terminology of system theory is used, but only in a classificatory way; the theoretical contributions of systems analysis, such as Easton's work on information input overload (1965, part 2), the work on information flow in systems—cognitive loops, cognitive reverberation, redundancy, encoding and decoding, etc.—is all missing. And so on.

What went wrong? The problem, I believe, is the limitations of the neoclassical perspective, which Kuhn of course does not recognize. Kuhn states that his purpose "is to provide a unified, parsimonious, and largely deductive conceptual set across a broad range of social science, not to provide new knowledge" (p. 329). But since Kuhn's standpoint is the neoclassical one of the small businessman out to maximize the returns from his available personal resources, only ideas that can be conceived from this perspective are included in the conceptual set. Ideas that do not fit are either distorted until they do fit, or are omitted entirely. Specifically, 1) satisficing is reduced to maximizing (pp. 125–126). 2) There is much discussion of Blau (1964); but the heart of Blau's theory is a distinction between two kinds of exchange, instrumental exchange of extrinsic rewards by universalistic norms, and expressive symbolic exchange within intrinsically reward-ing solidary groups by particularistic norms, and only the first category appears in Kuhn. In short, Kuhn has translated a number of more recent ideas into his categories, thereby discarding whatever does not fit into the neoclassical framework.

Where Kuhn recognizes that something does not fit into his system, he puts it into a residual category called "idiographic" (Chapter 16). All questions of change and dynamics belong here, as well as most of anthropology and personality theory. Homans has a similar residual category, "history," as Parsons has noted (1964). The fundamental error here is to assert, and believe, that everything that cannot fit into one's model is inherently unmodelable. History and the idiographic are the realm of particular fact, of intuition rather than scientific knowledge. One's own model thus becomes the whole of science. However, social science has progressed in part by devising new models to explain previously unmodelled phenomena; it continually captures new aspects of the "idiographic" or "historical" and re-expresses them as regular, orderly, mathematical, systemic.

Kuhn's justification for his deductive-and-definitional strategy is that he is merely proposing a set of 1000 hypotheses to be tested by someone else.

This is a smokescreen. Kuhn obviously thinks his propositions are true and admits he would have a hard time entertaining the possibility that any of the basic postulates are incorrect (p. 482). Boulding asserts in the Foreword that a logic of the social system has now been constructed (p. xi), saying nothing about testing. Since the book reports how the world looks from the neoclassical standpoint, Kuhn and Boulding cannot help believing that this is how the world really is.

However, disciples of Kuhn proposing to test a few of the propo-sitions would encounter three major difficulties. First, a deductive system of this sort is so unified that it is difficult to make a change in one part without extensive revision of the whole, as Kuhn recognizes (p. 482). Nor would one know, from decisively contrary evidence, just what corrections to make, since the error might be located almost anywhere in the deductive nexus. Second, Kuhn has paid only passing attention to the problem of operationalization. To take one example,

Riker (1962) has devoted some effort to the problem of testing the size principle in coalition theory, and has shown how "exceedingly difficult" to say the least, such a task is; Kuhn ignores the problem (p. 348).

Moreover, until the problem of operationalization is solved much of the deductive system is tautologous and therefore untestable in principle. Take for instance the bargaining variable of "being a good tactician" (p. 177, pp. 188-189). Without an independent measure of this—and none has yet been devised—any bargain can be explained by reference to it or to equally obscure changes of minimum effective preference. A similar problem occurs in measuring subjective expectations and preferences, as mentioned earlier. Kuhn tries to avoid the problem of tautology by defining irrational behavior as that based on preferences that change more often than usual or that are bizarre (pp. 124-125), but this is pretty vague too.

More seriously, it is doubtful that disciples of Kuhn would even be able to see contrary evidence. A testing program would resemble Homans' program of interpreting evidence to fit the neoclassical postulates, with the remainder being consigned to the "idiographic" category. To see evidence that contradicts a given postulate set it is necessary to look at data from the standpoint of a different set (Feyerabend, 1965). This in turn requires a perspective broad enough to appreciate two opposed sets of postulates. Kuhn's neoclassic perspective is too narrow for this task.

For example, there has been a long and often confused controversy over maximizing vs. satisficing (Ölander, 1975). Apart from the difficulty of specifying the theoretical issues exactly, it is difficult to test the comparative relevance of the two models because data on decision-making can sometimes—not always—be interpreted either way (Snyder & Diesing, 1977, Chapter 5). Kuhn cannot see the problem because he regards satisficing and maximizing as the same thing (pp. 125-126). Similarly, he cannot see the difference between his theory and Blau's (1964) or Walton and McKersie's (1965) to say nothing of Coddington's (1968).

III. The methodological difficulties of the work of Homans and Kuhn are avoided by a third line of development represented by Becker (1976). This tradition is an extension of the Chicago school's method to interpersonal relations and especially to family life. Becker et al. avoid Kuhn's deductive rigidity by constructing independent models for different areas of interpersonal relations—marriage, family life, crime, and racial discrimination. Consequently, one model could in principle be found wanting and corrected without affecting the others. Homans' tautologies and ad hoc explanations are avoided by avoiding the empirical question of what goods are exchanged and produced. People's desires or tastes determine what goods are exchanged and produced, and as Becker observes, there is no good neoclassical theory of tastes (1976, p. 133). Any sort of exchange or production could be explained by postulating a taste for it, and changes of prices or quantities could be explained by postulated changes of tastes. For instance, increased birth rates could be explained by an increased desire for large families (1976, p. 13). Becker avoids such pseudo-explanations by constructing models relevant to any tastes. For instance, in one model all the goods collectively produced in any family are summed up as "Z."

Becker's criticism of explanation by taste applies also to his own early work on racial discrimination (1957), in which the main explanatory variable is a "taste for discrimination" (1976, Chapter 2, esp. p. 25).

The method of this school is the *a priori* deductive partial equilibrium method. One postulates stable preferences over various interpersonal goods, individual maximization-rationality, and a long-run competitive equilibrium (1976, p. 5). Then one introduces a single change and deduces the redistribution of resources and changes of prices and quantities that must result. After a number of such derivations have been made one can try combining two changes to see what the combined result might be. However, the results rapidly become indeterminate. Eventually one relaxes some simplifying assumption such as perfect information, zero transaction costs, or constant production functions, and deduces what shifts from equilibrium this produces. Again, the results rapidly become indeterminate.

The assumption of long-run equilibrium is simply a device for holding all other factors constant so one can deduce the effect of one change. It is not intended to describe an actual state of affairs, since perfect equilibrium never occurs. Instead, such theories describe specific tendencies to change that result from specific independent variables.

For example, one model postulates an ideal family in which one member is a head (1976, Chapter 12). A head is defined as a person who cares equally for all other members, that is, whose utility is maximized only when all others' utilities are maximized. From this definition one can deduce that the head will transfer resources to other members until all marginal returns are equal; and that other members have no incentive to compete for family resources. Insofar as the head is less than impartial, sibling rivalry becomes rational for other members. The same model can also be applied to charity, with interesting results.

Becker follows the Friedman–Alchian argument (Friedman, 1953, Chapter 1) which says that the push toward equilibrium comes primarily from market forces rather than from individual rationality. Individuals may or may not be rational; their calculations may be conscious or subconscious, probably the latter, or nonexistent, but the long-run result is the same. It follows that an empirical investigation of allocation decisions is pointless. The only useful empirical question is whether the predicted results actually occur *ceteris paribus*. For instance, one model predicts that as family income rises expenditure on education also rises; this prediction can be checked empirically.

The models are in various stages of development. For some of them enthusiastic cheers may be a bit premature; but the models of the allocation of time (1976, Chapters 5–7) are in my opinion a considerable advance over the Walrasian general equilibrium model which deals only with monetary exchanges. Time is as obvious a resource as money and as easily measured; any model that ignores time is obviously deficient. The superiority of Becker's time models appears in their explanation of phenomena that seem perverse or unintelligible from a Walrasian perspective. A negatively sloped labor supply curve is perfectly rational (p. 101) and requires no sociological postulates or accusations of irrationality for its explanation. Increasing consumption after retirement, which seemed perverse to Milton Friedman (1962, p. 189) is also perfectly rational (Becker, p. 119). Becker also demonstrates that income inequality tends to increase steadily over time via differential investment in human capital, contrary to Friedman's argument (1957, pp. 39–40).

The deficiencies of the Becker type models are those common to all static partial equilibrium models. *First*, the interactions among the various *ceteris paribus* tendencies can be deduced only to a very limited extent because the results rapidly become indeterminate. Yet these tendencies obviously do interact in reality. *Second*, many factors that disappear at equilibrium cannot be studied well or at all. Power disappears at equilibrium (p. 36); profits disappear; uncertainty, mistaken expectations, misperceptions, and misinformation disappear; market imperfections like oligopoly disappear; labor and capital are perfectly mobile; and so on. Yet these factors are obviously important in reality.

Third, the rate of approach toward equilibrium cannot be deduced, or in other words the strength of the predicted tendencies against opposition cannot be deduced. If the rate of approach is slow, actual processes may be dominated by those factors like power and labor immobility which do not appear in the models, and the models become weak, useless, or misleading (Patinkin, 1972, Chapter 2; Mishan, 1975).

Fourth, the systemic or institutional context of markets is either treated as empirical fact or assumed away in the idealized models. There is no theory of institutional change. For example, lower wages paid to women doing the same work as men is treated as a simple fact by Becker.

Fifth, the "testing" of *ceteris paribus* predictions is not as straight-forward in practice as in Friedman's theory. Human cognitive processes intervene. There is a sensitivity to facts that conform to expectations, and such facts are reported as successes of the models. Seemingly disconfirming facts are studied more carefully to see whether the discrepancy with theory can be explained or removed by adjusting the facts; if it can, this correction is triumphantly reported (pp. 224, 228). All scientists do that. But in the case of *ceteris paribus* predictions there are always disturbing factors that can be searched out to explain the discrepancy of fact and prediction. Or one can postulate a taste or a change of tastes to explain the discrepant result, as in the case of low agricultural wages. Or one can simply blame market imperfections. When certain facts fit predictions, Becker can assert, "Apparently the marriage market . . . is more efficient than is commonly believed" (p. 224). If they had not fit, he could have said, "As is well known, the marriage market is somewhat imperfect" as he does for the political market (Chapter 3).

Consequently two or three different explanations of the same facts can each claim confirmation. An example is voting behavior. For Downs, the superficial information of many voters is rational, given the cost of getting accurate information and the low value of an individual vote. For Becker, explanations from individual rationality are suspect, and he prefers to call poor information a market imper-fection. For Riker and Ordeshook, information about candidates' policies is irrelevant to voting, since the real returns from voting are not policies but the satisfaction of identifying with a cause, affir-mation of allegiance, sense of efficacy, doing one's duty (1973, pp. 60–61) as the survey data on voting report. All three explanations above can claim empirical confirmation.

Nor can one pick the simplest explanation, since simplicity is a very complex concept as Mario Bunge has argued; one man's simplicity is another's complexity. As the neoclassicist would say, simplicity like beauty is a matter of taste.

In other words the construction of static partial equilibrium models is scarcely constrained by facts; it is much more creative than it appears to be. When a model is applied to facts, it is really being used to interpret the facts, and an interesting interpretation is mistakenly counted as confirmation. This does not imply that all such *a priori* models are invalid; rather, we cannot determine their validity. Nor do the other weaknesses imply automatic invalidity. Every method has its weaknesses; there is no royal road to guaranteed truth. Truth, however, is a much more difficult matter than it seems to the researcher who has just created a new model and finds to his delight that the facts all fit when properly interpreted. Facts speak in many languages.

Becker is quite explicit about the limits of his own perspective: the neoclassicist cannot explain tastes (1976, p. 133). Presumably what is required here is a theory of the formation of personality and of the non-rational cathexes, roles, and identifications that constitute personality.

III. Deterrence Theory

We now shift to a military setting. After World War II the US Air Force set up the RAND corporation as a research institute in the application of new mathematical techniques to military topics. The RAND researchers enthusiastically developed and applied systems analysis, game theory, linear programming, and the like to military topics; some of the early analyses were eventually declassified and published (Quade, 1966). The Navy also had an extensive research program, but when a pilot project concluded that deterrence does not work (Naroll et al., 1974), that line of research was hastily dropped. The RAND researchers used game theory to demonstrate scientifically that deterrence does work and is working (Wohlstetter, 1959), and received ample research support.

Daniel Ellsberg emerged from this exciting and dedicated milieu with three of the earliest game-theoretic works on deterrence (Ellsberg, 1956; 1968, originally 1959; 1964, originally 1960). Ellsberg's main argument is summed up in the critical risk model, which specifies what is necessary to make deterrence work. There are two players, an aggressor who is contemplating attack, and a defender who is threatening retaliation. The defender may be bluffing. The aggressor will attack if and only if attack minimaxes his expected utility, that is if attack is more profitable than keeping the peace. Accordingly, he must calculate costs and benefits—the benefit of winning multiplied by the subjective probability that the defender is bluffing, and the cost of war multiplied by the probability that the defender is not bluffing. There is a threshold probability of war at which the expected utilities of war and peace are equal; this is the critical risk level. At any higher probability of war aggression does not pay. The task of the defender is to lower the critical risk level and/or increase the aggressor's subjective probability of war, until the probability level is higher than the critical risk level. If he can do so, deterrence is successful.

In Ellsberg's blackmail model the tasks are reversed. Here the aggressor may be bluffing when he makes a demand under penalty of war, and the defender must estimate probabilities in order to calculate the costs and benefits of resisting.

Once the RAND thinking on deterrence had crystallized it came out with a great rush of excitement. All sorts of grandiose and spectacular pronouncements appeared: the unthinkable was now subject to exact mathematical study, international politics was a game of bluffing like poker, science had devised new tactics like invulnerable retaliatory force and irrevocable commitment that would preserve peace. Less noticed were the practical implications of this new science of deterrence—bigger budgets for the military and civil defense.

Some of these pronouncements were sincere expressions of the excitement and great hopes accompanying any new scientific development. Others were the self-display of tricksters and showmen of the Herman Kahn type who were interested in lining up military research contracts. The episode as a whole was a clear case of pseudoscience, in which old prejudices and annual budget requests were festooned with mathematical trappings and made to appear to have scientific support. Careful study can expose the trickery, as critics like Green (1966) have shown. Government spokesmen used one of the models, an escalation model, to argue that the Rolling Thunder bombing of North Vietnam was scientifically designed to end the war. As it happened, the bombing united the North Vietnamese, increased their determination, and contributed to the US defeat (Hoopes, 1973, p. 107).[3]

Some of the prejudices appear in the critical risk model. The defender is obviously the United States and the aggressor is the Soviet Union. The SU is assumed to be constantly ready to engage in aggression and to occasionally engage in blackmail, while the US is purely defensive. The SU is constantly estimating US resolve, the probability of US resistance to an aggressive move, so any show of weakness lowers the Soviet estimate. Consequently, a rational deterrence strategy requires absolutely firm US resistance to any SU move whatsoever.

The same prejudice underlies Schelling's obsession with Chicken games in his work from the 1960's. He plainly assumes that the SU has been regularly testing US resolve in a series of nuclear Chicken games. The Cuban crisis of 1962 is referred to as "about as direct a challenge as one could expect," and other Cold War crises are also interpreted as deliberate Soviet or Chinese challenges. The rational US strategy is to resist all challenges; the US is playing Prisoner's Dilemma, not Chicken.

There are two underlying prejudices here. One is the hawk or hard-line attitude (Snyder and Diesing, 1977, pp. 297-310; Halperin, 1974, pp. 11-12). The other is the partisan attitude of the military official who is convinced of the importance of his assignment and who needs more resources to do his job well (Snyder and Diesing, 1977, pp. 352ff.). Halperin's name for this attitude is "grooved thinking".

We can salvage the mathematical core of the critical risk model from these prejudices by eliminating the aggressor-defender heuristic. We postulate two indistinguishable players, SU and US, each deterring the other (Snyder, 1972; Snyder and Diesing, 1977, pp. 48-52). The model becomes a neutral device for classifying the tactics that any two rational bargainers would use to deter each other from attack, whether or not either one ever contemplates attacking.

The revised critical risk model turns out to be invalid empirically; actual crisis bargainers do not think that way, and their behavior can be better explained on other grounds (Snyder and Diesing, 1977, pp. 198-206, 484-485). It is also deficient mathematically (Hunter, 1971, 1972). Over the empirically relevant ranges of values, the model is sensitive to very small changes in values (Hunter, 1971, pp. 39ff.; Hunter, 1972), changes too small to be empirically estimable. Thus it cannot be used to predict the effects of proposed policies since two empirically indistinguishable policies will have opposite logical consequences. It is also internally inconsistent over some of its variable ranges. According to Hunter, Ellsberg's error was to depend on the neoclassical method of partial equilibrium analysis, which ignores interaction effects and multiple effects of single changes (1971, pp. 11, 58, 59). Thus he failed to find the deficiencies of the model, which result from interaction effects.

These deficiencies point to factors which must be included in an adequate deterrence model, factors which lie beyond the limits of the neoclassical perspective. First, the importance of probability estimates suggests that information processing should be included in the model, rather than externally appended; the model should be cybernetic. Second, the model is static and short run. It neglects the effects of deterrence strategies on long run relationships—with one exception, the effect of A's firmness on A's reputation for resolve. The effect of A's firmness on B, and other effects such as Nigel Howard's "preference deterioration" (1971, p. 199) are ignored. In addition it is necessary to face the question of what "rationality" means when applied to complex governmental processes. (George and Smoke, 1974, pp. 72-77). The assumption that governments act to minimax expected utility is an ideal at best rather than a simplified description. How do information processing, bureaucratic processes, and personality factors fit into rational decisions? To answer this question we need empirical studies of how foreign policy decisions are actually made (George and Smoke, 1974, p. 77). In short, we need an empirical, cybernetic, dynamic deterrence model rather than an *a priori* static partial equilibrium model. Such a model will be discussed in Chapter Five.

IV. Conclusions

The expansion of the neoclassical perspective to politics and interpersonal relations is a consequence of its claim to universality. If all men are all the time trying to maximize expected utility, then one should be able to see them doing this in politics and interpersonal relations, not just in business. But the attempt to expand into these areas has revealed the limits of the perspective more clearly than ever. Neoclassicists cannot develop an adequate concept of community, but can only point to some of its manifestations—a habit of obedience to law, nonrandom tastes, socialization, value consensus. But community in its various manifestations is a prerequisite for the successful operation of markets and of nonmarkets and thus for the empirical usefulness of the neoclassical perspective. In other words, the neoclassical-individualist perspective demands an opposite, complementary perspective.

In class terms, the expansion of the neoclassicist perspective expresses the claim that the small business class is a universal class, that we are all small businessmen living in a classless society. The claim cannot be so expressed, since classes are invisible from the neoclassical perspective. The limits of the perspective point to the dependence of the small businessman on other classes or segments of society.

Within these limits, however, the nonmonetary models have extended the relevance of neoclassical concepts considerably. Economizing, exchange, and quasi-market processes occur throughout society, at least in Western capitalism. They occur in a setting of social relations, power, and community, but they also maintain and change that setting.

The followers-and-critics of Homans have also shown that part of the neoclassical conceptual scheme—economizing, marginal utility, exchange, price, diminishing returns, opportunity costs—can be taken up into a larger conceptual scheme. Some concepts are left out—long-run competitive equilibrium and the *a priori* partial equilibrium method. This fragmenting raises the question of what, if anything, is central or essential to the neoclassic perspective. The neoclassicists themselves did not all share exactly the same conceptual scheme, and the interpretation in Chapter Two has focused on the Walrasian version of neoclassicism.

The contrast between the Becker school and the followers of Homans, and similarly between the Buchanan public choice school and the Riker–Davis–Rochester school, suggests that the maintenance of the complete neoclassic perspective is the result of sociological processes—identification and loyalty to a community and to one's ancestors, rather than simply the expression of a standpoint. The pure neoclassic perspective is preserved by schools—the Chicago school, the scattered Austrian–London school including Machlup, Hayek, Haberler, Kirzner, Robbins, and Fellner, and in Sweden followers of Bertil Ohlin. Outside such schools, neoclassic concepts are absorbed into other perspectives or are eclectically combined with pieces of other perspectives, as with the Homans school and the Rochester school.

Game theory has proved to be even more adaptable. In addition to the many fruitful applications to politics by the relatively neoclassic Rochester and Virginia schools, it has been absorbed into a number of other perspectives. First, international politics has long been dominated by the traditionalist conservative perspective of people like Morgenthau and Kissinger; yet some of these traditionalists have absorbed game concepts via the work of Morton Kaplan (1957, 1968, Chapters 11–14) and Arthur Lee Burns (1968). Traditionalist concepts like balance of power, bipolarity, and multipolarity have received a more precise definition, and game theory has become a technique for analyzing the dynamics of international systems.

Second, in Chapter Five I shall take up a cybernetic adaptation of game theory by recent deterrence theorists like George and Smoke.

Third, within the general social-problems perspective there is a broad tradition of experimental research into conflict resolution using game models going back to the work of Morton Deutsch in the 1950's. Fourth, Alker and Hurwitz (1979) also distinguish a school of behaviorist learning experimenters exemplified by Rapoport and Chammah's classic 1965 *Prisoner's Dilemma*. Alker and Hurwitz show how a single game, Prisoner's Dilemma, has been treated in very different ways within three different "paradigms"—the Morton Deutsch conflict resolution paradigm, the behavioral learning paradigm, and the original mathematical approach of Harsanyi, Shubik, Raiffa, and Howard. The varied adaptations of game theory have taken it far from its neoclassic origins and promise a very useful future for it.

Four Keynesian Economics

I. Keynes

Keynes' decisive achievement in the *General Theory* (1936) was to construct a formal model that could produce a short-term underemployment equilibrium.[4] No such model could be constructed on neoclassical postulates, and in fact one can deduce the logical impossibility of short-term underemployment *equilibrium* from them. The neoclassical models included the postulates of individual maximizing rationality, the existence of competition, and the flexibility of prices. Competition means that there is a market for labor, a market for capital, and a market for the commodities that can be produced from capital and labor. The commodity market brings together the consumers of commodities and their producers, the businessmen who hire capital and labor to produce commodities. The capital market brings savers together with investors (businessmen). The labor market brings workers together with employers (businessmen). Each market is governed by its own price: the commodity price vector, the interest rates, and the wage rate. Flexible prices serve to clear the three markets in the short run and to move them toward equilibrium in the long run. In the short run, an oversupply of commodities, or saved capital, or unemployed labor, can be sold by lowering the three prices; this brings more consumers, investors, and employers into the market temporarily to use up the surpluses. Conversely, a temporary shortage can be redistributed by raising the prices, a form of rationing. In the long run, higher prices draw more supplies permanently into the markets and lower prices drive them out; thus the simultaneous fluctuation of the three prices moves the markets toward equilibrium.

Now suppose there is an oversupply of labor. The short-term effect is a lower wage-rate, since the unemployed underbid those with work; that is, an employer lowers wages in the knowledge that labor will be available at the lower rate. This induces employers to increase investment, employment and production, which raises the interest rate and lowers commodity prices, which in turn increases savings and demand for commodities, and so on. The three prices continue fluctuating until the oversupply of labor has disappeared through increased employment, more labor-intensive production, and a reduced supply of labor. Thus long-term unemployment is logically impossible in neoclassical models.

Short-term unemployment is possible, but only as a disequilibrium phenomenon. Its occurrence shows either that the various markets have not yet had enough time to redistribute the shortages and surpluses, or that there is some persistent interference with markets. Fixed wage-rates, for instance, would prevent employers from hiring the surplus labor; too high an interest rate would discourage the investment required for additional employment; an interest rate fixed too low would discourage saving, cause a capital shortage, and frustrate some investment and employment plans. In general, any interference with prices will cause intractable unemployment directly or indirectly, and conversely continuing unemployment is a sign that somebody is interfering with prices somewhere.

From the above neoclassical perspective the persistent unemployment of the 1920's and 1930's was a temporary maladjustment of no great theoretical significance. It could easily be explained *after the fact* in a variety of ad hoc ways (Stoneman, 1979). Investment had overshot the equilibrium rate, perhaps encouraged by greedy, shortsighted bankers who granted too much credit (Simons, 1948, pp. 45–56; originally 1934). "If, as seems possible, both capitalism and democracy are soon to be swept away forever . . . then to commercial banking will belong the uncertain glory of having precipitated the transition to a new era" (p. 55). Then as investment turned back toward its proper level the accelerator took over and exaggerated the downturn (J.M. Clark). The resulting temporary unemployment was prolonged by rigid wages, for which Herbert Hoover or the trade unions were to blame (Sumner Slichter), or perhaps by rigid prices encouraged by the NRA (Arthur R. Burns). The panicky New Deal improvisations such as interest rate manipulations did not help either: "The worst feature of the situation, from the political point of view, is the panic type of thinking which seems to be natural to human beings in a crisis" (Knight, 1947, p. 380).

Thus the empirical fact of persistent unemployment posed no theoretical problem for neoclassical economists. There was no anomaly; the world was irrational, but economic theory was sound. Knight used to complain in class: "People are so *irrational*! When prices go down they buy less instead of more, because they expect prices to go down still further. No wonder we have depressions."

Keynes was brought up on the above neoclassical thinking and testified to the difficulties of shaking it off:

> The composition of this book has been for the author a long struggle to escape . . . from habitual modes of thought and expression. The ideas which are here expressed so laboriously are extremely simple and should be obvious. The difficulty lies, not in the new ideas, but in escaping from the old ones, which ramify, for those brought up as most of us have been, into every corner of our minds" (1936, p. viii).

We also have the testimony of Joan Robinson on the years of discussion and shifting of ideas (1951, pp. 52-58), and Klein's reconstruction of the many steps in the change of thinking of the Cambridge school (Klein, 1947). According to Keynes, the neoclassical assumptions he was shaking off were summed up in Say's Law "that supply creates its own demand in the sense that the aggregate demand price is equal to the aggregate supply price for all levels of output and employment" (1936, pp. 21-22).

It is not clear why Keynes chose to focus on Say's Law, and there has been much discussion on this point. One possible interpretation is that Say was thinking in terms of a barter economy paradigm, and that this barter paradigm continued to underlie neoclassical thinking. Money is then added to the barter economy as another commodity; its utility is its usefulness as a store of purchasing power, and its price is the other commodities that must be exchanged for it. In a barter economy individuals will produce or buy commodities only in order to use or exchange them, holding enough money to cover planned future purchases. But in such an economy, assuming price flexibility, there will be no surpluses or shortages, since unusable or unexchangeable commodities will not be produced. This paradigm plainly describes the economy from the perspective of the individual; the economy consists of all the other people ready to exchange with him. But when money is studied from the individual perspective, as a store of purchasing power, its system properties become invisible and must be handled ad hoc. And the system properties were precisely the important ones for Keynes.

Keynes conceived of the economy as a closed system within which money and commodities circulate in opposite directions, as depicted in Figure 4.1. The diagram shows the money flow; each box or module in the diagram has a reservoir in which it accumulates a stock of money and/or commodities. For the two production modules the main reservoirs contain inventories of finished goods available for sale. The household reservoir contains labor for hire, and the banks hold a stock of money. The other modules also hold stocks of money. The stock of money held by the banks can be expanded or contracted through the creation of credit, though this process is ultimately under the control of the government in various ways. The endogenous flexibility of the money supply and of the other inventories is a key aspect of the model, since it makes possible, though not necessary, the fluctuations in rate of flow that Keynes was trying to explain. It is this systemic aspect of money that is invisible from the individual-barter perspective. Nor is this aspect adequately expressed by saying that V, the velocity or turnover rate of money in the quantity equation $MV=PT$, is a variable, since the equation does not make the variability of V intelligible.

The flows are not automatic, but depend on decisions: decisions to save, to consume, to extend credit, and to invest. These decisions in turn depend on expectations about future demand levels, and expectations are formed in part on the basis of present information. Thus there is a third flow and stock in the model, the flow of information. Keynes did not work out the details of this flow, limiting himself to a few broad generalizations. However, from his and Kalecki's discussion of investment decisions it is clear that there are lags in the transmission of information. Investment is decided on the basis of expected future demand, which is based on information about past demand levels. Information about present forces determining future demand levels is not available in time to affect investment decisions. There are also other lags, such as the lagged effect of investment decisions on wage income.

The presence of lags implies that the rates of flow of money and commodities normally fluctuate even with flawless information processing (Tustin, 1953; Keynes, 1936, pp. 249-254; Kalecki, 1939, Chapter 6, p. 71, pp. 145-149). Investment and production decisions lag behind changes in demand levels, and output thus exceeds demand at the top part of a cycle and falls short at the bottom part. The

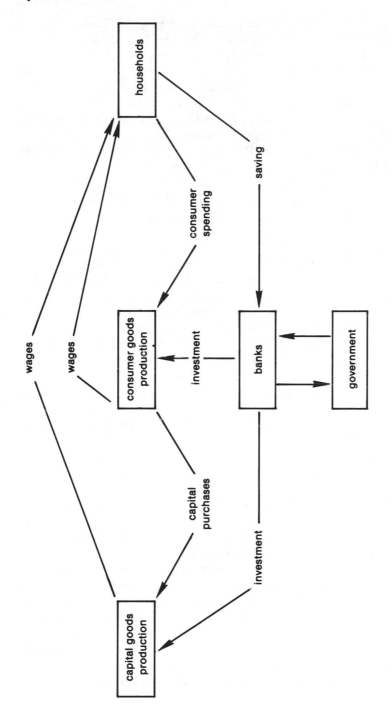

Figure 4.1. The Keynesian model of the economy.

dynamics are the same as those of Lotka's ecological model (Kemeny and Snell, 1962, pp. 24-29), where the key lag is located in the reproduction rate of the predator species. In this sort of system there is an equilibrium point E around which the flow rates move in an elliptical orbit. Exogenous shocks, and errors in expectations, keep shifting the system from one orbit to another, and E also shifts over time (cf. also Harrod, 1951, pp. 261-262). It is an equilibrium point only in the sense that if the system had been located there long enough to absorb all lags and errors, flow rates would be steady and remain steady apart from shocks. There are however no internal forces moving the system either toward it or away from it, so it is not a neoclassical type of equilibrium point. Fellner's discussion of this topic (1946, Chapter 1) is mistaken because he is thinking in neoclassical concepts.

The equilibrium is necessarily an underemployment equilibrium, since the peak flow rate cannot exceed full employment and the midpoint of the cycle thus is necessarily below full employment. The objectives of government policy therefore should be to moderate the size of fluctuations—move the system into orbits closer to E—and also to move E closer to the full employment ceiling. In Figure 4.1 government can do this by controlling the flow of money; left out of the model is the flow of information and the flow of taxes, government spending and investment, by which government can affect fluctuations more directly. Since there are lags in the flow of information to government and lags in the effects of government policies these policies may take effect at the wrong point of the cycle and aggravate it instead of damping it (A.W. Phillips, 1954). Lags also occur in the feedback about the effects of policy and in adjustments of mistaken policies; these lags make effective government action still more difficult.

There is a further difficulty which worried Keynes a great deal. The primary way to reduce unemployment is to increase investment. But investment faces in two directions: it employs labor now but it increases productive capacity for the future. Moreover investment during previous expansionary periods has already produced considerable surplus productive capacity. This produces an increasing downward pressure on employment, both directly in the producer goods industries via the accelerator and indirectly through reducing confidence in the profitability of further investment. To counteract this increasing downward pressure government has to continually increase the rate of investment, thereby aggravating its own future difficulties. There is a curse on the system: "Each time we secure today's equilibrium by increased investment we are aggravating the difficulty of securing equilibrium tomorrow" (Keynes, 1936, p. 105). "The tragedy of investment is that it causes crisis because it is useful" (Kalecki, 1939, p. 149). In other words the system is always off balance, in long-run disequilibrium, lurching into a troubled future (Tobin, 1975).

Many writers have argued that the Keynesian revolution involved a shift of paradigm, or perspective, or ideology, but they differ in their description of the new paradigm. For the neoclassicists, except Harry Johnson, there was no revolution and no new paradigm; Keynes merely proposed an empirical hypothesis about the marginal efficiency of capital, which has since been disconfirmed (Friedman, 1972, p. 908); or he provided practical advice on how to evade the effects of rigid wages; or he invented some technical puzzles like the liquidity trap.

For the Keynesians the new paradigm consisted of Keynes' particular models, either the fundamental equations in the *Treatise on Money* (Davidson, 1978; G. Mehta, 1978) or the underemployment equilibrium model in the *General Theory* of 1936 (Klein, 1947). For Schumpeter these models expressed Keynes' underlying ideology, his vision of a stagnant society with excess saving and his disapproval of rentiers (Schumpeter, 1954). Schumpeter finds the vision expressed already in 1919; thus he denies that the unemployment of the 1920's was the source of Keynes' new ideas.

Like Schumpeter, I wish to argue that Keynes' particular models express an underlying perspective, and the Keynesian Revolution involved a shift of perspective and not just a new model. It is immaterial whether Keynes developed this perspective as he worried about unemployment or whether he always had it; in any case he had it in 1930 when our study begins.

Keynes' standpoint was the government, and more specifically that of the British Treasury with which he had had a long and close association. If we ask of Keynes, Who are "we"? Who is free? Who is rational? To whom do we offer advice? The answer is always, the Treasury. " . . . if we are to control the economic system by changing the quantity of money . . ." (Keynes, 1936, p. 172). "If we have complete control of the Earnings System and of the Currency System . . . . But if . . . we have at least a partial control of the Currency System . . . " (Keynes, 1930, p. 169 in Davidson, 1978, p. 337). "Our final task might be to select those variables which can be deliberately controlled or managed by central authority in the kind of system in which we actually live" (1936, p. 247). Note the words "deliberately managed." Central authority takes advice, deliberates, manages; it is rational. Keynes' advice had to do with interest rates and budgets; he therefore implicity assumed that the Treasury was free to change both, and that changes would have some regular, intelligible effect on the economy. In terms of Figure 4.1, the control point of the system is government.

Businessmen, on the other hand, are not free; their behavior is determined by their class background, their temperament, the "animal spirits" and gambling propensities.

> In former times, when enterprises were mainly owned by those who undertook them or by their friends and associates, investment depended on a sufficient supply of individuals of sanguine temperament and constructive impulses who embarked on business as a way of life, not really relying on a precise calculation of prospective profit. The affair was partly a lottery, though with the ultimate result largely governed by whether the abilities and character of the managers were above or below the average. Some would fail and some would succeed . . . . If human nature felt no temptation to take a chance . . . there might not be so much investment merely as a result of cold calculation (1936, p. 150). Most, probably, of our decisions to do something positive, the full consequence of which will be drawn out over many days to come, can only be taken as a result of animal spirits—of a spontaneous urge to action rather than inaction, and not as the outcome of a weighted average of quantitative benefits multiplied by quantitative probabilities. Enterprise only pretends to itself to be mainly actuated by the statements in its own prospectus . . . (pp. 161–162).

The important theme in passages like these is not merely the rejection of the maximizing-rationality postulate. It is the distance Keynes is able to take from the individual businessman, which Minsky calls "the skeptical, aloof attitude toward capitalist enterprise . . . the basically critical attitude that permeated Keynes' work" (Minsky, 1975, p. 130). This distance enables Keynes to see the businessman as Object rather than Subject, as a determined part of a system. Another example:

> We recall that the motivations for the household sector and the business sector are lodged in the free decisions of their respective units. House-holders decide to spend or save their incomes as they wish. . . . Similarly, business firms exercise their own judgments on their capital expenditures, and as a result we have seen the indeterminacy and variability of investment decisions. But when we turn to the expenditures of the public sector, we enter an entirely new area of motivation. It is no longer fixed habit or profit that determines the rate of spending, but

political *decision*—that is, the collective will of the people as it is formulated and expressed through their local, state, and federal legislatures and executives . . . . Yet the presence of an explicit political will . . . gives to the public sector a special significance. *This is the only sector whose expenditures and receipts are open to deliberate control* (Heilbroner, 1968, p. 283).

In the Heilbroner quote even rational business decisions can be seen, from a distance, as "determined by profit," or as indeterminate and spontaneous, "as they wish," governed by the laws of chance.

Now that government rather than the businessman is the Subject, what characteristics does this produce in the Object? The Object is still the economy, but it no longer derives its intelligibility from its presumed source in decisions made by subjects. It is not derived from the Subject at all, but confronts the Subject (government) as its opposite. This means that it is separate, alien, having its own independent dynamics. These dynamics cannot be deduced a priori from postulates of maximizing rationality and diminishing returns, as in neoclassical science, but must be investigated empirically, objectively. In other words macroeconomics is fundamental and microeconomics derivative, the reverse of the neoclassical ordering.

The Subject-Object relation is not one of creation, but one of responsibility. Left to itself the economy performs unsatisfactorily; it fluctuates and generates persistent unemployment. The government ought therefore to manage the economy and counteract its inherent defects. This in turn means that the economy must have a size limit. It cannot be larger than the national boundary, the limit of government responsibility, though it could be smaller. For Keynes it was in fact limited by national boundaries; the Object was the British economy.

This means that the system is bounded, unlike the infinite neoclassical system; it is the whole national economy, abstracted from international transactions. Later these can be included, but transactions across a boundary are different from transactions within a boundary and must be handled separately. But in a bounded system practically everything has to come from somewhere else in the same system, and so on back in time. The system must run by means of circular flows, which divide and come together again, change rates and quantities, feed back on themselves, and so on. The infinite horizon of the neoclassical market, where more resources can always be drawn in by profit opportunities—and of the Game, where one can always add another player—is replaced by a national boundary across which limited transactions are possible.

This in turn means that the Keynesian system is inherently dynamic, no matter what sort of mathematics are used to think it. The proper mathematics is computer simulation—the Klein–Goldberger model and all its successors—that is, a closed system of lagged equations. More generally, all such macro models are composed of 2+ lagged, interdependent relations in two or more variables (Allen, 1960). Keynes however was still expressing himself in the neoclassical deductive set of equations, and this caused confusion both in his thinking and in others' interpretations of his thoughts. It made his system look comparative-static. For instance $S=I$ or $Y=C+I$ suggests a static identity; but these equations should really have time subscripts, or be read as Fortran equations, in which the equals sign means "change the value of the left-hand expression until it equals the right-hand expression." The equation expresses a flow, not an identity.

Given an inherently dynamic system, our concern as policy advisors is with its short-run dynamics. We have to deal with present unemployment, present inflation, etc., and we need a policy that will produce effects within a few years or even months, not only in the long run.

The focus on short-run dynamics in turn introduces, or recognizes, a radical uncertainty in individual decision-making. Uncertainty is absent in the long-run competitive equilibrium which is the core of neoclassical economics, and attempts to incorporate uncertainty concepts—treating information as a commodity and uncertainty management as an oracular skill—have always been unsatisfactory. Game theory introduces one kind of uncertainty management by substituting the personal opponent for given demand and supply curves. The information problem here is to predict the opponent's moves, and the unsatisfactory solution is the various decision rules. Keynesian economics introduces another kind by focusing on the short run: the information problem here is to estimate future demand levels and supply prices.

Keynes' inclusion of psychological factors in his model—the propensity to consume, animal spirits, expectations and liquidity preference—exemplifies another new characteristic of the Object. When our standpoint is external to the individual businessman we need not limit ourselves to factors present in his consciousness. The neoclassicals prided themselves on their subjective standpoint; and this was indeed a scientific advance *as of 1870*, since it produced the marginal calculus. But the emphasis on generic subjectivity had the defect of making the unconscious mind paradoxical if not invisible. If the economist did not dismiss such things as beyond all science he consigned them to the dubious sciences of sociology and psychology, well distant from his concerns. But for the Keynesians psychological factors that affect allocation decisions are included in the economy where they belong, and show up in the econometrician's models.

What characteristics does the Subject have in Keynes' work? The Subject, the government, remains completely empty; it was not part of the economy, and Keynes did not study it. There was a sharp distinction between Subject and Object for Keynes; the Object, the economy, was the proper domain of science, while the Subject remained outside of science.

The emptiness of the Keynesian Subject is not accidental. When government is Subject the scientist no longer has direct, immediate access to its inner workings, as the neoclassicist does. He is outside the Subject and must somehow define a role that relates him to government. There may be more than one way to do this, but for Keynes the relation was that of advisor. Keynes saw himself as a professional advisor to the Treasury, a person who could be called on for regular advice, temporary political assignments, and friendly support. He moved between Cambridge and London, putting his economic theory at the service of the government and using his government experience and contacts to enrich his theory. However, the advisor role obliges the scientist to focus his attention on the Object, the economy, the area of his expertise, and away from the official being advised. Hence the Subject is expelled from science.

II. Keynesian Economics, 1936-1966

The Keynesian Revolution transformed economics from a subjective to an objective science. Neoclassical economics, deriving from the marginalist revolution of the 1870's, was a science of individual rational decision, a science of the Subject. This meant that social science, the science of human subjects, was sharply distinct from natural science, the science of things (Mises, 1960, pp. 130-134; Knight, 1935, Chapter 4; 1947, Chapter 9; 1952, pp. 53-55). The social object, the economy, had to be approached indirectly through the subject, since *as social rather than natural*, it was a consequence of individual decisions.

Keynes effected this reversal, first through his professional detachment from the economy, and second through his policy-oriented attachment to the government as actor. In his science the government as actor confronts the economy as its object. The object is separate, alien, not of its making, having its own independent dynamics; however, it is an object for which the government has responsibility, and which therefore must have some handles by which it can be managed. The scientific task of the detached professional, therefore, is to trace out the dynamics of the object and to find those key variables by which the dynamics can be redirected in the proper direction.

To be sure, Keynes did not effect this reversal all by himself. He was only one part of a general movement of objectification and systematization occurring in the twenties and thirties and earlier. For one thing, other economists were moving in the same direction—Kalecki, the Swedish economists, even D.H. Robertson. Then there were the econometricians, achieving self-consciousness with the founding of the Econometric Society in 1930, who were developing techniques for measuring and modeling an objectified economy. In British anthropology Malinowski and Radcliffe-Brown developed the concept of primitive cultures as objective systems to be managed by the colonial administrator. Cultures were seen as closed, self-maintaining systems with their own dynamics, which could easily be damaged by careless, ignorant colonial administrators but which could also be maintained in a healthy state by wise management. The result was early functionalist theory, deriving from Durkheim and applicable to colonial areas but not of course to Britain, the managing and civilizing Subject (Ekeh, 1974, p. 7). American sociologists, for instance at Chicago in the 1920's, were focusing on problems of urban poverty and delinquency and explaining them with the Durkheimian concept of anomie, which they translated as "social disorganization." Rapid urban growth in Chicago had destroyed the web of shared expectations and understandings that gave life meaning and gave individuals self-respect, so they aimlessly turned to crime and drink and sank into poverty. Here was another bounded system, the city, spiraling into a social depression by itself, needing intelligent, sympathetic management to reverse its unsatisfactory trend.

The most direct consequence of the objectification of society was a proliferation of objective, empirical studies. In economics attention was given to the Keynesian magnitudes—national income, investment, employment levels, wage levels, and marginal propensity to consume (Klein, 1950, 1954). Problems of definition and measurement were examined and historical time series were estimated. Some of these studies, those of Kuznets, Douglas, and Colin Clark, preceded Keynes' 1936 work, but his work made them more relevant to economic theory and more timely. Studies of decision-making were also conducted: British and American studies of investment decisions that tested

Keynes' propositions about investment decisions; studies of consumption decisions by Katona and others (Katona, 1951; Mack, 1952); studies of managerial decisions. The empirical studies became the basis for revising specific Keynesian equations and for constructing large-scale simulation models of the economy. They also became the basis for annual claims by some neoclassical economist that Keynes had now been empirically refuted.

The neoclassicists doubted the usefulness of empirical studies for theory construction, especially studies of decision-making (Machlup, 1946; Hayek, 1952; Rothbard, 1960). For their a priori deductive theory any empirical studies that deviated from theory were merely evidence of short run irrationality, or complicating details, or interferences with competition, and therefore of no theoretical significance. Empirical studies, or in general Radcliffe-Brown's "Natural Science of Society" (1957; originally 1937) were scientistic; they reduced people to *things* suitable for government management. Incidentally, this neoclassic "scientism" is not to be confused with the traditionalist conservative "scientism" (Voegelin, 1952; Schoeck and Wiggins, 1960) which implies a condemnation of all social science including that of the neoclassicists.

The most important theoretical development was a theory of economic growth, by Harrod (1939), Domar (1957), Samuelson (1939), and others (Robinson, 1951, pp. 155–174). Keynes and Kalecki theorized about the dynamics of the system apart from government intervention, and argued that the system would fluctuate around an underemployment level if left to itself. But suppose that the government had learned this lesson and was ready to intervene; how large a stimulus ought it give the economy? If the economy tended toward underconsumption, underinvestment, and underemployment, more consumption and investment were needed, but how much more? What was the optimum rate of consumption (Lange, 1938) and investment? The optimum rate was one which maintained current and future full employment. But this meant that government could not simply stimulate enough investment to provide full employment now. Investment faces in two directions; it provides employment and income now but increased productive capacity in the future. This increased capacity requires increased demand to keep it busy. Consequently the future level of production, demand, and income must always be greater than the present level; investment for the future must always be greater than savings from the past (Domar, 1957, p. 92). The system *must* grow to avoid unemployment and depression, as Keynes recognized (1936, p. 105).

The optimum rate of growth or "equilibrium rate of growth" was the rate at which increase of income and demand equaled increase of productive capacity, thereby maintaining full employment (Domar, 1957, Chapters 3, 4). Harrod's "warranted rate of growth," G_w, was very similar; it was also an equilibrium rate, except that it could be specified for any desired level of unemployment (Eisner, 1952). However, the equilibrium is inherently unstable, since it involves a continually increasing excess capacity, which depresses private investment and makes more government action necessary. In addition, the lower the desired level of unemployment, the greater the problems from maldistribution of labor, structural unemployment, specialized labor shortages, and inflationary pressure. The quantity of money and the propensity to save must be just right as well (Davidson, 1978, Chapter 12). The target level is an equilibrium level only in the artificial sense that if government action maintains it there is a constant level of unemployment. It is a steady target for government, a requisite for optimal performance, not an equilibrium of the economy. Left to itself, the economy fluctuates around underemployment equilibrium.

The neoclassical long-run equilibrium concept is now left far behind. This state is a total chimera: the economy moves neither toward nor away from it, nor around it. A static economy is logically impossible: the economy must either grow or suffer depression and stagnation. Growth, for the neoclassicists, was an external addition to a static economy, derived from accidents of invention (new production functions). And indeed, this is how growth would look to the small businessman. For the Keynesians, growth due to government action is a vital necessity for the economy.

A second chimera is the neoclassical delusion that the rate of growth depends on arbitrary individual decisions (for example Alchian and Allen, 1964, pp. 516ff.). In this theory individuals decide what portion of their income they wish to consume and what portion they wish to save for future enjoyment. The aggregate of saving decisions is expressed by the interest rate, which is therefore the rate of growth that people desire. But in Keynesian science decisions to save are themselves part and product of an inherently unstable economy. Left to itself, the economy stagnates and fluctuates, generating both excess savings and capital shortages as part of its positive feedback cycles. Growth is a functional necessity for economic stability, rather than something that occurs automatically.

A third chimera is perfect competition. This notion implies many small firms, each with no market power; but as Domar observes (1957,

p. 30), these firms could also not afford the research and development required for, say, a 3% annual rate of growth. The result would be stagnation and chronic severe unemployment. (Here Schumpeter for once would agree). If big government were to provide the R & D, business and then labor would have to grow big to influence the course of research, and the dynamics of oligopoly would then take over. Bigness is inherent in the modern economy, along with growth; the development of oligopoly is essential to the continued development of capitalism.

Keynesian "expectations" also drop out of the Keynesian growth models. For Keynes economic fluctuations derive from cycles of optimism and pessimism; business optimism and the resulting boom cannot continue indefinitely, and once it breaks, pessimism takes over. So also for Kalecki (1939, pp. 134–135). But once the government takes responsibility for the economy and achieves an equilibrium rate of growth, pessimism becomes obsolete and optimism becomes permanent. Government controls expectations along with the economy, and expectations lose their destabilizing effects. This is not true for Harrod, who retains the Keynesian emphasis on optimism-pessimism cycles.

The curse that Keynes thought was on the system was also abolished. Keynes noted that the increased investment that provided employment would increase productive capacity in the future, thereby requiring still further increases to maintain full employment. But since investment opportunities are not infinite, investment would eventually stop expanding and a collapse would result. In a growth model this curse is transformed into a blessing. It remains true that a capitalist economy must expand at an ever-increasing rate to avoid misery; but once the government is educated to its responsibility, expansion can be politically guaranteed. If private investment and consumption should ever falter, government can make up the difference. The result is ever higher living standards and greater happiness for everybody.

The abolition of the curse was, however, a gradual process. For Harrod and Robinson (Robinson, 1952) G_w is a policy target for government but an unachievable one. Eisner agrees: ". . . my basic approach . . . is that the equilibria presented would be most difficult if not impossible to maintain . . ." (Eisner, 1953, pp. 389–390).

Domar, a few years later, was more optimistic: he noted the potential for trouble but trusted that the problem could be solved by a combination of increased consumption rate (military spending, perhaps) and more capital-intensive technology such as atomic power plants (1957, Chapter 5, esp. pp. 118–120). But in the 1960's, with the new economics triumphant, the US government converted to Keynesianism, and the economy booming at 4% unemployment, the curse was gone. Heller, Kennedy's chief economic advisor, was all optimism: "The significance of the great expansion of the 1960's lies not only in its striking statistics of employment, income, and growth but in its glowing promise of things to come" (1967, p. 58). "The discouraging pattern of recessions every two or three years . . . has been broken" (p. 73). We can afford to raise our aspiration level: ". . . the requirement today is for much more nimble and faster action than a chronically or repeatedly underemployed economy typically requires . . . policy tolerances become much narrower in the high-employment economic zone" (Friedman and Heller, 1969, p. 34). By 1973 the optimism was muted. Great depressions are most probably a thing of the past, but minor fluctuations can still occur; Heller's fine tuning does not work (Samuelson, 1973a, pp. 266–267, 345). Besides, there is the puzzling new problem of stagflation. Also the government's inept performance in managing the economy since 1966 is very discouraging.

Keynes' optimism–pessimism cycle, having been banished from the economy, reappears in the attitudes of economists.

The study of information flows in the economy was something that Keynes left to his followers, though they have not yet done much with it either. One theme that appears occasionally is that the price system in perfect competition cannot provide the necessary information for the firm (Sraffa, 1926, p. 543; Richardson, 1959; Shapiro, 1976; see also Leijonhufvud, 1968, p. 394). The firm must estimate future sales to decide present output levels. But in perfect competition the demand curve for the firm is horizontal by definition, and such a curve tells the firm that it can sell an infinite quantity at a given price. Since this is nonsense, the firm can get no information from price levels.

Information is provided by market imperfections. Each firm has its own quasi-monopolistic market of regular customers, whose size it can estimate from past demand levels. It also has specific "adjacent" competitors, whose market size can also be estimated. The cost of penetrating the opponents' market can be estimated, as well as the price differential that might induce an opponent to raid one's own market. The result is a downward sloping demand curve (and/or a game model) that gives the firm the information it needs. Market imperfections are thus an essential part of a market economy; as Shubik remarks, perfect competition is the best of all logically impossible worlds (1959, p. 180).

Meade (1972) provides a more systematic treatment of information

Figure 4.2. The controlled economy. After Meade (1972, p. 19).

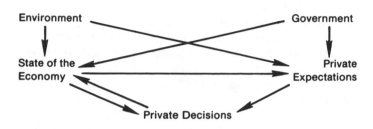

flows. In Meade's basic model (Fig. 4.2) information flows are combined with other influences into a single system. The basic feedback
cycle is expectations–decisions–state of the economy–expectations,
which produces the basic Keynesian fluctuations around underemployment equilibrium. Government breaks into this cycle with information (government→expectations) as well as monetary and fiscal
activity (government→state of the economy).

Meade deals first with the basic feedback cycle, showing the great
variations including both positive and negative feedback that can
result from variations in expectations (Chapter 5). Then he deals with
government information policies, including indicative forecasting and
indicative planning, that can correct expectations and induce a more
nearly optimal time-path for the economy (Chapters 9–13). "If the
formation of expectations is improved . . . then the behavioural relationships inside the economic system will themselves be changed in a
way which makes the system move through time in a more efficient
manner even without any governmental controls" (p. 148).

Note that the information flow to government is not included in
Meade's model. Government, the Subject, is outside the system; its
information comes from an econometric model operated by its advisors, the economists (Chapter 14). The natural environment is also
outside the system; it acts but is not acted on. There is no such thing
as pollution.

Another important development was a new theory of rational
decision to replace the destroyed theory of maximizing-rationality.
The new theory constitutes the "private decisions" and "private
expectations" modules of Figure 4.2. We need a new theory when we
introduce time, uncertainty, and information, because maximizing

under uncertainty makes no sense. The maximizing theorists evaded the problem by referring to *expected* utility, but they had no theory of how expectations are formed and changed by the flow of information, so the theory remained highly abstract.

The reason for the limitation was that the neoclassical theory was subjective and *a priori*. We human beings know a priori that we are rational, and the details have been worked out deductively in the marginal calculus. But the effect of information on expectations cannot be studied a priori; it is an empirical issue.

For the detached professionals of the Keynesian era businessmen were part of the Object, and business decisions could be studied empirically. There were many such empirical studies in the late 1930's, 1940's, and 1950's. These studies show businessmen interacting with their environment over time, and give us a theory of a flow of decisions corresponding to a flow of information. Some parts of the theory appear in Keynesians like Shackle, Sidney Weintraub, and Paul Davidson who emphasize expectations and uncertainty, but the theory was mainly developed by the Herbert Simon group at Carnegie-Mellon as the theory of bounded rationality or satisficing.

The theory of satisficing improves on the maximizing-rationality model in three ways. It allows for heterogeneous, incomparable goals; it allows for absolute goals, goals whose utility function is a step function; and most important, it incorporates uncertainty management directly into rational decision-making, instead of treating information as just another resource to be economized. Uncertainty management is incorporated by treating decision-making as a process over time, rather than as the solution of a maximum equation with $d=0$ in the neoclassical fashion. Thus the flow of information in the Keynesian system is matched continuously by the flow of decision in the individual firm. New alternatives appear and old ones drop out or are transformed; estimates of consequences are corrected; goals change, and so on.

Heterogeneous goals are allowed for by making each unique goal a constraint on an acceptable choice. Decision-making then consists of testing a proposed action against the list of constraints; if it fails to meet any one constraint to a criterion it is rejected, or revised until it meets all constraints. The criterion is the level of aspiration or acceptability for that goal; one level is set for each goal, and this level can be either fixed or changeable. An absolute goal is represented by a constraint with a fixed level of acceptability, while more open-ended goals or desires are represented by changeable levels of aspiration.

The concepts of heterogeneous goals and of absolute goals

correspond to several concepts and themes in the Keynesian literature. One theme that appears in various places is that business firms have at least two goals, survival and growth (Robinson, 1953). Suppose there is an investment opportunity that promises great profit if it pays off and ruin if it fails, and whose "expected value" by summing these two possible outcomes is positive. On maximization principles the opportunity ought to be taken if there are no better alternatives; on satisficing principles it fails to satisfy the survival goal and ought not be taken. The maximization principle is inapplicable here because the concept of expected value cannot apply to unique instances involving multiple possible outcomes (Chapter 2, Section 2). A third plausible goal is management continuity and independence; and market share is also discussed as a goal. Given a plurality of goals, a satisficing firm will reject all investment plans that do not meet all the fixed goals; the remaining possibilities can then be compared on the more open-ended profit criterion.

For middle management, a plausible absolute goal is avoidance of penalties imposed by top management (Mansfield and Wein, 1958). This is a "survival" goal for the manager. This goal rejects policies that carry a substantial risk of censure, and only low-risk policies are tested further against other constraints.

The consumption function can also be interpreted in satisficing terms. It is postulated that the household seeks to maintain a constant standard of living as part of the security it tries to provide for the children. Saving and dissaving insulate the standard of living from income fluctuations. However, if income is consistently above consumption level, the standard of living will gradually rise, and will gradually fall with consistently lower income (Brandis, 1968, p. 172). In satisficing terminology, standard of living is a level of aspiration concept in household budgeting. Income level provides the information by which the household evaluates and adjusts level of aspiration: with persistently higher income the level of aspiration is gradually raised, and with persistently lower income it is lowered. Or the information can flow in the reverse direction. Standard of living can be set by one's reference group (Blau, 1964, p. 318; Duesenberry, 1949) and the information about reference group standards used to set a level of aspiration for income. Income aspiration level then determines career choices or shifts, wage demands, and production levels on family farms, with production adjusted to provide constant satisfactory income for the farm family. It can also determine shifts in saving for retirement; if one's goal is a fixed retirement income, higher real interest rates imply a lower capital goal and lower saving rate, and vice versa for lower interest rates (Klein, 1947, p. 59). Thus the concept of income aspiration level enables one to interpret as rational those labor supply curves that the neoclassicists were forced to treat as irrational.

The strategy of full-cost pricing that appears prominently in the empirical studies is also a form of satisficing (cf. Tarshis, 1967, Chapter 7; Davidson, 1978, pp. 35-52). The firm sets a price that covers all costs including normal profit, sets a target or aspiration level of sales to cover average total costs, and then arranges a production process at this rate. Normal production is then insulated from fluctuating sales levels by shifting inventory levels and by delivery delays. The latter two also provide information feedback: steadily increasing inventories suggest the need to reduce production rates and perhaps costs, while short inventories and increasing delivery delays suggest overtime work.

The most important contribution of the bounded rationality theory is its incorporation of information processing into rational decision-making. I shall merely list the major information-processing concepts here.

1. Information feedback has already been mentioned. When the future is uncertain we cannot expect to get an investment or employment or pricing decision perfect immediately, but must devise a strategy for correcting initial estimates over time. The rational decision-maker is not one who has his preferences clearly ordered from the start and who "knows" the future, but rather one who can make maximal use of negative feedback to correct initial estimates (Snyder and Diesing, 1977, p. 333).

2. Level of aspiration already incorporates information feedback in its working. Aspiration level is initially determined by some standard operating level: standard of living, normal production process, normal share of the market, normal international sphere of influence. But when a policy or strategy is implemented, aspiration level becomes an estimate of the rate of activity that will be maintainable in the long run. As information feedback indicates that this rate is set too low or too high it can be adjusted, to the cumulative pattern of information rather than to every chance fluctuation. This kind of calculation is easy to perform, while the maximizing calculations based on new information of Cross (1969) and Modigliani and Brumberg (1954) are impossible and constitute an "as if" postulate.

3. Liquidity preference is a concept that Keynes devised to incorporate uncertainty into his monetary theory. Increase of liquidity is a way to postpone investment decisions until more information about the future is available. Preference for liquidity should therefore rise when uncertainty increases (Tobin, 1958). This concept can be generalized to all decisions: when the situation is not clear and postponement is possible, postpone part of a decision until adequate information is available. For instance, Herbert Simon argues that the standard employment contract incorporates liquidity preference in its failure to specify exactly what work is required; the boss specifies the required work as information becomes available, with the worker reserving veto power over unacceptable work through the grievance procedure (Simon, 1957, Chapter 11).

Another variant is the *stall*. In our research on crisis bargaining we found that when statesmen are faced with a choice between two unacceptable bargaining strategies—unacceptable in the sense that they fail to satisfice some goal—they refuse to make a choice. Instead of adding up the costs and benefits of each in maximizing fashion, they stall, and frantically search for an acceptable strategy or tactic. For example, in the period July 26 through October 16, 1941, Japanese soft-line leaders were faced with a choice between peace and war. Peace, given US embargoes and asset freezes, meant certain economic ruin in less than two years; war meant military ruin since Japan was almost certain to lose. Though they were under strong pressure from the military for a quick decision they refused to choose, and when several frantically devised alternatives also proved unacceptable they resigned rather than make a choice. This is an extreme example but not an isolated one.

Still another form of liquidity is *organizational slack* (Cyert and March, 1963, pp. 36-38). Slack is defined as payments to organizational members in excess of that required to maintain the organization. Among its many functions, slack serves to insulate organizations from environmental fluctuations and thus maintain stability: "1) by absorbing excess resources, it retards upward adjustment of aspirations during relatively good times; 2) by providing a pool of emergency resources, it permits aspirations to be maintained (and achieved) during relatively bad times" (p. 38). An earlier version of organizational slack is Robinson's "excess capacity" (1933), a firm's normal characteristic in imperfect competition.

4. Search: The two previous groups of concepts involve passive adaptation to uncertainty—waiting for information and reserving resources for environmental fluctuations. The main active concept is *search*. There is *random search*, a pattern of stochastic fluctuations in which the feedback pattern gradually narrows down the output range toward some optimum point (Quandt, 1956). There is *problemistic search* of various kinds in which the decision-maker seeks only that information which he needs to deal with his immediate problem (Cyert and March, 1963, pp. 120-122). Problem orientation can reduce the amount of needed information enormously (Simon, 1957, p. 249 fn. 4). Finally, the rational decision-maker also *evaluates his search procedures* by the quality of information they yield and fail to yield, and can search for better search procedures.

5. *Negotiation with the environment:* Another active process is to *negotiate with the environment* to reduce uncertainty (Cyert and March, 1963, pp. 118-120). For business firms, this includes long-term contracts with suppliers and purchasers, cultivation of market imperfections, stabilization of the industry, vertical integration, and cultivation of political influence. From a neoclassical standpoint, the standpoint of the small businessman faced with perfect competition and therefore no uncertainty, all these common practices are unintelligible and therefore to be explained away as irrationality or market imperfections.

A fifth major development accompanying Keynesian economics was the institutionalization of the professional advisor role. This role was institutionalized in the US in 1946 as the Council of Economic Advisors, an adjunct to the Keynes-inspired Full Employment Act. Later occupants of the role gave it a name: the "in-and-outer" (Heller, 1967, p. 24; Halperin, 1974, p. 89). Keynes had been an in-and-outer without knowing it; henceforth thousands of social scientists knew themselves as in-and -outers without being it, without actually getting the glorious call to Washington, London, or Bonn. They were in-and-outers in waiting, preparing themselves for the call.

But many people did make it. The war itself brought many social scientists and philosophers to London and Washington to help with price control, resource allocation planning, military intelligence, operations research. Many stayed on afterwards. Just as the war had been, for the Keynesians, the first major successful application of Keynesian full employment policies, so also it was the first large-scale occasion for the use of professional in-and-outers, except perhaps for the New Deal. After the war the military continued the use of professionals, forming the RAND corporation. Other wartime advisors moved their services to industry, and operations research and systems analysis was established as a professional discipline. Still others set up their own Hudson Institutes to advise and train officials. More generally, the whole postwar program of aid to scientific research was justified by the proposition that scientific knowledge is useful for government policy. These organizations controlled huge amounts of money by prewar standards, and through its disbursement controlled the direction of scientific research. Science policy was now made by the government rather than by the market for knowledge.

The Council of Economic Advisors was followed by other advisory roles. President Kennedy added several: a foreign policy advisor, a science policy advisor, systems analysts (PPBS), each including a whole department of assistant advisors. Sociologists also arrived in 1961, staffing the President's Committee on Juvenile Delinquency and Crime, the first stage of the 1964 poverty program (Moynihan, 1969, Chapters 2, 4). The Hoover Commission brought in public administration specialists.

The other side of this development was the professionalization of the university. If social scientists are professional advisors to government and industry, their time outside government must be spent preparing themselves for the call. This means, first, doing research in the particular specialty in which they stand ready to advise the government: fiscal policy, agricultural policy, juvenile delinquency, etc. It means communicating with others in the same area, in specialized journals and conferences, and training specialists like themselves. Conversely, as communication within a specialty increases, communication across specialties diminishes, and social scientists become less able to understand each other.

In short, a professional social science is organized in specialties, which in turn are grouped into fields. Students are trained not in social science or political science, but in American foreign policy, urban politics, international economic organization. Some people with broader inclinations maintain two specialties, which they juggle. Specialties tend to develop their own techniques—special kinds of mathematics, econometric models, statistical techniques, experimental apparatus—and their own theories and concepts and controversies. Over time new specialties are added—statistician, epidemiological sociologist, transportation economist, with new journals and professional societies to match.

The increasing size and bureaucratization of the university after the war also encouraged professional specialization. The bureaucratic mind requires specialization, set within a hierarchical control framework, so the professional and the bureaucratic impetus easily merged. On the Continent the problem of organization was much more difficult because the universities were still organized on the traditionalist conservative hierarchical pattern; each field had a single Professor-Interpreter who was supposed to embody the whole wisdom of his field, with assistants and subordinates to transmit it. The compromise was to establish a whole new Institute for each new professor, thereby maintaining the traditionalist fiction of universal wisdom alongside the new reality of professional specialization. But gradually the new bureaucratic organization comes to dominate here as well.

III. The Unification of Neoclassical and Keynesian Economics

According to Samuelson (Harris, 1947, p. 146) no one understood Keynes at first. This judgment, however, would seem to depend on some stipulation as to what the correct understanding of Keynes is. In any case, it seems exaggerated: Kalecki (1972, p. 13) and Shackle (1968, p. xviii), who were already thinking along Keynesian lines in 1936, recognized a close similarity to their own ideas and hurried off to Cambridge to join the movement.

Keynes himself declared that his two main innovations had been to draw the theoretical implications of uncertainty and to emphasize the relation between *total* investment, output, and consumption in the bounded macroeconomy (Keynes, 1937; Robinson, in Eichner, 1978, p. xi). Given an inherently uncertain future, money is needed for liquidity to postpone decisions or to cushion normal processes against fluctuations; the individualist-barter model is misleading, and Say's Law does not hold. The emphasis on total investment, output, and consumption leads to a conception of a bounded system within which resource flows must be maintained and nothing disappears, in contrast with the open neoclassical microeconomy in which excess labor disappears somewhere and conversely needed labor or capital can always be obtained at a price.

The neoclassical economists did not recognize these basic innovations, but picked instead on secondary details. Leontief (1966, pp. 88–89) declared in 1936 that Keynes' innovation was making the labor supply curve depend on money wages, not real wages; by neoclassical reasoning, which has learned nothing from game theory, this implies that labor is irrational. Hicks focused on the liquidity preference theory of interest, which he misinterpreted as a statement about the velocity of money (Hicks, 1937; Klein, 1947, p. 100; Minsky, 1975, p. 14); he declared that there was no real issue between Keynes and the traditional view on this topic (1939, pp. 153ff.), but failed to convince Keynes because of a regrettable imprecision of language (as he thought, p. 162). Actually for Keynes liquidity preference is a reaction to uncertainty and varies with expectations about the state of the economy rather than the daily interest rate, as Hicks realized much later in self-criticism (Hicks, 1974, pp. 38ff.). Röpke focused with revulsion on Keynes' attack on the foundation of civilization, the habit of thrift (1937). Viner (1937) had trouble with several Keynesian concepts; in particular he entirely missed the point of "liquidity preference" because he abstracted from uncertainty (pp. 152-159). Given perfect knowledge of the future, any degree of liquidity preference becomes an irrational "propensity to hoard," and Viner declared that such irrationality was rare "in ordinary times" (p. 159). But uncertainty about the future is an essential part of Keynesian economics, and there are no "ordinary times" for Keynes.

What happened here? Plainly the neoclassical reviewers were translating Keynes' theory into neoclassical terms in order to understand it. They began with the traditional postulate set and then looked for a particular low-level postulate that Keynes was rejecting; or they took a concept like liquidity preference or propensity to consume and translated it into traditional language before evaluating its usefulness. And this is the natural way to proceed. These people thought in neoclassical terms; so in order to think about Keynes' ideas they had to translate the ideas into concepts that they could think. They could not think them from the Keynesian systemic perspective because they did not have that perspective.

Translating Keynes into neoclassical terms, or thinking Keynesian ideas from the neoclassical perspective, consisted of assuming individual maximizing-rationality, perfect information, abstracting from money; and then relating Keynes' concepts to this framework. Viner, for instance, translates "propensity to consume," which for Keynes was based on habitual standard of living (Brandis, 1968, p. 172), into a rational schedule of consumer expenditure planned far into the future (Viner, 1937, pp. 151, 165). Fellner's perplexing discussion of Keynes (1946, pp. 94–103, passim.) is based on the assumption of individual maximizing-rationality under perfect information. The Keynesian propensities, including liquidity preference, become simply preferences that people happen to have; and uncertainty ("expectations") becomes simply another cost. Fellner recognizes that maximizing under uncertainty makes no sense, admits he has no solution to this problem, and then forgets it by assuming that businessmen solve it somehow (1946, pp. 152–156). The ensuing argument assumes perfect foresight plus a cost based on the degree of uncertainty. Given this translation, it is not surprising that the Keynesian arguments turn out to be invalid.

These early misinterpretations were not based on animosity, but on a simple inability to take the Keynesian perspective. Other economists who found Keynes' ideas useful and even exciting and innovative made the same misinterpretations. Pigou (1952) is an example. For Keynes, the System was a circular flow of resources and money, with the banks providing a variable reservoir of money, and with non-rational expectations and propensities determining rates of flow. Pigou transforms this into a set of simultaneous equations of the form "A varies with B." The plausibility of each equation is assessed on the basis of individual maximizing-rationality. For example, a change in the propensity to consume becomes "when people decide to consume less" (p. 51). Given rationality and certainty, the interest rate *does* determine both *ex ante* saving and investment (pp. 15-19, 32-35). The dependence of investment on consumption makes no sense and is discarded (pp. 13, 43-44). The dependence of investment on expectations is also discarded because expectations are too variable to generalize about (pp. 55-56). As Patinkin observes, "Once the Pandora's box of expectations and . . . uncertainty is opened . . . anything can happen." (1956, pp. 180-181). The whole set of equations describes a short-term equilibrium state (pp. 61-66); that is, the separate equations describe tendencies which are never completely realized. Thus the model becomes a static equilibrium model, not much different from the long-term equilibrium models. "Equilibrium" here means "the state toward which the system tends, at a diminishing rate," not "a point around which the system oscillates." There is no sign of a curse on this peaceful, well-behaved neoclassical system.

The standard translation of Keynes into neoclassical terms was developed by Hicks (1939), who was then in transition from the neoclassical London school of Hayek and Robbins, plus Robertson, toward a more thoroughly Keynesian perspective in the 1970's. The first step in his journey was the argument that there was nothing particularly new in Keynes' ideas (Hicks, 1937); the second step was the argument that Keynes had added a few new ideas to the neoclassical theory (1939). To specify just what was new in Keynes, Hicks worked out the IS-LM model which translates Keynes' ideas into simultaneous equations. This model has been frequently used by Keynesians.

The IS-LM model is a static short-term equilibrium model similar to Pigou's 1952 model. Reasoning to and from the model assumes static equilibrium, no money illusion, maximizing-rationality, and no destabilizing expectations (for example Ackley, 1961, pp. 390ff,

415–416). As a result the LM curve reduces the speculative demand for money to a rational preference function related to the interest rate rather than to uncertainty; the destabilizing effect of expectations on the money supply is pushed aside. Expectations in general, though empirically important in producing instability, cannot be reduced to a stable functional equation and must therefore be left out of the formal model (Hicks, 1939, pp. 256–272; Ackley, 1961, p. 416). The instability of the investment schedule, so that $S \neq I$, is likewise kept out of the model. Ackley notes with disapproval that Keynes attributed this instability to psychological factors (1961, p. 402).

In short, the Keynesian system dynamics remain outside the static IS-LM model as empirical deviations or complications of the model. They cannot be precisely stated in a static set of simultaneous equations.

Leijonhufvud (1968) provides a more recent example of well-intentioned neoclassical attempt to understand Keynes. This work is set firmly on a neoclassical foundation provided by Alchian, Clower, Friedman, Modigliani (as of 1960), and Strotz. Most of the discussion is on the micro level from the perspective of the individual firm, and Keynes' concepts are translated into concepts of individual decision-making under imperfect information. Keynes' contribution consists of dropping the perfect information assumption and showing that individual maximizing-rationality takes a somewhat different form as a result. The revolutionary consequence is the demonstration that in the Marshallian "day" it is quantity produced that varies, not price (p. 52). Keynes' long struggle to escape was not, as Keynes claimed, from Say's Law—here downgraded to a principle, and an invalid one at that (pp. 84, 98-102)—it was from the Marshallian paradigm in which P varies, not Q. Keynes' underemployment equilibrium becomes, in translation, short run disequilibrium (pp. 161, 95), thereby losing the systemic concept of a self-maintaining cycle with information lags, and substituting the micro concept of random individual search for an optimum price. On the other hand, Leijonhufvud does see and emphasize the important information element in Keynes' theory and thereby shows that it is not impossible for a neoclassicist to get some very limited understanding of Keynes.

To understand Keynes adequately it is necessary to take the Keynesian perspective. Particular concepts like liquidity preference or consumption function are not self-contained but take their meaning from the underlying conceptual scheme. Similarly, Keynes' real innovation did not consist of some particular concept or argument like fixed prices or the rejection of Say's Law. These concepts are results, and the real innovation lay in the way of thinking, the conceptual scheme, that produced such results. Once one has learned the way of thinking the results fall into place and can be changed when theory or data make that necessary. One can even use the IS-LM model, adding the missing factors informally in one's thinking.

The economists, however, focused their attention on the results. They were not conscious of underlying perspectives, nor of differences of perspective, and each probably assumed that everyone reasoned the same way he did. When differences of reasoning and conceptualization were noticed, they were criticized as errors rather than recognized as the products of a different perspective. Keynesians criticized neo-classicists for their a priori reasoning from postulates of individual rationality: "The theory proceeds with impeccable logic from un-realistic assumptions to conclusions that contradict the historical record" (R.A. Gordon, 1976, p. 5). And for their concern with long-run equilibrium: "A long run constructed to track the ultimate consequences of anything is a never-never land" (Tobin and Buiter, 1974, p. 273). Neoclassicists criticized Keynesians for their empirical interest in particular structural characteristics that could change at any time that individual tastes changed, and for their failure to put a micro foundation under their elaborate macromodels.

As a consequence of this focus on results rather than on underlying perspective, the real issues raised by the two conflicting perspectives were bypassed, and the arguments and data collecting were focused on particular issues: How much does saving depend on the interest rate? How different is money from credit? Are stock–flow or flow–flow relations more stable in the short run? Progress in economics seemed to depend on settling these issues by argument and evidence and then constructing a unified theory of the economy. Unfortunately as the decades passed the particular issues never did get settled, and unifi-cation proceeded without agreement. There were in fact two unifi-cations of Keynesian and neoclassical economics: Keynesians unified the two from a Keynesian perspective, and neoclassicists unified them within the neoclassical conceptual framework (Cf. Harry Johnson, 1971, Chapter 1).

The Keynesian unification is quite simple and direct. Samuelson is the example here (1948, 1973a), following Keynes' own arguments. Keynes argued that the neoclassical theory of Marshall and Pigou assumed full employment via Say's Law and therefore could not explain levels of employment and national income short of full employment. However, if full employment were given, the neoclassic theory would be valid in explaining the distribution of national income, production, and prices. Samuelson follows this scheme. Keynesian macroeconomics explains the level of national income and employment, including business cycles (1948, Chapters 12-18); neoclassical microeconomics explains the composition and pricing of national output (1948, Chapters 19-22). In the 1973 edition the amalgamation is even closer. Keynesian fiscal policy has produced continuous full employment and thereby made neoclassical theory valid again. Even the quantity theory is rehabilitated (pp. 286-287) since V is approximately a constant, though in the first edition it was a useless variable (1948, p. 290). The rehabilitation means that monetary policy is a suitable supplement to fiscal policy, but only for slowing inflation, not for correcting depressions (1973a, Chapter 18; 1973b, pp. 120-129).

In short, the neoclassical theory has the limited supplementary role of explaining the *short run* distribution of resources within a full-employment economy, and of reminding doctrinaire Keynesians that monetary policy should not be neglected.

The amalgamation from the neoclassical perspective is based on the long-run/short-run distinction. Neoclassical theory, including Say's Law (Fellner, 1946, pp. x, 112-113) is still valid, but only in the long run (Becker and Baumol, 1952). In the short run all sorts of peculiar disturbances can occur (Clower, 1960; Patinkin, 1956, pp. 235-237) and Keynes' concepts may or may not have some validity in describing and explaining them. Wages may be rigid, demand deficient, expectations perverse and destabilizing, investment and saving unequal, etc. In the short run, changes in the quantity of money do affect quantity produced, not price, just as Keynes taught (Milton Friedman, 1973, p. 28). But all these peculiarities disappear in the long run. "These feedback effects via wealth and income will work themselves out in time as income and employment are restored to their normal equilibrium levels" (Alchian and Allen, 1964, p. 541). The short run in which Keynesian concepts are valid may last only two weeks (M. Friedman, 1972, p. 922) or it may stretch out for two or three years. Alternatively, neoclassicists tacitly abandoned Say's Law long ago; it was a tautology anyway, representing an ideal limit in the long run, and the facts so obviously contradict it that neoclassicists could not have taken it seriously (Haberler, in Harris, 1947, pp. 172-175). In fact, claims Leijonhufvud, since Say's Law is invalid and no neoclassicist took it seriously, Keynes really meant to attack Walras' Law (1968, pp. 98-102), which also holds only in the long run.

Keynes' concepts, therefore, can be used to discuss short run disequilibrium phenomena, though most of Keynes' ideas can be found in the earlier work of Wicksell and Robertson (Fellner, 1957). Consequently Keynesian monetary and fiscal policies can occasionally be appropriate in moderating strictly short run disturbances. For example Patinkin argues, as does Fellner, that the short-run dynamics discussed by Keynes are all disequilibrium phenomena derived from wage-price inflexibility (Patinkin, 1972, Chapter 2; 1956, pp. 337-343; Fellner, 1946; 1960, pp. 93-94). Given flexibility, Patinkin argues, there is always a price level low enough to produce full employment. However, this long run equilibrium process is irrelevant for policy purposes beause 1) it might take several years to approach equilibrium; 2) during that time, increasing uncertainty might produce increasing liquidity preference, deficient demand, and a deflationary spiral; 3) the resulting bankruptcies would intensify the spiral. Therefore countercyclical policy is appropriate. Keynes' contribution to economics was to show that the economy cannot return to long run equilibrium smoothly in a reasonable time (see Patinkin, 1956, Chapter 14, for more detail).

In both cases, along with other variants not discussed here, the offending theory is granted a limited, subordinate status in one's own theory. It also proves to be a special case of one's own theory:

Either: Neoclassical theory, which deals with an economy at full employment only, is a special case; Keynesian theory, which explains all levels of employment, is the general case (Keynes, 1936, Chapter 1). Or: Keynesian theory, which assumes money illusion or wage rigidity (H. Johnson, 1973, p. 73) or a constant propensity to consume (Havrilesky and Boorman, 1976, pp. 10ff.) or a low interest rate (Modigliani, 1944, pp. 74-75) or imperfect information (Clower, 1965) or absolute liquidity preference (M. Friedman, 1972, pp. 908, 924-926) is a special case of neoclassical theory which makes none of these restrictive assumptions but can draw the special consequence of any of them. As it happens, the Keynesian special case is the one that fits the real world (Leijonhufvud, 1967).

Either: Maximizing-rationality is a special case of satisficing-rationality; it describes the limit which rational decisions approach, through endless corrections of estimates and aspiration levels, endless feedback and reduction of uncertainty, endless forced comparisons of incommensurable goals. Or: Satisficing is a special case of maximizing resulting from the assumption of absolute goals and limited knowledge, or it consists of choosing the best from a subset of alternatives (Riker), while the maximizing theory gives the general characteristics of all possible kinds of decision-making.

The positivist history of science in which science progresses from the special to the general (Kepler to Newton to Einstein) is only too accurate for the social sciences, since each theory describes itself as more general than its opponent. A further difficulty is that the predecessors do not vanish, as they do in the positivist history.

Both kinds of amalgamation, the Keynesian and the neoclassical, drastically change the absorbed theory by reinterpreting it from an alien perspective. The neoclassical perspective is that of the maximizing-rational small businessman in a competitive industry, faced with stable prices and adequate information. From this perspective, the Keynesian concepts are unscientific as they stand. They are merely empirical aggregates, and the equations connecting them are empirical and therefore arbitrary. Since the economy is a product of individual decisions all such superficial connections between observable aggregates can be changed at any time, if individual tastes change or cost-return ratios change. Friedman expresses the neoclassic attitude toward Keynesian variables:

> One variable that has traditionally been singled out . . . is the volume of transactions. . . . The idea that renders this approach attractive is that there is a mechanical link between a dollar of payments per unit time and the average stock of money required to affect it—a fixed technical coefficient of production, as it were. It is clear that this mechanical approach is very different in spirit from the one we have been following. On our approach, the average amount held per dollar of transactions is itself to be regarded as a resultant of an economic equilibrating process, not as a physical datum. If, for whatever reason, it becomes more expensive to hold money, then it is worth devoting resources to effecting money transactions in less expensive ways. . . . Similar remarks are relevant to various features of payment conditions, frequently described as "institutional conditions" affecting the velocity of circulation of money and taken as somehow mechanically determined . . . (Friedman, 1956; 1966 reprint, pp. 76–77; 1969 reprint, pp. 59–60).

Note the concept "somehow mechanically determined." For the neoclassicist, institutions are determined by individual rational decisions; if Keynesians or institutionalists forget or choose to deny this their theory becomes some kind of natural-science theory of mechanical or hydraulic determinism, not a social science of rational action. Another term used to criticize Keynesians is "sociological" (Brunner and Meltzer, 1977; Brunner, in Mayer, 1978, p. 77). Theories which do not derive institutions from rational decisions are implicitly deriving them from nonrational forces as yet beyond our understanding, and are consigned to quasisciences such as sociology.

To make sense of Keynesian theory its concepts must be related to a foundation in individual rationality. The consumption function must be reinterpreted as an aggregation of individual spending plans based on expected lifetime income, extending over a whole lifetime and beyond (Modigliani and Brumberg, 1954; see Hansen's critical comments, 1955, pp. 362–363). Keynes' distinction between transaction and speculative balances drops out, since people use their money in a variety of ways according to circumstances (Friedman, 1969, pp. 61, 136). The rate of growth of an economy is a consequence of aggregate individual decisions on consumption/saving ratios (Alchian and Allen, 1964). When these ratios change, unemployment results: "We see unemployment, therefore, as an attempt on the part of the system to cut down its rate of accumulation to a level that its people are willing to absorb" (Boulding, 1966, p. 60, p. 81). In other words, the unemployment of the 1930's was a consequence of people suddenly deciding in 1929 to consume much less—or so a Keynesian would misinterpret Boulding, by treating a long run equilibrium statement as short run.

The Keynesian standpoint is the government, which is responsible for keeping a balky, unstable economy performing at political target levels. Given this standpoint, we need an objective science composed of causal or statistical laws, which relate key system variables to levers which the government can control. But the neoclassic "laws," like diminishing returns, diminishing marginal rates of substitution, $MV=PT$, and Say's Law, do not provide handles for the government to control things; indeed, they produce the conclusion that the government is unable to do anything constructive and if it will only sit tight and do nothing the problem will go away by itself eventually. As Heller observes, the neoclassicist's advice to government is "Don't do something, just stand there" (Friedman and Heller, 1969, p. 34). This is unsatisfactory.

Neoclassic science therefore uses the wrong variables.

> A variable is not useful in explaining the behavior of an individual if its magnitude is just as much subject to his discretion as the behavior which it is supposed to explain. An explanation of spending decisions must relate the spending of a household to determinants outside its control. This is the fatal objection to the hypothesis that the spending of an individual unit depends on the size of its cash balances . . . (Tobin, 1952, p. 115).

It is also the fatal Keynesian objection to Friedman's "permanent income" hypothesis (1957) since permanent income is also a subjective concept. It is that portion of an individual's income which he estimates will continue permanently, which in practice means that portion of measurable income that Friedman estimates to be permanent (1957, p. 23). The Keynesian instead needs the objective concept of measurable income, the actual income that objectively circulates in the actual economy. Similarly, Tobin finds Friedman and Schwartz's individual-subjective definition of money—a temporary abode of purchasing power—too vague. He caricatures their position: "We don't know what money is, but whatever it is, its stock should grow steadily at 3 to 4% a year" (Tobin, 1965, p. 465). Heller has the same difficulty with Friedman's concept of money (Friedman and Heller, 1969, p. 20). Of course Friedman and Schwartz know exactly what money is: it is whatever individuals include in their calculations of available purchasing power. The precise items which individuals treat as money vary over time and over individuals and therefore the objective institutional characteristics of money change in unpredictable ways. However, the ultimate effects are what count, not the fluctuating institutional media, and the ultimate effects can be deduced logically and checked empirically. Consequently the precise definition of objective money is unimportant and one can use whatever definition happens to correlate well (Friedman, 1969, p. 208). But for the Keynesians it is crucial to distinguish objectively different assets: bonds, time deposits, demand deposits, stocks, etc., because these function differently in the objective monetary system, even if individuals treat them all as purchasing power (Tobin, 1965; Tobin, 1972b, p. 861; Gurley & Shaw, 1955). The manner in which government and banks change the quantity of money—change reserve ratios, discount rate, buy government bonds—is of the essence of monetary policy, so these variables must also be included in the category of money. Subjective "purchasing power" is not a proper variable, while the instruments of Federal control are (Tobin, 1961, pp. 29, 30).

In short, the neoclassicists need a subjective science that is compatible with individual freedom and rationality; the Keynesians, the operations researchers, systems analysts, functionalists, etc. need an objective science that is compatible with government responsibility. One of the purposes of this book is to show the importance and difficulty of interpreting a scientific tradition from its own perspective. If one neglects standpoints and perspectives and treats theories as products of abstract human creativity the result is misinterpretation and useless polemic, as each critic unconsciously reinterprets an opponent's theory from his own perspective. I have three examples: for a fourth see Tsiang (1956).

One is the Yeager–Meier exchange (Yeager, 1954; Meier, 1954).

Yeager complains that the Keynesian postulates are arbitrary since they are not founded on our inside, subjective knowledge of human decision-making. But how can arbitrary assumptions claim to apply to the real world? In addition the Keynesian magnitudes, S, G_w, etc., are not constants and the "laws" are therefore spurious. There are in fact no constants in human affairs, since men are free. Meier replies that the assumption of constancy is a first approximation for mathematical simplicity; the function can later be complicated. What is essential is that we find stable functional relations, unlike Yeager's MV, which is not stable, otherwise we have no science. Thus each finds the other's science unscientific.

Another example is the various arguments between Milton Friedman and his Keynesian critics on monetary vs. fiscal policy (Friedman and Heller, 1969; Samuelson, 1973b, Chapters 30, 31, 69, 71; Friedman, 1972; Davidson, 1972; Tobin, 1972b; Stein, 1976). Friedman's theory is that of Walras and his own teacher Simons. Of Walras he has said, "Walras has done more than perhaps any other economist to give us a framework for organizing our ideas, a way of looking at the economic system and describing it that facilitates the avoidance of mistakes in logic" (Friedman, 1955, p. 908). Friedman's deductive arguments apply to a Walrasian economy in long-term equilibrium, characterized by perfect competition, and occupied by individuals who behave as if they were maximizing-rational. It is a world in which Simons' 100% reserve requirement for banks is in effect so banks cannot cause trouble for his argument by extending credit (Friedman, 1952, p. 625; 1953, pp. 135, 265; 1960, pp. 71–78; 1969, p. 83). Friedman ignores credit in his theoretical arguments and in his monetary history (Tobin, 1965, p. 466) as though it were an artificial complication introduced into the normal Walrasian world by greedy bankers. He also assumes away Regulation Q, which sets maximum interest rates on time deposits, because it prevents money from behaving properly (Friedman and Heller, 1969, pp. 76–77), and he assumes free trade and floating exchange rates so there are no artificial interferences with the Walrasian adjustments. Friedman knows that the real world deviates from this ideal world, but the ideal world defines the trend toward or around which the actual world fluctuates in the short run. Some short run deviations are regular and must be recognized by slight adjustments in the argument and the equations; others are random and can be ignored. Friedman rarely mentions these adjustments in his debating statements, reserving them for replies to objections.

In a Walrasian world the quantity theory of money and the quantity equation MV=PT holds, so M determines P. Friedman interprets V through the postulate of individual rationality and deduces that V will act as a lagged accelerator of the effects of change in P (Samuelson, 1973b, Chapter 30; Friedman and Schwartz, 1963, pp. 303-305). In general static equilibrium T, the level of transactions, is a constant. That leaves M and P as variables, and they must vary in the same direction. Consequently changes in M will *necessarily* change P in the same direction. That is all that M, the money supply, does: it determines the price level given long run equilibrium (Friedman, 1968). It does not affect real income, whose changes are entirely outside the Walrasian model and therefore cannot be scientifically predicted (Friedman and Heller, 1969, pp. 46-47). Nor does it affect the economic fluctuations that so concern Keynesians (p. 48); these do not appear in the Walrasian model, so they are beyond human understanding and control (pp. 48-50). All that can be controlled is P, the price level.

Heller, Tobin, and Samuelson live in a quite different world, one where a balky, fluctuating economy must be managed in the short run to maintain target levels of growth, employment, and inflation rate. They see the issue as a question of government policy: fiscal vs. monetary techniques for controlling the economy (Samuelson, 1973b, Chapter 31). The answer obviously is that both techniques are useful (ibid.; Friedman and Heller, 1969, p. 16); the more control levers available to the government the better. They magnanimously praise Friedman for reminding us that the monetary lever is useful too, and are disappointed when Friedman does not reciprocate by admitting that fiscal policy could perhaps be effective. But Friedman does not want to provide more instruments of government control; he wishes to show that in this Walrasian world government cannot do anything good, except to leave M constant.

Each side finds the other's empirical evidence questionable and of little value. Heller complains, as have other economists, of Friedman and Schwartz's "complex and often quite arbitrary adjustments of their raw data" (Friedman and Heller, 1969, pp. 22-23). But what Friedman has done with his raw data is remove all the short run "noise" that obscures the long run ideal trend (Friedman, 1973, pp. 19ff.), such as business cycles (H. Johnson, 1971b, pp. 124-125), and then replace the adjusted objective-empirical magnitudes with subjective-theoretical magnitudes: permanent income, real velocity, permanent prices. These adjustments bring out the long run relation between subjective money and subjective prices.

The Keynesians, conversely, need short-run data about periods of deviation from normal—wars, depressions, inflation—so they can study the relative effectiveness of different fiscal and monetary policies. They are interested precisely in the noise that Friedman eliminates from his data (Friedman and Heller, 1969, p. 66; Modigliani, 1977). Friedman dismisses all such studies as "casual empiricism." They are selected instances of atypical episodes. But for Keynesians atypical episodes are precisely the ones in which stabilization policy is most needed.

Friedman caricatures the Keynesian data by suggesting that Keynesians are mainly interested in first-round effects of government policy, which may last only two weeks, while monetarists are concerned with long-run cumulative impact (Friedman, 1972, pp. 917-922). Conversely, for Keynesians Friedman's long run never really arrives, so he must read it into the data with arbitrary manipulations, while their own short run models can be run by computer as far into the future as one wishes.

In addition there are the usual problems of translating concepts from one system to the other. For Keynesians the price of money is the set of interest rates (Friedman and Heller, 1969, p. 21) while for Friedman it is the Walrasian $1/p$ (pp. 74-75). Characteristically Friedman treats this difference as a simple logical error by his opponents; he refuses to admit the possibility of any other logic than the Walrasian.

A third example of translation problems and misunderstanding is the neoclassical concept of money illusion. It is asserted, from Leontief in 1936 to the present, that Keynes assumed money illusion in order to get his peculiar results. Money illusion consists in being fooled by money wages, and assuming that an increase in money wages means an equivalent increase in real wages. It may be, says Friedman (1975), that labor could be fooled that way in the 1930's; government could produce real wage cuts through deliberate inflation, thereby increasing employment. But people have by now learned to watch the price level; "you can't fool all the people all the time" (p. 28) so money illusion no longer works and government should stop depending on it with its dishonest Keynesian policies. Note that for Friedman uncertainty comes from government interference in an otherwise stable economy.

"No money illusion" is the standard neoclassical assumption (for example Patinkin, 1956, pp. 22-23). This of course is a simplified first approximation. Money illusion does occur, but it is rapidly corrected: "The main difference between the post-Keynesians and the monetarists appears to be how rapidly households develop correct perceptions of price and wage developments" (Rasche, in Havrilesky and Boorman, 1976, p. 27). But what does "no money illusion" mean, asks the

Keynesian (Minsky, 1975, p. 41; Bramson and Klevornick, 1969). It must mean that people know in advance what the price level is going to be for the duration of their labor contract or bondholding or houseowning. Only by knowing forward prices can one estimate the real value of a long term contract. But this is possible only in long term general equilibrium. We seem always to arrive at this fictitious state when we try to understand some neoclassical concept. In the real world we cannot know future prices and therefore real wages and costs. "Money illusion" is a misleading way of referring to the inescapable fact that we live in an uncertain world (Leijonhufvud, 1968, pp. 383–385). "Absence of money illusion" has become one of the great fudge-phrases of economic theory by which uncertainty is assumed away (p. 80). Since we cannot know the future, we have to form expectations on the basis of extrapolations from some past period, and these will inevitably overshoot or undershoot the mark as the economy goes on its fluctuating way. This was the point of Keynes' emphasis on expectations as an integral contributory part of the business cycle.

But for the neoclassicist we do live in a stable Walrasian world, which is thrown off its normal course by bad government policies and bad institutions. The disturbing effects of these policies and institutions can in principle be calculated after a little study. "Money illusion" merely means that it takes a little while to see just what trickery the government is up to this time. Assuming away money illusion is not fudging, it is merely a way to look past this short period of Keynesian confusion, of estimation and adjustment, to the real equilibrium effects of some policy.

In the 1970's, after over three decades of continuous misunderstanding ("we seem to be talking at cross-purposes" comments Friedman, 1972, p. 918) the Keynesian-neoclassical distinction has become more difficult to trace, and in the opinion of many economists the distinction has nearly disappeared. "We are all Keynesians now" assert the neoclassical monetarists. Instead of two sharply distinct schools one sees numerous minor disagreements and controversies among a variety of groups. However, the unification has occurred at the surface level of concepts and propositions, while the two underlying perspectives remain as different as ever. Both sides have borrowed each others' concepts and arguments—always with appropriate reinterpretations—so there seems on the surface to be a community of interpretation enclosing minor disagreements.

The monetarists long ago adopted Keynesian terminology like "consumption function." Next they incorporated "Keynesian" concepts like wage rigidity, money illusion, the multipliers, correlation of the demand for money assets with the interest rate (for example, H. Johnson, 1971b). They learned to use the IS–LM formalization in discussions with Keynesians. Finally, they provided a micro foundation for these "Keynesian" concepts by deducing them from individual preferences and rational decisions. They corrected "Keynes' failure to reinforce the concept of the propensity to consume with any explicit utility-maximizing rationale" (H. Johnson, 1973, p. 123). They could then contrast "Keynesian" and monetarist models according to different assumptions about effects of interest rates, stability of expectations, size of the multiplier, and could engage in elaborate disputes and econometric tests.

The Keynesians incorporated the competitive equilibrium model as a partial account of one aspect of the economy. Other aspects, however, could be oligopolistic (Modigliani, 1977). They used the assumption of individual rational choice in constructing portfolio models, and incorporated the neoclassical life cycle theory in the MPS model of the economy.

Despite the surface similarities, the underlying differences of perspective still appear in characteristic differences of reasoning and empirical testing. For Keynesians like Klein, Tobin, and Modigliani the economy is a complex objective system of flows and interdependences. Consequently it must be modeled by a 300-equation structural model, the MPS model, whose individual equations can be continually corrected. There are no independent causes in this system—except for government policy, the Subject, which remains outside the model. In particular, money is not a cause, though it can be used as a policy variable.

For neoclassicists like the St. Louis Federal Reserve group and the Chicago school the economy is the ultimate outcome of countless individual rational decisions. The particular institutional channels through which these decisions work toward equilibrium vary according to changing preferences, and therefore are beyond the range of scientific inquiry. Some of the channels may not have been discovered yet, and in any case the subjective variables that operate in individual decisions are not objectively observable (Havrilesky and Boorman, 1976, p. 66). Consequently the large structural models are an exercise in futility and their "empirical" findings are worthless. They stay on the fluctuating observable surface of things, confusing random noise with short run irregularities. Their theory is also scientifically worthless; it asserts that everything depends on everything else, and such a blanket assertion is immune to refutation (Brunner, in Mayer, 1978, pp. 79ff.). A proper scientific theory asserts a refutable claim about the relation between two variables. Consequently the proper method is still deductive partial equilibrium analysis: hold everything constant except one variable, say money, and then trace the consequences of this change via individual decisions all the way forward to equilibrium. Mathematically such deductions take the form of a "reduced" model of eight equations or less in which one variable acts as cause *ceteris paribus* and others act as effects.

For the Keynesians a model which holds everything constant except one variable assumes precisely the long run equilibrium, full employment, full information, flexible wages, etc. (always with one exception) that Keynes long ago discarded. In addition such a model ignores interaction effects and reverse causation, so its outputs are pure makebelieve, even if at times they happen to match empirical data. In any case the models are miserable failures at forecasting (Modigliani, 1977; cf. also Anderson and Carlson, Chapter 13, in Havrilesky and Boorman, 1976). For the neoclassicists, of course, the demand for a model that forecasts makes one focus precisely on the endless short-run fluctuations that are intrinsically unknowable, rather than on the inexorable long-run dynamics that are knowable.

The Keynesian standpoint has completely replaced the neoclassical standpoint in one respect: the professionalization and professional-bureaucratic organization of the social sciences. Milton Friedman has stated the neoclassic, free market objection to professionalization: it is a trade union or cartel arrangement which restricts entry, thereby raising salaries above the free market level and reducing services (Friedman, 1962, Chapter 9). Friedman discusses mainly doctors and lawyers, but his arguments apply as well to PhD's. Friedman's free market proposal is that anyone should be free to declare himself a doctor or lawyer—or teacher—and the buyers of these services would have to estimate their worth. In the long run the skillful practitioners would flourish, the hacks would go out of business or charge lower rates, and everyone would get the services for which he was prepared to pay.

The free-market mode of organization became archaic in universities long ago, and the PhD union card became universal by the 1940's. Even Friedman participates in the PhD trade-union apprenticeship ritual, and inconsistently does not refer to it in his 1962 chapter.

The well-institutionalized role of professional advisor to government is also open to neoclassicists, traditionalists, and indeed any kind of scientist. If the Keynesian can advise government on how best to control the economy, the neoclassicist can advise it to practice benign neglect so the economy can right itself, and the traditionalist can remind it of the eternal laws of power politics and government.

IV. One Goes Into Two: Left, Right, And Center Keynesians

In recent years the Keynesians have divided into a variety of groups, with names like right and left Keynesians, post Keynesians, post-Keynesians, bastard Keynesians, hydraulic Keynesians, and neo-Ricardians. Davidson's classification of these groups is as good as any (1978, Chapter 1). He distinguishes three groups: the neoclassical Keynesians like Samuelson on the right, the neo-Keynesians like Robinson on the left, and the true or genuine Keynesians like himself in the center. The right group are the most numerous by far in the US, and think of themselves as simply Keynesians. Like Davidson, they see themselves as ideologically neutral, neither left nor right: ". . . fiscal policy . . . is . . . an important modern technique of economic management, as ideological in its implications as a dental drill" (Lekachman, 1966, p. 275). Section III above has concentrated on the right or neoclassical Keynesians, since only this group has had any interest in unifying neoclassical and Keynesian theory. The other groups regard neoclassical theory as false or absurd and try only to refute and replace it.

This section will concentrate on the policy differences between right and left Keynesians in the United States.

The triumph of Keynesian thinking in the US is dated at 1961, when for the first time a new President took a solid array of Keynesian advisers into office with him. It was high time; the economy was stagnating after the 1958 and 1960 recessions, unemployment was high, and a fiscal stimulus was badly needed. The issue was what form the stimulus should take. As discussion continued into 1962, Kennedy's advisers found themselves dividing into two groups. One group, led by Walter Heller, advised a general tax cut, increased investment tax credit, and liberalized depreciation allowances. The other group, which included Galbraith, advised increased public welfare spending, increased public housing, and more technical education to increase labor skills.

Both policies could be justified equally well on Keynesian grounds. Both involved a similar budget deficit; both would stimulate the economy to a similar extent. They represented two different but equally plausible ways of breaking into the sluggish flow of investment and enlivening it.

Heller's proposal involved primarily an improvement in the marginal efficiency of capital. Investment tax credits and depreciation allowances reduced the cost of investment projects and thereby directly increased their profitability. A tax cut would convince businessmen that consumer demand would soon improve; this would increase business and banking optimism and thereby increase the estimated profitability of new investment. For both reasons some investment projects that might otherwise be judged unprofitable would now appear profitable, more bank credit would be available, and aggregate investment would increase. Second, the tax cut would stimulate consumption, and the increased employment from the new investment projects would also stimulate demand. There would also be multiplier effects. The result would be increased investment, employment, demand, and GNP.

Galbraith's proposals were intended mainly to increase demand. Public welfare outlays would go directly into consumer demand, since people on welfare spend their whole income; and purchase of public housing was itself a demand for consumer durables. These demands would induce businessmen to increase production and employment. A secondary stimulus to investment took the form of investment in human capital via education, thereby increasing labor productivity. Consequently when the additional demand became manifest there would be additional skilled labor available to increase production.

The same kind of policy split has appeared elsewhere among Keynesians when they were influential enough to be able to disagree among themselves. Bronfenbrenner (1954, p. 34) describes two opposite Keynesian ways to reduce inflation. Government could increase taxes, reduce investment credits, raise interest rates, and reduce its own spending. This would be the obverse version of the Heller proposal, since it would reduce investment, employment, (or at least excess demand for labor), and consumer demand, thereby reducing prices and wages. Or one could set up price controls and rationing, thereby halting the wage–price spiral and reducing excess profits and excess investment without actually lowering consumer demand and employment. This is also the obverse of the Galbraith proposal since it maintains employment, purchasing power, and consumption but kills off the speculative investment boom that inevitably overreaches itself and turns into a bust.

More generally, the one type of proposal involves a solicitude for business confidence and investment incentives in depressed times and a reduction of consumer demand in inflationary times. The other type involves a concern with consumer demand deficiency, the purchasing power of poor people, in depressed times and a reduction of business speculation and excess profits in inflationary times.

I shall call the first type of policy right Keynesian and the second left Keynesian, though both groups in 1961 thought of themselves as simply Keynesian, or in Galbraith's case ex-Keynesian. The difference of policy results from a characteristic difference of practical concern, not from a difference of standpoint.

The right Keynesians are concerned with the optimal performance and growth of the whole economy. They are in principle neutral toward the various possible fiscal and monetary policies, and ask only which policy mix is best for the whole economy at a particular time. This year it might be tax credits to certain depressed industries; next year it might be welfare measures or direct government investment. Their concern is not with the distribution of income within the economy but with the optimal growth of total GNP. The efficient allocation of resources within the economy is achieved quite well by the market system, as Keynes himself observed. As for redistribution of income toward greater equality, that is a valid government responsibility *up to a point* (Kurihara, 1954, p. 366) but one that is distinct from the overriding responsibility to maintain stability and growth.

The left Keynesians reject this distinction. Optimal growth depends on a steadily increasing level of investment, which in turn is stimulated by the prospect of normal or better profits; profits depend on sales, which depend on adequate consumer purchasing power. All Keynesians agree on this. But left Keynesians, following Kalecki, point out that consumer demand depends, not on GNP in general, but on the level of wages, since wage-earners constitute the great bulk of the consumers. The portion of GNP going to the wealthy capitalists is mainly saved, not consumed (Kregel, 1973). Consequently adequate economic growth depends on maintaining and improving the incomes of wage-earners. Consumer purchasing power must steadily increase to provide the stimulus to steady and increasing investment. Without increasing demand, direct stimulation of investment can be only a temporary remedy for stagnation.

Consequently government must maintain stability and growth by reducing inequality.

> The failure of the advanced capitalist system to move toward a more
> equal distribution of income (and the actual movement toward a more
> unequal distribution of wealth) would seem to be the heart of the

problem—the conflict between productive potential and consumption.
... Investment in greater productivity would appear to be futile and
even wasteful as long as people with unsatisfied basic needs still do not
have the wherewithal to keep the resulting new productive capacity
operating at optimum rates for spreading overhead costs. Turgeon,
1980, p. 101. An angry god may have endowed capitalism with inherent
contradictions. But at least as an afterthought he was kind enough to
make social reform surprisingly consistent with improved operation of
the system. Galbraith, 1955, p. 198.

Reform involves not simply income transfers, but capital transfers
in the form of education in labor skills (Schultz, 1971; C. Bell, 1977)
which will permanently increase labor's share of GNP and thus reduce
structural demand deficiency. Education, of course, is a form of
socialized investment, and Keynes himself regarded socialized investment as the ultimate solution to economic instability. By taking a
direct part in investment decisions government can correct the misal-
location of resources resulting from the "whims and fancies of profit-
seeking industry" and make sure that poverty and an unemployable
underclass does not continually drag the economy down (Robinson,
1951, p. 108; 1965, "Beyond Full Employment"; 1972).

The unemployable underclass is a moral anomaly in a society that
otherwise is growing happier every year as GNP rises. In addition it
makes the Keynesian goal of full employment more and more difficult
to reach. Ordinary countercyclical measures cannot reach this "structural unemployment" since these people are barely employable even
in prosperous times. They are last hired, first fired during business
cycles; they cannot accumulate seniority and skills; they get discouraged and defeated by endless struggle and failure, and develop
compensatory culture and personality characteristics like present-
orientation and indifference to work. These people are not so different
from the "socially disorganized" slum dwellers that the Chicago
sociologists studied in the 1920's, except that the causes of their
poverty are located in the unstable economy rather than in value
breakdowns. Over the generations this underclass becomes more
culturally deprived, technologically obsolete, and victimized by discrimination. What is needed is to devote some of our surplus resources
to job training, cultural enrichment, better schools, and income
maintenance in a concerted program to bring these people back into
the regular skilled labor force.

This was the thinking behind the 1962 Galbraith proposals for
welfare and technical education programs. The Heller group, though
they sympathized with income redistribution in the abstract, could not

pay attention to the specific structural problem that concerned Galbraith and his supporters. The overriding problem for them was how best to stimulate the economy.

As it happened, the right Keynesians won the argument in 1962, and the 1962 and 1964 tax cuts with several years of prosperity and relatively full employment followed. In Britain in 1946 the left Keynesians apparently won with their Beveridge plan, and several years of full employment and rising GNP followed.

The defeat of the US left in 1962 created a problem for them. The government had not taken their advice; how is this to be explained? Lekachman offers the most obvious explanation: government made a mistake. The politicians had not yet fully absorbed Keynesian (read "left Keynesian") thinking, and suffered from remnants of pre-Keynesian prejudices against government spending (Lekachman, 1966, pp. 266ff.). There was another possibility, however: perhaps government was not entirely neutral. Perhaps specific business groups had too much influence on policymaking and distorted otherwise sound policies (pp. 295ff.). If so, it would be necessary to educate the business community to the soundness of left Keynesian thinking (p. 301). This should not be too difficult, as businessmen had already learned to think in right Keynesian terms—tax cuts and government deficits—so a little more education would do it.

The discouragement at government rejection of sound professional advice provided a stimulus for left Keynesians like Lekachman to take a look at the Subject, government. The Subject was not entirely featureless, a mere technical device for expressing "the collective will of the people" (Heilbroner, 1968, p. 283). For one thing, it made mistakes—or were they really mistakes? There was, after all, a great deal of business influence on government. A continuation of this line of thinking gradually made government part of the Object. One could scientifically study the influences on government and explain policy outcomes. Policy was not the result of rational deliberation by responsible public managers; it was the effect of systemic influences. Robinson, for instance, sourly argues that "in fact Keynesian prosperity has been a byproduct of the Cold War" (1965, p. 115). In the case of Galbraith, his left Keynesian ideas of the early 1940's are still evident in his explanation of the 1929 crash (1955, pp. 182-199). In his 1952 work government is still Subject, with the responsibility of mediating between conflicting powers and supporting the weaker power; but by 1967 government is completely part of the Object, an integral part of the corporate technostructure.

In short, some left Keynesians move farther left over the decades and may even become ex-Keynesians. I know of four left Keynesians like this—Lekachman (1976), Robinson, Galbraith, and Schumacher, the British Coal Board economist. The further adventures of the latter two will be taken up in Chapters Eight and Ten. Conversely, if we look at the right Keynesians over a period of decades we find some of them moving rightward, dental drills and all. This occurs both politically and in economic theory.

Politically, Heller's proposals of 1962-1964 were not simply the result of an impartial judgment of what was best for the economy. There was a political component in the judgment. The Kennedy liberals saw themselves as a thin majority both in Congress and in the country, and wanted to widen their base of support. Tax cuts and investment credits were a bid for business support, "a bet on business" (Lekachman, 1966, pp. 270ff). And if business support were to be maintained and consolidated through successive elections, business advice and worries would have to be taken seriously. The Heller proposals thus pointed rightward politically. Heller's subsequent work as advisor to bankers and corporations also points rightward.

In economic theory, the Heller–Samuelson type of Keynesian has been concerned with reaching an accommodation with the neo-classicists, a grand synthesis of mainstream economics. Such an accommodation involves accepting monetarist ideas where possible and playing down differences, so it points rightward. The left Keynesians show no such interest in rapprochement, and discuss monetarists only to show the empirical falsity and theoretical absurdity of their ideas. Galbraith, from his left vantage point of 1973, sees right Keynesians and neoclassicists fused together as a pack of pseudoscientific propagandists whose sole achievement is to blind people to economic reality by inventing fairy tales and nonsense wholesale (1973, Chapter 1). If we compare Galbraith, 1973 with Samuelson, 1973a and remember their similarity of views in 1939, we realize that the Keynesian economics of 1939 is no more. It has become two—or three plus, if we add Weintraub, 1977 and Eichner, 1978.

Five The Objectification of Society; The Systems Approach

My purpose in Chapter Four was not to interpret Keynes simply as a great economist but to interpret him as the most spectacular example of the escape from the individualist-subjectivist standpoint. When we turn to sociology and related fields in this chapter, we find that others have made the same transition both before and after Keynes. The objectification of society or the "systems approach," with government as the responsible Subject and social scientists as professional advisors to government, is a general development in the policy sciences during the 1930's to the 1950's. The present chapter surveys a few prominent examples of this development, contrasts them with the individualist theories of Chapters Two and Three, and estimates the relative strengths and weaknesses of this approach.

The most influential system theorist in sociology and in political science is Talcott Parsons. As it happens, Parsons' model of society is quite similar to that of Keynes, partly because they share the same perspective and partly because Parsons has adapted and generalized some of Keynes' ideas. We turn now to Parsons' ideas and a few examples of their use and development by others.

I. Parsons

Parsons' work is divided into three stages: early, middle, and late. In the early stage up to about 1940, the main work is *The Structure of Social Action* (1937); there are also articles on economics and economists. Parsons' concern in this stage was to argue against utilitarianism in its various forms and especially the form it takes in neoclassical economics (1937, Chapters 1, 2). The theory he argued against is that wants are arbitrary and individual, that rationality is identical with individual maximizing-rationality, and that social relations are entirely exchange and production relations. This is the theoretical expression of the individualist standpoint of Chapters Two and Three above. Against this theory he argued, for instance in his debate with Frank Knight (Parsons, 1940), that wants and motivation in general are socially determined and are systematic, not arbitrary; and that social relations are governed by norms, including role-expectations, which are themselves systematic. In short, he argued that the economy is a dependent part of an inclusive social system rather than a product of individual rational choices. His standpoint was an objective system standpoint; he looked at a whole society from somewhere outside it just as the early anthropologists looked at a primitive society from a distance as temporary visitors to it.

Parsons' critique of utilitarianism is an extension of Durkheim's critique; like Durkheim, he emphasized the noncontractual basis of contract, the normative and sacred basis of economic activity. He also drew ideas and support from Marshall and Weber, both of whom argued that economic activity depends on a larger cultural or moral-religious setting.

In his middle period (1938-1952) Parsons moved beyond the "sociological basis of economic activity" theme and developed a Durkheimian functionalism culminating in *The Social System* (1951). He showed that the norms governing social action form a self-maintaining system. The system is a unity of opposites: a) instrumental norms govern economic activity and in general any action concerned with getting things done in the external world, and b) expressive norms govern the ritual activities in which people experience their emotional unity. A third category, moral norms, completes the Kantian triad and unifies the two opposite aspects of the system.

Parsons' late period, beginning about 1950, is a collaborative period in which he and many collaborators developed Parsonian functionalism. In terms of standpoints this involves a shift from the

Durkheimian-anthropological standpoint in which the Object is a small self-sufficient and self-maintaining primitive society, a stationary unity of opposites held together by common values, to a Keynes-type standpoint in which the Object is a highly differentiated modern society undergoing continuous fluctuation and growth and is held together by political leadership as much as by common values. The Subject shifts from the external colonial administrator to the political leader inside the system. The three categories of *The Social System* (1951) are supplemented by a fourth, the political.

Parsonian functionalism focuses on the functional prerequisites that a system must satisfy in order to maintain itself in changing equilibrium, but which it can never fully satisfy. It is thus analogous to the Harrod–Domar–Hicks models in which a target or equilibrium rate of growth is specified. The four prerequisites are contradictory, so that action to satisfy one causes trouble with respect to an opposite one. Small systems manage these contradictions by phase movement (Parsons, Bales, and Shils, 1953, Chapters 4, 5) in which the system cycles around the four prerequisites, dealing with each in turn and shifting structure and leadership with each phase. Larger organizations manage them by hierarchical functional specialization (Parsons, 1960, Chapters 1, 2). Whole societies manage them by developing specialized subsystems, each in turn tending to develop its own four specialized sub-subsystems (Parsons and Smelser, 1956). Functional specialization separates the contradictory structures and processes in society and thus mutes the inevitable conflict. In fact, it partly converts conflict into cooperation—each subsystem, by meeting its own functional prerequisite, contributes to the solution of the other three functional problems. Parsons' main concern then is with "interchanges"—the ways in which action satisfying one prerequisite also contributes resources for satisfying the other prerequisites. For instance, insofar as the socialization subsystem achieves its goal effectively, it produces socialized adults, including labor, which is available to the economy for meeting its goal. The result is a system model of multiple flows into which the Keynesian models can easily fit (Figure 5.1). As in the Keynesian model, money flows in the opposite direction to balance the interchanges.

The economy is the subsystem specialized to the "A" function of providing generalized material resources for meeting system goals. Its four sub-systems are specialized to the four Marshallian factors of production—land, labor, capital, and organization. Since the economy is the most thoroughly studied subsystem of society (Parsons and Smelser, 1956, pp. 308–309), Parsons uses economic categories to study

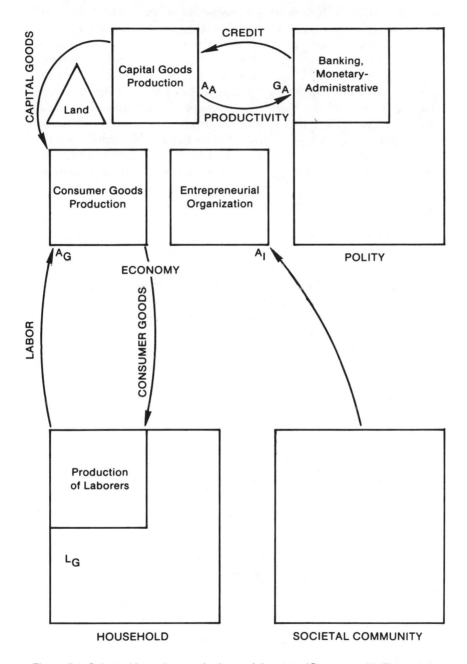

Figure 5.1. Selected interchanges in the social system (Compare with Figure 4.1)

the other three subsystems, beginning with the polity. His basic argument is 1) the economy is not the whole of society, contra utilitarianism; 2) the other aspects of society are analogous to the economy in their internal structure, rather than being irrational residues à la Pareto; 3) relations between economy and other subsystems are systematic. Point 1 is a repeat of the early Parsons thesis. Point 2 is new. If the three other subsystems are analogous to the economy, this means that they have their own structure, their own system-goal, their own productive process or mode of action, and their own mode of decision-making or control. This in turn means that when they are functioning effectively, achieving their system-goal steadily, they also exhibit their own mode of rationality, analogous to economic rationality. It is however the system that is rational, not necessarily the individuals in it. "Rationality refers to a mode of organization relative to a standard of effective attainment of a system's paramount goal" (Parsons and Smelser, 1956, p. 176). We may call this kind of rationality "functional rationality," following Weber's argument, since it characterizes a system that is functioning effectively by reference to its own functional prerequisite-goal. There are thus four analogous kinds of rationality, four kinds of decisions (1956, pp. 71, 77, 79) and four kinds of social problems.

The four kinds of functional rationality are examined in Diesing (1962), a work very much in the Parsonian tradition though differing in details of the I and L subsystems. The economy is taken as a reference point and its structure is contrasted with that of the integrative system (Parsons's "societal community"), the legal-moral value system, and the polity or system of communication, decision, and control. The primacy of the political or control system comes out clearly in this work. Its emphasis is on distinguishing different kinds of social problems, so that the social problem-solver—usually some agency of government—can solve each problem in the appropriate way and with the appropriate resources.

Parsons makes direct use of Keynesian ideas when he spells out the systematic relations between the economy and the other subsystems. Unlike the neoclassicists, Keynes pointed beyond the economy with his three psychological propensities—the animal spirits controlling decisions to invest, the consumption function, and liquidity preference. These three "propensities" are obvious place-holders for some noneconomic theory, and Parsons argues that the three noneconomic subsystems provide a systematic understanding of these propensities. In addition Parsons includes Keynesian monetary and fiscal policy as an important responsibility of government.

To begin with monetary policy: according to Parsons the creation of credit is a political act, since it determines the direction of investment and therefore the kinds of resources that will be available for goal-achievement (Parsons and Smelser, 1956, pp. 56–77). Since the polity is responsible for achieving overall system goals, it is also responsible for determining what resources will be available for achieving system-goals in the future. Whoever or whatever makes investment decisions—banks, insurance companies, the Defense Department—is therefore performing a political function.

This argument extends Keynes' suggestion that investment will eventually have to be socialized to bring the economy under rational political control. Parsons is arguing that government is necessarily responsible for investment decisions, though operative responsibility must normally be delegated via the administrative hierarchy to banks and other agencies. Among the control techniques Parsons and Smelser mention are tax policy, tariff, and subsidies (p. 73).

The "animal spirits" have to do with business confidence in the future investment climate, and this is another government responsibility. Insofar as government maintains general social harmony and stability (I function via G-I interchange) and guarantees the value of credit with proper monetary policy (G-A interchange), the basis for business confidence is there. Domar and Harrod mention another detail that Parsons overlooks—the guarantee of adequate purchasing power, via full employment and welfare, to purchase the future products.

Parsons interprets the consumption function in terms of the L subsystem, whose goal is to produce socialized, educated adults and to maintain them in good mental health. The family performs a good part of this function, along with schools, churches, recreational and cultural facilities. In order to socialize effectively, all these institutions must be structured to fit the requirements of growing personalities— close interpersonal relations, openness to emotions, drives, fantasies and symbolic meanings. Action is ceremonial and esthetic, inducing emotional participation and identification. But this kind of structure and its required integrative-expressive leadership (Parsons and Bales, 1955, Chapters 5–6; 1953, Chapter 4) conflicts with the impersonal, external, measuring and calculating orientation required to solve the economic problem of maximizing productivity. Consequently, if families etc. are to be structured to solve the L-problem, socialization, they must be partly exempt from solving the A-problem, the economic problem, which requires a conflicting structure for its solution. But the economic problem is solved insofar as the family (church, school, recreational and cultural facilities) can count on a stable flow of consumption goods, a fairly fixed standard of living (1956, pp. 221ff., pp. 61–63). Insofar as this flow is not guaranteed by the economy and ultimately by the political credit system, the family etc. is strained and eventually disorganized. With resource shortages parental roles cannot be performed properly, parents experience failure and defeat and children suffer in many ways. Conversely with sudden wealth traditional standards and practices lose their meaning and life becomes an aimless chaos of consumption, as Durkheim argued. Only a fixed level of consumption, appearing statistically as a stable consumption function, is compatible with successful socialization.

One could even speculate that in lower middle-class households under constant economic pressure to maintain a threatened relative standard of living, the economic problem (thriftiness) pervades the socialization process, and this sort of warped socialization produces economists who believe economizing to be all-pervasive.

The standard of living required varies according to class and reference group and thus changes over time. The changes are induced partly by changes in the class structure as the I-function is performed well or badly; and partly by the rising consumption standards that a growing economy must induce (Parsons and Smelser, 1956, p. 158) in order to maintain effective consumer demand. The latter is an interchange between A_I and I_I, part of the entrepreneurial and advertising process. Schumpeter's heroic entrepreneur is here reduced to a functionary in the A_I sub-subsystem.

Finally, liquidity preference is the consequence of an *institutionalized* uncertainty (Parsons and Smelser, 1956, pp. 234 ff.). Since the economy must adapt to changing environmental circumstances, it inherently fluctuates continuously. Information about these fluctuations must be transmitted to the polity so that the fluctuations can be controlled via credit and fiscal mechanisms. The information is transmitted by the fluctuations of the investment market.

Insofar as uncertainty is collected in the investment market it is removed from the labor market, thereby providing the stability needed for performance of the socialization and mental health function (p. 235). Insofar as wages and employment absorb economic uncertainty, this acts as a destabilizer for family and personality. The fixed wage levels that Davidson (1978, pp. 231ff.) argues are necessary for monetary stability are also necessary for family stability according to Parsons.

The reaction of the individual investor to uncertainty, the liquidity preference phenomenon, is irrational—though functional for the system because it transmits information to the polity. Sociologists are familiar with this sort of irrationality; it appears in panics, riots, and other mass phenomena, and exhibits standard time profiles and leadership patterns. The anxiety it produces is controlled by magic and ritual, including the magic of "inside tips" and the ritual expressions of confidence by bankers and politicians.

In Parsons' later work during the 1960's he focuses, among other things, on the medium through which the interchanges among subsystems occur. Here the borrowing of Keynesian concepts is direct. Money is treated systemically as a medium for transmitting the flow of real social resources, rather than from the individual standpoint as a store of purchasing power or as another Walrasian commodity. But since there are four subsystems of society of which the economy is one, there must be four media of circulation of which money is one. The other three—power, influence, and commitments—are studied by analogy with the properties of money (Parsons, 1969b, Chapters 13-16).

In particular, Parsons argues that the other media undergo inflation-deflation cycles analogous to those studied by Keynesians in the economy (1969b, pp. 463-467, 426-429, 392-394). Deflation spirals in all cases involve a loss of confidence in credit and an increase of liquidity preference; this reduces the quantity of the circulating medium and hinders the performance of the relevant functions; this reduction in real output circulates through the four subsystems in a cumulative fashion, and output declines until a balance is reestablished and confidence returns. One can also distinguish an artificial deflation based mainly on expectations, which reverses rapidly, from a real deflation based on reduced output. Parsons treats the McCarthy "twenty years of treason" episode of 1950-1954 as an example of deflation in the commitment medium (1969b, pp. 179-180, 392-393). It had a real basis in structural conflicts in the societal community, which McCarthy used to weaken confidence in commitments (loyalty); the deflation of commitments served to deflate power and reduce the real output of government, which circulated back and caused increased strains in the societal community. Inflation consists of an overexpansion of some medium—overcommitment, too much power delegation, too much credit—beyond the capacity of the relevant subsystem to expand its real output. Consequently, the returns from the credit are deficient, the delegated bits of power get into conflict, the commitments cannot all be honored, and their value declines. The system must either move to a lower level of real output, which may become a deflationary spiral, or increase its credit, commitments, etc. still further in an inflationary spiral.

However, if the political leadership expands credit etc., just the right amount it can stimulate expanded real production in the other three subsystems and thus promote system growth (1969b, pp. 389–392, 345–348). Since all four media of circulation are connected to the polity, the polity can expand them all, though only if there is unused productive capacity. In reference to commitments it works only if the collectivity and its members are ready to assume new binding obligations (p. 390). The increased real output returns to the polity in the form of increased power, which can be re-invested in further growth. This political growth spiral is analogous to the economic spiral of the Keynesian growth models, in which controlled credit creation and demand expansion stimulate real growth.

Parsons' main example of growth is the prospective full inclusion of the Negro American in the American societal community (1969b, Chapter 11). This is an integrative problem, one of reducing racial conflict, but its solution must be undertaken by government. "Thus the problem of coping with mass unemployment in the great depression was largely economic, but the agencies of doing so were largely political. The problem of the status of the Negro American is . . . integrative, but political agency is fundamental in attempts to cope with it" (1969b, p. 476). The mechanism is for political leadership—in this case President Johnson—to mobilize the American value-commitment to equality for all, extend financial credit for job training and employment, delegate power to enforce nondiscrimination laws, and persuade (influence) voluntary organizations to accept Negroes as equals (pp. 280–284). Of these tactics the economic one, credits for upgrading of labor skills of Negroes and all victims of discrimination, is the most important (p. 284). Note that for Parsons an effective policy should use all four media—money, power, influence, and commitment—to activate all four subsystems simultaneously. Inclusion of the Negro will reduce social conflict and increase American power—it will show the world the superiority of democracy over Communism and justify U.S. world leadership (p. 289). Here Parsons the propagandist contributes some of the persuasion that is needed.

Conversely, if political leadership allocates its power and other liquid resources unwisely the result could be inflation and reduced real returns of power. At the extreme such a declining spiral of power and other resources can end in political bankruptcy—withdrawal of loyalty, loss of political support, unwillingness of officials to follow orders, flight of capital. Parsons cites Weimar Germany and the French Fourth Republic as two examples of political systems that gradually ran out of power and went politically bankrupt (1969b, p. 493).

If we ask whether Parsons' affinity is with the right or the left Keynesians, there is evidence that places him with the right Keynesians. Functionalism itself faces in two directions: it can be used to justify the detailed working of institutions by showing what functions they perform and how well the system is working, or it can be used to locate conflict, strain, and social problems that the system is failing to solve. The emphasis can be on functional unity or on the contradictory prerequisites.

Parsons has always been able to see contradiction and conflict, including especially class conflict. In 1953 Bales asserted, "The problem of equilibrium is essentially the problem of establishing arrangements whereby the system goes through a repetitive cycle, within which all the disturbances created in one phase are reduced in some other. The dilemma of all action systems is that no one disturbance can be reduced without creating another" (Parsons, Bales, and Shils, 1953, p. 123). In 1956 Parsons and Smelser noted: "Since the American value system and its institutionalization is skewed in the direction of a strong adaptive emphasis, we would expect a relatively heavy general input of labor services relative to corresponding outputs from the economy. . . . The labour market is skewed toward the economy in its G-component" (Parsons and Smelser, 1956, p. 146). That is, the socialization process produces a surplus commitment to work in the personality, which gives employers a heavy advantage in wage bargaining and produces a chronic money shortage in the L-subsystem. If we add to this Parsons' emphasis on the family's need for economic security and especially security from intermittent unemployment, there is material for a left-liberal analysis of the intolerable strain put on the lower class family by structural exploitation and structural unemployment. Joan Robinson has already given us such an analysis. However, Parsons leaves the matter there, as a Durkheimian problem of values. Similarly, Parsons is much concerned about racial discrimination; yet in 1965 he was as confident that liberal government will solve this problem as Heller was in 1966 that permanent full employment was then guaranteed. In 1968 Parsons was very much opposed to the student movement (Rapoport and Kirshbaum, 1969, pp. 88–95). One cannot imagine him writing in 1969: "Since the American university is skewed in the direction of a strong professional emphasis, we would expect a relatively heavy general input of student services relative to corresponding outputs from the professors . . . ." No, he writes of the superior competence and deeper educational commitment of the faculty, and assigns students the right to learn and to ask questions (Parsons, 1969a). Whereas in the 1940's and 1950's Parsons noted the many strains and conflicts in American life, his writings of the 1960's emphasize how well U.S. society is solving the four functional problems (1967, 1969b), and the University, as of 1969, seems to be about perfect.

In the 1960's the inherent contradictions between the opposite functional prerequisites are no longer mentioned, and as a result the source of social problems in systemic contradictions is no longer investigated. Social problems are just there, somehow, waiting to be solved.

This slow rightward drift suggests an affinity to the rightward Keynesians.

II. Diffusions of Parsonian Functionalism

Parsons' functionalism has been most influential among political scientists, especially among the developmental functionalists. These are students of the developing nations of the 1950's and 1960's, the new states whose governments were trying to create a whole new society—political, economic, cultural, social—as fast as possible. The lines of diffusion run via Levy, Apter, and Almond as well as directly from Parsons. The method is the large case study of a whole country, or the still larger comparative study of two to four countries (Almond and Coleman, 1960; Almond, 1970). Parsons' categories have also been used to study the development of societies in previous centuries, especially the development of capitalist societies.

A society evolves from one historical type to another when the old functional unity is broken up, when social conflicts become extreme, and the functional prerequisites can no longer be fulfilled. The breakdown diffuses through the subsystems as each failure increases the strain on some other subsystem, the media of circulation lose their value, and real output declines drastically. This problem is more serious than mere political bankruptcy within a badly crippled but still viable society, as in Weimar Germany. As long as the other subsystems are still operating, a bankrupt polity can be replaced by a new political structure that then adapts to and maintains much of the old society. But when all subsystems break down the whole society changes to a new type, with a new mode of production, a new political structure, different classes, a different family-educational system, and different basic personality and cultural values. The new structures relate to new versions of the four functional prerequisites, and a new functional unity develops.

This process has been best studied in two excellent works by Eisenstadt (1963) and Holt and Turner (1966), as well as in studies by Binder, Bellah, Geertz, and others. Eisenstadt studies the bureaucratic empires, the type of society that immediately preceded capitalism, and shows how the central administration was continuously in trouble meeting the contradictory functional requirements of these empires. In mode of production it had to balance feudal production with small scale capitalist production and commerce; in values it balanced ascription and achievement values. Sooner or later all these empires collapsed (the most recent being Binder's modern Iran) and changed into either feudal or capitalist societies depending on the degree of development of the productive forces and the degree of liquidity of the four media of circulation (Eisenstadt's "free-floating resources").

Holt and Turner study the same process of breakdown from the capitalist side. Focusing mainly on the A and I functions, they show how two modernizing governments, Britain and Japan, could gradually break up the various feudal structures and build up capitalist economic and social structures in their place. From these cases they derive advice for the modernizing governments of the 1960's. For instance, they suggest encouragement of small-scale technology not requiring elaborate bureaucratic management, as bureaucratic management would adapt itself to the old bureaucratic–imperial structures and values (1966, p. 338). They also emphasize the importance of government control of investment and credit (the G_A function) and conversely nongovernment management of production (the A_I function) (1966, p. 308). It is questionable whether such advice based on the transition from bureaucratic empires to capitalism is appropriate to the transition from capitalist colonialism to socialism. They also study the contrasting cases of France and China where anti-modernizing governments maintained imperial structures and satisfied the functional prerequisites for empires with increasing difficulty until the whole system collapsed in revolution.

The problem for the ex-colonial developing nations is that all four functional prerequisites of a modern society have to be satisfied simultaneously, when almost none of the structures for doing so are yet in place (Almond, 1970, Chapter 5; pp. 175–177, 322–325). Failure of such a project is almost guaranteed.

Another line of diffusion of Parsonian functionalism runs via Easton's 1965 theory of the political support system—the G_G-I_G interchange—to the study of aspects of American politics. The various interest groups in the societal community make demands on the polity; the polity processes these demands and outputs policies that more or less satisfy the demands. The interest groups respond with political support, an input of power that the polity can use to manage other problems. Insofar as the class structure is well integrated, its demands will be compatible enough so that policy outputs can satisfy most of them, thus producing increased support, increased power to solve social problems. Conversely, a society experiencing intense class or racial conflict makes incompatible demands on the polity (input overload) with resulting output failure and loss of support. Similarly, a disorganized polity will be unable to process demands effectively and produce satisfactory policies, again leading to reduced support. Easton's many followers have turned out case studies of the demand-policymaking–support cycle with its many characteristic problems, for example Wirt (1974), a study of San Francisco politics. Easton and others have also studied political socialization, a part of the L-function carried out by families, educational, and cultural institutions.

III. Objective Studies of Social Problems

The commonest sort of policy study in the last two decades has been the study of some domestic or international problem. These studies share the Keynesian-functionalist perspective which treats government as the general problem-solver responsible for the well-being of all sectors of society. They are objective and empirical, professional and specialized.

Domestic social problems

If government is responsible for the adequate functioning of all the subsystems of a society, then it needs technical advice on the dynamics and performance of each subsystem. Just as economists continually monitor the economic indicators, interpret their meaning, and advise on corrective policy, so other professionals should keep watch on the other subsystems—transportation, class and race relations, education and juvenile delinquency, science and technology, welfare, the arts, etc. First it is necessary to model each inadequately functioning subsystem so a problem can be diagnosed. Then indicators must be devised and continuous data gathering mechanisms set up. The analyst must also locate control points at which government can intervene, and must develop a theory of how these controls work to correct malfunctioning.

For functionalists the proper subsystems are defined by some model of the whole society. In contrast, systems analysts define any interrelated actions and institutions as a system, without reference to the whole. For instance, all the public agencies that deal with blind people can be called a "blindness system" (Schon, 1970). It happens that this system maintains its own functioning without reference to the changing needs of the blind; it runs for itself, not for its supposed clients. It is a nonsystem in that there is no control unit and no communication channel through which the changing needs of the blind could feed back to change agency programs.

More commonly systems analysts and operations researchers are hired to study and improve some system already defined for them. Management defines the system and provides the criteria for optimum system performance. The analyst may question and revise these criteria somewhat and shift system boundaries a bit, but he is eventually guided by his employer's decisions (Churchman, 1968). Science becomes an instrument of management, control, social welfare. This development was already implicit in the earliest work of Malinowski, the founder of functionalism; Malinowski's concern was that the colonial administrator through ignorance was not managing the native societies properly.

Deterrence as crisis management

This development is a foreign policy analogue of the social problems approach. If science is an instrument of management, then it should help governments manage foreign policy problems as well as domestic social problems. Foreign policy problems occur in the various international systems—the diplomatic system, the financial system, the trade system, and the regional alliance system. Each system has one or more administrative structures through which the US or other governments can manage it—the United Nations, the International Monetary Fund, the General Agreement on Tariffs and Trade, and the Organization of American States, among others. Each system tends to operate crankily or even to break down if left to itself. The task of the foreign relations professional is to describe the normal dynamics of some system, point out the chronic or acute problems, evaluate the effectiveness of actual or possible government policies, and advise on an improved policy. Examples are Bergsten, *Dilemmas of the Dollar* (1975) for the financial system; Bergsten et al., *American Multinationals and American Interests* (1978) for trade; Slater, *The OAS and U.S. Foreign Policy* (1967) for the regional alliance system.

The international diplomatic system is an anarchy, since power is controlled by the member states rather than by a world government. This system exhibits both chronic problems like hostility spirals and arms races, and the acute problems of crises which can lead to war. There are two corresponding kinds of deterrence: general deterrence, whose goal is to reduce tension between potentially hostile powers and prevent a hostility spiral, and immediate deterrence, whose goal is to protect threatened interests in a crisis but also preserve peace (Morgan, 1977, Chapters 2, 3). Immediate deterrence is also called "crisis management" (Williams, 1976).

The theory of crisis management, in which a cybernetic-rational government has responsibility for the smooth running of an objective system, differs in characteristic ways from the strategic deterrence approach of Chapter Three. The following summary is based on George, et al. (1971), George and Smoke (1974), Jervis (1976), Williams (1976), Morgan (1977), Snyder and Diesing (1977), and Lockhart (1973, 1979). First, its method is empirical, using comparative case studies of crisis management rather than *a priori* deductions. This means that the theory is short run; each case is a separate problem, though conditions and consequences can be traced a short distance into past and future. There is no need for the unrealistic assumptions of pure game rationality, such as well ordered preferences, complete information, and perfect calculating ability. It is assumed that each government is rational enough to listen to advice and limited enough to need advice, otherwise the whole research program would be pointless; but the details can be investigated empirically. We find "sensible" rationality (Morgan, 1977, Chapters 4, 5) or more usually Herbert Simon's bounded rationality. This means that information processing is mixed in with crisis decision-making and that the whole process takes place over time rather than instantly as in game theory. At the start of a crisis it is necessary to diagnose the problem, estimate the opponent's intentions and strategy and goals, locate other actors who might get involved, and clarify one's own goals and constraints. Most of the crisis management process consists of communication and search for information. It is necessary to communicate to opponents and allies that their goals are unrealizable and their diagnosis mistaken, and conversely it is necessary to use feedback to correct one's own misperceptions, diagnosis, and strategy (George, et al., 1971, p. 229). It is often necessary to lower levels of aspiration, reassess preferences, and search for new alternatives. The rational crisis manager is one who can make use of the flow of information to correct his own mistakes of diagnosis and tactics rather than one who reasons flawlessly from perfect information. Most governments have fallen short of this modest standard of rationality in varying degrees.

The "critical risk" model of Chapter Three produces the policy advice of absolute firmness, plus Schelling's various tactics like irrevocable commitments and automatic use of coercion. These tactics are supposed to increase one's reputation for resolve, so that the opponent's estimated costs of aggression exceed his critical risk. In contrast, the crisis management approach emphasizes the uncertainty, confusion, and misinterpretation that permeates most crises, on all sides (Williams, 1976, Chapter 7; George and Smoke, 1974, Chapters 3, 19). Subordinates in the bureaucracy are likely to get their instructions wrong, or act at the wrong time; the opponent is likely to be guided by a mistaken historical analogy, so that one's own past firmness or conciliation are irrelevant to one's reputation for resolve; and so on. In such circumstances a threat of coercion is likely to deter only if it is clear and clearly communicated, if it supports a clear and limited objective that is clearly vital to oneself and of little importance to the opponent, and if there are positive compensations to the opponent (George et al., 1971, Chapter 5); and if both sides agree in their diagnosis of the situation (Lockhart, 1973).

The crisis management approach produces a characteristic interpretation of the Vietnam War: it was a mistake. It was a case of extremely poor crisis management by the US (George et al., 1971, passim.) US objectives were not clearly formulated and of course not clearly communicated; the diagnosis of the opponent's goals and strength of commitment was mistaken and was not corrected; coercive threats were vaguely and inconsistently communicated and the demands on the opponent were also not clear. The coercive strategy was inappropriate for many reasons: the situation was too complex for any participant to interpret clearly, US vital interests were not clearly involved, popular support was consequently lacking, many governments with their own diagnosis and goals were involved, and there were too many constraints on US actions. Also the coercive strategy was poorly carried out and mistaken diagnoses were not corrected until too late. In short, the US should never have "intervened"; it should not have intervened militarily; and it should have realized its errors and have withdrawn sooner.

Other interpretations of the Vietnam war will appear in later chapters, to illustrate differences of perspective.

IV. Contrast Between Functionalist and Neoclassical Categories

Household consumption

From a neoclassicist perspective household consumption is the implementation of a plan that is designed to maximize the expected utility of consumption (Modigliani and Brumbaugh, 1954; Friedman, 1957). From a functionalist perspective consumption expresses the attempt to maintain an expected or proper standard of living (Parsons and Smelser, 1956, pp. 221ff.). In the first case consumption is freely and rationally chosen; in the second case it is determined by the socialization subsystem and by the pattern of community reference groups.

In the functionalist interpretation, families socialized into a certain class position have a concept of the proper way to live, and this standard of living requires a certain income level. Maintaining this standard and thereby maintaining self-respect requires a certain occupational level for the wage-earner(s). Note the satisficing concepts here. The amount of savings required, for instance for children's professional education, also varies with class. Savings and debt also cushion the standard of living against income fluctuations. Over time the standard of living changes upward as a result of entrepreneurial efforts to increase consumption, since a growing economy requires an increase to maintain effective demand. Insofar as families cannot maintain their expected standard of living, or insofar as they exceed it, they are subjected to stress and strain, with resulting personality maladjustments.

In a mobile society where families move up or down in the class structure, living standards are determined less by childhood socialization and more by the family's reference group. That is, the newcomers to a class learn proper consumption standards from established members whom they respect (Duesenberry, 1949; Parsons and Smelser, 1956, pp. 230–232: "Duesenberry moves a little closer to the incorporation of a structured role-expectation system within the community," p. 231). Consequently lower-income members of a reference group will save less and higher income members will save more, as both maintain the same living standards.

In the subjective-individualist interpretation, the household works out a spending and saving plan that uses up its expected income in such a distribution as to maximize its expected utility over some time period. For Friedman the period is three years, estimated from his data; for Modigliani it is a whole lifetime, and the lifetime spending plan is recalculated each time income diverges from expected income. Presumably those adolescents who seem to be lying around doing nothing are actually working out their lifetime spending plan, and one should be able to find page after page of mathematical calculations in their wastebaskets.

Both types of theory can explain the gross data on consumption equally well. For both, spending levels should remain relatively constant despite income fluctuations, aggregate consumption should rise with GNP, and poor people should spend as much or more than they earn. A comparative evaluation of the two approaches must depend therefore on more detailed empirical tests, plus theoretical considerations of testability, breadth, discrimination power, etc. We begin with the tests of Friedman's theory of the consumption function (Friedman, 1957).

Formally, Friedman's theory is $C_p=k(i,w,u)Y_p$(1957, p. 26). That is, permanent or planned consumption is a constant percentage of permanent income, the percentage depending on a) interest rate, which is the reward for postponing consumption; b) wealth/income ratio, which measures the savings protection against uncertainty; and c) tastes, or how one likes to spend money. Friedman recognizes that this equation is empirically empty, since any variability in k can be attributed to changes in i, w, or u. He gives it content by postulating that transitory income Y_t is uncorrelated with transitory consumption C_t, where $Y_p + Y_t = Y$, $C_p + C_t = C$. The problem then is to estimate C_t and Y_t from the data, and this requires a great deal of statistical manipulation and estimation. Friedman also makes other predictions, and these require further data adjustment and estimation of non-observable magnitudes.

This work is a good example of how Friedman's "Methodology of Positive Economics" works in practice. There is an "as if" postulate: people behave as if they had fit an exponential series of weights to their income of the past seventeen years, or perhaps nine years, and used the result plus information about the capital market to plan next year's consumption. This postulate is supposed to be justified by *some* of the empirical predictions it yields. Attention then focuses on complex statistical manipulations, estimates and adjustments of data, computations, regressions, and correlation coefficients. *But Friedman's theory is never tested.* Sometimes the adjusted data fit Friedman's theory and sometimes they do not. If they fit, Friedman reports the fit as confirmation (pp. 40, 44-46, 58-69, 97-103, 116-119, 125-134, 190). If they do not fit, Friedman either rejects the data as bad (pp.

48-53, 85-90, 107-108, 136-137, 149-150, 191-192, 194-195) or offers ad hoc explanations for the poor fit (pp. 53-54, 54-58, 61, 69-85, 95-96, 120-124). Sometimes he re-estimates or revises data that do not fit, reporting the improved fit as confirmation (pp. 90-94). Clearly Friedman is testing data and estimation procedures, not theory. When data and theory do not fit, the data or estimation procedures are revised, not the theory. This process may be justified by poor data and difficult econometric problems, but the result should not be reported as theory confirmation.

Thomas Mayer (1972) has made a detailed study of all known "tests" of Friedman's theory and of other household consumption theories, and we cannot do better than to accept his judgment of their comparative validity. Mayer's own perspective is neoclassical. He observes first that Friedman's main hypothesis is not clearly testable (p. 10) as I have already mentioned, and that the subsidiary hypothesis (Y_t is uncorrelated with C_t) is not really testable either (p. 40). He records Friedman's arbitrary data manipulations (pp. 63, 79-81, 94) and his tricky interpretations of data to fit his theory (pp. 62-63, 68, 69, 70, 74n. 24, 75). More important, he shows that Friedman's adjusted data fit alternative theories as well as his own, so that Friedman has provided no confirmation of his own theory.

Mayer then surveys other "tests," and concludes that Friedman's two hypotheses are strongly disconfirmed if one accepts the tests as valid (Mayer, 1972, Chapter 16). One can always reject a test by using a different measure of C_p etc. or by asserting that tastes have changed; in this sense Friedman's hypotheses are not testable because any negative data can be rejected. Modigliani's life cycle hypothesis performs very badly, though some data are compatible with it; and, like Friedman's theory, it can be modified to fit almost any data. Duesenberry's theory is disconfirmed by one test but supported by several others (pp. 187-195). On the other hand the general principle of distinguishing permanent and transitory income in *some* fashion is strongly confirmed (pp. 349-350, passim.). Mayer concludes that households do plan their consumption ahead to some extent on the basis of expected income.

The functionalist theory is based on case studies, such as W. L. Warner's "Yankee City" series, that show regular class differences in consumption patterns, differences that are maintained by diffuse criticisms of households that do not consume properly. However, Thomas Mayer's neoclassical "standard income" theory is probably compatible with such data too, so that empirical tests do not choose between them. We turn therefore to the issue of relative conceptual adequacy.

The key conceptual difference is in the treatment of tastes. For the neoclassicist tastes are arbitrary and beyond the scope of science; for the functionalist tastes express a class or reference group determined standard of living.

The functional theory of consumption is plainly broader in its categories, since it explains the neoclassicist's arbitrary tastes in terms of socialization needs, class structure, and demand requirements of the economy. Moreover, functionalists have a theory of what happens when those needs and demand requirements are not met. These categories are invisible for the neoclassicist because from his standpoint within the lower middle-class masculine individual the socialization process is "beyond" or "behind" his consciousness and his preferences really do seem uncaused. The same point can be made for Friedman's explanation of saving, which is summed up in the statement that money is a luxury good—people demand more as they get richer. But as Tobin observes (1965) this repeats the facts in the form of a postulated arbitrary preference, without explaining anything.

The functionalist does not deny that people make spending decisions and even, in the middle classes, plan ahead; but these decisions occur within an objective systemic context and thus are determined by complex system dynamics. Moreover the decisions themselves are better described in satisficing than in maximizing terms, as I argued in Chapter Four. For one thing, raising a family is not a maximizing problem at all, but a problem of meeting a multiplicity of fixed targets: "We must have a color TV in our trailer, and a snowmobile, or we would be living like animals" or "If we don't give our children a good start in life by putting them through college we will have failed as parents." In Parsons's terminology "household" decisions are not "economic" decisions.

At the same time the neoclassical emphasis on planning and calculating which Mayer salvages from dozens of confusing studies is a part of the picture, however small. We need a theory that recognizes individual and organizational rationality in the context of institutions. The functionalist theory meets this requirement fairly well in principle since it leaves room for individual planning.

Social behavior as exchange

Homans' standard example of exchange is taken from Blau's case study of interaction in an office. A needs help with some report he is writing and goes to B, a more experienced employee. B helps A, and A says, "Thank you." This exchange continues intermittently; sometimes A goes to C for help and also says, "Thank you."

In Homans' maximizing-rational interpretation (Homans, 1961) A has a surplus of thanks and B a surplus of help; the exchange of help for thanks benefits both. These utilities are not measurable, so thus far the explanation is a tautology, as Morton Deutsch observes (1964). The empirical content comes from the principle of diminishing returns. Sooner or later B collects so many thanks that additional units become less valuable, and he requires larger amounts of thanks to pay for his help. Meanwhile A's supply of thanks is getting smaller and it costs him more in self-respect to say, "Thank you." At some point the cost of B's help in "thank yous" gets too high for A, and he goes for help to C, whose price is still low. And sure enough, it works out that way empirically.

In Parsons's and Blau's interpretation (Blau, 1964; Parsons and Smelser, 1956, pp. 104–113) a continuing exchange sets up a bipolar social system with its own four functional prerequisites that must be satisfied if the system is to continue. Blau discusses the latent or L-prerequisite of common values. "Exchange processes utilize, as it were, the self-interests of individuals to produce a differentiated social structure within which norms tend to develop that require individuals to set aside some of their personal interests for the sake of those of the collectivity" (1964, p. 92). In Parsons and Smelser's account (1956, p. 111) the G and I prerequisites are the important ones for interpreting Homans' example, with L tacitly in the background. G, the goal of an exchange relationship, is to exchange things beneficial to both parties. I, the integration of the parties in a system, is accomplished by symbolic gestures of mutual approval, esteem, or recognition of joint success. G and I are contradictory, since G sets the two poles of the system in opposition and I unites them. Small systems moderate this contradiction by phase movement, in which hard bargaining over exchange terms alternates with conviviality, joking, and expressions of mutual esteem.

In a Parsonian interpretation Homans' example is of an unbalanced system under strain. There are two levels of exchange, G (help) and I (thanks). A is benefiting at the G level of help and B is not; but conversely A is contributing most of the solidarity and esteem at the I level, though presumably B at least acknowledges A's thanks. This is a common situation; Parsons observes that "apparent imbalances on the primary level are often compensated by an imbalance in the opposite direction on the secondary level" (Parsons and Smelser, 1956, pp. 109–110). Balance must now be restored by A helping B and B thanking A. If the doubly unbalanced exchange continues the system soon collapses under the strain. Subjectively, A's "thanks" expresses diffuse indebtedness to B, and when the debt is not paid B feels cheated; tension rises, and the L-subsystem is activated in B's disapproval of A.

The functionalist categories are plainly superior to the individualist-maximizing categories because they are more complex and precise and can differentiate and explain a wider range of empirical events. The only empirical component of Homans' theory is diminishing returns; the other categories include arbitrary tastes, subjective utilities, and unobservable calculations. Nor does a translation into learning theory increase the empirical content, since "degree of reinforcement" is also unobservable. Parsons' system dynamics explain why returns diminish in value, and also point to other empirical factors— tension, strain, phase movement—not present in Homans' categories.

In addition Blau observes that the above system is one of two types of primary exchange systems, a distinction that disappears in Homans' theory (Blau, 1964, pp. 35-36). It is a system in which exchange is instrumental to extrinsic, extra-system rewards, and norms are universalistic. The opposite kind of system is one in which exchange is expressive-symbolic of the intrinsic rewards of system membership and identification, and norms are particularistic. Shibutani, 1964, provides a further discussion of the expressive-symbolic type of exchange system. Most systems are mixtures of these two polar opposite types.

Security dilemma vs. hostility spiral

Game theorists and objective system theorists have provided contrasting interpretations of the Cold War. Game theorists, who assume that both governments are game-rational, see the Cold War as a Prisoner's Dilemma game with its characteristic paradox of rationality. The paradox expresses itself to each player as an insoluble security dilemma. Cybernetic system theorists, who assume bounded rationality at most, see the Cold War as a hostility spiral, a positive feedback system based on inadequate communication and information processing.

The security dilemma is an $n \times n$ Prisoner's Dilemma, of which each 2×2 submatrix looks like Figure 5.2. If we expand this to a 6×6 or 10×10 matrix as in Figure 5.3, the movement down the main diagonal is an arms race, and up the main diagonal is a disarmament process. See Nardin, 1968, for a 6×6 matrix.

A closely associated Prisoner's Dilemma is the conflict of interest dilemma, which moves down the main diagonal toward crisis,

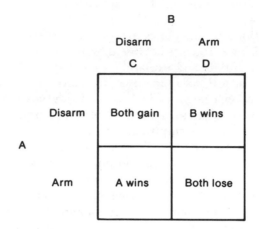

Figure 5.2. The security dilemma.

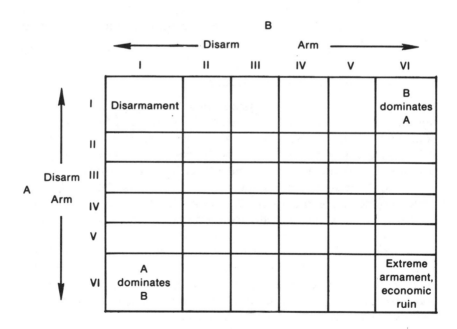

Figure 5.3. The arms race.

deadlock, and war; and up the main diagonal toward détente, good relations, and entente.

There is no rational solution to the security dilemma and the conflict of interest dilemma. This is either a tragic paradox in international relations or a deficiency of game theory. No matter how much either A or B would like to disarm and reduce tensions, they cannot afford to for fear of being doublecrossed; and the precautions each must take against being doublecrossed force the other to take the same precautions. Disarmament negotiations are bound to fail, since each side must ensure that the other gets no unilateral advantage and each knows it is rational for the other to evade any agreement that may be reached. The most obvious way to evade is to invent new weapons not covered by the agreement, and each must make every effort to do so, justifying the new weapons as "bargaining chips," knowing that it is rational for the other side to do so as well.

If we look at the arms race from an objective system standpoint we see it as a system of distorted communication, with lags in the correction of misinterpretations that produce a positive feedback of initial misinterpretations and therefore an explosive time-path. Any two information processors with very different coding systems, like the United States and the Soviet Union, are bound to produce garbled decoding a good deal of the time. For example, as we all "know" the United States has been sincerely interested in disarmament and re-laxation of tensions for some years, (up to 1981) and has sent many messages including a disarmament proposal to express its interest. According to Boris Rabbot, a Soviet sociologist who recently emi-grated to the US, these messages were interpreted in three different ways in Moscow. "According to the first, the United States wanted to exacerbate the Sino-Soviet conflict, even to the point of war. Accord-ing to the second, the Americans wanted to destroy the very basis of the Soviet system by introducing profound liberalizing social change as a result of Western influence on Russia. The third explanation offered was that America simply wanted to reduce the nuclear threat to humanity . . ." (Washington Post, July 20, 1977, p. A23). See also Hans Morgenthau's alarmed preface to Anatol Gromyko, 1973, which sums up to: if the Soviet interpretation of US foreign policy is as wildly inaccurate as Gromyko's book suggests, we are in real trouble.

When there is disagreement on the meaning of a series of messages, as in the above example, a well-functioning, rational information processor will wait for additional information to clarify the situation, or may take actions that test the varying hypotheses about the meaning of the messages. The lag involved in this waiting and testing process can easily be a year or more. Meanwhile, processor A is getting very strange responses, or none at all, to its perfectly clear and sincere messages; and if A is a well-functioning information processor it will suspiciously search, probe, and test for the meaning of B's strange messages or silence. But this change of message coming in to B, even before the original messages have been interpreted, will confuse the interpretation still more; in particular the correct interpretation will be disconfirmed by the shift of message and some incorrect interpretation will be confirmed. B's hypothesis will now be further off the mark, and its testing responses or clear replies will confuse A's picture still more; and so on.

If the information processors are poorly functioning (irrational), each will confidently misinterpret the well-intentioned disarmament proposals of the other as some sort of trick, will rebuff them, and will thereby confirm the other's misinterpretation that sinister intentions are involved. Once each is convinced of the other's sinister intentions an explosive hostility spiral will develop.

There is a solution to the hostility spiral (C. Osgood, 1962). The first step is to work for the election of a liberal, internationally responsible US government. Just as the Keynesian fiscal policies could not be carried out until the Keynesian Kennedy administration was elected, so an administration dominated by conservative cold warriors and friends of the military could not carry out a genuine detente and disarmament policy. Once a Kennedy or Carter is elected, he should call in professional specialists in distorted communication to advise on how to correctly communicate our sincere desires for disarmament and détente. For one thing, we should use a variety of channels over a long period of time, so that the various messages can confirm each other and drown out misinterpretations. For another thing, we should combine words and actions to lend force to each other. We should announce our desire to disarm and should disarm—cancel the B-1 bomber, close some overseas base, withdraw some troops—as evidence that we are sincere. We can then announce that if our gesture is reciprocated we will make another specific arms cut; and so on. We should more than match any cuts the opponent makes, to allow for differences of valuation, and should clearly connect our cuts to his with short time lags, to prevent misinterpretation. Only if the op-ponent consistently rebuffs our messages for many years can we conclude that he has aggressive intentions, and move to defend ourselves.

The game theorist can easily criticize the unilateral disarmament strategy, which is simply a play of C in Prisoner's Dilemma. If the disarmament is trivial, as was the Soviet unilateral disarmament of

1979–1980, it could easily be a trick to lure the US into real disarmament. If the disarmament is extensive it leaves the disarmer vulnerable to local "incidents." No rational government would intentionally leave itself vulnerable, so any apparent unilateral disarmament by the Soviet Union must be studied with great suspicion before it is reciprocated.

This sort of suspicion is precisely the main component of the hostility spiral.

It is not immediately clear that either of these sets of categories, game theory and system theory, is superior to the other in precision, empirical scope, and complex unity. Neither is directly included in or superseded by the other; each brings out something that is missing in the other. It would seem desirable to combine the two sets of categories, and this can easily be done within the framework of the objective system perspective.

The security dilemma does not depend on the absurd postulate that either government is game-rational, since it describes an objective dilemma, the Game, that transcends the subjective calculations of the actors. The dilemma is still there if we substitute bounded rationality. Consequently we can regard the Prisoner's Dilemma game as a description of the objective conflict of interest, though this conflict is continually changing as a result of the players' general deterrence policies. The hostility spiral theory focuses on the information processing and communication moves of the players, tending to overlook the effects of communication moves on the objective conflict of interest. A bounded rational policymaker will be attentive to both problems and to their interactions.

A similar synthesis is possible in the theory of crisis management. If we drop the assumptions of game-rationality and perfect information, the various games describe the unknown but objective structure of various kinds of crises. The theory of crisis management focuses on the subjective decision-making, search, and communication processes of the players. We combine the two by asserting that the main task of crisis management is first to discover the structure of the crisis game and then to solve the game problem either by changing the game or by choosing the correct strategy for that game (Snyder and Diesing, 1977, pp. 79–88, 408–418).

The international economy

The neoclassical approach to the international economy begins with a long run equilibrium state in which all resources except land are freely mobile worldwide, there are no trade or monetary barriers, prices are the same in all countries, and trade is based on comparative advantage. Each country will export those goods which it can produce more cheaply than other countries and import goods that are more expensive to produce. Actual trade shows little or no resemblance to this ideal pattern, as Leontief pointed out in 1956 by observing that US exports were exactly the opposite from those predicted by the model (Freeman, 1977, pp. 264–265). Next the neoclassicist takes up each factor that prevents international trade from approaching the ideal open pattern—fixed exchange rates, tariffs, quotas, subsidies, licenses, immobility of capital, labor, and technology—and estimates the distorting effect of each factor separately. Attempts are made to explain the "Leontief paradox" by redefining comparative advantage or searching for additional advantages and costs, and the search reveals additional factors that distort the trade pattern.

The Keynesian begins with a short run closed national economy and eventually adds the complicating effects of international trade. In the Keynesian textbooks the chapter on the international economy occurs near the end of the book and qualifies the model developed in earlier chapters. International trade and capital mobility open the national economy to a variety of influences good and bad, and thereby endanger government efforts to maintain stability and growth. Consequently it is also necessary to manage trade and mobility for the national benefit. Some trade, immigration, emigration, capital or technology transfers, are to be encouraged and others discouraged, according to circumstances. The means of control include those same "interferences" studied by neoclassicists, now transformed into policy instruments.

Systemically, the international economy is a set of managed national economies (Bergsten, 1975). Each government tries to manage its foreign trade for its own benefit, but in the process tends to create problems for other governments. It can use devaluation and import controls to export its own unemployment, and can produce a balance of payments surplus by forcing deficits on other countries. When all or most governments follow such policies the result (as in an n-person Prisoner's Dilemma) is erratic and sluggish international trade and frequent balance of payments crises. This situation hurts all economies but especially the weaker and more open ones, who cannot protect themselves.

Thus the international economy, like the national economy, performs erratically and unsatisfactorily if left to itself. It must be managed by the strongest nation or by a coalition of strong nations for the benefit of all. There must be well-understood rules against export dumping, dirty floats, high tariffs and low quotas, and governments that stubbornly follow a selfish neomercantilist policy must be punished. There must be an international bank or banks that manage money and credit and cushion national economies against balance of payments fluctuations and speculation. The leading countries get their reward for good management in the form of high, steady, and profitable levels of international trade.

The open international economy of which neoclassicists dream was approximated in the nineteenth century because of the equilibrating effect of the gold standard, which can no longer be re-established (Horie, 1960, Chapters 1-3). In addition there was a leading country, Britain, which managed the world economy and world monetary flows for the benefit of all, including especially itself (Bergsten, 1975, pp. 51-52; Block, 1978, pp. 4-6, 12-14). The gold standard collapsed in 1914 when Britain lost its leading economic position, just as the Bretton Woods system collapsed in 1973 when the US could no longer sustain it.

Neoclassicists and Keynesians approach international trade and finance from two opposite sides. One begins with long run open or openable economies and later studies partial closures; the other begins with short run closed or closable economies and later studies partial openings. It would seem that these two approaches are supplementary but not unifiable.

The Keynesian approach is obviously superior in its ability to deal with actual short run system dynamics. The neoclassicists must treat actual trends as temporary deviations from an imaginary ideal, and must study them one by one *ceteris paribus* rather than systemically. The neoclassical "small country" assumption, that the market sets prices and that all countries are price-takers, assumes away large-government influences on the international price level, and thereby assumes away the system management problems that Keynesians study. The neoclassicist can study only the problems of adapting to market forces.

Conversely, the Keynesian approach has not to my knowledge been used to study long-run dynamics, which transcend the immediate problems of system management. But it is not clear that the neoclassical approach is suitable for long run dynamics either. The neoclassical open world economy is an idealization of the nineteenth century British free trade system with British system management concealed; the relevance of this ideal to the present is very limited. Its main usefulness is to conceal US–World Bank–IMF system management. An adequate approach to long run dynamics requires the perspectives of Chapters Six, Nine, and Ten.

Racism

The one neoclassical treatment of racism known to me, that of Gary Becker, 1976, is so superficial that it shows how far racism is beyond the limits of the neoclassical perspective. Becker assumes the whole problem as given: whites have a taste for discrimination, blacks have less human capital, whites have nearly all the nonhuman capital. Given this situation, Becker deduces that blacks benefit from working for white employers, even at wages lower than their meager skills would justify. He ignores the benefits to whites.

The givens that are part of the nature of things for Becker are variables in Downs' analysis (*Urban Problems and Prospects*, 1970, Chapter 3). Low skill levels are part of a self-maintaining system of institutional racism, in which the residential segregation resulting from previous discrimination causes many continuing disadvantages for blacks: inferior education, poor transportation, poor work opportunities, poor information channels about available work, high indirect costs from urban renewal and highway construction (Downs, 1970, Chapter 8). These disadvantages in turn discourage blacks who try to increase their skills and income, and contribute to feelings of low confidence and low self-respect. Feelings of discouragement, resignation, and apathy which express black adaptation to a depriving situation also serve to maintain that situation, in part by supporting white prejudice.

Whites benefit from institutional racism in many ways: reduced competition for jobs and other opportunities, a sense of superiority, an opportunity to project undesirable traits on minority groups and to blame them for social problems, availability of cheap labor and captive customers with low market power. And since the institutionalized subordination of blacks and other minorities is not openly discriminatory, whites can continue to enjoy these benefits while believing with good conscience that they are free of prejudice.

Institutional racism is invisible to whites because it depends on the social and personality structures produced by overt racism in the past. For instance, a white employer may be sincerely ready to hire any qualified applicant regardless of color; but if information about openings flows through informal contacts with present white employees, if the workplace is in a white suburb, if the necessary skills are taught in mainly white schools, if previous experience is an advantage and whites have the experience, then the result will be that whites are hired (Boesel and Rossi, 1971, pp. 311ff.).

Downs' proposed remedies are broader than those recommended by Parsons (p. 128 above) in that they require not only government action but also black participation in reform programs, extensive education of whites, and black power to enforce reforms. Even black nationalism, which Becker's superficial analysis depicts as irrational, can encourage self-respect and build political power.

Downs' analysis was made possible by his shift from a neoclassical to a systems analysis and social problems perspective about 1960. He brought his neoclassical concepts and techniques with him and uses them where they are appropriate, for example in analyzing transportation systems (1970, Chapter 7). Here is another way to broaden a perspective and produce better science; Downs is equipped with two perspectives.

V. Summary: Comparative Advantages of the Objective System Perspective

By "comparative advantage" I mean the topics that can be thought and studied with the objective system categories but that are invisible or highly distorted when subjective-individualist categories are used.

1. The objective system perspective enables us to study system structures and dynamics as such, without having to reduce them to individual rational choices. This is the big advantage of Keynesian economics, as Chapter Four argued, and the various kinds of functionalism and systems analysis have the same advantage.

In particular the information aspect of economic systems and the information processing aspect of national and international political systems can be analyzed more adequately. Information is not simply a commodity, and uncertainty not simply another cost; this standard neoclassic way of treating information is highly distorting. We need system concepts like encoding and decoding, channel capacity and overload, filters, feedbacks, wishful thinking, organizational memory, search, to deal with information properly. These concepts probably look mechanistic from a subjective-individualist perspective, but this merely indicates an inability to think in system concepts.

Similarly, money is not simply another commodity, a luxury good, and it is absurd to think that one can study the demand for money as a separate topic abstracted from systemic fluctuations. Money is a systemic variable like information, and is more adequately studied in terms of expansion and contraction processes with positive and negative feedbacks.

Power is another systemic variable that is highly distorted in neoclassic theories. The typical neoclassic account (for example Hayek, 1960, Alfred Kuhn, 1974, Weidenbaum and Rockwood, 1977) treats the economy as devoid of power and government as possessing an apparently inexhaustible supply of power. Power is treated as a simple interference with individual freedom, and the circulation of power, its systemic buildup or dissipation over time, is entirely missing.

2. By extension, we can also study noneconomic systems and can locate noneconomic components in an economic system. Socialization as a systematic intelligible process replaces the concept of arbitrary individual preferences—"people want the damndest things," in Homans' language—and the functional necessities of political systems replace neoclassical moralizing about individual power drives. The concept of functional rationality—of structures analogous to the economy but performing different functions well or poorly—enables us to study strain and conflict and diagnose social problems suitable for political solution. In other words, we get a policy-oriented science to replace a science that announces the impotence of government.

Neoclassical attempts to study the noneconomic aspect of life systematically have failed because their individualist maximizing-rational categories have closed off such areas to inquiry. Marshall and Pigou were quite clear that economic categories apply adequately only to business affairs involving money, and Marshall especially tried to conceptualize other areas of life, but in the end had to treat them as empirical deviations from theory. Pareto tried to focus on the noneconomic, but his two categories of irrational residues and derivations are entirely inadequate. Knight poked around into anthropology, psychology, and all sorts of places but like Pareto could find only irrationality. J.M. Clark called for a concept of community to supplement market concepts, but could not provide one himself. Boulding has referred since 1953 to the integrative or love system, but his deeply engrained supply-and-demand thinking has closed off the topic to him.

3. One particular social system that has been opened to study is the corporation, and formal organizations in general. It is notorious that there is no neoclassic theory of the firm as a system; the firm is treated as another individual producing and exchanging goods and accumulating capital. Or if one looks inside the firm one is constrained

to see individuals exchanging commodities—money for labor etc.—
and the firm becomes a market. It is instructive to see Herbert Simon,
in the first edition of his *Administrative Behavior* (1947), struggling to
break out of the neoclassic categories and succeeding brilliantly in his
Models of Man (1957) and March and Simon (1958). Operations
research led the way here with its system–flow concepts like line
balancing and queuing, though there were also functionalist organization theories in the 1950's like that of E. Wight Bakke. The functionalist approach allows one to study the large corporation as a
political system, in addition to studying it as a community with
common values or "organization charter" (Bakke's term). March and
Simon also discuss the community or common-values aspect of
organizations (1958, pp. 65ff.), which is maintained by individuals
identifying with an organization and taking its goals as their own.

4. We now have a concept of community and of the "feminine"
role. The concept comes from Durkheim and farther back in history
(Hegel, *Philosophy of Right*, section on the family), but it gets a new
precision in the Bales-Parsons-Blau categories (Parsons and Bales,
1955, Chapters 5, 6). A community is a unity of opposites, the
outward-looking instrumental role and the inward-looking expressive
role. The duality includes dual values, dual structures, dual leadership
roles and dual modes of communication. The feminine or expressive
or best-liked role continually recreates the unity that is always being
put under strain by the outward-oriented achievement role and its
corresponding impersonal-authoritarian structure. It includes 1) a
certain kind of information reception and processing, focusing on
emotions and unconscious attitudes; 2) in game-theoretic terms, a
propensity to play C in Leader, accommodate to the other's leadership; 3) the ability to identify, that is to take the other's "tastes,"
values etc. as one's own. Parsons and Bales also observe that a certain
amount of role specialization is functionally necessary, but extreme
role specialization imposes intolerable strains on the system. That is, if
one of the two leaders always takes the expressive role, always plays C,
does all the identifying, the two leaders are split apart, lose rapport,
come into conflict, and break up the system.

The blatant sexism of the neoclassic theory is one of its many blind
spots, and the more subtle, refined sexism of the functionalist categories is a real improvement. Woman now has her own personality
and her own place, even though that place is—the home.

5. The shortcomings of the objective system perspective will
become apparent in later chapters, but I shall mention two of them
here. First, those scientists like Keynes, Parsons, and Almond who

reacted against neoclassic individualist categories are still constrained by the categories they reject. Keynes saw the impossibility of constructing a system model of the economy by aggregating individual decisions; yet he continued to believe that the internal allocation of resources followed the neoclassic model of perfect competition. Parsons rejected the utilitarian theory that the whole of society is an economy and all social relations are entirely an exchange of utilities; yet like Keynes he accepted the neoclassic models of the allocative workings of the economy. Almond and Easton reject the neoclassic concept of government as men given sovereign power by constitutions, and focus instead on the maintenance and structural problems of the political system. Yet they retain a vague residual notion of government as a non-market aggregator of individual preferences whose ideal goal is maximum aggregate utility. Bergsten (1975) consistently rejects the neoclassic theory of the international economy, and insists that the international economy must be managed collectively by the leading governments if it is to run at all well. Yet he retains the neoclassic model of a long run equilibrium distribution of resources as an ideal objective of government policy. The result in all cases is that the internal dynamics of the economy or polity or international economy are too readily interpreted as arbitrary preferences, economic calculation, and perfect competition, while the actual institutional structure of multinational corporations and bureaucratic interlocks is treated too casually or ignored.

A second shortcoming is that the concept of US imperialism is unintelligible in both its economic and its military aspects. Whether or not such imperialism actually exists, there are theories that assert that it does exist, and these theories are unintelligible to system theorists who treat their own government as Subject. There are two main reasons.

First, the System for a Keynesian or a functionalist is bounded by a national boundary that sets the limit to the government's responsibility. The economy for Keynes was the British economy. There were of course external influences on it, but these could be taken up later after the basic model was worked out. Similarly for Parsons, the American social system stops at the Canadian and Mexican border; the Old Country is left behind and forgotten, relatives and all, and Negroes are Negro-Americans. The developmental functionalists influenced by Parsons study whole countries as units, a large topic to be sure, but treat each country as a separate case.

Professional specialization also follows national and subsystem boundaries. Foreign policy specialists who are in training to advise the

State Department study foreign diplomatic policy only; internal politics, to say nothing of internal economics and international trade, are someone else's professional specialty. International relations specialists understand political colonialism and the operations of Colonial Offices; but once a country attains political independence and has its own embassies and UN delegates, its internal affairs are no longer Colonial Office responsibility, and pass into the professional domain of comparative politics. The comparativist in turn avoids studying US or British foreign policy toward the new states, to say nothing of international economics which belongs in an entirely different department.

Consequently there is no one who covers the area of modern imperialism. Phenomena that might be called imperialist by some are seen through specialists' eyes as something else. For instance, US troops have occasionally appeared in places where they were not especially welcome, such as the Dominican Republic and Vietnam in 1965. These appearances are called "interventions" by foreign policy specialists (Slater, *Intervention and Negotiation*, 1970; Hoopes, *The Limitations of Intervention*, 1973). US troops crossed a boundary and meddled in another country where they did not belong. These were mistakes in foreign policy decision-making, and the writers focus on how the mistakes were made—bad information, misjudgments, anti-communist paranoia, bad advice from fanatics like Walt Rostow—and in the Hoopes volume, how the mistake was finally corrected. The purpose of such studies is to locate the faulty decision-making procedures and human errors that might be corrected to avoid future mistakes.

Second, when government is the responsible problem-solving Subject, to be advised on how to improve its performance, the theoretical categories must be subjective ones. If the advice is to be intelligible to government officials it must be expressed in the concepts with which those officials think. This means that case studies of foreign policy must seek out the concepts that officials actually use when they diagnose a problem and make decisions. "Imperialism" must be understood subjectively as an imperialist foreign policy. But the US has no imperialist foreign policy; in fact sometimes it is hard to find any consistent policy at all: "The US has no consistent, coherent policy toward foreign direct investment and multinational enterprises. Nor has it ever had one." (Bergsten, 1978, p. 16). British and French policy is the post-imperialist one of helping former colonies get on their feet economically and protecting them against temporary dangers. Soviet imperialism, in contrast, is easy to see; the Soviet Union is part of the Object, and the objective facts of Soviet troop deployments and unfair trade agreements with satellites, or assistance to unviable satellites like Cuba, are public knowledge. The subjective categories by which Soviet diplomats deceive themselves about their own imperialist actions are brushed aside as irrelevant fictions.

Traditional histories of the origins of the Cold War exhibit the same dualism—subjective categories for us, objective categories for them. The standpoint of these historians is Truman and Byrnes in 1945, or further back to Roosevelt's advisors in 1944. They watch the Soviet Union doing suspicious things in Poland and Iran and speculate from afar on Stalin's motives. Truman's and Byrnes' motives they know intimately from the many memoirs, speeches, and State Department documents of the period. The US was trying to stay on friendly terms with the Soviet Union, reconstruct a peaceful and prosperous world by US foreign aid, and settle disputes peacefully in the UN, without meddling in anyone's internal affairs. But what was the crafty, enigmatic Stalin up to with his troop movements and puppet governments? At any rate things went wrong through no fault of Truman and Byrnes who were doing their best to preserve good relations with everybody.

The "hostility spiral" writers of the 1960's take the same standpoint but find errors in US foreign policy. The US was sincerely interested in peace, disarmament and good relations with the Soviet Union but seriously underestimated the difficulty of communicating with the traditionally suspicious, isolationist, and Oriental-minded Soviet leaders. Truman and Byrnes mistakenly assumed that their friendly intentions had been made clear, and therefore misinterpreted the Soviet defensive responses in Poland and Iran. They too hastily assumed aggressive intentions where probably none existed, and a systemic hostility spiral resulted through US errors of communication and interpretation.

What is needed here is an ability to see the US government as Object, as part of the system. Parsons comes close to this, and the lower reaches of the government hierarchy are objectified in his theory and tied to their functional tasks. But the top leadership somehow slips out; it is free and ultimately responsible for solving the many problems of the whole social system. After all, somebody must be responsible. To see the whole government as Object it is necessary to have a different standpoint, and this will be taken up in Chapter Eight.

Six Schumpeter and the Intellectuals

"Why is there no Schumpeter school?" Haberler raises this question at the end of his obituary article on Schumpeter (Haberler, 1950). If by "school" he meant a group of student disciples, then Schumpeter's reluctance to teach his own ideas in class would be a good reason (Sweezy, preface in Schumpeter, 1951,). But if he meant intellectual influence, the question was simply premature. Schumpeter's most influential work, *Capitalism, Socialism and Democracy* (1942), was only eight years in print, and other works were yet to be published or translated. Schumpeter's ideas became quite influential in the late 1950's and the 1960's and, along with certain ideas of Michels, Mosca, Pareto, and Weber, can be described as the foundation of a school or loose grouping of theorists. One social focus of this grouping was the journal, *The Public Interest*, edited by Bell, Kristol, and Glazer, though occasional representatives of other standpoints, especially Chapter Two and Three types, appear in its pages. Publications of the group reached a high point about 1960 with the appearance of Rostow (1960a, b); J. Schlesinger and A. Phillips (1959); Bell (1960); Lipset (1960); Kornhauser (1959); Huntington (1960); Dahl (1961); and D. Lerner (1958). Earlier works were Lasswell and Lerner (1951), Dahl (1956).

The grouping was too loose to develop a self-definition as of 1960, but later interpreters and disciples have given its central ideas the name "elite theory" (Prewitt and Stone, 1973; Dye and Zeigler, 1975). A subset of elite theory is the theory of democratic elitism (Bachrach, 1967), which derives from Schumpeter (1942), and Mosca. The term "democratic elitism" was coined by Lipset in 1962 (Walker, 1967).

I shall first sketch the main categories and propositions of elite theory, by way of stipulating what is being discussed in this chapter. Then I shall interpret the work of Schumpeter and W. Rostow, the two most influential economists within elite theory; I take them together because their theories are very similar. The purpose here will be to locate the Schumpeterian standpoint. Finally, I consider the theoretical developments in elite theory since Schumpeter, to estimate the strengths and weaknesses of this standpoint.

I. Elite Theory

This is a theory of the kinds of human beings there are by nature, the social processes that sort them out and locate them in society, and the contributions each kind and process makes to society. The theory of democratic elitism deals with the nature of democracy and the contributions each kind makes to the preservation or weakening of democracy.

The three main kinds by nature are elite, mass, and intellectuals. Since the elite are the most important kind, they have many subdivisions—entrepreneurs, aristocrats, political elite, modernizing elite, traditional elite, cultural elite or "elite of integrative symbols" (Bell), colonial elite, counterelite—and many of the theoretical developments of the 1960's consist in distinguishing and studying various kinds of elites.

In defining the kinds it is important to distinguish the initial stipulations that locate each empirically, from the theoretical conclusions about the characteristics of each. As in all science, theoretical conclusions turn into definitions and are used to reclassify the kinds for further study, and this is sound procedure as long as a theoretical definition is not confused with the initial arbitrary stipulation.

The elite, initially, are those few who actually make the most important decisions in a society. They make the decisions either because they occupy the institutional positions authorized to make such decisions (Mills, 1956) or because they have the most influence (Lasswell and Lerner, 1965, p. 4). Pareto tried to combine this stipulative definition—the elites are those who rule—with a more theoretical definition—the elites are the best by nature, the most capable and intelligent (Prewitt and Stone, 1973, pp. 160–161). Plainly, the two sets are not identical, and only one can be used as the initial definition. Similarly, in the 1930's, Lasswell defined the elite as those who get the most benefits out of the political system, but this category is more properly part of a theoretical hypothesis rather than an initial definition, since it is difficult to locate empirically.

From the initial stipulation it follows that there has always and will always be an elite, since only a few people can occupy particular positions or have the most influence at a particular time. This is the *a priori* or tautological core of elite theory, comparable to the neo-classical proposition that a rational person chooses the better rather than the worse, and the Keynesian "aggregate income = consumption plus investment" or "investment = saving." The basic theoretical proposition, appearing in a variety of forms, is that the elite are also as a rule the best and the brightest by nature. An alternative proposition asserted by some intellectuals is that they themselves, the intellectuals, are the brightest if not also the best. Mills, for instance, used to say that the elite have no ideas of their own and need us to think for them.

The small discrepancies between the two sets, the best and those who rule, leads directly to the theory of circulation of elites, which appears in Pareto and indeed in Plato's *Republic*. Circulation is ideally the process by which those who are the most capable of ruling rise into the ruling positions and those who inherit ruling positions but are incapable are displaced. The well-being of society depends on a smooth, gradual, but prompt circulation of elites, and on a circulation that filters out the merely ambitious and the crude powerseekers. Michels' theory can be interpreted as an assertion that in some or all political parties the circulation of elites is blocked. If it is interpreted as an assertion that only a few people occupy the top positions at any one time it merges with the core tautology of the theory.

The mass are the obverse of the elite. By stipulation they are the many who do not occupy the top positions; by theory they are incompetent, passive, and apathetic. "Homo civicus is not by nature a political animal," asserts Dahl (1961, p. 225), referring to the mass.

The intellectuals are those who are specialists in verbal communication—writers, journalists, advertising men, scientists, students, teachers, philosophers. The basic theory is that they are somewhat detached emotionally from society—alienated, irresponsible, objective, utopian—and therefore by nature critical of it.

On the topic of how each kind acts, and how its actions affect society, there is great disagreement among elite theorists. Some assert that in fact the elite rule in their own interest (Pareto, early Lasswell, Mills); others assert that they try to serve the whole society (Schumpeter). The elite may be described as in fact destroyers of democracy, necessary evils to be controlled, or preservers of democracy; and conversely for the mass. The intellectuals may be described as in fact preservers of democracy (Mills, late Berle), as gadflies valuable within limits (Lipset as of 1972) or as destroyers of democracy (Schumpeter, Feuer).

A second subdivision of elite theory consists of the theorist's evaluation of the kinds and of their contributions to society. Many writers insist that their personal evaluations are quite different from their scientific descriptions. A writer will assert that the existence of elites, or the apathy of masses, or the antidemocratic, prototalitarian contributions of intellectuals, is a scientific fact; but we may very well deplore this situation and wish to change it. We may fervently desire more mass participation than actually occurs (Dahl, in Bachrach 1971). We may study elites whom we believe to be bad and whom we wish to displace (Lasswell and Lerner 1965, p. v). Mills, for instance, studied the "power elite" (1956) in order to promote controls on them (cf. also Michels; Feuer 1969, introduction). More generally, a theorist may regard some elites as bad and others as good, some modes of mass influence on elites as good and others as bad. Whether the theorists' evaluation of elites, masses, intellectuals, and their contributions is as independent of his scientific description as he claims is an open question, which I shall later answer in the negative.

A third subdivision, or annex, to elite theory is the theorist's prognosis and his evaluation of the expected future. Pareto's and Schumpeter's pessimism is well known: they expected inexorable social processes to replace the good elites by mediocrities, but deplored this fact. Most recent elite theorists are optimists, expecting the good elites to stay in power. The democratic elitists have generally been optimists about the prospects of democracy in the US but have shifted from optimism to pessimism about its prospects in the developing nations.

II. Schumpeter and Rostow

Schumpeter's social theory is summarized in his influential 1942 work, *Capitalism, Socialism and Democracy*, and Rostow's main works are his *Stages of Economic Growth* (1960b) and *Politics and the Stages of Growth* (1971).

Both theories are historical theories of the development of capitalist society over the last several centuries. Capitalism develops in a series of jumps or waves rather than smoothly (Schumpeter, 1942, pp. 83ff.; Rostow 1960b, Chapter 2), qualitatively rather than quantitatively. Each jump begins in some particular sector of the economy, transforms that sector, spreads its influence to other sectors, and then dies down and is followed by a jump in some other sector. "The process as a whole works incessantly however, in the sense that there always is either revolution or absorption of the results of revolution, both together forming what are known as business cycles" (Schumpeter, 1942, p. 83).

A jump or revolution results from, first, an opportunity of some sort—new lands or resources or energy sources to exploit, a high potential demand for some new product (Rostow, 1960a, 1960b, Chapter 2), a groundbreaking invention like the internal combustion engine—in short an opportunity for vast profits and a whole new industry. Second, there must be entrepreneurs who see the opportunity and create the new industry and the way of life that goes with it, thereby incidentally destroying an old way of life and the class attached to it. The new mode of production spreads its influence throughout the economy, polity, and culture over a period of approximately a century: for instance the cultural effects of the mass-produced automobile are still spreading. Gradually the new mode of production becomes routinized, the new class associated with it accepted and established in the social system, and the new consumption habits standardized—until a new revolution in some other sector changes everything again. "If . . . a society is to sustain a high average rate of growth, it must engage in an endless struggle against deceleration" (Rostow, 1960b, p. 175).

The growth of capitalism has thus depended on the appearance of unique opportunities and on the availability of bold, imaginative, creative individuals to exploit them. And these have resulted from the breakdown of feudal and despotic structures. The Chinese empire was the extreme case of despotism: travel and invention were discouraged, a rigid scholastic education destroyed creative intelligence, and a strict class structure provided no rewards for initiative (Wittfogel, 1957). As a result the few creative minds that survived mandarin education found no social outlets or rewards, and the Chinese empire stagnated for thousands of years. Nomadic, horse cultures were more open to individual creativity, but only in military affairs, since these cultures were specialized in horsemanship and vigorous individual prowess. Consequently, the religious innovation of Mohammed turned almost immediately in a military direction, producing a military code, holy wars, and conquest (Schumpeter, 1951, Chapter 3).

Similarly, in European feudalism the opportunities for individual creativity were located in military and church affairs and later in national politics, attracting the creative minds into these fields (Schumpeter, 1942, pp. 124–125). But over the centuries the creative minds expanded the range of innovation possible in these fields, producing ideas and techniques effective outside religious and military affairs. Scholastic learning shifted from the texts of Aristotle to the development of rational thought, science, technology; military campaigns and crusades shifted to voyages of commercial discovery; and the new resources and techniques began to attract creative minds into trade and manufacturing.

Thus the religious–military innovators gradually created a society hospitable to their successors, the scientists, inventors, and explorers, who in turn opened the way for commercial and manufacturing entrepreneurs.

In today's mature capitalism the entrepreneurs are to be found in the monopoly sector (Schumpeter, 1942, Chapter 8 esp. p. 101) where plenty of opportunity for bold creativity still exists (Chapter 10). The competitive sector is the routine, obsolescent sector that gets destroyed by the innovative big businessman (pp. 84–86, 106; cf. W. Shepherd, 1970, pp. 142–143). The small corner grocery is wiped out by the supermarket chain with its powerful buying system and efficient packaging and distribution system; the small auto manufacturers were eliminated by the big three in the US by 1925 (p. 90). However, each new innovative wave brings a backwash of small service, distribution, and secondary businesses as the innovation is routinized.

Each sector of the capitalist economy, as of earlier economies, produces and is occupied by its own appropriate social class. The capitalist class structure consists, first, of big business, where the best brains and greatest financial power are located; there are in addition remnants of the old aristocracy, who inherited their intelligence and ability to govern (pp. 136–139) and who are mainly active in politics. Together these two constitute the Schumpeterian elite. They are the best, the most creative, the most intelligent. They get their rewards from the opportunity to act, to display their talents and energies on a grand scale. Second, there are the small bourgeoisie and in general the obsolescent classes and trades being displaced by big business, doomed

to join the candlemakers, blacksmiths, slaves, and peasants in ob-
livion. There are no rewards for them in a dynamic, progressive
capitalism. Then there are the masses, people of mediocre intelligence
and no ideas of their own (Schumpeter, 1942, p. 145), who are suited
to performing the routine tasks of everyday life. For them the rewards
of capitalism are very great—a standard of living incomparably higher
than that of the medieval nobility (Chapter Five), ever increasing
leisure, and in the near future the elimination of poverty and
insecurity (pp. 66, 70). For Rostow also the stage of high mass
consumption is the final stage and end goal in the development of
capitalism up to now (1960b).

Finally there are the intellectuals (1942, pp. 145-155). These are
educated people who live by the spoken and written word but have no
direct responsibility for practical affairs (p. 147). This is Schumpeter
the Austrian finance minister speaking. Their reward is public esteem,
fame, and power, achieved by voicing the grievances of the masses and
criticizing the existing order. In particular the intellectuals have
invaded the labor movement through flattery, incitement, and maneuvering, and do the staff work in political parties. Intellectuals are
as much a product of capitalist economic progress as the entrepreneurs
are. The printing press and cheap newspapers gave them their
opportunity just as the new lands and new energy sources gave the
entrepreneur his opportunity. The expansion of education with economic progress turned out increasing numbers of mediocrities who do
not have the ability to become good professionals, let alone businessmen, but are glib enough with words. These become the critical
intellectuals (pp. 152-153). Note that the main argument of Feuer,
1975, appears on these two pages of Schumpeter.

What of the future? According to Schumpeter, the same process of
economic development that produced the entrepreneur will eventually
make him obsolete. The routinization of innovation in R&D departments will leave him with nothing to do so he will be pushed to the
fringes of society as the nobility were in their time. The result will be
socialism, a dull routine period of high mass consumption, in which
the masses will get the rewards of capitalist progress (pp. 131-139).

Here Rostow and the other Schumpeterians like James Schlesinger
disagree. Rostow sees plenty of challenge and excitement in the
international sphere, helping the new nations modernize and holding
off the menace of Communism (1960b, Chapter 7; Millikan and
Rostow, 1957). Domestically also there are plenty of political challenges left for the foreseeable future: control of the business cycle,
provision of social security, income redistribution, the organization of

leisure time (1960b, Chapter 5; 1971, preface, Chapter 6). The implication seems to be that with economic development substantially
completed and routinized in the US the best brains will now be
attracted by the challenges of politics, including political management
of the economy. Schlesinger and Phillips (1959) also focus on the
challenging political problems posed by the Cold War, and argue that
the intellectuals can be isolated and rendered harmless by timely and
creative political leadership. Schumpeter's argument that only European aristocrats are qualified to be innovative statesmen (1942,
pp. 134–139) is rightly ignored.

In interpreting Schumpeter's theory it is essential to distinguish the
unique elements that come from Schumpeter's own experiences and
personality, from the general elements that can be shared by followers
as the basis of a scientific school. Schumpeter's pessimism is one
unique element, scientifically irrelevant as he himself knew; whether
this comes from his close emotional association with the dying
Austrian aristocracy or from other personal experiences is irrelevant.
Bell (1960, p. 77) suggests that Schumpeter's pessimism comes from
his European experience and does not apply for American capitalism.
Even Brzezinski, with a similar class background, does not share
Schumpeter's pessimism. Schumpeter's standpoint and intellectual
categories are the general elements that other scientists can work with
to develop and test scientific theories; his specific hypotheses and
arguments have been tested and in part discarded.

The Schumpeterian Subject is plainly the entrepreneur. He is
characterized by superior creative intelligence and by vigor and
boldness; his aim in life is to do great things on a grand scale. The
entrepreneur is a subtype of a more general type that occurs throughout history, the "best brains." Some people are more creative by nature
than others, but the development of this creativity depends on the
opportunities and rewards in a particular society. In capitalism the
best brains were attracted into trade, manufacturing, finance, and
industrial management in successive periods, and their creativity took
a practical commodity-management orientation. Other subtypes in the
past were the military geniuses and speculative philosophers, now
rendered obsolete by the routinization of warfare and professionalization of science. Still another subtype, nearly obsolete, is the aristocratic
statesman like DeGaulle who long performed the political tasks of the
bourgeoisie. Schumpeter's followers, dealing with the developing
nations, use the concept of the "modernizing elite" (Rostow, 1960b,
Chapter 3). These are the nation builders, who introduce new modes
of production, political organization, values and ideologies, and

destroy the old tribal and colonial cultures and societies. "The modernizing elite" includes the entrepreneur as the special case for Western Europe and the US, and therefore is a more general conceptualization of the Subject.

The Object, the System, is the whole society as it develops historically. It includes semi-autonomous subsystems: production and distribution, the classes associated with particular occupations, the political order, and the cultural–value–ideological system. Each of these has its own dynamics but is influenced by changes in the other systems. Classes, for instance, come into existence and are made obsolete by changes in the mode of production; but an obsolescent class can take on a new economic position and modify conditions of production accordingly (1942, p. 13).

The dynamics of all these systems combine the two opposed tendencies of routinization and qualitative change. Left to themselves, all social systems stagnate: classes are stratified into castes, production is routinized and traditionalized, ideas become scholastic dogmas. But the modernizing elite, the Subject, is always innovating and reorganizing, and the consequences of previous innovations—in capitalism, not in Oriental despotism—are still reverberating through the system as new innovations occur. For example Huntington argues that the standard pattern of US military policy decisions has been innovation to meet new problems despite resistance by established interests; the interests were established by previous successful innovations (1960, Chapter 5, p. 429). Schumpeter argues that in Western society the major innovations have as a rule and on the whole appeared in the economy and later reverberated through the other systems.

The Subject/Object relation is dialectical: the innovative Subject creates changes in the Object, and the Object shapes and limits the Subject. "Things economic and social move by their own momentum and the ensuing situations compel individuals and groups to behave in certain ways whatever they may wish to do ... by shaping the choosing mentalities and by narrowing the list of possibilities from which to choose" (1942, pp. 129-130). The elite "make patterns of choice within the framework permitted by the changing setting of society: a setting itself the product both of objective real conditions and of the prior choices made by men which help determine the current setting which men confront." (Rostow, 1960b, p. 149). Cf. Marx's "Men make history . . . ."

The appearance of the subject-object dialectic brings out an important fact: *Schumpeter is influenced by Marx and so is Rostow.*

Rostow's similarity to Marx is hidden from him by his superficial understanding of Marx, as evidenced by his attribution of a simple economic determinism to Marx (1960b, preface to first edition) of the sort that Schumpeter correctly dismisses as misunderstanding (1942, pp. 10–11).

Schumpeter is influenced by Marx, and knows it, first in the use of the subject-object dialectic. Second, this brings historicism with it: history is the story of man making himself, by continually changing the objective conditions that shape his mentality, his creativity. Social science must combine history with analysis (1942, pp. 43–44). By "man," however, we mean here only the modernizing elite. The masses do not create anything, and the traditionalist elite actively oppose change. Third, this dialectic includes a Marxist sort of determinism: men cannot make history in accordance with utopian fantasies, but only within the narrow limits set by present objective possibilities. In particular, they cannot choose between capitalism and socialism (1942, pp. 129–130). Socialism is inevitable sooner or later, one way or another. Schumpeter's followers disagree with him on this point. Fourth, Schumpeter uses the base-superstructure scheme, not as dogma à la Rostow (1960b, Chapter 1) but as a list of the primary subsystems of society and a set of hypotheses as to their probable interrelations. This, I submit, is the proper Marxist use of the scheme.

Fifth, Rostow like Marx expected all or most countries to follow the path of development charted by the leading country, Britain or the US. History moves through a series of stages, and some countries are now in stage three, some in stage four, and some in stage five. In contrast, a developmental functionalist like Apter (1968) or Almond recognizes several different paths of development resulting from the different combinations of structures, ideologies, and functional problems.

Schumpeter is of course also anti-Marxist in his opposition to the socialist parties who try to hasten the inevitable doom of elitist civilization. This double relation to Marx—using his categories, but rejecting socialism on moral grounds and/or opposing some Socialist movement—is characteristic of the Schumpeterians. Rostow's parents were socialist, but his whole ambition from college on was to provide an alternative theory to (a caricature of) Marx (1971, preface) while unwittingly using Marxist categories. His mentality too was apparently shaped by the narrow alternatives present in his early cultural milieu. Then there is Wittfogel the ex-Communist; Kornhauser and Kristol, ex-Socialists; Feuer, a Marxist in his youth; Lipset, that "Man of the Left," student of the CCF and ITU and faculty adviser to the Young People's Socialist League in 1964; Bell, the ex-*New Leader* editor who surprised everybody by taking a job at *Fortune*, that bastion of capitalism, and who writes of the contradictions of capitalism (1976) in quite Schumpeterian fashion; and Heilbroner the ex-Socialist (1977). As for Schlesinger, Huntington, and Brzezinski, their preoccupation with and opposition to Communism equals Rostow's, though without the Socialist background.

The pattern here may be called the Sidney Hook syndrome: the Old Left Marxist, an enthusiastic socialist in his youth, disillusioned by Stalinist brutality and horrified by postwar Soviet expansion, coming to appreciate the value and fragility of democracy while still hoping for Socialism some day, who is then attacked *from the Left* by those outrageous idiots, the student radicals of the 1960's. The result was a series of counterattacks: Bell and Kristol, 1969; Lipset, 1972; Feuer, 1969, 1975. Another pattern is simply anticommunism and antisocialism.

What sort of science is required by this standpoint? I find two basic methods in use. One is large-scale historical studies—all of Schumpeter's major works; Rostow's *Stages of Economic Growth* and his *Politics and the Stages of Growth*; Huntington's *Political Order in Changing Societies* (1968); Lipset's *The First New Nation* (1963), among other works; Bell's *Cultural Contradictions of Capitalism* (1976); Feuer's *The Conflict of Generations* (1969); Lipset and Solari's *Elites in Latin America* (1967); Wittfogel's *Oriental Despotism* (1957). Since the Object is a historically-developing society it must be understood by a combination of history and analysis. Social science must be historical through and through. Theoretical categories, such as Rostow's five stages (1960b, Chapter 1) or threefold political imperatives (1971, Chapter 1) or Feuer's principles of wings and generations (1975) are devices for analyzing cases to bring out their uniformities and uniqueness. The studies are primarily objective in that they trace out the dynamics of some subsystem and list the factors involved; but one constant factor is the availability of the modernizing elite, and this introduces subjectivity into the history. The mentality of the elites, such as the growth of universalist values, must be imaginatively portrayed to understand their decisions; their performances must be evaluated since they may well fail to produce the required innovative solutions (Rostow, 1960b, pp. 193–195), or act irresponsibly (Schumpeter, 1942, p. 69), or may even decide to reverse the modernization process, as in Burma (Rostow, 1960b, p. 176). In short, a dialectical historicism must study both elite-subjective and society-objective factors and see how each produces the other.

Statistics can be used in these historical studies, but they must be disaggregated to the separate economic sectors, so that entrepreneurial innovation can be found and its effects traced (Rostow, 1960b; preface to 1971 edition). Keynesian-type aggregate statistics are not useful because they merely describe overall results without explaining them: that is without locating the entrepreneurial decisions that produce growth (Rostow, 1960b, p. 190). Keynesian data are purely objective and therefore merely descriptive.

The other kind of study is small-scale sample surveys, chiefly of the masses but also of the elite. These studies mix objective census-type data with subjective attitude data. Sometimes the objective data are used to explain the subjective, sometimes vice versa; or attitudes can be an intervening variable, for instance in studies of political participation. There are also large-scale comparative surveys like Wilensky, 1975 and Huntington, 1968. And of course there are also technical studies designed to develop measuring instruments, scales, variables, dimensions, etc. These studies will be discussed in a later section. They become components of the large historical studies.

The Object here is an aggregate, usually the masses or some portion of them, and the laws of large numbers therefore apply. The purpose of the surveys is to locate regularities in the Object. These are not eternal laws, since for a historicist science there are very few eternal laws, if any. They are rather the routines into which some sector of the Object has stagnated for the time being. The dynamics of the social system always involve an oscillation between creativity and routine, and the routine aspect is suitable for study by survey techniques. However any of these regularities can be changed by the creative subject, the modernizing elite, or is already changing as a result of past actions. For example some of Lipset's regularities have already changed (1960, pp. 32–38) and some of Huntington's (1968) as well.

If we compare this kind of science with the two kinds studied previously, we find a good deal of similarity with Keynesian-Parsonian-systems science. In both cases the Object is a whole social system composed of interdependent subsystems and having its own objective dynamics. In both cases the system continues to run well only because the Subject manages it from a control point or points within it. The similarity is even closer when one compares the developmental functionalists like Holt and Turner (1966) with studies of the modernizing elite in the developing nations. The developmental functionalists are also concerned with the efforts of a modernizing political elite to destroy an old social system and set up a new one in its place. In addition their theory is a long run theory of the development of one system out of another, thus matching the

Schumpeter-Rostow long-run analysis, while regular Keynesian theory is short run.

The differences are, first, that the dynamics of the Object are much more complex for Keynesians-Parsonians-systems analysts than for Schumpeterians. For the latter the dynamics are simply a combination of regularities—production techniques, bureaucratic routines, styles of living, art styles—and of unpredictable innovations. The regularities, themselves the consequence of past innovations, can be studied objectively by survey and other statistical techniques. The innovations can be understood subjectively by study of the entrepreneurial mentality but not predicted. For the Keynesians and systems analysts system dynamics include mechanisms like positive and negative feedbacks, lags, filters, channel capacities, decoders, transformers, which cannot be uncovered by aggregate data. Complex models must be used to interpret the data and to locate key indicators. For instance, for the Keynesians business cycles (and for Parsons social inflation-deflation cycles) are an inherent kind of system dynamic composed of lagged feedbacks. Left to themselves, cycles can expand and cause much trouble; but they can in principle be controlled and moderated by a government possessing an adequate econometric model. For Schumpeter cycles are merely the reverberations of past innovations, tending inherently to die down and having no internal dynamics. The destruction they cause is part of the creative destruction of the dead wood by which society advances.

A resulting second difference is that the Parsonian, Keynesian, or systems analyst has a much more complex conceptual apparatus for analyzing systems. In the fullblown Parsonian scheme Schumpeter's entrepreneur is only one of eighteen possible functionaries, each with a different task to perform in maintaining a social system or establishing a new one. There are also cultural functionaries. Schumpeter recognizes a few of these other functional prerequisites under the headings of "protecting strata" and "institutional framework" but his theorizing is ad hoc, unsystematic, and superficial. Or, if we just consider the political elite, the A-G-I-L scheme as used by Holt and Turner, Eisenstadt, or in another version by Almond is more systematic than Rostow's three imperatives and three dilemmas (1971, preface), which seem, like the five stages, to be another "arbitrary and limited way of looking at history."

As a result the elitist histories are more narrative and less analytical than the developmental functionalist histories. In the elite histories innovations occur in sectors whose opportunities have attracted and produced a modernizing elite, and the innovations spread or are blocked by other strategically located elites; but the details of the process are always unique, and only the overall results show a broad statistical uniformity. The functionalist studies are guided by the list of functional prerequisites, the interchanges, the media or "free floating resources," the typology of structures, and the pattern variables in one version or another, the result being a good deal of analytical interpretation of the facts.

This difference is related to a third difference already discussed: the functionalist histories and Keynesian growth models are purely objective, while the elite histories exemplify the subject–object dialectic. Functionalist–Keynesian studies of existing systems describe what must be done to maintain or establish the system in a moving equilibrium with target rates of growth, investment, employment; mobilization of support, socialization, stratification, etc.—and what alternative ways of doing these things are available. They describe the systemic consequences of doing them or failing to do them, and end with advice to the political leadership. Studies of past systems describe analytically what was done or failed to be done, what strains and systemic changes resulted, and what new functional tasks resulted. Or they describe structural uniformities, necessities, dilemmas (R. Needham, C. Lévi-Strauss, E. Evans-Pritchard) or systemic oscillations (E.R. Leach, Max Gluckman). The omission is the same one that bothered Left Keynesians in the 1960's: the Subject remains outside of science. The political leaders or colonial administrators are advised but not studied. In contrast the elite histories focus on the development of the modernizing elite (or their repression and failure to develop, as in Wittfogel's 1957 history). For instance Lipset's excellent study of Latin American elites (Lipset and Solari, 1967, Chapter 1) locates the entrepreneurs as social deviants in several senses, contrasts their class position and mentality with those of the traditionalist elites and those rats, the intellectuals (Lipset's attitude, not mine), and traces several paths by which the modernizing mentality—universalism, achievement, technical-engineering rationalism, willingness to take risks and innovate—can achieve power in a society. He also traces the objective systemic consequences of changes in elite mentality and changes in the location of the "best brains."

These three differences produce one typical misunderstanding. For the Schumpeterian the system minus the Subject is mere routine, stagnation. Functionalist and Keynesian objective studies thus seem static, even mechanical. Schumpeter regarded Keynesian economics as static, and described Keynesian studies of imperfect competition as Hamlet without the prince (1942, p. 86). His followers similarly criticize

functionalism for its static bias (Rostow, 1971, appendix). Functionalists and Keynesians, in turn, have found the charge of static bias
incomprehensible, since their models are inherently dynamic, with in
fact more complex dynamics than the Schumpeterian innovation-
routinization dialectic. The contrast comes out nicely if one compares
Wittfogel's interpretation of the Chinese empire with Eisenstadt's
(1960), or Schumpeter's interpretation of the French empire (1942,
pp. 134-136) with Eisenstadt's. Eisenstadt's history is incomparably
more dynamic in a functionalist sense, but static in a Schumpeterian
sense—there are no entrepreneurs in Eisenstadt's history (1963,
Chapter 7).

There is a much greater gap between Schumpeterian and neoclassic
science. According to Schumpeter the classical economists' vision was
commendable—they were trying to defend capitalism—but their
theory was almost totally wrong (1942, pp. 74-76). The neoclassicists
were better theorists, but as a result their static theory of perfect
competition is almost totally irrelevant (1942, pp. 76-82, 103-106).
They completely missed the importance of big business, cartels and
monopolistic practices, rigid prices, government enterprise, and in
short completely fail to understand modern capitalism. To this list of
criticisms Rostow, Huntington, Schlesinger etc., add capitalism's need
for an active foreign and domestic politics to deal with problems of
unemployment, poverty, economic development, income redistribution, Communist subversion, etc. (Rostow, 1952, 1960b, 1971; Schlesinger and Phillips, 1959; Huntington, 1960). The Schumpeterian
emphasis on active, innovative government and business is quite the
opposite of the neoclassicists' critique of both government coercion
and big business inefficiency.

The neoclassic concept of maximizing-rationality is also quite
foreign to Schumpeterian science. Man does not maximize, Rostow
argues (1960b, ca p. 170; 1971, Chapter 1); he balances conflicting
objectives, either in an unimaginative, restless shift of desire to
whatever is missing at the time (the masses) or in a bold creative
synthesis that resolves the dilemmas temporarily (the elite) (cf. Huntington, 1960, pp. 2-3 for the same argument). Maximizing is characteristic of the routine action of the small businessman, for whom
routinization has eliminated uncertainty; and from a Schumpeterian
perspective the whole of neoclassical economics expresses the narrow,
unimaginative mentality of the thrifty petit-bourgeois businessman.
And just as that class is obsolescent, the science that expresses its
mentality is incapable of dealing with modern capitalism, in spite of
its highly polished analytical apparatus.

How does the scientist himself fit into Schumpeterian science? The Keynesian and functionalist scientists are professionals, trained specialists with technical skills; but what sort of person is the Schumpeterian scientist? Here we come to a difficulty. If we accept Schumpeter's own definition of the term, *Schumpeter was an intellectual*. To be sure, he arranged the detailed descriptions of these wreckers of civilization so they would fit only people he despised, like Keynes; but if we generalize they apply to him as well (Sievers, 1962, pp. 55–56).

Schumpeter's followers, however, have recognized that they themselves were intellectuals and have engaged in considerable self-analysis. We turn to them, therefore, for an account of the scientist as intellectual.

III. The Intellectuals

The proper way for a Schumpeterian to study intellectuals or any other social stratum is historically and statistically, by tracing the objective conditions that shape its mentality. Examples of such self-studies are Bell (1960, epilogue), Feuer (1975, 1969), Lipset (1960, Chapter 10; 1972a, Chapters 1, 4–6), and Horowitz (1968, Chapter 14). In these studies several characteristics appear that change Schumpeter's picture a little. Intellectuals tend to be somewhat detached from their society and critical of it; they find the weaknesses that every society has, exaggerate them perhaps, but thereby provide a stimulus to reform. They are also self-critical and semi-detached from their own values, not wholly committed to anything, but used to seeing several sides to everything. In the US they come primarily from white collar and professional, Jewish or university backgrounds. In the 1950's and 1960's they were strongly anti-Communist and realized that the US, in spite of its few remaining weaknesses, is the best society we have and well worth defending. They have given up the utopian dreams of their youth and realize that the welfare state, the mixed economy, and pluralist democracy is about as good a society as we are going to get. Thus they experienced a commitment pull which countered their normal tendency to detachment. This sort of sobering-up with maturation is characteristic of intellectuals; the younger ones always want to transform the world immediately.

According to Kadushin (1972) the top or elite intellectuals in the US live mainly in the New York City-Boston Area. Socially they are organized in several overlapping groups or circles, largely centered in the journals *Public Interest, Commentary, Partisan Review,* and *Dissent.* As these journals suggest, most of the elite intellectuals of the 1960's were radical in their youth (1930's, 1940's) but are no longer so. The Number One intellectual is Daniel Bell.

Intellectuals are creative and innovative, and therefore personal freedom is their highest value. "Intellectuals, that is, those concerned with the creation of art, culture, literature, science, and knowledge, whether academics or not, are involved with creation and innovation. . . . many of the brightest people who seek to be innovative and free of the ideological restrictions and materialistic commitments which they believe are inherent in the corporate and professional worlds . . ." (Lipset, 1972a, pp. 31–32).

In the university, intellectuals are different from both professionals and scholars. (Gouldner, 1963; Bell, 1960, epilogue). For Horowitz, there are two kinds of "mainliners" (1968, Chapter 14). The scholar is a selfless worker in some old tradition to which he patiently adds his bit. The professional is a specialist and technician, using abstruse mathematical techniques or jargon and communicating only with other specialists in his own field. The intellectual acquires broad and diffuse learning and knows history as well as current events. He is weak on technique or even opposed to it, as with the Latin-American intellectuals, but substitutes bold, imaginative creation for the technical virtuosity of the professional. The career lines of professionals and intellectuals are also different. The professional gets his training in a specialized research project, rapidly produces some technical innovation, goes on to his own specialized research, and finally trains others as director of larger and larger projects. His whole career lies within a particular academic field at a University, except for short consulting trips or a longer tour of duty in Washington. The intellectual is not limited to academic life; he may teach somewhere for a dozen years, then work for a journal or newspaper, or become an independent writer or critic, or a Unitarian minister, then teach again at a liberal arts college, edit books or journals, and so on.

It appears that the intellectual is similar to the entrepreneur— creative, innovative, intelligent, restless, always on the lookout for new opportunities.

There is a term that expresses this similarity: "cultural elite," which includes the most creative leaders in art, literature, and science. The culture they continually create gradually filters down and is "reproduced mechanically by the cultural mass" (Bell, 1976, p. 81) including presumably the unimaginative professionals. Schumpeter's, Rostow's, and Huntington's waves of innovation and routinization appear in culture as well as in the economy and political system.

But if the cultural elite are themselves part of the modernizing elite, the Subject, then there is another difference between them and the professionals. The professionals always distinguish themselves, as advisors, from the politicians who bear responsibility for the actual decisions. They are not qualified as scientists to make value judgments about goals; their science is ethically neutral, like a dental drill. But when the intellectuals look for someone to advise, they see no one but other members of the elite like themselves. They can advise members of the political elite, but the relationship is more like colleagues consulting than it is like two quite different specialists each sticking to his own province. The cultural elite must therefore share responsibility for the governing of society. The sense of responsibility for the well-being of society, the sense of duty or service, that Schumpeter attributes to the entrepreneur (1942, p. 127) is shared by the committed intellectuals (for example, Rostow, 1977). This means that their science is politically engaged, not value-free. The problems they select for study are the real problems of industrial society, and they are not stopped by artificial professional boundaries.

Organizationally also, the intellectual's ideal career does not lead to the Council of Economic Advisors; it leads straight to the centers of power: the White House, the Cabinet, State Department, Congress. The ideal is a Rostow or Kissinger, who after a brilliant career in the university moves into government and supervises mass bloodshed and violence, the destruction of whole countries, then retires to write more books or memoirs. Today one reads encomiums of Senator Moynihan the ex-professional, who stopped advising others and became his own politician in order better to deal with the problem of poverty (Horo-witz, 1977). Or the intellectual can bypass existing political forms to set up his own organization for direct participation in politics; the Trilateral Commission is a recent example.

The same contrast occurs in the government careers of Schumpeter and Keynes. Schumpeter had direct responsibility for managing a ruinous inflation as Austrian finance minister; Keynes was always the in-and-outer who gave advice, drew up policy papers, or carried out bargaining assignments, but never was directly in charge. Political power was not part of his career.

One problem remains: what about Schumpeter's and Lipset's and Huntington's bad intellectuals, who infiltrate labor unions and politi-cal parties, stir up the masses with wild accusations and romantic visions, and generally undermine the stability of democracy? How do they differ from the good, responsible intellectuals who are seriously working on the world's problems? The student left of the 1960's was plainly part of the bad, but their counterpart in the Soviet Union, the dissidents, are good because they are calling for freedom of speech and research. Thus Feuer, after devoting a long volume to furious denunciation and pseudopsychoanalytic namecalling of student protest movements through the ages, ends by calling Soviet student protesters "the historical bearers of humanity's highest hopes" (1969, p. 531). According to Feuer, students have always had suicidal impulses, among other disreputable things; but how about Jan Palach the martyr, who committed suicide to protest the Soviet occupation of Czechoslovakia? What makes the students in the East so different?

Brzezinski (1970, pp. 44–46), Schumpeter, and Feuer suggest that the bad ones are the mediocrities, the "pseudo-intelligentsia" who slip into a rapidly expanding educational system and get by with little or no serious training (for instance, in black studies programs—Brzezinski, 1970, p. 211). Instead they pick up a few utopian ideas and then vent their frustrations in political agitation. This suggests that the Soviet educational system must be pretty good, to produce the bearers of humanity's highest hopes. Rostow suggests that the "revolutionary romantics" like Ho Chi Minh are the ones who cause trouble (1971, p. 279), and Feuer distinguishes the ideologists from the more sober intellectuals like himself whose romantic visions have been dissolved by the encounter with reality (1975, p. 81 and passim.). Brzezinski calls the bad ones "counter revolutionaries" and "historical irrelevants" (1968); he seems to mean that they are reacting emotionally against the inevitable technetronic revolution (1970, pp. 94–110). The good ones are those who carry the revolution forward.

Lipset's study (1972a), the most careful one known to me, brings out amid many complex historical determinants the theme of "student youth." The bad intellectuals throughout history have mostly been the young students, who despise the halfway decent society laboriously created by generations of responsible elites, and who want to sweep it all away and create a Utopia in four years. As they mature, most of them face reality, see the good as well as the bad, realize how little can actually be done, and become responsible. A few, like Ho Chi Minh, never give up their youthful romanticism, and these are the troublemakers. Soviet officials could easily accept this characterization as they worry about their own youthful dissidents.

Still, it is good for a society, even a nearly perfect one like ours (Lipset, 1972a, Chapter 7; Glazer, 1968) in which the university is even better (Bell and Kristol, 1969, introduction, pp. 67–74) to have troublemakers to remind us that improvement is still needed. Liberals were perhaps too complacent about the improvement in race relations in the 1960's; the student radicals were useful in pointing out that the problem was still not completely solved. Even extremists and violent protesters may be useful (Lipset, 1972b, p. 261). Lipset expresses well the Old Left intellectual's ambivalence toward the students. When his students accuse him of having sold out to capitalism for prestige, security, and a fat salary, it is his own youth, in a double sense, that is accusing him. The charge is angrily denied; he is still a Man of the Left, a member of the SPUSA, but one who has been sobered by reality—what reality? The awful reality of world Communism!—and besides, it is normal historically for intellectuals to move right as they mature. But the charge is intelligible and painful, as it would not be to a functionalist, systems analyst, or Keynesian.

Perhaps as a reflection of this ambivalence, there is also an ambivalence about the modernizing elite as a whole. The elite *are* the best brains, the most creative, the most responsible, the makers and protectors of our civilization. The mass are mediocre, plodding, self-centered, apathetic about politics, without ideas of their own but swayed by fashion. And yet—perhaps the elite dominate the mass too much. Perhaps there are unrealized potentialities somewhere in the mass that could be brought out (Lipset, 1972a, introduction; Rostow, 1971, pp. 298–301; Bell, 1976, p. 179; Bell and Kristol, 1969, p. 106).

Huntington and Nelson (1976) express this ambivalence in detail. Increased political participation is one goal of political elites, especially in the US (Chapter 2), along with economic growth, mass economic wellbeing and equality, national independence; (and international prestige and power; Huntington, 1968, pp. 441–466), but these objectives conflict, and participation may have to be suppressed temporarily for the sake of other goals. In particular, radical elites who desire to improve the position of the lower class may have to temporarily suppress middle-class participation in politics while simultaneously mobilizing the lower class, as in Chile from 1970 to 1973. Technical decisions needed for economic growth may have to be shielded from mass interference. In the long run economic development generally leads to increased mass participation, but in the short run there are many complications.

Note that throughout Huntington and Nelson (1976) participation is a problem for the modernizing elite, the Subject. "Autonomous participation can occur at reasonable costs only if political elites encourage it, permit it, or are unable or unwilling to suppress it" (p. 28; see also summary, pp. 168–171). The masses surge up (Rostow,

1960b, p. 118), follow fashions, get mobilized; the elites decide how much participation is appropriate. This is the same Huntington who in 1968 argued that today's increased mass participation was a source of political instability and violence, and in 1974 reported to the Trilateral Commission that some democracies are becoming ungovernable because of insufficient mass apathy (Huntington, 1968; 1975, esp. p. 37; Crozier et al., 1975). Critics have fastened on these statements to accuse Huntington of being an authoritarian elitist like Schumpeter; but they miss the ambivalence. He, like the others, is an anti-elitist elitist.

IV. Developments in Elite Theory

There are four topics here: 1) Elites, especially the modernizing elites; 2) The masses and the counterelite; 3) Democracy (democratic elitism), including the contributions of elite, mass, intellectuals, and elite circulation; 4) The Soviet Union, headquarters of the counterelite.

1. Schumpeter's entrepreneur serves as a pattern for a number of case studies and evaluations. Dahl (1961) sketches a picture of New Haven's Mayor Lee as political entrepreneur. His predecessor "was politically somewhat timid and unadventurous" (pp. 117-118), content with the existing political structure of petty sovereignties, stalemate, and small piecemeal actions (p. 201). Lee saw an opportunity in the urban renewal issue and moved boldly in, organizing a winning coalition and taking power. Once in office, he swiftly transformed the political order (p. 200), centralizing control in his own hands by continuous bargaining and persuasion. He used his power to make sweeping changes in the city, changes that benefited the apolitical masses as well as the elite members of his coalition—and of course ultimately expanded the power of his political empire. "To the political entrepreneur who has skill and drive, the political system offers unusual opportunities for pyramiding a small amount of initial resources into a sizeable political holding" (p. 227). The ultimate basis of the opportunity was the availability of a new exploitable resource promising huge political profits, namely Federal urban renewal funds.

Kennedy is the hero of other such accounts. He is pictured as eager to take bold new initiatives in foreign policy, to "get the country moving again," but stymied by the entrenched bureaucracy, the State Department "bowlful of jelly," the petty local interests (for example, Campbell, 1971). Khrushchev is almost never given such treatment; he is the bullying, aggressive, bluffing adventurer, threatening war to get his way. The exception is Brzezinski and Huntington (1965), where Khrushchev, too, is an entrepreneur. Huntington (1960, Chapter 5) extols the bold innovator in military policy, who champions a new weapon or strategic program to meet some foreign danger, and is opposed by a bureaucracy with vested interests in obsolescent weapons and programs. Selznick (1957) urges the importance of bold innovations from the top to keep organizations from stagnating.

Heilbroner expresses the hope that the capitalist and managerial classes will understand the ecological crisis we now face and make the bold and drastic economic changes needed to solve it—even though this involves giving up their economic privileges (1970, pp. 283–285). Bell and Kristol (1969, introduction, p. 101) criticize university leaders for failing to meet the challenges of the post-industrial era and the emerging meritocratic society with far-sighted innovations.

The accounts summarized above treat the political entrepreneur as Subject; they describe the opportunities, challenges, and resources that lie before him and then show how he creatively seizes the opportunities and builds himself an organization, or fails to innovate and goes down to defeat, like Grayson Kirk of Columbia University, who brought a student strike down on himself.

The other kind of study deals with the objective historical conditions in which modernizing elites appear, and with their resulting characteristics. Lipset and Solari (1967) assert that the Latin American modernizer is a social deviant, often an immigrant, sometimes even a Protestant; this enables him to maintain his own universalist-achievement values amid an ascriptive-particularist society. In some countries he may be a Socialist; again this deviant ideology serves to protect his universalist–achievement values. The traditionalist elite have ascriptive-particularistic values and are integrated into the society. Huntington (1960) similarly notes that the organizational innovator tends to come from outside the military bureaucracy and have unconventional attitudes and values. But the modernizing US businessman, Lipset adds, is not a deviant, since the dominant US values support his own achievement orientation. He comes, other studies have shown, from the well-educated, urban, white, Anglo-Saxon, upper and upper middle class male population (Dye and Zeigler, 1975, Chapter 4).

The first type of study, of the entrepreneur as heroic Subject, consists of case studies; the second type, of objective conditions and characteristics, present statistical surveys.

2. Statistical surveys of the masses support Schumpeter's characterization of them. They are politically inert; they live by habit, unexamined loyalties, emotions, transient impulses (Dahl, 1961, p. 90).

Not only are they inert, they actively avoid involvement in politics and reject available political information (pp. 264–267, contra Downs, 1957). They are anti-intellectual, intolerant, authoritarian, and racist (Dye and Zeigler, 1975, Chapter 5; Lipset, 1960, Chapter 4, p. 366; Kornhauser, 1959). However, they can be politically activated when their own narrow private interests are threatened. At such times they become emotional and violent, demanding extreme and immediate solutions to complex problems, and intolerant of dissent. "Any genuine 'people's' revolution in America would undoubtedly take the form of a right-wing nationalist, patriotic, religious-fundamentalist, antiblack, anti-intellectual, antistudent 'law and order' movement" (Dye and Zeigler, 1975, citing Lipset and Raab, 1970, p. 348).

Mass unrest is often mobilized and exploited by a counterelite. These people are the successors to Schumpeter's "intellectuals." They appeal to the masses' racism, anti-intellectualism, anti-elitism, emotionalism, and proclivity to violence, offering simplistic solutions, calling for immediate action, and expressing contempt for due process and constitutional procedures. Joseph McCarthy and George Wallace are often cited as examples of counterelite figures, though the counterelite may be either right or left extremists. In the third world they are, of course, the Communists, who seize on the discontents associated with early modernization to mobilize the masses; Communism is "a disease of the transition" to complete modernity (Rostow, 1960b; Lipset, 1960, Chapter 2). Unless the established elites successfully organize the masses in support of the existing political system the counterelite will organize them to overthrow that system (Huntington, 1968, pp. 461, 78).

The objective of the counterelite agitator is to get power for himself. Either he is impatient of the slow, uncertain advancement and long training that the elite offer him in a meritocratic society, or he is barred from power for racial, religious, ideological, or class reasons. The existence of a counterelite thus indicates a deficiency in the circulation of elites. Lasswell and Lerner (1965) find that the German (1930) and Russian (1910) counterelite came from the lower middle class, bearing a century of political frustration, failed to get into office by legitimate means and so shifted to extremism and violence (Chapter 7). The Chinese counterelite both left and right were composed of alienated intellectuals (pp. 465ff.). Among the US counterelite of the 1960's Lipset (1972a) finds two types: the renouncers (Brzezinski's "counter-revolutionaries"), who disown and reject all of Western culture, technology, urbanization, and discipline, because they reject their own traditionalist parents, and the radicals, who identify with their liberal or radical parents' ideals and demand to achieve them immediately, in four years, and who therefore wish to take power and change society.

Note that elite science offers us *two* subjects, a good and a bad. The good is portrayed lovingly from the inside, by subjective case-study. The good subject is consciously motivated by his own achievement values and by his sense of responsibility; the object is seen as a field of action, composed of opportunities, challenges, and resources. The categories of conscious, rational action are used, categories that the subject could use to describe his own actions. The bad subject is portrayed with hate, or at least with concern and disgust, from the outside, from the standpoint of the good, responsible intellectual. Unconscious drives are ascribed to him: a century of frustration, a drive for power, a rejection of the father. Of course the counterelite themselves, the George Wallaces and Ho Chi Minhs, could not describe their own behavior in those categories, but would speak of responsibilities, challenges, values, opportunities, just like the elite. For both subjects the social conditions of their appearance and socialization are studied objectively, by census data and the like. Both alike are a product of social conditions; the subject-object dialectic occurs in both cases.

Contemporary history is the story of the dramatic global struggle between these two subjects, the modernizing elite and the counterelite, taking place over the inert corpses of the apathetic mass. The tactics of each side can be evaluated and advice offered to the good ones (Brzezinski, 1968); the outcome is still in doubt.

This constitutes our second explanation of the Vietnam war. It was not just a bureaucratic mistake, in which US troops crossed a boundary where they did not belong, as the foreign policy professionals assert; it was a bitter episode in the continuing struggle with the world counterelite. Boundaries are irrelevant to this struggle; US troops belong wherever democracy is threatened.

3. Schumpeter's theory of democracy has not been changed much by the democratic elitists. According to Schumpeter the elite always rule everywhere, but they rule democratically when two or more groups of elite compete periodically for popular approval. A democratic elite is a plural elite (Dye and Zeigler, 1975, Chapter 1). This does not mean that the elite compete by offering reasoned policy arguments; policy issues are beyond mass comprehension, and would only stir them up. Rather, the elite present themselves in slogans, symbols, and images. The masses choose their leaders but do not make policy (see Dahl, 1956, and Prewitt and Stone, 1973, pp. 200–211). In

recent political science this theory has been generalized beyond elections to the whole political process. Politics is democratic when power
is divided among a plurality of conflicting interest groups, each of
course led by its own elite. The elite compete among each other for
popular support, and form opposing coalitions which check the
accumulation of too much power by any group. But they are united
on the fundamentals of democracy—free speech and mutual toleration
among the elite—and work together against any threat to democracy.

The main threat to democracy comes from the counterelite of left
and right, who exploit mass discontent and mobilize the masses in
attempts to get power for themselves. To protect democracy against
this threat the elite must do two things: first, they must reduce mass
discontent by managing the problems that continually appear in every
society, even the best—the business cycle, racial conflicts, population
mobility, unemployment, alienation (Bell, 1976, p. 180ff.; Moynihan,
1969, Chapter 1). Constant reform is needed; if the reforms are prompt
and imaginative the masses will lapse back into their habitual inertia
and the troublemaking intellectuals will be isolated and rendered
harmless (Schlesinger and Phillips, 1959). The business elite can also
act co-operatively to reduce economic instability (Phillips, 1960).

Second, the elite can make sure that no counterelite slip into their
ranks. Elite consensus on democratic values is the key to success here;
all aspirants to elite membership must be screened for extremism and
educated to democratic values as they move up. Conversely, the elite
must co-opt potential leaders so that the latter do not turn extremist in
frustration. Roosevelt is cited as a master of co-optation, appointing
potential troublemakers like Sidney Hillman to high, responsible, but
supervised posts in the government (cf. also Selznick, 1950). This is
Pareto's circulation of elites. The elite preserve democracy by ar-
ranging a smooth, steady circulation, as well as by setting an example
of responsible, tolerant, lawful conduct (Lasswell and Lerner, 1965,
pp. 27–28).

The above theory of democracy is called "democratic elitism" by
some (Lipset, Bachrach, Dye and Zeigler) and "pluralism" by others
(Dahl, Polsby, Rose). The former term emphasizes the crucial role of
elites in preserving democracy and in governing; the latter term
emphasizes the divisions among the elite. The pluralist-elitist controversy is about whether the elite in Western societies is plural or
unified, but both sides agree that the elite dominates politics. I have
been calling the supporters of the pluralist theory "democratic elitists"
or "elitist intellectuals" to emphasize their own location in society,
their standpoint. In Chapter Seven I shall call the supporters of the

elitist theory "critical intellectuals," again to emphasize their self-defined location in society.

The pluralist or democratic elitist theory of democracy is sharply different from the individualist or "rational actor" theory of Chapter Three. In the latter theory the rational individual faces government as a nonmarket which sells public goods or policies, and decides which policies he should buy. Government officials are also individuals, selling policies for votes, so the whole political arena is composed of individuals buying and selling. In the pluralist theory the actors are groups, each led by its own elite. Government is the arena in which groups struggle and bargain, and each group has allies and access at some point in the vast government bureaucracy. Thus the bureaucratic struggles within government express larger interest group struggles outside government. The existing distribution of power and authority is the routinized outcome of earlier group struggles. The only significant individual in the pluralist-elitist theory is the political entrepreneur who reorganizes government and groups into a new pattern of domination that brings him power. In the one theory politics consists of buying, selling, and calculation; in the other theory it consists of maneuvering, innovation, and routine.

The democratic elitists differ with Schumpeter mainly in their ambivalence about the masses. For Schumpeter the masses were stupid by nature, and the few exceptions could be located and circulated into the lower reaches of the elite—Bell's meritocratic principle. The democratic elitists accept this as fact but reject it as value. Realistically, at the present time, the masses are hopeless as many surveys have demonstrated. Realistically, mass participation is a threat to democracy and must be curbed (Huntington, 1975) and buffered (Kornhauser, 1959). Indeed in view of the serious problems of population explosion, pollution, and resource scarcity now appearing, mass participation may have to be entirely eliminated (Dye and Zeigler, 1975, pp. 457–458). But in aspiration things could be different. There may be some way to educate the masses to responsible, moderate, tolerant participation in democratic processes (Huntington and Nelson, 1976; Lipset, 1960, Chapter 6)—that is, participation on elite terms.

4. The Soviet Union, as the world headquarters of the counterelite, has been the object of intense scientific study, beginning with Leites' work of the early 1950's. This is the first standpoint for which the Soviet Union is a central focus of attention; for all previous standpoints it is an incidental, rather trivial topic. To bring out the contrast, let us review quickly how the SU looks from previous perspectives.

First, for the traditionalists like Morgenthau the fact that the SU happens to be communist is quite irrelevant. Governments come and go, but the eternal strategic necessities of power and security remain valid for all governments. Soviet foreign policy is determined by its geopolitical situation in the Eurasian heartland, blocked from most warm water ports and open to invasion along the Napoleonic and Hitlerian route across the indefensible Polish–Ukrainian flatlands. Second, for the neoclassical deterrence theorists the Soviet Union must be presumed to be rational since its government is composed of human beings. Consequently deterrence theory applies to it, as to all other governments. It happens that the Soviet government has a taste for aggression, as governments sometimes do; that is what deterrence theory is about. The deterrence problem consists of estimating the value of a piece of territory for the defending power (us, of course), estimating its value to the Soviet aggressor, and then deducing whether it is worth defending—or for the Soviets, worth demanding. The problem is solved by information exchange, including the testing of messages for deceptiveness. The Soviet government is quite rational about this; it probes, tests, negotiates, and does not advance or withdraw until it has sufficient information to act rationally. If both sides are rational there will be a long-run equilibrium in which each side controls the territory of highest value to it and joint utility is thus maximized. Third, for the Keynesians the Soviet government practices a different kind of economic planning and thus furnishes a useful comparative case for studying resource allocation policy (for example Brandis, 1968, Chapter 34). Fourth, for the system theorists both the SU and the US are caught in the security dilemma and the arms race, in which a purely defensive motivation for both sides leads to war. It is in the interest of both to work out a co-operative solution that avoids the explosive outcome. Whether the US is free to do this the systems theorist does not inquire; his task is merely to advise the government on what ought to be done and goverment, the Subject, has to take it from there. In any case, for the system theorist the deterrent theorist's long-run equilibrium is illusory; the interdependence of commitments plus bureaucratic inertia and the cognitive limits on rationality make an explosive outcome probable, unless the system is deliberately managed by the US.

In all four cases attention is concentrated on the systemic theory, and the Soviet Union shows up only as another case for the theory. But for the democratic elitists the Soviet Union is a unique substantive focus of attention. As such it has elicited a tremendous amount of research.

Most of this work is scientifically worthless. By "most of this work" I mean:

1. During our research on crisis bargaining (Snyder and Diesing, 1977; Lockhart, 1979) I read about forty works on Soviet politics, Soviet foreign policy, the Cold War, the West Berlin crisis of 1958–1962, and the 1962 Cuban crisis, written from the elite-counterelite perspective, works like H. Speier, 1961, K. Schultz, 1962, and J. Smith, 1963. These works were almost uniformly worthless, moralistic fairy tales based on twisted, selected facts. Their moral was always the same: Communists are aggressive, unscrupulous bluffers who will take whatever we are not willing to defend but will back down if we are firm. Therefore we must resist all Communist aggression. Facts are twisted and interpreted to fit this moral or are omitted; to get even a partial account of what happened one must go elsewhere.

For example, in Jean Smith's 1963 fairy tale about the Berlin crisis the high point of the story is Lucius Clay's activities in Berlin in September and October 1961, and especially his tank confrontation with Soviet tanks on October 27. The account reads like fiction:

> Twice more that day American cars were escorted through the East Berlin checkpoint by military police. The East Germans, chagrined and humiliated, made no effort to interfere. By now the Ulbricht regime was close to panic . . . Late in the afternoon, after the US had forced the barrier once more (the East Germans now were thoroughly disgraced) . . . For the first time since 1958, the West had successfully exposed the puppet relationship between Ulbricht and Moscow. A vital Communist argument had been demolished. . . . And once more, when confronted by a show of American determination, the East had backed down . . . the tide of Communist encroachment had been checked. (Smith, 1963, pp. 322–323).

Apart from the moralistic interpretations and the imputations of an evil consciousness to the East Germans this account focuses on a sideshow, since neither Kennedy nor Khrushchev took Clay's actions seriously. The main events of September and October were the Kennedy-Khrushchev letters and accompanying statements, as well as a series of discussions at the UN, all of which Smith ignores.

The accounts of Soviet politics give us a picture of the Soviet counterelite as engaged domestically in a pure, endless struggle for power, a war of all against all unrelated to any larger purpose; and in foreign policy in an endless attempt to expand anywhere and by any means. US leaders, in contrast, are described as defensive and cautious, motivated purely by a sense of responsibility and restrained by moral principles. They suffer moral agony when they have to permit the CIA to counter communist aggression (Payne, 1970, p. 126). Soviet leaders are aware of these moral restraints and take advantage of them in their unscrupulous aggressive gambles (ibid., p. 161; Horelick and Rush, 1966, pp. 8ff., 105ff.).

2. A few works, including Brzezinski and Huntington, 1965 and works by Conquest, J. Schick, Zimmerman, and Slusser, show some care and method in checking their facts and can be taken seriously as historical studies.

3. A number of works, like Aspaturian (1966) and works by Fainsod and Ploss move in varying degrees toward the bureaucratic politics perspective of Chapter Eight and away from the devil-image of the counterelite concept. These works are scientifically useful case studies in bureaucratic politics, not moralistic denunciations of the counterelite.

The diplomatic histories are not included in the above judgment. Some of them, such as Langer and Gleason (1953), with its State Department *nihil obstat*, and Dörnberg (1968), are essentially official government histories and obviously one-sided. These works give us an insight into the thinking of some government, which is certainly part of the whole picture, while the Horelick and Rush type moralistic fairy tales tell us nothing. Other histories such as Ulam (1968) and Shulman (1963) are more rounded accounts and quite useful. In addition, works written from the systems perspective of Chapter Five, such as Gamson and Modigliani (1971), are not included. The systems perspective is the opposite of the elite/counterelite perspective since it views both elites as equally determined by systemic forces.

V. Preliminary Evaluation

What does the Schumpeterian perspective reveal to us that we could not see before? Its biggest contribution is an empirical science of the Subject, though as it happens this science is applied only to the modernizing elite and the intellectuals. The masses seem to be untouched by history in this kind of science. In former times the neoclassicists thought they had an *a priori* subjective science, but we have already discussed the difficulties that resulted.

There are two phases of this science. First, the modernizing elite are a product of society—of its values, status system, power distribution, socialization processes. The origins of the elite can therefore be studied objectively, by census data, attitude surveys, documentary materials on education, and content analysis to locate values. Second, the modernizing elite creatively change society. Creativity can be studied subjectively, by participant observation, intensive interviewing (Dahl,

1961), and other case study methods. Third, the continuity between the two, the whole Subject-Object dialectic, can be studied in large economic and social histories.

The obverse weakness is the difficulty in conceptualizing objective system dynamics in Keynesian-functionalist-systems fashion. Keynes produced an objective science by completely pushing the Subject outside of science, thereby positing the economy as something that runs by itself. But the subject-object dialectic blocks this perspective on the economy. The Schumpeterian, looking at the economy, sees everywhere the creative handiwork of the entrepreneur, or of the modernizing elite in the new states, and if one abstracts from this only stagnation remains. In the case studies the modernizing elite—Mayor Lee, General Lucius Clay, Nehru—is faced with a field of problems, opportunities, resources, the raw materials for creativity rather than an autonomous System. This difference expresses itself in Rostow's complaint about Keynesian aggregate data. The aggregate data are needed to describe the circular flow of resources and money; but, Rostow complains, they obscure the entrepreneurial innovations in certain sectors and the stagnation in others and thus make economic growth unintelligible. Conversely, Rostow's sectoral data enable one to locate bursts of innovation in particular sectors and their sub-sequent diffusion; but they obscure the picture of the whole system that is essential for the systems theorist.

On the level of concepts the contrast comes out in the concepts used by Lipset and Parsons. Lipset's categories—apathy, authoritarianism, intolerance, utopian moralism—characterize classes of people, while functionalist categories refer to stocks and flows of resources, inputs and outputs of subsystems. Lipset is sometimes called a functionalist because he uses the pattern variables; but he uses them to describe elite values in various societies, while Parsons uses them to describe the values that are functionally appropriate for various subsystems, or to describe cultural systems. The other functionalist categories—func-tional prerequisites, structural types, interchange systems, media of circulation, do not appear in Lipset's works.

Another advantage of the democratic elitist perspective is that for elitists the System is global, not confined within national boundaries as with Keynesians and functionalists. The responsibilities of the capitalist elite are global, not national, and the struggle between the forces of good and evil is likewise global. This means that the Schumpeterians are able to perceive and study economic and military imperialism. To be sure, it is mainly Soviet imperialism that is studied, but capitalist imperialism also gets some attention. Bell refers to a US "imperial role" (1976, p. 179) but does not develop the point. Lipset (1950) has a clear discussion of capitalist imperialism; he shows that the powerful economic elite in Toronto and Montreal severely limited the Saskatchewan CCF government's socialist projects. Schumpeter's own work on capitalist imperialism (1951) discusses tariffs, export monopolies, capital exports to colonies to exploit cheap labor, raw material controls, war profits, monopolistic prices, and payoffs to domestic workers to promote national solidarity, all as imperialist mechanisms that benefit the monopoly sector.

The elitist perspective also supplements and extends functionalist treatments of social classes. Functionalists argue that stratification is a functional necessity in all but the simplest social systems, that certain structural characteristics are necessary for an integrated stratification system, that these characteristics never completely exist and there is always class conflict, and that government has the responsibility to mediate and moderate the inevitable conflict. Classes are also related to the economy, but since the economy is studied by professional economists and stratification is studied by professional sociologists, the connection remains vague.

The elitist intellectuals disdain such artificial boundaries and are able to study the dependence of classes on changes in the economy. Schumpeter gives us a historical account of the origin, rise, and decay of classes (1951). In capitalist times each great innovation in the mode of production or exchange brings a new class into existence, forces some older classes to adapt, and makes still others obsolescent. In precapitalist times religious and military innovations had the same effect. Class conflict is the friction that accompanies the ascendance of new classes and the economic obsolescence and decay of old classes.

Classes are invisible from the neoclassicist perspective, since we are all rational individuals and since the tastes and resources that differentiate us are given prior to economic analysis. I do not mean to assert that neoclassicists are unaware of class differences; I mean they are unable to construct a theory of classes with their categories.

Finally we should look at the one glaring weakness of the elitist perspective where it regularly produces monstrous distortions—the Soviet Union and the counterelite. The difficulty here is not in the concepts of elite theory, which could in principle be applied as readily to counterelite as to elite. The counterelite are an elite of sorts, and Communists are even a modernizing elite of sorts (cf. Brzezinski, 1970, pp. 139ff.), so their creative efforts could in principle be described subjectively and empathetically just as Mayor Lee's were. The Soviet Union, like the US, has a political system, that is, a field of resources and opportunities that a political entrepreneur could use to build himself an empire as he rises to the top, making system innovations as he goes. The conclusive evidence that this is conceptually possible is Brzezinski and Huntington, 1965, where it is actually done.

The difficulty then is not with the scientist's stock of concepts, but with his strong identification and commitment to the US. The Soviet leaders are the Enemy, and responsible intellectuals must constantly strain to avoid being duped by them or by their dupes; student radicals are wreckers of our superb universities, perhaps inciters of another McCarthy or Wallace movement. These strong emotions block application of the usual elite study methods to the counterelite.

Brzezinski and Huntington were aware of this problem and went to some trouble to overcome it. "To avoid approaching the subject purely from the American perspective . . . we visited several foreign countries, where we held extensive conversations . . . in Kyoto . . . in Tokyo . . . in Calcutta . . . with various helpful Soviet professors and intellectuals in Moscow, Leningrad, and Tashkent; and with many distinguished western European scholars" (1965, preface). They note the common practice of using black and white stereotypes and observe that a comparative study should look for similarities as well as differences (1965, introduction). Their assertion that "we aim to keep our analyses free of our preferences for constitutional democracy" is a standard one among the elitist intellectuals; but in my opinion they are the only ones to actually succeed in doing so.

This failure to separate historical interpretation from personal evaluations suggests two plausible hypotheses (cf. also Schumpeter, 1954, p. 43).

1. *Extreme hatred is a hindrance to scientific objectivity*. I believe the elitists' intense anti-communism is what distorts their Soviet studies. Their hatred blocks all empathy with the enemy; they cannot even try to look at events from a Soviet perspective, or even from a neutral perspective. There is only one way to interpret Soviet actions, and facts that do not fit that interpretation are rejected as misleading or fallacious. In particular all statements coming from the Soviet side are ignored or treated as lies. The Soviet and East German leaders of course have to lie to disguise their aggressive schemes, and their historians and political scientists of course have to follow the official line. Ambassadors like Kroll or Thompson who portray Soviet intentions as defensive have been duped, and are objects of pity or contempt. Then, having rejected all information that could be used to empathetically construct a plausible picture of a Soviet mentality, the writer *ascribes* an evil consciousness to the Soviet leaders by fiat:

"Stalin *had to know*" that he was proposing to change the status quo and was therefore by definition aggressive (Payne, 1970, pp. 67, 68). Payne argues that his own conception of the status quo *must* be shared by Soviet leaders because it is the only possible conception.

Jack Schick (1971), a far from extreme example, does a very careful job of reconstructing the thought processes of Dulles and other US leaders, using their publications and biographical materials; but he refuses to do the same for Soviet leaders, despite the considerable material available, relying instead on Kremlinological speculation about the nefarious motives behind their aggressive behavior. Feuer, in a study of the conflict of generations (1969), defines a generation by some overwhelming experience that defines reality for an age cohort, and gives as an example postwar Soviet aggressiveness in his generation. Yet when he comes to his hated enemy the New Left the whole topic of generational experience is clouded over with much "the issue is not the issue" kind of discussion which rejects the New Left's accounts of its own experiences. The New Left seems not to have had any experience, but only unconscious Oedipal drives, death wishes, etc. In his *Ideology and Ideologists* (1975) we get a clue to a possible explanation. As in his 1969 work, the Vietnam war is barely mentioned, only on pages 16 and 127. At the second reference he asserts that support for North Vietnam is a form of masochism, since it improves the chances for a triumph of world Communism. It seems that the awful prospect of a future victory of world Communism prevents him from focusing on the present bloodshed and misery in Vietnam. But this bloodshed plus the Civil Rights movement is the "generational experience" of the New Left. It is a moral experience; and this fact could be used to explain some of the weaknesses of the New Left, some of its theorizing, the scope of its appeal, even in part the violence of its extremists. Instead, Feuer ascribes unconscious motives by fiat.

2. *Strong commitment is a barrier to objectivity.* This less plausible hypothesis is the obverse of the previous one. The Schumpeterian intellectuals are so eager to defend the US, the best society we have and are likely to get, that they are very reluctant to focus on its few remaining faults. They would rather stress its good points. The result is an idealized picture of US government and society. We have a meritocratic society, they say, in which everyone can rise to his proper station. The universities are excellent; their involvement with the War is minimal, perhaps one or two professors, or token representation on military research institutes (Bell and Kristol, 1969, pp. 67–74 and introduction). The Peace Corps was pure

idealism (Feuer, 1969, pp. 402–403), though Moynihan in supplement suggests that at $7800 per person per annum it was a cheap way to keep hotheaded middle-class activists busy and quiet (1969, p. 72). Our opinions really are discussed in Washington: "we have in the U.S. a representative democracy, a Congress and a Senate, to which we elect representatives whose debate presumably becomes a sifted mirroring of our views" (Feuer, 1969, p. 412). And since our opinions are already known, any attempt to express them directly to government representatives is a form of elitism, a claim to be listened to twice. One must wonder if Feuer knows what a lobbyist is.

In international politics the elitists accept all US government statements at face value, both in their factual assertions and in their assertion of US aims and principles, just as they reject all Soviet statements as systematically deceptive. Then they build layer upon layer of theorizing on that "factual" foundation; they refine concepts, evaluate statistical techniques, test hypotheses against their "facts," and pass off the whole as science.

One could argue that the democratic elitists' blindness toward the SU and the US is not an essential characteristic of their standpoint and could be reduced in time. It so happened that the standpoint came into prominence during the Cold War period when many social scientists got infected with a hysterical dualist view of the world and produced piles of propaganda. Their belief that their personal preferences did not affect their scientific work was pure self-delusion. Perhaps future social scientists with a more sober, detached attitude toward the US and the SU could study the two sets of elites more objectively, following the example of Brzezinski and Huntington.

Conceptually this would involve dropping the concept of counter-elite, with its associated baggage like "disease of the transition" and "a century of frustration". Communists of various kinds could be treated as modernizing elites working in mobilization systems (to use Apter's functionalist term). The Wallaces and Reagans could be treated as a traditionalist elite, and that category could be given a more differentiated, sympathetic treatment than it has received. Conflicts among the various kinds of elites would no longer be an apocalyptic struggle of good and evil, but a conflict among various forms and combinations of modernization and traditionalism. I believe such a change would open the way for realization of the very considerable potential of the elite standpoint.

Seven The Critical Intellectuals

If we take the same categories as before—elite, intellectuals, and mass—and rearrange them, we get a different kind of science. The scientist still sees himself as an intellectual, but his focus of concern is for the mass, rather than the elite. Instead of identifying with the elite—the cultural elite, who have risen to the top through sheer intellectual brilliance in this meritocratic society of ours—he identifies or rather empathizes with the oppressed victim, the mass. Instead of worrying about the problems of our elitist democracy, beset by extremists of right and left, he worries about what is happening to the victims of that democracy. "And so the issue is not the relative merit of work itself; it is rather how some men are made to do the harshest work for the least reward" (Piven and Cloward, *Regulating the Poor*, 1971, p. xvii).

> To be out of the moiling street
> With its swelter and its sin!
> Who has given me this sweet
> And given my brother dust to eat?
> And when will his wage come in?

Hayes, *Power Structure and Urban Policy* (1972, p. v), quoting a poem by William Vaughn Moody.

189

There is some change of subcategories as a result of this shift. "Mass" is much too vague a category—indeed, for the elitists it is a residual category, referring to all those not good enough by nature to be part of the elite. One needs instead more differentiated categories— the poor, the black, the unemployed, the non-union coal miners, the welfare clients, the deviants, the imprisoned, the asylum inmates, the migrant workers, the Indians, the colonial peoples. Conversely, the many subtypes of elite no longer need to be distinguished; they are all equally oppressors, all part of the ruling class. The simple concept "elite" is sufficient.

In particular the concept of counterelite drops out. This is an instance of a familiar propaganda category, the "outside agitator" who is stirring up our happy and contented Negroes. When such individuals show up in the mass case-studies they appear as leaders of the black community or as organizers and activists; they seem to emerge from some group as its temporary spokesmen. Martin Luther King, for example, was elected to head the Montgomery, Alabama boycott committee in 1955 because he was a newcomer in town and thus not yet identified with any of the local factions (Piven and Cloward, 1979, p. 209). The active Subject is the community itself, the unemployed or the inmates, rather than their temporary spokesmen. The intellectual's empathy and concern for the mass enables him to see these people as Subject, making the best of their sorry situation with considerable ingenuity and dignity. Thus there are still two opposed Subjects, but they are the elite and the mass rather than the elite and the counterelite. Consider for instance the various studies of the student movement of the 1960's: for such as Bell and Kristol (1969) and Brzezinski (1968) the opponents are the administration, or elite, and the extremist students, or Maoists or counterelite; they are contending for the allegiance of the confused moderate students, the mass. For Horowitz and Friedland (1970) the opponents are the administration and the students.

The instruments of struggle are those same "reforms" that the theorists of elitist democracy celebrate as means of making the masses happy, contented, and apathetic, and of isolating the critical intellectuals. From the mass perspective these same reforms appear as coercive, destructive, divisive, or at best as frauds, in short as violence against people.

When this point is developed, it will constitute the *third* explanation of the Vietnam war, the poverty program, and the welfare system.

The distinction between those intellectuals who identify with the elite and those who empathize with the masses is not a static one. As I indicated in Chapter Six, many of the theorists of elitist democracy are ambivalent about their identification with the elite and retain a submerged anti-elite bias—at least in the form of a wish that more of the masses could be as good as the elite. For the theorists to be discussed in this chapter the ambivalence is reversed and the anti-elite stance is the manifest one. In a few instances, such as Mills, both components are present about equally. The empathy with the oppressed makes his *White Collar* (1951) a vivid, powerful book, and his identification with the intellectual elite comes out in his later works.

Perhaps the distinction can be made in terms of rightward vs. leftward movement. The theorists of elitist democracy have moved right, in those cases I have examined; indeed in their self-conception they argue that rightward movement is normal for good intellectuals. The theorists we will now discuss declare that a left bias is normal for intellectuals. They themselves are left and move left, in the cases I have examined, and indeed there is an easy transition from the standpoint of Chapter Seven to standpoints farther left. This movement produces transitional works in which components of the mass perspective combine with left-liberal or Marxist components. The paradigm contrast for me is Moynihan and Cloward from 1960 to 1977. In 1960 their views were very similar; then they diverged.

I will divide the mass perspective researches into three groups: studies of the elite, studies of the intellectuals, and studies of the masses.

I. Studies of the Elite

The initial works in this tradition are Hunter (1954, 1959) and Mills (1956), or farther back the Lynd "Middletown" studies. These case studies attempt to demonstrate that in one city and in the whole US the economic and political elite work closely together to make the important policy decisions. The opposing pluralist thesis is that political power is normally rather widely dispersed, with different politicians making decisions in different issue areas; that the elite disagree on most issues and use their power to block each other and to bargain and compromise; that an enterprising politician can sometimes collect a good deal of political power but is always in danger of losing it again to other politicians; and that the economic elite are one among several elites that influence politicians and are often unsuccessful in their influence attempts.

To counter the pluralist thesis, later elitists produced case studies which showed a unitary economic elite dominating political decisions in particular cities (Bachrach and Baratz, 1970; Crenson, 1971; Hayes, 1972; Domhoff, 1978; cf. also Vidich and Bensman, 1958), at the state level (Orren, 1974), and nationally (Domhoff, 1974; Engler, 1961; 1978). They have also pointed out that investment and price decisions, which directly affect people's lives, are made by the economic elite with little or no political interference (Bachrach, 1967, Chapter 5; Orren, 1974). The case studies show that the economic elite dominates political decision-making by their direct participation in government and by their control of the economy. They also dominate indirectly, through their reputation for power; their ability to veto or nullify is sufficient to keep some issues off the political agenda (Schattschneider, 1960; Bachrach and Baratz, 1970; Crenson, 1971). Other studies show that the political system is not neutral, as pluralists have asserted; some interest groups are favored and others are actively excluded (Greer, 1971; Parenti, 1970).

The power of the economic-political elite is not unchallengeable; there have been mass revolts (Hayes, 1972, pp. 19-23; Boesel and Rossi, 1971; Greer, 1971) which have failed, but have induced minor concessions from the elite to the protesting groups (Hayes, 1972, pp. 151–155; Bachrach and Baratz, 1970; Piven and Cloward, 1979). In historical perspective, elite power grew steadily during the period 1850–1950, as earlier mass challenges were defeated in numerous struggles (Orren, 1974). Orren's history neatly reverses Dahl's pluralist history (1961) which claims that in New Haven the economic elite dominated politics before 1900 but lost ground since then, until by 1950 it was on the sidelines.

The elitist studies also deal with the question of who benefits directly from political and corporate decisions, and show that the corporations benefit. The Federal program to help the unemployed actually provided capital gifts or low-cost loans to businessmen in Oakland and produced almost no new jobs (Hayes, 1972); the insurance industries' urban investment program produced profits and some loans to businesses but almost no jobs (Orren, 1974, Chapter 6).

The pluralists have countered with a variety of methodological arguments, such as that the elite thesis is too vague to be testable (Wildavsky, 1964, p. 322) and that Hunter's reputational method automatically produces an elite. But the main disagreement is on the facts. Wildavsky admits that there may be an occasional US city dominated by a single employer, but lists the many pluralist cities, including Hunter's Atlanta which Hunter misrepresented as elitist, to show that pluralism is the normal case (Wildavsky, 1964, pp. 344ff.). Conversely, Domhoff (1978) restudies Dahl's New Haven to show that Dahl's finding of pluralism in that elite-dominated city is the result of superficial observation and a neglect of the evidence. What is remarkable is that each side is thoroughly convinced that it has proved its case with facts many times over (Rose, 1967, introduction; Domhoff, 1974, pp. 109-110) and remains completely unconvinced by the evidence and the arguments of the other side. For example Polsby (1980) completely rejects Domhoff's 1978 restudy of New Haven.

My interpretation of this deadlock is that it is not based on methodological differences, as are some continuing disagreements in science, since both sides use variants of case study methods. The variants were originally devised to fit the guiding theory, and each variant produced the desired data. Consequently the methodological differences are derivative. The real basis of the deadlock is the difference of standpoint. The pluralists identify the elite as Subject and see society from inside an elite consciousness; consequently they take for granted an elite consensus on the fundamentals of the democratic polity and the mixed economy, and concentrate their attention on the many disagreements spread around them. Or, if not with the elite, they identify with the Horatio Alger types, the upwardly mobile Bill Longs (Wildavsky, 1964, pp. 328ff.). Also as committed intellectuals their responsibility is to defend democracy against extremist criticism and counterelite agitation. They are willing in principle to admit that American democracy has faults but in practice they need extremely strong evidence to be convinced that the fault is genuine and not an extremist fabrication. And even a genuine fault, they remind us, must be evaluated in comparison to alternative governments such as the Soviet Union, rather than by reference to a utopian ideal of democracy. Our democracy is not perfect, but it is the best government we are likely to get; and as realists we must be careful that irresponsible criticism or hasty reforms do not make it worse instead of better.

The elitists empathize with the mass victims of our elite-run democracy and are interested in what it is doing for the masses. They realize that the economic elite disagree on whether weapons system A or B should be developed, on whether to tear down a slum and build luxury housing or to grant investment credits, but they note that the effect on the masses is about the same either way. The masses lose. They are interested in results, not procedure, and they note that the condition of the poor, the black, the unemployed is getting worse, not better. Improvements have occurred at times, but only because of mass protest, not elite benevolence. And as realists they are not interested in Dahl's or Truman's idealizations of democracy, their arguments about what is ideally possible for a well-organized interest group of the poor, but in what actually does happen. They are willing in principle to admit the possibility that the victims, not their oppressors, are in part responsible for their situation but in practice they need extremely strong evidence to be convinced.

The disagreement is not based on a difference of conceptual framework, since both kinds of intellectuals use pretty much the same basic concepts, but on a difference of standpoint, that is on which group one identifies with or empathizes with. In contrast, the neoclassic-Keynesian disagreements are based on a difference of conceptual framework, so that no real argument even occurs. And since each must misinterpret the other's argument in terms of his own categories, debaters of good will, like Samuelson, can even convince themselves that a broad measure of agreement has been achieved, though in fact no rational discussion has occurred.

By about 1968 the professionals, the functionalists and system theorists, had taken over the whole pluralist-elitist dispute except that the original proponents continued to support their original positions with new case studies. The professionals focused their attention on operational definitions of power and leadership, and projected vast and ever-expanding comparative research projects to find the power structure of one city after another, for one issue-area after another, in one decade after another, all over the world. I have in mind here articles and studies by Clark, Frey, D. Miller, G. Hoskin, Wirt, Morlock, among others. With the professional takeover of the dispute the categories shifted from the elite-mass categories to system categories like power structures, socialization subsystems and processes, and linkages among structures. Questions shifted from "Who governs," "Who decides," "Who benefits" to functionalist questions of system self-maintenance processes and structuralist questions of channels and linkages. For example:

> . . . as part of its capacity for "interest aggregation", every durable social system has to say no to various actors. On saying no, it must face the consequences of what the denied actor will do next. Ordinarily, it possesses formidable "cooling out" processes whereby the disappointed are led to accept their lot, at least temporarily, without disrupting the system too severely. . . . Mechanisms to put an early and inconspicuous *quietus* on some potential issues are probably essential to every large political system . . . (Frey, 1971, p. 1100).

Here the Object is a self-maintaining system in which nondecisions, the mobilization of bias, have a positive function. Similarly, Hawley and Wirt (1974) argue that the categories of Easton's system theory provide the conceptual framework for transcending the pluralist-elitist dispute.

II. Studies of the Intellectuals

Recent self-studies of critical intellectuals include Horowitz (1968), Gouldner (1974, 1976, 1979), B. and J. Ehrenreich (1977). The picture is similar to that provided by the Schumpeterian intellectuals. Intellectuals are relatively detached from the conventions of their society and even from their class. They deal with words, language, ideas, and believe in the power of ideas; their characteristic virtue is creativity. In contrast with the professionals or technicians, Gouldner's technical intelligentsia, intellectuals engage in a broad, unspecialized scholarship.

The differences between the two kinds of intellectuals appears on the issue of detachment. The elitist intellectuals see themselves as engaged or committed to American democracy, a commitment that counteracts the normal intellectual detachment. The experience that produced this commitment was the experience of Soviet totalitarianism in the 1930's and Soviet expansion in the 1940's, interpreted as a threat to democracy and to the freedom of speech prized so highly by intellectuals. The commitment to democracy and the mixed economy makes the intellectual responsible; he takes on the obligation to defend democracy against its critics. In contrast, Gouldner declares that critical detachment is the defining characteristic of the true intellectual. "Intellectuals, then, are scholars who reject, make problematic, or critically focalize the boundaries hitherto implicit in normal scholarship and the scholarly paradigms on which the scholarly community had, till then, centered . . ." (1976, p. 23); "this . . . alienation—in the case of intellectuals—is also conducive to a politically revolutionizing potential that *rejects* the conventional political and economic institutions" (p. 21).

Here we have the self-definition of the critical intellectual. He rejects the status quo both in science and in society. He questions the assumptions underlying accepted science and existing social institutions. His creativity is devoted to exposing the deficiencies of his own society, his own science—and also his fellow critical intellectuals. Gouldner's account expresses the self-concept of a long line of critical intellectuals, including the Frankfurt School in Germany and the *Praxis* group in Yugoslavia. Compare for instance: "Philosophie ist das ganze, rationale and kritische Bewusstsein des Menschen von der Welt, in der er lebt . . . Philosophie [war] stets das kritische Bewusstsein im menschlichen situation . . . " (Markovic, 1968, pp. 7-8; cf. also Stojanovic, 1973, Chapter 1 for the same view).

One can discern here the irresponsible, troublemaking intellectual of whom Schumpeter complained, the one who was always stirring up the masses with utopian visions. Similarly, Gouldner's third world intellectuals who "give authentic expression to national resistance to exploitation by aliens" (1976, p. 11) and even lead peasant revolts, are recognizable as the same troublemakers who disgust Lipset and Solari (1967), Huntington (1968), and Wilensky (1975, p. 116): "these intellectuals who claim to articulate the discontents of the oppressed." The conflict between these two kinds of intellectuals is an old one. One example in sociology is Shils' criticism of Adorno for failing to be anti-communist: Adorno focused on the authoritarianism of US conservatives, when he should have realized that Communists are just as authoritarian (Shils, in Christie and Jahoda, 1954).

The critical intellectual naturally sides with the oppressed masses against the elite; his fundamental commitment is to the alleviation of suffering, exploitation, and inequality (Gouldner, 1974). His vision is of a society in which the elite have lost their power to oppress and the masses will finally be able to live in dignity. In pursuit of this vision intellectuals have articulated mass aspirations, mobilized the masses, and transformed themselves into disciplined party intellectuals. The Leninist vanguard party is the typical instrument of mass mobilization and intellectual self-discipline.

These activities are not purely selfless; they have a selfish side as well. The socialist society to which the intellectuals aspire always includes a large and important role for the intellectuals themselves (Ehrenreich, 1977; Gouldner, 1976, p. 11). They expect to do the planning, managing, administering, and educating on behalf of the masses, with the purpose of eventually raising the masses to their own level. Indeed, this has already happened in countries where the revolutionary intellectuals have successfully taken power; they have become a modernizing elite, in their turn repressing the new critical intellectuals who have sprung up. Similarly Piven and Cloward, 1977, criticize the intellectual leaders of New York City rent strikes for killing the tenants' movement. When the tenants were aroused enough to join protest marches on City Hall, the organizers diverted them into the prosaic tasks of organization maintenance like checking membership lists, answering the telephone, and setting up building organizations. Soon the intellectuals had a large paper organization with them at the top; but with mass enthusiasm worn out the organization had no power and could be ignored by City Hall.

In short, the critical intellectuals—self-critical intellectuals—see themselves as elite anti-elitists; they have opposed interests as well as common interests with the masses.

To illustrate: Horowitz and Friedland (1970) provide a critical study of student protest that contrasts nicely with the elitist Bell-Kristol-Lipset-Feuer—Brzezinski studies. The latter studies are from the outside, treating students as an object of study; they inquire into the psychological and social causes of this disturbing phenomenon, and use statistical surveys to locate the regularities (even while questioning the validity of such surveys). Statistical surveys deal equally well with subjective and objective causes or correlations, and both appear in these studies in great numbers. Objective factors include parentage, nationality, socioeconomic status, IQ, and marginality of the student status. Subjective factors include personal problems, opposition to the war, lack of experience with conflicting role obligations, romanticism, mass conversion hysteria. Such studies also conclude that there is nothing new in the student movement of the 1960's—students have always been middle class romantic, idealistic troublemakers; there has always been domestic opposition to US wars; universities have always expanded, etc

Note that the statistical survey method used in these studies focuses attention on the troublemaking students. The question asked is, "How are these students different from ordinary students?" The discovered correlations that provide the answers also serve to explain the troublesome behavior: they act differently because they are different.

The Horowitz and Friedland study comes from the inside, from sharing the experiences of students. The method is participant observation supplemented by reports of experiences at a few other universities. The result is an account of the "generational experience" of the New Left, the events that organized our world for us. There were two: the civil rights movement and the Vietnam war. The war in particular enabled students to relate their personal concerns to their concern for society: the war was dangerous as well as immoral.

The participant-observer method used in this study focuses outward on the world as experienced by students. The question asked is, "What was it about the experienced world that called for protest and resistance?" The answer serves to interpret student protest as an appropriate or intelligible response in that situation. And since many nonprotesting students also experienced pretty much the same world, the method enables one to understand student activists as spokesmen for the most passive students against the administration.

The perspective of Horowitz and Friedland is that of the critical intellectual who empathizes with the oppressed and shares their hostility toward the elite, those who think they are better than others and have the right to push other people around. The ambivalence or dual identity of the critical intellectual comes out in the last section, on crisis management (pp. 208ff.). The authors list the tactics that shrewd administrators have used to pacify the students, such as co-optation of leaders and potential leaders. Then they end with advice— to the administrators, not the students! They advise administrators to share power with students by including them on various university committees. If one looks carefully, this is precisely the co-optation tactic shrewd administrators had already been using to pacify students. The students are to be appointed individually on the basis of their demonstrated maturity and responsibility, not elected by other students as a matter of right, so their constituency is the administration and the faculty, where their reputation rests.

Horowitz and Friedland express well the attitude liberal faculty felt toward student protesters about 1968. We sympathized with their bafflement at confronting the bureaucratic labyrinth, and with their eager, perplexed search for the committees with the *real* power so they could demand a share. As insiders who "knew" which committees had the real power we wanted to help them through the maze. We wanted to share our "power" with them and in fact guide them to a spot just below us on the pyramid of power: faculty first, students second, administration third, nonacademics last (Horowitz and Friedland, 1970, p. 218).

III. Studies of the Masses

Many of the mass studies of the last thirty years have grown out of the Chicago school of the 1920's (Becker, 1970, Chapter 4). The object of study was the city, Chicago, and especially its slums, ghettos, and delinquency. The main theoretical framework was the social problem-social disorganization-anomie framework deriving from Durkheim among others; urbanization was seen as producing social problems that government ought to deal with, and the sociologist's task was to map out the slum-poverty-delinquency cycle to find points at which government can intervene to correct it. Arnold Rose, who associated with Chicago sociologists, provides a recent example of this social problems perspective and theoretical framework (1967, pp. 196ff.). His discussion of mass society is really a discussion of urbanization à la Louis Wirth; the problems of mass society result from individual failures to cope with the liberating potential of urban life. These individuals, overcome by feelings cf helplessness and anomie, retreat to the ghetto and get caught in its cycle of crime and disorganization. Rose's proposed solution is government control of depressions and unemployment but also ghetto self-help in the form of more voluntary associations, hobbies, and camping. (In Minneapolis camping might make sense.) Another recent example of the social problems perspective is Matza (1966), who locates the problem of poverty (apart from cyclical unemployment) in the dregs, the skidders, the perverts, the aged and infirm—those who cannot cope with urban life.

The early Chicago studies made heavy use of statistics—census data, house-to-house canvassing, questionnaires, indices such as the Index of Status Characteristics which the interviewer could surreptitiously compute while seated in the respondent's living room. Statistical methods were also important in studies of delinquency and poverty at other universities such as Columbia.

The Chicago school also made use of participant observation and life histories; the theoretical framework was provided by Mead, Park, and W.I. Thomas rather than Durkheim or Wirth. The purpose of participant observation was to learn to see the world from the subject's perspective—his definition of the situation, his self-concept including I and me, self-presentation, his concepts of the other and the generalized other. Once the subject's perspective had been thoroughly absorbed, her actions could be understood as attempts to cope with the situation. Collective action then consisted of a plurality of subjects coping with each other and developing shared understandings. Sociology was the study of "people doing things together" (Becker, 1970, p. v) rather than the study of systems, structures, cyclic mechanisms of the sort discussed in Chapter Five.

In short, participant observation gives us an empirical science of the subject, sharply different from the objective science of the Keynesians, system theorists, and Parsonian functionalists presented in Chapter Five. If we compare it with the Schumpeter-type empirical science of the subject (Chapter Six), we see that the subject–object dialectic is missing in participant observation and is replaced by Mead's self- other dialectic. Instead of the subject changing society and society changing the subject, Mead's subjects perceive and introject each other, each defining herself through the other's perceptions. For a Schumpeterian one must understand the subject, the entrepreneur or modernizing elite, by examining the social system that produced him, and then show how he in turn recreates that system. This sort of science ideally requires large historical and statistical studies of whole cultures—values, status systems, etc. But for a participant observer the subject is immediately there in a context of other people. We get therefore small studies of everyday life, in which intimate shared understandings rather than whole cultures are sustained.

Every social science method requires a certain kind of personality to bring it to life and to bring out its potentialities. Participant observation in its Chicago school version requires a Goffman-type person who is sensitive to the unspoken nuances of an interpersonal situation, who can blend unobtrusively into an ongoing activity and who can take her self-concept (the "me") and role from others' expectations and thereby put others at ease rather than on guard. Or in Mitroff's terms (1974) it requires a "feminine" Riesman rather than a "masculine" Watson (Hammond, 1964, Chapter 10).

This kind of person is antistatistical, since statistics, fixed questionnaires, pre-established indices get at people from the outside by imposing the observer's categories and therefore miss the complex reality of life (Becker, 1970, pp. 44–51; Cicourel, 1964). In contrast, for the Schumpeter-type scientist statistics are essential to locate the work of the modernizing elite and/or to describe the culture which produced them. Case studies like Dahl, 1961 are also used, but these focus outward on the work and accomplishments of the political entrepreneur rather than on his inner life.

The other big difference between the two empirical sciences of the Subject is that for Schumpeterians the Subject is always the elite, while for participant observers the subject is always the masses, the ordinary people. According to Becker "Most sociologists are politically liberal . . . we usually take the side of the underdog" (1970, p. 130).

This is the tradition out of which the "mass" studies of the last twenty-five years or so have come, except for some historical studies like Piven and Cloward, 1979, which emphasize the objective conditions that determine mass consciousness. Garfinkel's ethnomethodology is also an outgrowth of the Chicago tradition, as is Berger and Luckman (1966). Saul Alinsky also comes out of this tradition; his first participant observer study as a young criminologist involved associating with the Capone gang for a year or so. We have studies of students (Becker and Geer, 1958), gamblers (Goffman, 1967,

Chapter 6), inmates (Goffman, 1961), prisoners (Jackson, 1972), unemployed coal miners (Jackson, 1971), hustlers and petty crooks (Polsky, 1967), addicts (Lindesmith, 1968), Indians (Gearing et al., 1960; Gearing, 1970), lower class barrio inhabitants (Peattie, 1968), lower class education (Becker, 1970, Chapters 9-11), and the more recent studies of the slum (Suttles, 1968; Lewis, 1969; Portes, 1972) and the black ghetto (Stack, 1974, connected to the Chicago school via Ed Bruner).

These studies show people constructing a meaningful and livable world for themselves in very difficult and sometimes hopeless circumstances; at the extreme, "making it in Hell" in Jackson's phrase (1972, p. xvi). Behavior that from the outside looks irrational or "governed by the pleasure principle" is actually part of an effective strategy for survival in the hostile and dangerous slum (Rainwater, 1967). We see nothing of disorganization, anomie, social problems, or even deviance; such concepts are imposed on people from without (for deviance as an imposed category, see Rubington and Weinberg, 1968 Part I; Becker, ed., 1964). People are social problems, anomic, etc. *for others*, usually for the government. Such concepts belong to the perspectives of Chapters Five and Six, where the government or the elite are Subject and the masses are part of the Object. Piven and Cloward (1971, Epilogue) note that the explosive increase in welfare in the 1960's might be a crisis from some perspectives but is a reform from the perspective of the poor.

What is visible instead from the mass or underdog perspective is oppression and exploitation. The desperate and even hopeless situation of some of these people is a consequence of elite oppression, government social programs, welfare policies. The unemployed coal miners were cheated out of the mineral rights of their lands long ago by unscrupulous entrepreneurs, assisted by crooked lawyers and judges; the coal companies can now legally ruin farmland and water supplies by strip mining. The miners' health was ruined by unhealthful working conditions, permitted by a Bureau of Mines subservient to the coal companies. When the mines or the miners are worked out the miners are discarded like used beer cans (Lockard, 1971, Chapter 1; Jackson, 1971). The lower-class child inevitably gets poor education from a system geared to middle-class institutions and motivations (Becker, 1970, Chapter 9); the textbooks and teachers insult lower-class children by describing them as slum dwellers, delinquents, immoral, shiftless, social problems (E. Diesing, 1952). For example the Fox Project (Gearing, 1960) at first defined the problem as a local one, in "social problems" fashion; it was a vicious cycle of poverty and discrimination involving loss of traditional masculine occupations, cultural differences, loss of male self-respect. But as time went by the pervasive hand of the Indian Bureau enforcing dependency and helplessness became apparent. The Bureau, in an economy move, had decided to withdraw certain services from the community, and resorted to its usual duplicity and chicanery in the process of implementation. Finally at one stormy meeting Sol Tax, our project director and hero, repudiated the government agent standing next to him and took the side of the Indians against the government (Gearing, 1960, pp. 198-204). One project member went on to find neo-colonial oppression in a Venezuelan barrio (Peattie, 1968). A US-owned corporation was constructing a plant nearby and ran the plant's sewer pipe through the barrio where Peattie was living as a participant observer; the pipe's outlet was on the bathing beach. Here was the reverse side of Schumpeter's responsible, creative entrepreneur and Rostow's idealistic foreign aid: the corporation got the profits and the barrio inhabitants got the sewage.

Stack shows how the welfare system itself traps people in poverty (1974, pp. 105-107, 126-128). Welfare rules prevent people from accumulating any kind of savings and equity; AFDC rules discriminate against fathers, penalize nuclear families, and encourage the existing kinship networks that sustain but also trap people. All welfare does is alleviate the symptoms of poverty, while maintaining poverty itself. Piven and Cloward (1971) generalize this point; they argue that historically relief has been expanded in periods of high unemployment and especially civil disorder—riots, strikes, hunger marches. As soon as people are pacified, relief is cut back and restricted by rules forcing people to work at anything they can get. As Fusfeld's Rule states, "Welfare payments to the poor are set at that level at which the resultant unrest can be held in check by the existing instruments of law and order" (Fusfeld, 1972, p. 694). In addition, the arbitrary use of bureaucratic discretion reinforces the dependency and helplessness of welfare clients (Cloward and Piven, 1975, pp. 23-26), exactly the same effect we had seen in our Fox Indian project.

A second characteristic of welfare programs that becomes visible from the mass perspective is their divisiveness. When welfare benefits are given to the poor, the black, the unemployed, they are paid for by those one step up the status ladder—the blue-collar worker. Special job-training for blacks, the favored solution for Parsons and for Downs, puts them into competition with white workers who are precariously holding on to those same jobs, since no new jobs are being created. Local welfare costs are paid for by property taxes, which are felt most acutely by those who have just managed to buy a small home. The very existence of a permanent reserve pool of unemployed is a threat to those who have jobs (Stack, 1974, p. 128; Cloward and Piven, 1975, pp. 141–150; Piven and Cloward, 1971). The resulting resentment by blue-collar workers is duly discovered by McClosky-type survey researchers and labeled "working class conservatism" as though it were an inherent characteristic of the ignorant masses.

A third point that comes through clearly in the mass studies is the powerlessness of the poor. If American society is characterized by a struggle between two Subjects, the elite and the masses, it is an extremely one-sided struggle. Abandoned coal miners, barrio and ghetto and reservation inhabitants, welfare clients, lower-class school children have no bargaining power because they make no economic contributions that they can threaten to take away or promise to deliver. Consequently the political system is closed to them (Cloward and Piven, 1975, Chapter 1; Parenti, 1970). The only power they have is the power to disrupt—to riot, block traffic, dynamite the sewer pipe, organize a rent strike. Disruptions produce only temporary, token concessions, but even these are better than nothing and the best they are likely to get (Bachrach and Baratz, 1970, pp. 87–91; Cloward and Piven, 1975, Part Two). The gains are often illusory (Bachrach, 1971, p. 5); if they are real, they are likely to be reduced or withdrawn once the protesters quiet down, or the ruling elite modify them into a new support for the status quo and a new instrument of oppression (Piven and Cloward, 1979, Chapter 1). Naturally the elitist intellectuals condemn disruptive tactics and call for patience and regular interest group politics; they want the masses to depend on elite benevolence.

The contrast between the mass perspective and the elite or the social problems perspectives comes out nicely in the various criticisms of Piven and Cloward's work. Take for example Albritten (1979). Albritten argues that if Piven and Cloward's work is significant at all, if it is science rather than journalism, its significant content must consist of a new causal model to explain urban crime. He then reconstructs their model by locating the constants, the independent, intervening, and dependent variables, and the causal paths. Piven and Cloward are hypothesizing that mass migration of blacks caused the breakdown of traditional political channels in the cities, which caused increased mass insurgency, which caused an increase in welfare. A constant was black electoral power. He tests this model against Piven and Cloward's own statistics and finds no significant correlations. The model is disconfirmed. Albritten's alternative explanation is that the welfare increase resulted from the 1965 poverty program which was intended to help the poor.

Piven and Cloward reply that they were misunderstood. They were interested in finding the conditions in which mass insurgency might provide benefits, as their title indicates (*Poor People's Movements; Why They Succeed, How They Fail*). They argued that a ruling stratum—here, the Democrats—if weakened in some way might respond to mass insurgency by appeasing the poor. But if the ruling stratum were strong enough it would ignore or repress the insurgency. The Democrats were weakened in the 1950's by a split between Southern whites and civil rights protesters among their constituents; Kennedy and Johnson chose to respond by placating on civil rights and repressing the Southern whites.

For Albritten, there is one Subject, Johnson and his liberal congress, who are motivated by high humanitarian ideals. Mass behavior is subject-matter for a quantitative behavioral science which tests causal models against statistical data. Piven and Cloward write as participant observers of poor people's movements. They see two Subjects: a ruling stratum that above all tries to maintain its own dominance, and the poor who are trying to better their lot. They try to bring out the conditions in which mass insurgency has a chance of success, although in a situation of strategic interaction success cannot be guaranteed. For a game theorist an indeterminate outcome is a normal and mathematically significant outcome of a two-person game, but for a causal modeler a model that says "A sometimes causes B somewhat"—the poor sometimes get something—is terribly weak. Piven and Cloward have the participant observer's skeptical attitude toward statistics (Diesing, 1971, p. 171). They revise *their own* data upward or downward according to the varying conditions in particular cities and particular years; one must know the actual conditions to avoid being misled by numbers. Consequently they find Albritten's tests to be worthless, just as they reject the causal model he imputes to them. They were not using "or," "and," "resulted in" as causal-model terms but as part of the detailed story of what happened. As Albritten complains, they "do not understand the logic of comparative analysis" (p. 1022). Piven and Cloward could have replied that Albritten does not understand the logic of participant observation.

Albritten concludes by reminding Piven and Cloward of the real class situation: "In any case, mass insurgency is a highly dubious strategy for middle-class academics to urge upon the poor" (p. 1023). But Piven and Cloward are not academics who construct causal models relevant to public policy; they are critical intellectuals committed to the cause of the poor. A dialogue between these two kinds of science is very difficult.

IV. Preliminary Evaluation

Views of Oppression and Injustice

The mass perspective shows us vividly, for the first time, oppression, violence, and injustice. There is no substitute for the victim's point of view: the Keynesian aggregate statistics point to poverty, unemployment, and discrimination as objective facts, but not as oppression of the weak by the powerful. The power relation, or as Parsons calls it, the zero-sum conception of power, does not fit into the Keynesian-Parsonian-cybernetic conceptual framework. The conception is rather that of a living system maintaining itself via its government, and power is the ability of the system through its government to act in its environment. Poverty, unemployment, and discrimination are system-problems, objective and impersonal. The violence that police and others regularly use against mass protesters is simply an exercise of government regulatory power. Moreover, the Keynesian-Parsonian-cybernetic idealization of government (the control function) as a neutral, benevolent problem solver is incompatible with the conception of government as a powerful oppressor. If, for instance, an urban renewal program makes the poor worse off (Downs, 1970, Chapter 8), then government or its professional advisors made a mistake somewhere, and we should learn to do better next time. "I" cannot be an oppressor.

Similarly, the elite-perspective studies of poverty, such as Moynihan (1969), are founded on the premise of elite responsibility for the welfare of the masses. Particular elite may fail to carry out their responsibilities, may act stupidly or selfishly or negligently; but if someone were to actually be malicious or unjust he does not belong in the elite. Power in the zero-sum sense is a part of this conceptual framework (unlike the Keynesian–Parsonian framework), but the opponent is that elusive but ever-present scoundrel, the counterelite. Mass power, when it is legitimate, is exercised through an interest group with its own elite leadership and thus is part of the pluralist bargaining process. Consequently systematic use of elite power to oppress the masses is an unintelligible concept. The elite qua elite simply cannot do such a thing.

If poverty and unemployment continue or get worse despite expensive welfare programs, the elite-perspective studies use one of two kinds of explanation.

A. We do not know scientifically how bad the problem is; survey data are unreliable, many questionnaires are badly constructed and poorly administered, we need better social indicators (for example, Wilensky, 1975, Chapter 5). Criticism of survey research by those who use it is common and is as thoroughgoing as criticism of it by its opponents like Blumer and Cicourel. But they would never think of studying poverty from a mass perspective via participant observation; that would be unscientific, impressionistic, subjective.

B. Perhaps our expectations are too high (Wildavsky, 1975, pp. 45–59). Poverty and unemployment are very difficult problems and we should not get up utopian expectations; even at best welfare programs should not be expected to accomplish much (Wilensky, 1975, Chapter 5). There has always been poverty and probably always will be; we were too optimistic in 1960. "In every society the overwhelming majority of the people lead lives of considerable frustration, and if society is to endure, it needs to be able to rely on a goodly measure of stoical resignation" (Kristol, 1973b, p. 10).

In both cases the problem is located out there in the slums where the poor people are, not here with us; so elite oppression and injustice have no possible location in the problem. This is known to the mass-perspective scientists as "blaming the victim" (Ryan, 1976). The problem with blacks is their broken, fatherless families (Moynihan, 1965), their lack of skills, poor work habits, low literacy, inability to postpone gratification, or more generally the "culture of poverty" that traps them in a self-reinforcing poverty system. But "blaming the victim" is an incorrect description of elite-perspective studies. One does not blame a social problem; only people, subjects, can be blamed and thereby assigned responsibility. Moynihan certainly did not intend to blame blacks for their fatherless families; that situation was caused by unemployment, discrimination, and ultimately by slavery. His intention was rather to stir up pity and concern in the White House so that blacks would be helped by an employment program (Rainwater and Yancey, 1966); he was in the Labor Department at that time. In a later work (1969) Moynihan blames everyone but the victim: first the professional specialists, the Keynesians, for their ignorance of politics and poor understanding of poverty (Chapter 2); the conservatives, for cutting out liberal aspects of the program (p. 91) and generally making trouble (Chapter 6); the Washington liberals, for their confusion, romanticism, and improvisation (Chapter 4, 5); and of course the counterelite, for taking advantage of liberal confusion to move in and wreck the whole program (Chapter 7). More recently, as he has moved farther right, he has come to center blame on the liberals for blocking Nixon's humanitarian welfare reform, the Family Assistance Program (Moynihan, 1973). Marris and Rein (1967) similarly scatter blame about, but do not blame the poor, the problem. Matza (1966) deserves first prize for blaming the British governments of 1795 and 1834, plus the Irish landlord system and US slavery, for the American poverty of the 1960's. However, these errors of judgment occurred long ago and their effects are finally dissipating, he argues; the Irish have finally gotten respectable, the Negroes are on the march upward, and the whole problem of the disreputable poor should shortly shrink to insignificance. He certainly does not blame the poor themselves, the dregs and skidders and aged and sick, for their incompetence; that is just a fact.

In short, the elite-perspective studies focus, in sorrow and pity, on alleged characteristics of the victims in order to explain the persistence of poverty, but they do not *blame* the victim. The effect, however, is to make their oppression invisible.

In addition, the elite perspective and the perspectives of Chapters Two and Five have concepts that provide alternative interpretations and thereby block recognition that there is anything left to be explained by the concept of oppression.

Take for example the sewer pipe that was laid through Peattie's barrio (1968). For the neoclassicist this is a familiar pricing problem. The sewage is an external cost, and it has always been difficult to price such costs accurately. If economists were to develop an adequate pricing mechanism one could estimate just how much the pipe was costing the barrio inhabitants and could charge this cost to the iron corporation, who would of course have to pass it on to the consumer. The revenue then could be used to clean up the river or build a swimming pool, and everyone would benefit. For the Keynesian this is a temporary side effect of economic progress which will disappear at higher levels of GNP; meanwhile the government can alleviate the problem in various ways such as a pollution measurement station or municipal swimming pool. For the elitist intellectual this is another aspect of the "revolution of rising expectations." Mankind has always had sewage; when has it ever been different? (cf. Kristol, 1973a). The medieval cities must have stunk awfully. Besides, we are at least free to complain; in the Soviet Union one would go to jail for protesting about *Soviet* sewage.

What all three perspectives hide are the questions, Who pays? And who benefits? And who decides? That is oppression.

Doubts About Survey Data

The mass-perspective studies cast strong doubt on the survey and census and administrative data used or produced in the elite-perspective studies. Consequently the elite-perspective account of the masses as stupid, apathetic, and authoritarian is shown to be highly suspect. I have three examples.

First, Moynihan (1965; 1969, Chapter 8), citing several studies, focuses on the matriarchal black family as an important intervening variable. When there is no father, or only a weak, despised father, the male adolescent must go to heroic lengths to assert his confused masculine identity and either becomes a delinquent or gives up in apathy. This was also my original interpretation of the Fox problem (Gearing, 1960). The independent variable might be slavery, or job discrimination against Negro males, or sexual jealousy, or whatever. Some of Moynihan's numerous critics have disputed his argument on statistical grounds, pointing out that only 25% of Negro families are matriarchal and that this is not statistically significant in some sense, etc. (Ryan, 1976, Chapter 3; pp. 310–314). One can always argue about statistics. But Stack's participant–observer study of a black ghetto (1974) makes nonsense of Moynihan's data. First, the census and administrative (AFDC) data used by the matriarch theorists are inaccurate. Second, the data collectors use kinship concepts that do not apply to the kinship system of the ghetto. Once one learns the kinship concepts these people actually use one sees that kin networks are not broken, that fathers are very much a part of them, that there is a clear system of expectations and obligations centered on kinship and friendship and therefore no social disorganization and anomie, and consequently there is no unusual masculine identity problem. There is a very serious employment problem, to be sure, and the welfare agencies are highly oppressive. In short, the perspective from inside the subject via participant observation throws doubt not only on the matriarch data but on all survey and census-type data collection imposed on the mass from the elite perspective. Some of these data no doubt are valid; but which? Probably the public opinion and marketing surveys, where the scientist's categories are the same as those of the respondent. But here one faces the familiar problem of creating opinion with the question rather than measuring it. Matza's counter-complaint about "the contrived relativism that currently misleads some anthropologists and sociologists" (1966, p. 652) expresses the survey researcher's desire for universally valid objective data, and therefore his rejection of participant observation as relativistic; but it is precisely Matza's own statistical data that are relativistic—relative to a social problems perspective on the masses.

Second, the universal survey findings of mass apathy are shown up as worthless. Apathy is commonly defined by reference to participation in our elitist democracy and our elite-led voluntary organizations; but this means participation on elite terms and in support of elite programs and leadership. But if there are no rewards for the poor, why should they participate (Wolfe, 1973, pp. 82–85)? Moynihan, Kramer (1969), and others have noted the low rates of ghetto participation in the poverty programs' "community action organization" elections; but if these organizations had no power and no jobs, why should anyone bother? As Marris and Rein note, (1967, Chapter 7, esp. pp. 184–185) community members were induced to get involved early in these programs, but later dropped out; they found a familiar pattern of elite deception—"symbolic rewards"—in operation. And when there were tangible benefits to distribute, the poor did get very actively involved (Mahler, 1976; Portes, 1972).

In addition, apathy is defined as a variable attribute of the poor rather than as a relation between oppressor and oppressed, since the "oppressor" part of this relation is invisible from the elite perspective. As such it is a descendant of an older elite misconcept, "our happy, contented negroes." If resistance to oppression is hopeless, one must make the best of it; and from the outside this looks like apathy.

More generally, elite-perspective studies and all the "social problems" studies produce distorted data insofar as they define an isolated problem out there in the slums. These studies are blind to the sources of poverty in the economic system; poverty is conceived as a universal human problem that we are finally rich enough to be able to solve. Matza asserts that there is no evidence that the US political economy fosters poverty (1966, p. 699); but Cloward and Piven point to the mechanization of Southern agriculture (1940–1960) which produced a huge migration of blacks into Northern cities where there were no jobs (1975, p. x; Piven and Cloward, 1979, pp. 189-205)—a mechanization encouraged by government agricultural policy. Matza discusses the English poor laws of 1795 and 1834 as errors of judgment, but Piven and Cloward point to soaring grain prices and mass starvation and unrest in 1795, resulting from wars with America and France 1971, Chapter 1). I suppose social problems sociologists are not expected to discuss economic problems, and vice versa; that would be unprofessional.

Lack of Overall View

One thing missing from the mass perspective, as also from the elite perspective, is a view of the whole economic system and its dynamics. To conceptualize a dynamic system one needs a formal model of some sort, and this kind of thinking is alien to the mentality of the participant observer. If one feels comfortable seeing society as "people doing things together," as subjects building a common world of meanings or as struggling against oppression, then the view of society as a structure, system, or "mechanism" seems alien and inhuman. The kind of person who goes into social science to get closer to people is different from the kind who likes to build big machines or take things apart to see how they run.

The participant observer can notice the economic-political system affecting his small, vivid world, but the sources of that effect come from beyond his limited horizon. Where did all these poor people of the 1960's come from? They came from the South, Cloward and Piven note (1975, p. x)—Stack's friends came from Mississippi (Stack, 1974)—where they used to be sharecroppers. They were thrown off their farms when the landlords mechanized. Why did Southern agriculture get mechanized from 1940 to 1960? Federal subsidies (Cloward and Piven, 1975, p. 129). Why? This question takes us beyond the horizon of the participant observer. Others came up during the war in the 1940's and were later laid off more or less permanently. Why does the economy work that way? More generally, is it the case that poverty, unemployment, and housing shortages are persistent products of our economic system (Hayes, 1972, p. xiii, Chapter 3)? If so, the elite welfare programs are only a side issue, a small part of a larger problem. Unemployment and bad housing are not simply a result of elite oppression but rather of larger systemic causes beyond even elite control. Similarly, if our social system needs and produces deviants as part of its normal operation, the detailed processes of stigmatization are only a part of a larger process, and could change drastically without reducing the number of deviants or their problems.

Both the elite and the mass conceptual frameworks have readymade categories that obscure this type of problem. The Schumpeterian intellectuals can easily see poverty, bad housing, etc. as part of the human condition to be endured, and can blame utopian intellectuals for stirring up mass expectations unrealistically. The critical intellectuals can easily blame the conditions they see so vividly on elite oppression. In addition there are the usual methodological objections:

it is unscientific to study human beings mathematically or "mechanistically", mathematical models are untestable and therefore unscientific, or they are premature because our survey data on which they ought to be based are not good enough yet.

Tendency to Exaggeration

Mass perspective studies tend to exaggerate the power, foresight, and malevolence of the ruling class. When one views the powerful from the standpoint of the powerless it is easy to attribute responsibility for everything that happens to those distant demons. But the pluralist studies of elite decision-making give us a more human picture of bumbling confusion and hasty expedients, with Dahl's Mayor Lee a remarkable exception. When Moynihan (1969 pp. 75ff.) tells us that the poverty program was almost not adopted at all, that it was primarily an election gimmick for 1965, that it was hastily patched together from existing programs and budget appropriations, that nobody was clear on what it was supposed to do, if anything; or when Pressman and Wildavsky (1973) describe the Oakland employment program as a poorly conceived idea of Foley and Bradford's that immediately aroused bureaucratic opposition because it never even belonged in Foley's agency; then we recognize people pretty much like ourselves, and the malevolent scheming that appears in the mass-perspective studies seems to dissolve into accident and confusion. For instance, Piven (Cloward and Piven, 1975, pp. 320-322) interprets the attacks on city government by local poverty organizations as a deliberate Washington strategy to shake up and reform city government. The community organizers and lawyers were paid for by Federal poverty funds, and city government was in need of reform; so it must all have been planned in advance. But the evidence Moynihan presents about some of the actual decision-making makes such craftiness highly implausible. Similarly, from Hayes' account the Oakland program could be interpreted by the hasty reader as a disguised adjunct to the Vietnam war effort, since the primary recipient of initial grants, World Airways, was heavily involved in transporting materials to Vietnam (1972, pp. 176-177). But from Pressman and Wildavsky's bureaucratic politics account it looks more like a problem of getting money committed—anywhere— by the end of the budget year (1973, pp. 11-13). On the other hand Hayes' account of seventy years of Oakland politics shows that, for all the confusion that one may find in a particular program, the total picture is that of a business elite-dominated political system that has consistently benefited business and oppressed the poor and the working class. The close-up short-run bureaucratic politics perspective does not reveal the whole story either.

Eight Galbraith and the Objectification of Government

This chapter is an immediate continuation of Chapters Four and Five. The standpoint of those chapters was government, the neutral manager and problem-solver, facing an economic-social-political system that needed constant supervision and repair. First, the system's inherent and incurable fluctuations had to be moderated—the economic depression-inflation cycle by countercyclical policy and the political fluctuations in the support system by persuasion and symbolic reassurance. Second, the system's inadequate growth rates had to be brought up to target levels by mobilization of investment capital, social influence, and personal commitments. Economic growth was necessary to maintain full employment; social growth to overcome ethnic and racial conflict; and political growth to bring more Americans into active participation in the political system. Third, there was a set of subsystem problems whose connection to overall system dynamics was not well understood but which might be partly solved by ad hoc efforts, by suboptimizing. These included juvenile delinquency, the pockets of poverty that were somehow bypassed by economic growth, the various growing pains of the new states we were helping into full international status, urban decay, pollution, and depletion of the society's natural resources.

The task of science was to delineate system dynamics and to locate the control points from which the system could be managed. For the smaller social problems the task was similarly to describe the particular vicious circles, information overloads or blocks, imbalances, etc. that maintained some unsatisfactory situation. This was an objective, system-oriented science. As objective, it was also value-free in the sense that the ultimate decision to commit resources to some problem had to be a political decision. Government was the problem-solver, and since there were always more problems than could be handled at any one time, government had to establish the priorities and commit the resources—"find the political will" or the "political courage" to take on the problem. The scientist, as professional specialist in the dynamics of some particular problem, could advise on that problem but could not mobilize the needed resources or estimate its relative urgency.

This standpoint broke down simultaneously on several fronts from about 1966. The economic growth measures designed to maintain full employment produced (or were followed by) inflation, increasing unemployment, and decreasing growth. The civil rights measures designed to bring "full citizenship for the Negro American" were halted by determined resistance, and produced increasing racial polarization. The multifaceted assault on juvenile delinquency did not halt the increase of delinquency rates. The multifaceted poverty program produced small local improvements in employment and education in community projects in New Haven, Pittsburgh, Brooklyn, Oakland but had negligible effects elsewhere and failed to appreciably reduce overall poverty. The foreign aid designed to assist democratic self-development in Vietnam somehow got the US bogged down in an Asian civil war, and foreign aid to other poor countries did not help much either. There were also earlier examples of failure: in the 1950's it had become clear to agricultural economists that the farm program designed to save the family farm was actually destroying the family farm and promoting corporate agriculture. And even earlier, it had become clear that the attempt to redistribute income to the poor via the progressive income tax had failed because of those "loopholes" that had inadvertently been built into it.

Liberal social scientists could explain all these developments perfectly well: in each case government had made a mistake. The economic growth measures were only temporarily effective because government had primarily encouraged business investment, a short-term remedy, rather than income redistribution and investment in human skills, a longer-term remedy. In addition government spent far too much on military equipment and military aid, leaving insufficient funds for expenditures that would encourage growth (Samuelson, 1973a). The civil rights measures were stalled because of inadequate government commitment of resources and persistent white resistance. The juvenile delinquency measures failed to produce jobs, other than temporary dead-end ones. The poverty program never had nearly enough funds, among many other reasons; Vietnam took the funds that should have gone into the poverty program. We got into Vietnam because Truman laid down a rigid, overgeneral containment doctrine that trapped his successors and prevented flexible problem-solving (Gelb, 1979, pp. 365–369). Once in, we backed the wrong man, Diem, and should have looked for the real democrats among the non-communist population. And in 1965, when Kennedy might have extricated us, Johnson took the US reverses as a personal insult and consequently was receptive to the bad advice of people like Rostow, that "fanatic in sheep's clothing" (Hoopes, 1973, p. 61). So we blundered into the quagmire (Arthur Schlesinger). In the Dominican Republic the government was obsessed by the thought, "No More Cubas!" and got panicked by the hasty misjudgment of an incompetent ambassador, Tapley Bennett (Slater, 1970). The farm program centered on measures to maintain market prices when it should have provided direct income maintenance with an upper limit of $20,000 per family. The income tax loopholes were sheer oversight, compounded by the skills of smart income tax lawyers hired by the rich.

In each case, the liberal could add, we learned from our early mistakes and now can offer better advice on all these problems. (For example, Sar Levitan.) In addition we learned that we were over-optimistic in the early 1960's; these problems are very complex and difficult, and we should not expect much success even after decades of continuous effort (Rustin, 1976, p. 63). As a result of this over-optimism we overextended ourselves, and by trying to resolve all problems at once failed to solve any of them.

The above was the dominant reaction in the late 1960's; it enabled the liberal social scientist to deepen his professional researches into some social problem, calling for ever more research funds because of the ever greater complexity of the problem. As for the poor, the unemployed, the Vietnamese, they would have to wait; we were not yet ready to help them. Perhaps another century of professional research would be necessary before we would have enough valid scientific knowledge to deal with social problems (Naroll, et al., 1974, introduction; an extreme estimate).

The other reaction was to question the assumption that the US government was a neutral problem-solver that invariably took the wrong advice. In domestic politics it was always conservative or business-oriented advice that was taken, even by the liberal Kennedy and Johnson administrations; and even in the unusually liberal 1964-1966 Congress the seemingly liberal legislation was spoiled by conservative amendments, or was enforced in a conservative spirit or not at all. The income tax loopholes, for instance, were put there deliberately (Lockard, 1971, Chapters 1, 5). Perhaps the government was not neutral, but dominated by conservatives. In Congress the conservatives controlled most key positions and maintained close working relations with big business; the executive departments similarly worked closely with business, banking and insurance, commercial agriculture, and mining.

But if we come to think of government as dominated by big business, the Southern conservatives, the military–industrial coalition, the agribusiness bloc, then government becomes part of the Object. It no longer stands apart from and above the system it is supposed to manage but becomes a dependent or interdependent part of that same system.

At first sight this might seem to be a simple and obvious development. If science is the objective study of objective system dynamics, then political systems are logically no different from economic or social systems. More generally, the government of any living system, whether organism, personality, family, small group, formal organization, society, or world society, is an integral part of the system and must necessarily be studied by an adequate system science or functionalist science. And indeed such a development, the objective study of political systems and of organizations treated as political systems, was occurring in the 1950's. But all such studies and theories exempted the top leadership, the chairman of the board or the President and his immediate advisers. The top leadership was studied subjectively, by case study that portrayed a problematic situation and its attempted solution. The President faces pressures coming from everywhere: "Congress and the press tried to keep the President's feet to the fire and had several other pots boiling for him no matter which way he jumped" (Gelb, 1979, p. 274). He studies these pressures, takes advice, deliberates, and decides on a policy. The reason for treating the President subjectively is simple. If the purpose of our science is to provide advice on how to maintain or reform some system, to whom do we offer that advice? Whoever it is, we must assume that person to be free, not system-determined, otherwise our advice and our science would be pointless.

And in fact the shift of standpoint in which government becomes part of the Object, part of the problem, has been difficult and sometimes painful. It has involved giving up a personal loyalty to

Presidents Kennedy and Johnson for some; for others, resignation from government service and/or RAND, followed by tapped telephones and both legal and illegal government persecution (Ellsberg, Halperin). In general, government could not become a neutral part of the Object until one had become emotionally detached from it, even disloyal to it. The social problems scientists and systems analysts were value-free only in the sense that they did not presume to judge the relative importance of their problem compared to other problems; their loyalty and respect for the government was unquestioned. The Vietnam war was the primary cause of disillusionment and therefore the primary source of the objectification of government (for example Schurmann, 1974, pp. xvii, 561–562; Lockard, 1971, p. vii), though the same shift occurred in individual cases before 1965.

The best known and most influential economist to undergo this shift is Galbraith. Based on his published writings, the shift occurred between 1961 and 1970 as part of a steady leftward drift lasting at least twenty years. In 1952, his government is the impartial arbiter that maintains a power equilibrium, and in 1955 his government is the impartial Keynesian manager of the economy. In 1958 he can still be seen as giving urgent advice to government on our perverted priorities, and in 1960 he did agree to advise Kennedy. But by 1967 government is part of the technostructure, and as head of Americans for Democratic Action in 1968 Galbraith opposed both Johnson and Johnson's war in Vietnam (cf. Destler's comment on Galbraith's striking shift of position between 1961 and 1967, 1972, pp. 32, 79). Galbraith's 1973 work develops more systematically the 1967 view of government as part of the Object.

Galbraith's recent views are representative of the institutionalists, a sizeable group of economists organized around the *Journal of Economic Issues*, and tracing their ancestry back to Veblen and Ayres.

We begin therefore with the categories and main arguments of Galbraith's *Economics and the Public Purpose* (1973), the most developed example of the standpoint treating government as part of the Object. Then we turn to other studies, chiefly in bureaucratic politics, that supplement Galbraith's work.

I. Galbraith

Over the last century the economy has steadily polarized into two opposites, the planning sector and the market sector. Other economists have called them the monopoly sector and the competitive sector.

Polarization results directly from the competitive process, understood not in the neoclassical sense as an impersonal movement of resources but in the game-theoretic sense as the attempts of individual businessmen to survive and prosper among and against other players. Survival in an uncertain environment depends partly on adapting oneself to the environment and partly on controlling and adapting the environment to one's own needs. The neoclassical economists emphasized the former process; Galbraith emphasizes the latter (1973, p. 39, 47). But control requires power, and market power depends mainly on relative size (pp. 40, 83); so the imperative of survival brings with it the imperative of growth. Galbraith calls these two imperatives the protective and affirmative purposes of the business firm (Chapter 10).

The two imperatives are valid for all firms, but in some sectors of the economy growth is technically difficult or impossible at present. The firms in these sectors must limit their control efforts to the cultivation of market imperfections (p. 47). The firms in the remaining sectors must expand without limit, or go under; so over time the planning and the market sectors become increasingly different.

As firms expand and become corporations, internal motivations to grow supplement the original survival motivation. An expanding corporation opens more opportunities for promotion than a static one, and thus is better able to attract and retain managerial staff. Also the expansion of a division or department in terms of sales or profit margins is likely to be taken as evidence of competence and to be rewarded by top management (pp. 100–102; cf. Williamson, 1970, pp. 50–52).

Profit is a closely interconnected part of the survival-growth goal set, so that the much-discussed issue of profit vs. growth is a false one (R. Marris, 1968). Short-run profit is necessary for both survival and growth, and growth is a means to long-run profit. Profit rates are one set of measures of growth, along with dividends, sales, and market share (Galbraith, 1971, Chapters 14, 15). However, maximum profit is not a goal, because as Galbraith observes (1973, p. 107) there is no way of specifying it empirically. The concept of maximum long-run profit is as objectively meaningless as that of maximum utility, under uncertainty and oligopoly (cf. Chapter 2 Section 2 above) and over a long time-span.

The corporation controls its environment in several different ways. It controls other corporations, both suppliers and customers, by negotiating contracts, preferably continuing ones (1973, Chapter 8; cf. Cyert and March, 1963, pp. 119-120). It also negotiates contracts with labor unions and with government customers. As in all negotiation, the advantage goes to the most powerful, but there is also a substantial common interest in mutual survival against competitors; it is often more like alliance bargaining than adversary bargaining, Leader or Protector rather than Chicken. It controls scarce raw materials by long-range acquisition programs; when the raw materials are in another country or area, this constitutes economic imperialism (p. 123). Imperialism is a form of exploitation because the superior market power of the corporation enables it to set favorable terms of trade both in acquisition and in later exploitation of the raw materials.

Corporations also use their government friends, their allies or partners, to control various threats—threats to their material supplies in other countries, legal restrictions on production or marketing, entry of new competitors. The latter can be kept out by legal restrictions. National barriers to production and trade—import and export controls, currency controls, etc.—are evaded by setting up or buying branch firms in the target country (Chapter 17; cf. also Aharoni, 1966).

Consumers are controlled by advertising, which both induces wants for one's products and a general probusiness, consumption-oriented culture (Chapter 14; R. Marris, 1968). Neoclassical economic theory is also useful in promoting the endless expansion of frivolous consumption. In addition it mystifies the whole process with its myth of consumer sovereignty; the illusion of freedom prevents the consumer from realizing what has happened to him. Technical innovation and planned obsolescence is also used to increase consumption (pp. 150ff.). Labor-saving innovations are aimed more at controllability than at efficiency, since machines are more controllable than people.

The executive branch of government is organizationally analogous to a large corporation, and therefore has the same *internal* motivation to expand without limit (pp. 141–144). Each department is in competition with every other for the budget dollar, though coalitions form, and the President and his assistants have to keep the total down without alienating any of the more powerful departments. Each department has as natural allies its suppliers and customers among the private corporations, since public expansion benefits the private corporation as well; the best known example is the Pentagon and the weapons manufacturers. Galbraith calls this "bureaucratic symbiosis." The analogy between government and private corporation is only sketched by Galbraith and is developed more fully by bureaucratic politics theorists.

Portions of the market sector also try to make alliances and get help from government. Individual firms cannot do this because they have no market power and therefore nothing to offer government in return;

but organizations of firms can meet some divisions of government on an equal level. Market-sector organizations usually make alliances in the weak legislative branch, while large corporations mainly connect with the strong executive branch and the regulatory agencies (Chapter 16, p. 159). Farm organizations, controlled by the planning sector, have been especially successful in getting government assistance in the form of technical research and protection of capital investment via price supports (pp. 48–49). This has enabled the agriculture sector to increase efficiency greatly and to reduce labor costs since 1940.

Note how the perspective on government as part of the Object produces a different interpretation of agribusiness policy. Price supports were not a misguided attempt to save the family farm that accidentally produced exactly the opposite effect. They were a product of bureaucratic symbiosis between the Department of Agriculture, agribusiness, the agricultural marketing corporations, and plantation owners like Senator Eastland. Their purpose was to help the planning sector in agriculture; and this help successfully speeded up the expansion of the planning sector and the decline of the market or family farm sector. The propaganda about saving the family farm, provided by the liberal agricultural economists like Rainer Schickele and T.W. Schultz, was a smokescreen that kept the family farmers quiet while they were being ruined.

If we consider the dynamics of the whole system including the planning sector, market sector, and government, we see that the system must necessarily expand without limit. There is no check on the growth drive of the corporations and their allies in government bureaus. In former times expansion was chronically slowed down by demand deficiency in which production expanded faster than consumption and investment (Chapter 18). However, by 1945 Western governments learned to cope with demand deficiency by increasing public spending and by encouraging increased investment; "the Keynesian Revolution was, in effect, absorbed by the planning system" (p. 183).

A second dynamic is the continuous redistribution of wealth from the market sector to the planning sector, so that the disparity between the two grows even greater. One mechanism of redistribution is direct bargaining over exchange prices; since the planning sector has the power to set prices, it can guarantee itself favorable terms of trade (pp. 50–51, 77). Another mechanism is the recession cycle brought on by demand deficiency. Recession is brought on by overinvestment, overexpansion, in the planning sector, but the resulting unemployment and bankruptcies are felt mostly in the market sector. The large corporation can produce for inventory or can cut production rather than prices in recession, and can survive a long period of losses, but the small businessman has no cushion against recession and must close or go bankrupt. Similarly, the unionized worker in the planning sector has several cushions against unemployment, while the non-unionized worker without seniority in the dead-end market sector has none.

Another mechanism of redistribution is inflation, which inevitably accompanies system growth (Chapter 19). One source of inflation is bargaining within the planning sector: union-management bargaining in which unions get wage increases and management raises prices; bargaining between the Defense Department and its weapons suppliers, in which the suppliers get cost-plus contracts and the Defense Department gets a dependable supply of new weapons. Since corporations have the power to pass cost increases on via price increases (p. 187), these increases accelerate through the planning-government sectors and come to rest in the market sector which cannot pass them on. The market sector must ultimately pay for corporate wage increases, R&D expenses, and government cost-plus contracts. Another source of inflation is the continuous bureaucratic pressure for unbalanced budgets. The President's task is to slow down departmental expansion without alienating key departments and their corporate allies, that is without damaging business confidence, but it is much easier to pass on the needed increases via unbalanced budgets.

Government fiscal and monetary policy also helps the planning sector and hurts the market sector—and this is to be expected, given the symbiotic relationship of government with the planning sector (pp. 183-184, 192-194). The same alliance also explains the ineffectiveness of anti-inflation policies—the only true remedy for inflation, permanent wage and price controls, will not be adopted by a corporation-dominated government because it destroys the corporations' market power, so inflation is a permanent part of the present system (pp. 194-197).

In summary, we are living in a system that grows without limit, with periodic recessions and continuous inflation, that continually redistributes wealth and power from market-sector businessmen and workers to large corporations, and that continually teaches people to desire and consume what is being produced and to believe in the inevitability and goodness of the system.

If we compare Galbraith's conceptual framework with those presented in earlier chapters, we see first that his treatment of the planning sector is the opposite of Schumpeter's. The Schumpeterian glorification of big business as the locus of creativity, intelligence, and responsibility is replaced by a study of objective system dynamics; there is a shift from subjective freedom to objective necessity. The businessman still has some freedom, and a few may be extremely creative, but his creativity must be shaped by the necessary goal of expanding without limit, and of maintaining control within his own organization. Even the most creative entrepreneur, a Henry Ford or Robert Moses, has his goals set by the expansionist and organizational dynamics of the planning sector. Moreover, the day of the creative Henry Ford types is over; today's board chairmen are organization men (1971, Chapter 8).

Galbraith's similarity is rather with the Keynesian and the Cyert-March-Simon organization theory frameworks of Chapter Four. Galbraith's account of the corporation follows closely the Cyert and March 1963 account, including corporate goals, bounded rationality in decisionmaking, and the emphasis on control of the environment through bargaining and advertising. The Keynesian conception of the economy as a circular-flow system that must grow at an ever-increasing rate to absorb its own products is also similar to Galbraith's conception. Also both are theories of the short run. The kinship is with the left Keynesians, who share Galbraith's concern for the poor, unemployed, and small business victims of economic progress. What Galbraith does is combine the micro organization theory concepts with the macro Keynesian concepts to produce a more adequate, more integrated theory of system dynamics. The "micro-macro problem" that was used to torment so many economics students of the 1950's disappears in Galbraith; it was a pseudoproblem resulting from Keynes' mistaken belief that the neoclassical theory was an adequate microtheory.

Farther in the background is evidence that the neoclassical models have been absorbed and assigned a minor explanatory role as ideal limits, principally in the competitive sector (pp. 186, 187, 180-181). However, for Galbraith the neoclassical models are almost entirely a distortion and disguise of reality, propaganda rather than science, because they systematically deny the existence of power in the economy. For Galbraith power pervades the economy: first in the oligopolistic games of the planning sector, second in government-business relations, third in planning sector control of the terms of trade with the market sector, fourth in the imperialist control of resources in weaker countries, and fifth in the general scramble forced on everyone by permanent inflation. The powerful stay ahead in this scramble, not simply "the more active members of society" (Boulding.)

The combination of organizational and system dynamics enables Galbraith to transcend both organization and system theories by including government in the system. Government as an organization is similar to a private corporation and therefore determined by similar dynamics. Government budgets and prices therefore can be explained objectively as the consequences of bureaucratic symbiosis, rather than subjectively as bad advice, mistakes of judgment, or Presidential bias. The top man in an organization is not exempt from organization and system dynamics, as he is for the organization theorists. Systemically he is bound by the imperative of growth; internally, he must hold down his subordinates' push for ever more resources and must mediate their disputes. This argument applies to government as well, though Galbraith does not develop it, asserting merely that top government officials are the captives of their subordinates (p. 87).

The scientific advance, as well as the close similarity of conceptual framework, can be seen by comparing Galbraith, 1973, and Williamson, 1970, a carrier of the Cyert–March–Simon tradition. Williamson's discussion of organization goals and dynamics is in agreement with Galbraith's until the last few pages. However, Williamson avoids the whole question of power struggles within an organization and tacitly assumes that the board chairman is a dictator able to reorganize the structure at will. On page 164 he mentions that division managers may get too much influence over policymaking due to carelessness and other errors at the top, but trusts that survival pressures will force restoration of power to the top where it belongs. Here Williamson's systems perspective in which the top of an organization is Subject has interfered with scientific objectivity. It is simply assumed that the *normal* distribution of power is one of total control by the Subject, and departures from the norm are blamed on carelessness or other errors by the Subject, just as failures to control inflation or end the Vietnam war are explained by others as accidental mistakes by government. The proper scientific procedure would be to study organizational power struggles as they occur, without assuming any particular outcome as the normal one. Surely every division manager must try to increase the power and resources of his division, or at least be alert to prevent them from being whittled away, and the central authority must balance these pressures to maintain his independence. But such study requires detachment from any particular standpoint within an organization; it requires Galbraith's standpoint in which the whole system including government is Object.

It seems, then, that for Galbraith we are all part of the system and no one is free. Many people have a maneuver space, which they can expand somewhat, but they must use this space to meet the imperatives of growth and survival for their department, division, bureau, corporation. Even the consumer has a range of choice over which food additive is going to poison him. But no one, including the government, has the power to halt the endless growth of the system or to correct its many evils.

That the system is morally evil is obvious (Chapter 20). It fosters ever-increasing inequality and therefore poverty and misery; it produces useless and harmful commodities in abundance and endemic shortages of necessary commodities; it corrupts people's values so they will desire to consume the harmful commodities, turning women into exploited domestic servants in the process; it pollutes the environment; it keeps underdeveloped countries in imperialist oppression.

We can not expect government to correct any of the evils of the system. The objectification of government has enabled Galbraith to see that government is too much a dependent part of the planning sector to have any substantial freedom of action toward the corporations. Government is part of the problem.

To whom then do we report these findings? Who will reform this evil system? Who is Subject? The answer is—the government. "The government is a major part of the problem; it is also central to the remedy" (p. 242). There are actually two governments from Galbraith's perspective. One, the existing government, is not free to reform anything; it is determined by its own bureaucratic growth imperatives and its myriad alliances with the corporate sector. It is both corrupt and helpless. We ignore this government; we offer it no advice. The other is the ideal government that could be voted into office by an aroused electorate. This government would derive its power from the people and would therefore be independent of the corporations. Consequently it need not show any favoritism and could in fact control the planning sector and subordinate it to the public purpose. The main instruments of control, comprehensive planning and permanent price and wage controls, would work because of the impartiality of a people's government, in contrast to the biased controls exercised by past governments. (See Gruchy, 1974, for the same argument.)

But there are also two electorates, the real and the ideal ones. The present, real electorate is not free; it has been corrupted by governmental symbolic politics, corporate advertising, and the propaganda of the neoclassical economists. The real electorate believes in consumer sovereignty, free enterprise, endlessly increasing consumption, symbolic democracy, and the wisdom and morality of the elite. Consequently, it has no power and only a narrow range of freedom. The ideal electorate would be emancipated from this indoctrination (Chapter 22) and would therefore vote for Galbraith's ADA-sponsored candidates. The result would be a reform liberal government emancipated from the power of the corporations, which would move decisively to break that power and reform the system (Chapter 24).

"The first step in reform, it follows, is to win emancipation of belief" (p. 221). Freedom, from this perspective, is emancipation from the false beliefs and values of an evil system, and adoption of socialist values in which men and women will live in harmony with one another and with Nature (pp. 225–226). Few people are free today; we have arrived at the opposite extreme from the neoclassical standpoint in which all men, with insignificant exceptions, are free. Nor are the prospects for emancipation bright; the vast propaganda resources of the planning sector will most likely keep the public mind in bondage. However, we know that emancipation is not impossible because it does actually occur. Galbraith is encouraged by recent loss of confidence in government, business, and the military, by the New Left counterculture (pp. 230–231) and the women's movement (p. 233).

Since people have been corrupted by false beliefs, emancipation is achieved by spreading true beliefs. Here is the scientist's proper role: to be the professional advisor and teacher of the people, not of government. The truly liberal scientist is one who liberates people, not one who becomes a technical servant of the planning system. The odds against success are great because of the vastly superior resources of corporations and government, but he makes the attempt against the odds because he sees no alternative way to reform the system.

The theme of reeducating the people so they will reform an evil system is one mark of the reform liberal. When Ellsberg discovered the extensive US war crimes in Indochina, he felt a responsibility to tell the full truth to the American people. The people had to be made aware of the constant Government deception and of what was actually happening; they had to recognize their own complicity in these crimes so they could repent and vote out the gang of war criminals in Washington. This was an act of faith and hope in the people (Ellsberg, 1972, p. 40) and in their repesentative, Senator Fulbright (1972, Chapter 3). We find Halperin becoming a radio commentator, moving from the liberal Brookings Institution to the farther left Center for National Security Studies, and meanwhile suing the government in an attempt to publicize some of its secret crooked dealings; one could not imagine a Cold War liberal, a Harlan Cleveland or Theodore Sorenson, suing the government. Similarly, after Lockard

(1971) details the evils of the present system, including the biased judiciary that Galbraith does not discuss, he declares that the American people are ultimately responsible; they are just as militarist and imperialist and racist and plain mad as government officials are (Lockard, 1971, pp. 304, 318–319, Chapter 8). The remedy is to spread correct ideas (Chapter 9); the power of ideas will emancipate the people from error and madness.

Here we see another similarity between the Galbraithian standpoint and the Keynesian-systems-social problems standpoint. In both cases a sharp fact-value distinction coincides with a sharp object-subject distinction. Science is purely objective and factual; moral evaluation, exhortation, responsibility, faith and hope are in the domain of the Subject. There is no science of the Subject. The professional scientist mediates and relates Object and Subject in his dual role as scientist and advisor. Howard Becker's question, "Whose Side Are We On?" (1970, Chapter 8) and his argument that the social scientist *as scientist necessarily* sides with either the superior or the subordinate power in his evaluation of data and his choice of problems makes sense to the elitist intellectuals and the critical intellectuals, but makes no sense to the Chapters Four, Five, and Eight perspectives. For these people taking sides is a personal, not a scientific issue; as scientists they are neutral.

The separation of fact and value also brings with it a separation of determinism and freedom, of material conditions (Object) and ideas (Subject). Either the public mind is determined by the objective routines of work, the pressures of organizational maintenance, the propaganda of marketing departments, or it is freed by the power of ideas. Changing material conditions bring with them changes in mentality, but no freedom. To be sure, ideas get their power in part from the supporting evidence that material conditions provide; pain and discomfort are more persuasive than mere abstract argument (Galbraith, 1973, Chapter 22). However, many of the evils of the present system, like the Vietnam war, provide no direct pain and discomfort, so we have to depend on the power of ideas. In contrast, for Schumpeter ideas and values are a reflection of material conditions and change only as those conditions change; but conditions are changed by the Subject. There is an object-subject dialectic rather than an object-subject dualism.

II. Organizational Dynamics and Bureaucratic Politics

The central empirical topic opened up by the objectification of government is government itself. Objectively speaking, the Executive Branch in particular is a large organization whose dynamics are much the same as those of other large organizations. The Defense Department controls its supplier corporations much like the central office of a large corporation controls its branches and subsidiaries (Melman, 1970). The President and his staff are subjected to organizational pressures and action imperatives similar to those at the top of any corporation. There are also differences, of course.

The dynamics of large organizations are simple: they persist and they expand (Kharasch, 1973; Melman, 1974, p. 186). The basis of persistence is the fact that an official's mentality is conditioned by his or her official responsibilities, in a variety of ways, and she comes to believe that her work is important and should be continued. The basis of expansion is the fact that any department can do a better job with slightly more resources, jurisdiction, and influence with superiors, so the conscientious official pushes for more.

The internal politics of an organization is a consequence of these two dynamics. Given that each department believes in the importance of its own work and is constantly trying to get or retain the resources and support needed to do its work well, then internal politics is a struggle for resources, jurisdiction, and influence. The way to win is to get the whole organization to define its current problems in terms of one's departmental outlook. Each departmental view of the world, of course, is one in which its own work and the work of its allies is important. In other words, the material struggle for resources appears as a rational argument over what problems face the organization and how they should be solved.

The opposite relation is also possible: "Advocacy by the military of a particular weapons system is, in fact, advocacy of a certain foreign policy current" (Schurmann, 1974, p. 425). That is, the policy struggle can appear as a material struggle for resources.

This does not mean that the argument is hypocritical. On the contrary, the participants are sincere and earnest. It merely means that their mentality has been conditioned by their departmental responsibilities: their sensitivity to problems and resources in the environment, their practical principles and common sense rules, their tactical ingenuity all express their departmental socialization and experience.

The results of bureaucratic struggle are expressed in the organization's policy decisions—its assessment of the problematic situation, its preferred strategy, and its budget. Policy decisions normally express a compromise, either among the main factions of a winning coalition or between two opposing coalitions. The struggle does not end when a policy decision is made; it continues in discussion of tactics, in implementation, in feedback of results and in their evaluation, and in the later memoirs and histories.

Here we have the bureaucratic politics perspective. Its essence is the attempt to understand organizational decisions not as a rational response to an external problem but as an expression of internal struggle rooted in organizational dynamics. The former approach treats government as Subject; the latter treats it as Object.

The bureaucratic politics writers of the 1970's mostly trace their ideas back to Neustadt's *Presidential Power* (1960). This work, as well as Neustadt, 1970 and 1975, is squarely in the social problems-systems analysis perspective of Chapter Five. Thus the shift from Neustadt to the bureaucratic politics perspective parallels Galbraith's shift from a Keynesian perspective some ten years earlier. In both cases the shift involved the objectification of government. To see what conceptual changes were involved in this shift, let us compare Neustadt with his followers of the 1970's.

For Neustadt the President is responsible for managing the many domestic and foreign problems facing the country (1960, Chapter 4, pp. 188–191). His instrument for managing problems is the Executive Branch, the organization. But in order to use his instrument he must first achieve control over it; his first and fundamental responsibility is to get power over the organization. Most of *Presidential Power* is an account of how difficult this task is, plus advice on how a President can and must do it. The President ought, however, exercise moral self-restraint in the use of this power once he collects it (1975). Thus the President and his advisers, as Subject, confront the organization as Object. This is a perspective on government from the standpoint of the White House—where Neustadt himself later served as adviser to Kennedy.

The resistance of the organization is not the result of the routinization inherent in bureaucracy, as it is for elite-perspective theorists like Huntington (1960) and Campbell (1971), the two editors of *Foreign Policy*. Remember that for the Schumpeterian elitist the subject-object categories are creativity and routinization; the political entrepreneur, Kennedy or Rickover or Moses, must break through bureaucratic inertia to deal creatively with new problems and opportunities. Also he must counteract the organization's inherent tendency to routinize by periodically reorganizing it.

For Neustadt the resistance of the organization comes from organizational dynamics, which in turn are based on officials' sense of responsibility. The conscientious official wishes to do a good job and therefore needs resources and the support of his superiors. He views other agencies and the outside world from the perspective of his own job: other agencies are competitors for resources and support and in any case have a warped view of the world and always project their own narrow problems onto it. Some agencies are allies, with a more sensible view of the world, and the world itself is the source of the problem his department must manage. In short, the official's mentality is conditioned by his experience in office. His resistance to pressures from other officials—who may have talked the President into supporting them—is not a matter of inertia but of conscientiousness, though some bureaucratic inertia does occur. His office is not a fudge factory (Campbell) or bowlful of jelly (Kennedy); the State department's resistance to Kennedy was not based on inertia but on the opinion that he had been misled by bad advice into pursuing bad policies. Consequently for Neustadt the President cannot deal with the organization by simply "getting it moving", shaking it up, reorganizing it; he must persuade officials that they can do their job better his way, or get their co-operation in his policies by helping them with their problems.

Neustadt's White House perspective on the organization was shared by other writers of the 1960's and 1970's coming out of various traditions, such as Wilensky (1967), Williamson (1970), and Destler (1972), the best work in this field. Destler comments on his work, "The author adopted a Hamiltonian, Rooseveltian view of government as the developer and pursuer of positive national purposes" (Destler, in Wildavsky, 1975b, p. 312). These writers share Neustadt's concern with Presidential control; they study the structural characteristics and deficiencies of organizations, and recommend improvements. For instance Wilensky (1967) studies how information is distorted as it moves through an organization; Destler (1972) studies deficiencies in decision-making and implementation and concludes that the president ought to coordinate his foreign policy apparatus through the Secretary of State rather than through his own foreign policy advisor. The ideal for these writers is an organization that adequately filters and organizes incoming information, provides correct and varied information and advice to the central decision-maker, and faithfully carries out decisions once they are made, within constraints set by previous decisions.

The shift to the bureaucratic politics perspective involves simply including the top man in one's theory—a simple and obvious shift scientifically, but a difficult divide to cross in practice (cf. Ellsberg, 1972, p. 34: "The President was part of the problem."). The impetus for the shift in many though not all cases was the Vietnam war, which alienated the scientist from the whole Executive Branch including the President. These people no longer write about U.S. foreign policy, shield of the Republic, but about (ugh) foreign policy (Kharasch, 1973, Chapter 14).

Halperin (1974) and Schurmann (1974) are two outstanding products of this shift. Halperin distinguishes three general kinds of mentality in an organization. 1) *Partisan thinking* or "grooved" thinking characterizes the permanent officials in an organization. Their mentality is determined primarily by their departmental responsibilities and standard operating practices; their goal is the successful implementation of departmental programs. To achieve this goal they must strive for growth in their department's power and resources. The partisan can be counted on to push his departmental viewpoint in contacts with his superiors. This whole concept is taken directly from Neustadt.

2) *Ideological thinking* generally characterizes the in-and-outer, the temporary official coming from business, law, or academic life. Department officials are also more or less ideological. This mentality is dominated by the belief systems of the political culture, in the US from 1945 to 1970, by the Cold War consensus (pp. 11-12). (At other times conflicting ideologies can be present in an organization and produce sharp divisions, even within the same department, for instance Britain 1900-1914; France, 1920-1924 and 1936-1940—P.D.) The ideologue can be counted on to push his view of the world at conferences, and the power of his opinions derive from the fact that influential groups in the country share them. The most influential group in the US is the Eastern Liberal Foreign Policy Establishment centered in the Council on Foreign Relations (p. 74), a group closely associated with big business. The Cold War consensus has also been broadly shared by the voters, but this is itself a consequence of political propaganda put out by the government and the Liberal Establishment since 1945 (pp. 78-79; cf. Edelman, 1964, Chapter 9).

3) *Uncommitted thinking* characterizes the top decision-maker and his allies. He is continually under pressure from various directions, continually receiving conflicting information and advice. He is not free to ignore this advice because it is backed by power, either the power of key departments whose animosity would ruin him (partisans) or the power of broad groups in the country who could defeat him in the next election or in Congress (ideologues). But he usually

cannot accept it all because it conflicts. Consequently he must stall, accepting what he must, compromising where possible, postponing where possible, maneuvering and bargaining. The pressures on him broadly determine his decision, though he is free to determine the details by much maneuvering and bargaining. Halperin's account gives substance to Galbraith's laconic statement that the President—in government and industry—is the captive of his subordinates. This is not invariably true for Halperin, and there are many qualifications. Point three is Halperin's principal addition to Neustadt's ideas.

Schurmann (1974), using a broader historical data base than Halperin, comes to a somewhat different arrangement of Halperin's three categories. Schurmann deals with the bureaucratic foreign politics of the US, SU, and China from 1943-1973, and his paradigm example is the Chinese Cultural Revolution. He distinguishes a politics of interests and one of ideology. Interests include Halperin's categories of partisan and uncommitted thinking, and also bureaucratic symbiosis with the corporations. But ideology does not just blunder awkwardly into government via Rostow-type ideologues, as for Halperin; it comes directly from the President or Party chairman. The Cold War ideology that vaguely but pervasively annoys Halperin comes directly from Truman, who adapted Roosevelt's grand ideological vision of a world New Deal to the partisan thinking of 1945. Ideology is the President's way of marshalling power against his subordinates, as Mao did in 1965, Khrushchev did in 1956, and Roosevelt tried to do in 1944. It expresses and mobilizes the aspirations of the masses, sweeps them into politics behind their leader, and may—as in revolutions—sweep away the entrenched interests and their politics. Ideological politics are always democratic, mobilizing the masses, and interest politics are always elitist. (Schurmann, incidentally, has absorbed the Schumpeterian perspective into a bureaucratic-politics perspective, a remarkable achievement.) Interest politics tend to stagnate; ideologies are creative visions (Schumpeter's creative destruction) that reorganize political forces, until they are gradually routinized by interest politics (Schurmann, 1974, p. 29).

The source of possible ideological visions is the aspirations of the masses—which may in turn have been conditioned by previous ideological politics. Also, mass aspirations are only mobilizable in critical or crisis periods; at other times the leader has to carry on with the ideological weapon of his predecessor.

Halperin's chief example is the decision in 1967 to build a limited antiballistic missile system; he shows that this decision was a stall by the President, who accommodated himself after much maneuvering to the sharply opposed pressures on him (cf. also Hoopes, 1973, p. 84). Ellsberg (1972, Chapter 1) provides a much longer example, the US involvement in Vietnam from 1947-1972. He shows that this was one long stall in which contradictory decision axioms immobilized five successive Presidents. The power of the axioms—a combination of partisan and ideological pressures—came from the departments and public opinion groups supporting them.

Here is a *fourth* explanation of the Vietnam war (for the previous three see pp. 135, 178, 190), which must be completed by describing the power of the groups supporting the contradictory axioms (cf. Melman, 1974, and Schurmann, 1974).

According to Melman (1974, pp. 264ff.) the forces pushing for involvement and escalation in Vietnam, namely the national security bureaucracy, were simultaneously partisan and ideological. The military defined Vietnam as a military problem and wished to test and improve their weapons systems there. But the whole Cold War ideology shared by the National Security Council, the CIA, and the military, made involvement obligatory. If the US were to fulfill its historic responsibility of defending the Free World against Communist aggression it must seek out and support democratic governments everywhere. Then, having given a guarantee of support, it must keep its word to demonstrate its reliability and resolve. Accordingly, its purpose was not to win or even to save Vietnam from ruin but rather to *avoid defeat*, thereby showing Communists all over the world that aggression would be costly for them (p. 267). Note that this is a deterrence argument. Barnet (1972, Chapters 4, 5) adds a detailed analysis of various phrases and concepts in the Cold War ideology— "the operational code of the national security managers"—showing how they serve to justify and disguise bureaucratic homicide. Or rather genocide, disguised as body counts and doing one's job (Schurmann, 1974, p. 458).

Schurmann describes Vietnam as "a bureaucratic war from beginning to end" (p. 458). He locates two opposed partisan-ideological forces within the national security bureaucracy, and explains detailed changes in US policy in terms of the continuing struggle between them (pp. 401-561). The stronger of the two forces, the push, was the "conservative" rollback ideology, which defined the opponent as the Sino-Soviet block and whose favored tactics led via North Vietnam to war with China. The ideologues ranged from the China lobby through Congressional forces in both parties to military spokesmen like Chennault and MacArthur. Their allies were the rollback regimes in South Vietnam, Taiwan, and South Korea. The partisans included the Navy, the Air Force, and the CIA, the departments that would be active in a war with China. The actual guerilla war in China was already being conducted by the CIA from bases in northern Laos and Quemoy and used mercenaries in Burma, Laos, and Taiwan–Quemoy. A larger war would be an air war conducted by the Air Force and carriers of the Seventh Fleet.

The opposing force, the drag, was the "liberal" containment ideology, which defined the US goal as maintaining the integrity of the 17th parallel border of South Vietnam and maintaining the credibility of US commitments (for example, Payne, 1970). The ideologues included Dean Rusk and the Eastern Liberal Foreign Policy Establishment like Dean Acheson. The partisans were the Army, the least influential of the military services, which would be the most active in defending the 17th parallel, and whose military advice was often refuted by the rollback CIA. The five Presidents were forced to support the weaker side to maintain their independence of the dominant military coalition and thereby their own power. This is Schurmann's version of Halperin's "uncommitted thinking." However, each rejection of rollback advice had to be compensated by some appropriate concession, and the result was the long stalemate that Ellsberg chronicles.

The bureaucratic politics perspective does not force us to assume that the President or managing director is invariably a captive of his subordinates or, conversely, invariably the creative entrepreneur. It asserts rather that both the President and his subordinates must try to maintain and expand their power, and that the outcomes are varied. In the realm of interests, Schurmann agrees with Halperin that the President tends to become a captive of the strongest partisan force, and the phenomena of stall and compromise are common; but ideological politics free the President or Party chairman by mobilizing the masses behind his charismatic leadership. Ideology mobilizes the masses by announcing a great crisis and a great vision of a better world, and at times of crisis and reorganization power flows toward the top (p. 497). Thus the Truman Doctrine was not a mistake, the mistake that got us into Vietnam as Gelb (1979) asserts; it was Truman's way to take power over his government. It was the only way he could do his job properly. The particular distribution of influence, both between President and subordinates and among bureaus, thus becomes an empirical question.

In contrast, the systems or social-problems perspective closes off the empirical question of how much power the top man has, because it defines him as Subject who is beyond objective investigation. In effect this perspective forces one to assume that the top man normally has all the power he needs, and if he does not, this is due to carelessness, inattention, or errors on his part (for example Williamson, 1970, pp. 164–166; Krasner, 1972). As Krasner argues, if the top man has no power we cannot blame him for the continual mistakes of government, and we need someone to blame.

The contrast comes out in Murdock's study of PPBS in the Defense Department (1974; cf. also Wildavsky, 1967). PPBS is a form of systems analysis that enables the analyst to estimate the costs and returns of alternate expenditures of a department's funds. The department head then can choose the particular combination of programs that maximizes expected returns from a given budgetary level. Systems analysis does not deal with bureaucratic power, so it tacitly assumes that the department head has enough power to choose the best alternative; or if he does not, it assumes that power is a political question beyond the professional competence of the systems analyst. Murdock shows that PPBS was in fact a political device that Defense Secretary McNamara used to take power away from the four military branches, a device to centralize power. As Wildavsky observes, centralization is inherently demanded by PPBS (1967, pp. 41–44). Murdock also shows that the military learned to fight back, effectively, using the same systems-analysis technicalities to block McNamara, and that the outcome was a draw. But even this outcome left McNamara with more power than any Secretary of Defense before or since; PPBS was temporarily an effective device. This whole struggle, which is of the essence of politics from the bureaucratic politics perspective, is necessarily invisible to the systems analyst, who can say at most that McNamara tried to rationalize the Defense Department and failed.

The bureaucratic politics perspective also broadens our empirical grasp of international diplomatic relations. Much of Halperin's argument (1974) as also of Allison (1971) is devoted to showing that deterrence theory, the "rational actor" perspective of Chapter Three above, misses much of what goes on empirically because no government is remotely like a rational actor. But the systems perspective of Chapter Five is also inadequate. The systems perspective enables one to see positive feedback systems, Richardson process models, that trap governments into courses of action with disastrous consequences like war. One such system is the arms race, in which a country's defensive armaments force the opponent to defensively improve his armaments, and so on to disaster. The bureaucratic politics perspective enables one to see an alternative interpretation of armament expansion: it could simply be the bureaucratic imperative to expand without limit. The opponent's armaments or potential armaments simply provide a convenient excuse for military departments to use at budget time. The issue between the two hypotheses then becomes an empirical one: to what extent is military budget expansion determined internally and to what extent is it determined by an international action–reaction system? Senghaas (1972, 1973) and Rattinger (1974, 1975) have investigated this question empirically and concluded that for both NATO and the Warsaw Pact the bureaucratic variables explain 65–90% of the variance. Whether or not these empirical results stand up (and all such statistical studies are fallible and improvable), the bureaucratic politics perspective has broadened our vision of the possible explanations of international tensions and the Cold War.

The bureaucratic politics perspective gives us still another conception of the Soviet Union, summed up in the terms "bureaucratic socialism," or "bureaucratic collectivism" (Carlo, 1974). Here "socialism" refers to all countries whose governments call themselves socialist; within this group the Soviet Union and its satellites are distinguished from the others as "bureaucratic," that is as characterized by the same kind of bureaucratic politics as in the United States and other Western countries. Like the US, the SU has a Defense Department, a Bureau of Heavy Industry analogous to our planning sector, and therefore a military-industrial complex; a consumer goods sector; a Foreign Affairs Department; and so on. Policymaking therefore takes the same form as in the US (Aspaturian, 1966; Hahn, 1972). As in the US the central leadership must try to increase its power by ideological appeals while remaining uncommitted in the face of partisan pressures, except that in the SU the central leadership is a committee that itself reflects partisan pressures. Like the US the SU must helplessly expand without limit; even more than in the US, Soviet armament increases are determined internally, bureaucratically, rather than externally by the international armaments races (Rattinger, 1974, 1975). The Soviet government has been dominated by the heavy industry–military coalition, which defeated Malenkov's attempt to shift to consumer goods and Khrushchev's attempt to shift resources to agriculture (Aspaturian, 1966; Carlo, 1974, pp. 52–61); hence the enormous amounts of steel in Soviet airplanes and tanks.

The bureaucratic standpoint also gives us another perspective on the pluralist–elitist controversy. Organizational decision-making is explained in a series of ever-broadening stages. In the narrowest focus we see organizational power dispersed through an interlocking set of organizations and bureaus, Galbraith's technostructure. Within this structure individuals and departments maneuver with and against one another, amassing and losing influence, transmitting information and advice. Explanation at this stage is subjective and pluralistic: decisions result from the interplay of the many mentalities whose power gives them a piece of the action. In a wider focus we explain the mentalities themselves in terms of the organizational position of the occupants, as Halperin does. Explanation is objective and pluralistic. Next, the widely shared beliefs and values in a country's political culture, Galbraith's "conventional wisdom" and Halperin's "Cold War mentality" are explained in terms of symbolic politics, the mass media, doctrines in economics textbooks (Melman, 1974, p. 149) and in general the propaganda efforts of the elite. Explanation is objective and elitist. Finally, the relative power of the various departments in government is explained by their corporate alliances and by their relation to the political agencies of the planning sector of the economy: the Council on Foreign Relations, the Committee on Economic Development, the Business Council, etc. Explanation is objective and elitist.

The pluralist, with his subjective cases of decision-making, takes the narrowest focus and sees widely dispersed power and sharp disagreement. The elitist, with his national studies of corporate influence, takes the wider focuses. The Galbraithian adds one observation: both dispersal and concentration of power work for big business and against the poor, black, and unemployed. Dispersed power blocks liberal efforts to help the poor, and concentrated power ensures that government policies benefit the planning sector (Lockard, 1971, pp. 311–317, 165–167). "Minority elements face just as much difficulty from the dispersal of power as they do from the unequal power held by the elites, for both serve to create the priorities that exclude the poor or racial minorities from consideration" (ibid., p. 314).

The method of the bureaucratic politics theorist, and of his partner the Galbraith-type institutional economist, is rather loose and varied. The subject-matter is always a case: either bureaucratic struggle and policy-making, or a large organization, or a whole political economy including government. The method therefore is case study, ranging from the detailed history of some policy decision to a large, loose survey of some economy or organization over twenty years.

Theory is generally intermixed with the case history. At one extreme the theory is loose inductive generalizations from the case. Or the theory might be derived from comparative cases and used to illuminate the present case. In a few works theory is dominant and some large case is brought in periodically for illustration. Always, however, the theory is nonmathematical and loosely presented and is supported by historical evidence rather than formal deduction. This differentiates the bureaucratic–institutional theorist from his ancestors the Keynesians and systems analysts. One can see evidence of the mastery of formal thinking, but this is a holdover from the theorists' earlier standpoints, such as game theory for Ellsberg and Keynesian modelling for Galbraith. In other cases such as Halperin the previous standpoint was a subjectivistic policy analysis and advice to policy-makers, and no formal background is in evidence.

The writing style tends to be popular and vivid rather than technical and precise. These professional specialists are not writing primarily for fellow-specialists, nor are they demonstrating technical competence as potential advisors to government. They have left government, some of them at least, and their audience is the American people, whom they are trying to alert to how their government actually operates.

Data in the smaller case studies are mainly memoirs, interview data, and government documents. Here there is a serious access problem (Melman, 1974, pp. 13-14), similar to that facing students of the Soviet economy. Governments have no objection to official Langer and Gleason or Dörnberg-type histories, but they do not like outsiders studying them critically and poking into their secrets. The scientist must therefore depend on interviews with "refugees," on reading between the lines in technical journals and Congressional hearings, and on information derived by suing the Government under the Freedom of Information Act. A good many of the bureaucratic-institutionalist people were formerly in government or government research institutes themselves—Barnet, Ellsberg, Galbraith, Halperin, Murdock—and can use their own experience and privately declassified documents.

The larger studies must depend more on institutional statistics as well as documents and interviews. Here again, as for Rostow, the Keynes-type aggregate statistics are useless because they obscure the difference between different sectors of the economy. "If the economists' categories of undifferentiated growth are used as a basic unit of analysis, then the special effects of the military economy are blotted from view" (Melman, 1974, p. 155). For the Keynesian, aggregate investment is an important datum, but for the Galbraithian it is misleading, because investment in the military sector, the planning sector, and the market sector has in each case quite different effects. Similarly, aggregate unemployment is meaningless because unem-ployed aerospace engineers cannot be absorbed by investment in the

planning or market sectors (Melman, 1974, pp. 244-246) and unemployed chambermaids cannot be absorbed by military investment.
Keynes' key theoretical error of assuming the adequacy of neoclassical
economics as a microtheory—that is, assuming free mobility of capital
and labor across the three sectors—reappears as a source of erroneous
data selection, according to the Galbraithian.

The Schumpeterian and the Galbraithian economists do not use the
same kind of disaggregation, however. The Schumpeterian must
disaggregate by technology, since he wishes to trace the consequences
of some epoch-making invention, first in transforming its own sector
such as heavy industry, electronics, or the chemical industry, and then
in gradually diffusing to other sectors. The Galbraithian disaggregates
by type of market: competitive, monopoly, and government contract.
In some cases he must disaggregate down to individual corporations
so he can study their performance in various circumstances; he must
draw up long lists of corporations with detailed data for each.

The problem with disaggregated statistics, documents, and testimony is that they lend themselves readily to selective use and to
selective interpretation. The whole story of any complex organization
or system is too complex to be told, so the scientist must select the
essential aspects. This problem does not come up with the Keynes-type
aggregate data. But those statistics that are crucial evidence for one
interpretation are irrelevant for another interpretation, and the
scientist naturally selects those data that support his own view, rather
than confusing the reader with endless irrelevant statistics. Similarly,
all documents can either be accepted as unbiased evidence or as
misleading testimony requiring interpretation. Are the CIA reports on
Vietnam unbiased facts which can be used to bring out the bureaucratic distortions of Army reports and predictions? Or are they instances of
bureaucratic struggle in which the "rollback" faction tried to discredit
the "containment" faction? Was Acheson's famous 1946 remark that
US expansion is necessary to protect markets and raw materials needed
by our capitalist economy a sudden revelation of the real inside truth?
Or was it propaganda designed to get conservative congressmen to
support Acheson's containment policy? Was McNamara's speech
about the futility of spending $4-$40-$400 billion on ABM because
the Russians would just reciprocate, an authoritative recognition of an
arms race? Or was it a predictable attempt by a department head to
control the competitive expansionism of his subordinates? Scientists
can easily pick the component that fits their theory and ignore the
other component. Barnet (1972) provides instance after instance of
selecting facts and interpretations to fit his (Barnet's) theories.

The problem of selective evidence is fundamental for the social sciences, taking different forms in different methods, and will be discussed more thoroughly in Chapter Fourteen.

III. Preliminary Evaluation

This standpoint represents the maximum of detachment from the existing system and therefore the maximum of objectivity in some sense, compared with earlier standpoints. The objectivity makes it possible to invent objective explanations for phenomena that other standpoints must treat as subjective.

In particular, the "government" standpoint of Chapters Four and Five obliges its adherents to treat government as a free, somewhat rational problem-solver. Government policies must be interpreted as attempts to solve subjectively defined problems. Some policies seem wise, some foolish; some succeed, some fail. The task of the scientist is to study the failures so they can be corrected or avoided next time. However, persistent error and persistent failure to correct a mistaken policy is inexplicable and discouraging (for example, Thompson, 1980, pp. 146–147, discussing Vietnam war strategy).

The bureaucratic-institutionalist perspective of Chapter Eight sees government policies as objectively determined, not free. Consequently errors and persistent failures are in principle as easy to explain as successes; they all are equally determined by the pattern of pressures outside and inside governments and ultimately by organizational dynamics. For example the farm policies of the last forty years which had the stated goal of saving the family farm were actually shaped by pressures from the agricultural planning sector and achieved their intended effects of protecting corporate investments in agriculture. The transformation of the Appalachian poverty program into a road-building program that helped mining and construction companies but not the poor is similarly explained. Kennedy's reluctance to move on civil rights is explained by his lack of power in relation to the Southern bloc. The failure to carry out Keynesian countercyclical measures against inflation is explained by the expansionist imperatives of the government departments and the planning sector.

In contrast to the mass-perspective theorists of Chapter Seven, who attribute immense power to the elite, Galbraith and the bureaucratic theorists argue that the elite themselves are determined by imperatives of growth and survival and are themselves captives of the ideological thinking that they continually inculcate in the masses. The Southern plantation owners who used government price supports to protect their capital investment in new machinery (Galbraith, 1973, p. 49) thereby pushing sharecroppers off the farm and into the Northern ghettos to rot (Cloward and Piven, 1975, p. x) did not do so out of malevolence towards blacks; rather, they were under intense competitive pressure, for instance from the insurance company agribusinesses in the Western states.

It is not immediately clear whether the subjective-free or the objective-determined approach to government and the elite is superior. They seem to be opposite, complementary perspectives on the same phenomena. When a policy persists despite decades of obvious failure, an objective explanation by persistent determining forces seems superior; but other policies may call for a subjective-rational interpretation to supplement the objective explanation. In any case there may be good and bad objective explanations, good or bad subjective explanations. The bureaucratic-institutionalist perspective makes objective explanations of government policy possible but does not guarantee valid explanations; only scientists can produce valid explanations.

The bureaucratic-institutionalist perspective is unquestionably superior in one respect: its concern for facts. Both the "government" and the "elite" standpoints require a loyalty to government, a faith and trust in the integrity of the President or Congress or at least the Supreme Court. This trust carries over to official government statements, such as executive reports at Congressional hearings. Our government would not lie to us; or if in the national interest it must deceive or keep some things secret, as all governments must, we ought to trust the Presidential decision that such deception is necessary. Consequently government and elite-standpoint scientists normally accept the official facts as true, though they have learned to make an exception for the later Nixon years.

The ex-government servants of Chapter Eight have learned from experience that behind the official politics that gets into the newspapers there is an unofficial politics of a quite different sort—bureaucratic maneuverings, CIA "dirty tricks," guerrilla wars and destabilization programs, secret diplomacy. An objective science must therefore look behind the official facts to find the real facts, and even behind those to find the secret facts, just as we are used to doing in studying foreign governments. Any theorizing that limits itself to official facts is in danger of becoming a scholarly version of government propaganda.

In this context Daniel Ellsberg's publication of the Pentagon Papers was a fundamental and heroic stand for scientific objectivity—a stand that naturally earned him the contempt of government-perspective scientists for betraying a trust. The various publications of ex-CIA agents fall in the same category. An objective political science requires facts of this sort; and it requires the sort of mentality that will search out such facts.

For example, the Pentagon Papers report that the CIA was using Quemoy in the 1950's as a base for raids and sabotage on the Chinese mainland. None of the government-perspective studies of the Quemoy crisis of 1958 report such a fact or even speculate as to its possibility. Consequently they give us a picture of unprovoked Chinese aggression, however much they disagree on other details. Quemoy goes down in "history" as one more instance of Communist expansionism. These "facts," in turn, provide the basis of much theorizing in international relations in the 1960's—Schelling's "chicken" models and tactics, Possony's theory about Mao's plans for global expansion, Rusk's warnings about the dangers of appeasement, and so on. How much scientific value can such theorizing have? An objective scientist in the 1960's would have said that since we do not yet know what happened at Quemoy we can draw no firm theoretical implications from the case. But such a statement is possible only for a person who is inherently suspicious of all official histories, and this requires the perspective of Chapters Eight or Nine.

Having made a distinction, let us be wary of it. There is no sharp line between the government perspective of Chapter Five and the bureaucratic perspective of Chapter Eight. Policy scientists combine loyalty and suspicion of government in varying degrees, and many of them are in movement toward a Galbraithian position, or back again. Many policy analysts and social problems professionals have a certain degree of suspicion of official facts; and conversely it is conceivable that some antigovernment scientists could be too suspicious of official facts, just as the elitist intellectuals are too suspicious of official Soviet facts. There must be an optimum range of detachment from government, whose exact boundaries no one can draw.

The bureaucratic perspective also enables one to see things that are invisible or barely visible from other perspectives. The possibility of explaining the increase of US or Soviet armaments in bureaucratic-industrial terms has been mentioned above; another example is economic imperialism, the result of the competitive drive to control raw material sources, which is visible from the elite perspective of Chapter Six but rarely discussed. The political-military imperialism of the national security managers ("Pentagonism"), with foreign bases and occupational troops, foreign military aid, and CIA guerrilla war and internal subversion, is another new concept that has been thoroughly worked out empirically. The control of the consumer by advertising has been discussed by organization theorists and of course by the marketing economists, but Galbraith and Edelman have generalized it to government and the university in an extended discussion of political control and public opinion. This concept is an alternative to the elite-perspective theorists' interpretation of the mass as placid, contented, and apathetic. Galbraith also provides an extended discussion of sexism as an adjunct to the conspicuous consumption mentality. Both these concepts as well as others of Galbraith's are found in Veblen; but the present study is complicated enough already without bringing in Veblen, who died in 1929.

On the negative side, the Keynesian faith in a neutral, wise, and benevolent government, has reappeared as a faith in a potentially neutral, wise, and benevolent American people. The Keynesian Subject has been shown up as a fiction, but another fiction has been put in its place. Faith in this Subject requires the Galbraithian to distinguish between the people as it is and the people as it could and ought to be; it requires him to hope that his Pentagon Papers or his latest book will be more powerful than the combined propaganda of Government, Corporations, and Universities; and it requires him to believe, or hope, in the pluralistic democracy that his science has shown up as a fraud.

How long can such a faith continue? It seems to me that the Galbraithian perspective is inherently unstable because of the sharp contradiction between what is and what ought to be. After, say, twenty years of waiting for the "emancipation of belief" the Galbraithian institutionalist will have to move either left or right. On the left, the Marxist perspective provides a long-run theory that can explain a long continuation of "false consciousness" and a way to deal with it. On the right, the Galbraithian New Socialist is continually tempted by some new liberal image, a McGovern or a Carter/Young/Mondale, to return to the Keynesian and social problems perspective, which after all is very similar. The tempting argument always is, this is about as liberal a government as we are going to get for a while; the alternatives are worse; it is better to help this government along, perhaps move it left, than to stand on the sidelines and complain; and there are pressing problems of poverty, inflation, unemployment, racism, sexism, imperialism that cannot wait. So the refugee from government is tempted to fall for the symbolic politics of some liberal's Presidential campaign and to see himself again as advisor to an idealized government, forgetting his own teaching about corporate control of government and bureaucratic control of the President. Some people never learn.

IV. The Consumer-Environmental Movement

There are three wings to this movement: the consumer movement, which began its latest phase with Ralph Nader's work of the 1960's and was institutionalized with the Public Interest Research Groups and other Nader organizations in 1970; the environmental movement, which began its latest phase about 1967 with the founding of the Environmental Defense Fund and many similar groups; and the people's advocates, who began working in the inner cities in the late 1960's (Cloward and Piven, 1975, pp. 43–65) and are still active.

The standpoint and conceptual scheme is the same as that of Galbraith (1973), though not as fully worked out. The Object is the politico-economic system in which government and corporations work in bureaucratic symbiosis to expand their power and resources. The Subject is the people in their dual capacity as victim and savior, problem and solution. In fact, scientifically, the people are victimized by pollution, by deceptive advertising and dangerous products from cars to nuclear power, by ever-rising taxes to pay for the military bureaucracy. They are corrupted by the mass media and symbolic politics into consenting to their own victimization. In hope, politically, the people can be emancipated and organized to fight the corporations and their government. Note that "people" here means "consumers." The scientist is the mediator between these two aspects of the people, between fact and value, science and politics. He or she is the professional advisor who can emancipate the people with information about the system, and then adivse them on how to fight the corporations and the government.

The scientist's tactics are primarily research and information. She investigates what the corporations-government are daily doing to the people, and then publicizes the results in consumers' handbooks, environmental journals, newspaper columns, newsletters, broadcasts. The audience, as for the bureaucratic-institutionalist scientists, is the people rather than fellow professionals. The information is technical—complex chemical, biological, and physical processes, lumbering and steel technology, legal trickery in bills and administrative regulations, legislative and administrative processes—but it is not simplified down to a popular, nontechnical level. The consumer-environmentalist does not share the Schumpeterians' contempt for the stupid masses; she has faith and hope in the capacity of the people for self-government, and works, like Galbraith, for the emancipation of belief. For the same reason, the people are encouraged to participate in research, in the Public Interest Research Groups.

In addition to research and information, the scientist represents the people in technical dealings with government. This includes suing or threatening to sue the government; lobbying for more effective laws; and testifying before regulatory commissions. The lawsuit tactic was greatly facilitated by a change in the "standing to sue" doctrine by the Supreme Court in 1970 (Orren, 1976), and by clauses in recent environmental laws that give every citizen the right to sue.

The contradictions characterizing the Galbraithian-bureaucratic standpoint are abundantly evident in the consumer-environmental movement. They are contradictions between fact and value, between science and hope. These scientists "know" (believe) that Congress, the Executive, the administrative commissions, and the lower courts are in symbiotic alliance with the corporations, yet they prod the government to act against the corporations. They know that regulatory agency public hearings are formalities because the commissioners have been thoroughly captured by the industry they are supposed to regulate; yet they prepare careful testimony for these hearings, hoping that the commissioners will this one time listen to reason. They even lobbied for a new regulatory agency to protect consumers; yet when the new agency promptly showed an acute sensitivity to the needs of industry they reproached the commissioner, rather than tallying another confirmation of their political theory. In this case they were rewarded by a slight shift in agency policy a few years later. They know that bills are written or amended by industry lobbyists; yet they lobby and testify at Congressional hearings. They sue the government knowing that even a clear win in court is only the start of a long legal–political battle in which their financial resources are matched against corporate financial resources. For example when they got a court order for New York City to carry out its own anti-pollution plans nothing happened; eventually after more court appearances the city pleaded financial inability to implement its plans, and there were several years of legal maneuvering before the city agreed to a slow partial implementation. They know that if they finally, after five years of legal pressure, get some harmful food additive or industrial chemical or pesticide banned another one will promptly take its place, but they sue nevertheless.

They "know" that the actual political system is essentially elitist and that big money controls Congress (Green et al., 1972, *Who Runs*

Congress?, the Ralph Nader Congress project), but they continue to
believe in the pluralist fringes because these fringes offer the only
hope for popular participation in government, for real democracy.
This hope is expressed in the Common Cause-type people's lobbies,
in the recommendations to write your congressman, and in the
publication of environmental newsletters that are supposed to
counteract the corporate-controlled mass media, indoctrination by
the entire educational system, and systematic deception by
politicians.[5]

To understand how people live with these contradictions it is
necessary to see how the contradictions developed and continue to
develop. The conceptual schema in the conservation movement since
at least Pinchot's time, 1910, was the people and the administration
(Forest Service) vs. the special interests. The people, organized and led
by professionals, protected the public interest: our natural resources,
public recreation, endangered species. The special interests represented
the legitimate need for economic development, but also in the process
tried for excessive private enrichment at public expense. The impartial
arbitrator between these two interest groups was Congress. The democratic ideal was for the two opposed interests to present their claims
openly and fully, so Congress could decide how much each interest
should get in each case. This is still the ideal for some environmentalists (Sax, 1971, pp. 156, 167). However, for Pinchot the ideal was
something to be achieved eventually through his organizing efforts,
while for Sax the ideal is something that used to happen.

In contrast, for the Keynesians and others discussed in Chapter Five
the legislature was seen as the domain of the special interests; and the
President, the only person elected by the whole country, was the one
responsible for the public interest and the health of the whole
economy. And along with the legislature, the courts too were part of
the Object: the lower courts were under the control of local political
machines representing the status quo, and the Supreme Court was the
dead hand of past conservative administrations.

In the 1960's the environmentalist schema was still the people vs.
the special interests, but the executive branch was now on the side of
the special interests. Administrative routines and bureaucratic politics
were added to the list of barriers to achieving the public interest.
Congress might clearly declare itself in a Clean Air Act or a Water
Pollution Control Act, but the agencies responsible for the acts would
fail to carry them out, or would compromise with the special interests
(Rosenbaum, 1973, Chapter 4 and passim.; Sax, 1971, p. 239 and
passim.). In contrast, for the bureaucratic theorists of the Neustadt

type the administration was seen as an obstacle to the President's attempt to serve the public interest.

One environmentalist solution was to bring in the courts to reestablish a balance. The role of the courts was to block special interests and administrators and thereby induce Congress to rethink its policies, clarify its priorities, and reassert its control over the errant administrators (Sax, 1971, pp. 151ff.). Congress was still Subject responsible for the public interest, but it was a careless, slumbering Subject that needed to be prodded into alertness.

Both Keynesians and environmentalists treated one part of government as Subject—the President, or Congress, or the Supreme Court—and readily objectified other parts. In the gradual objectification of government one part was always exempted. Government in general might exemplify organizational dynamics and be determined by the imperatives of growth and survival, but one part was treated as free to serve the public interest. For Galbraith it might be the left wing of the Democratic Party, which could someday elect a people's congress; for Ellsberg it was Senator Fulbright; and for the consumer-environmentalists it was the Supreme Court or the Consumer Protection Agency. In each case the exempted part served as the point of entry for the people to reform a special-interest government and restore democracy. In each case the exempted part served as an idealized focus for the hope of reform. The sharpening contradiction between fact and value, science and hope, Object and Subject, remains manageable as long as the "hope" side can be attached to some actual point—even if this point has long ago been written off by some other tradition.

The one unique contribution of the consumer-environmentalist movement to science is its critique of professionalism. This is different from the well-established antiprofessionalism of the intellectuals, whose critique centers on specialization, mathematics, and technical language.

Both critiques have become even more relevant in the 1970's after several decades of luxuriant professionalization. Professional specialization began with the demarcation of economics, sociology, political science, etc. but continued with the subdivision of these fields ad infinitum. Each new field brings its own specialized journal, professional association, terminology, and controversies with it. Some specializations, like the theory of the military–industrial complex, disappear after a few years and are replaced by equally short-lived specialties. Education follows suit, as students are examined on the details of the latest esoteric controversy and aspire to write their first article reviewing some such controversy or providing experimental evidence for it. Some sociologists of science measure the scientific status of a field by the recency of the citations in the footnotes, that is by the speed with which last year's trivial disputes are forgotten and replaced by this year's equally ephemeral disputes. (Experimental psychology wins the race).

Along with specialization comes what Ravetz (1971) has described as the industrialization of research. This includes the familiar phenomenon of grantsmanship, the technique of winning a steady succession of research grants and keeping several projects running simultaneously. Research and writing become automated, and a steady stream of multiple-authored journal articles is produced both to justify past grants and to lay the basis for future ones. Quality and originality are unimportant in these articles, as their purpose is to justify grants and promotions. Ravetz calls this phenomenon "shoddy science." Along with automated research comes a specialization of research roles: at the top the principal investigator, concerned mainly with keeping his various projects on schedule, writing progress reports and budgets, hiring researchers, and organizing new projects; then the co-investigators, who supervise and write; and finally the student employees who do the actual work and get paid off with degrees and co-authored publications (Ravetz, 1971, pp. 44ff.). In short, it appears that the dynamics of a professionalized social science include ever-increasing specialization, division of labor in research, ever-expanding research budgets, geometrically expanding publication rates, and ever more rapid obsolescence of research.

The consumer–environmentalist does not criticize specialization as such; he criticizes the *kind* of specialization now occurring. Specialization now is hierarchical and departmental, by fields, subfields, and subsubfields. This kind of specialization cuts through the complex interdependences of our society and produces a trained incapacity to understand the dynamics of the whole system (cf. Ravetz, 1971, p. 114 fn. 6). The social-problems professional sees only the superficial appearances of his problem—delinquency, poor education, poor health care, alcoholism—and is unable to understand its complex interdependence with, say, aerospace R & D or (ugh) foreign policy. Consequently the solutions he proposes touch only the surface and preserve the corporate-military status quo. What is needed, therefore, is specialization by problems, interdisciplinary specialization.

For example, one of my environmentalist colleagues is a specialist in sulfur dioxide (Tobin, 1979). That means he knows its chemical and biological characteristics in professional detail; its economic geography, that is the location of low and high sulfur fuels, mining and transportation costs, etc.; its technology, that is the techniques and costs of recovering it at each stage of the production cycle; the administrative law and the politics of the regulatory commission at whose hearings he testifies (to no effect, of course), and the Congressional politics and political history of the utility industry. The same interdisciplinary expertise is necessary for nuclear-energy-and-cancer specialists, urban land-use politics–architect–geographers, or molecular biochemist–epidemiologist–home economists.

This critique of professionalism is therefore a professional critique. It argues that a professionalized social science has become a tool for maintenance of the status quo, and the social scientist a bureaucratized servant of the corporate-bureaucratic-military system. 1) the bureaucratic mentality of a professionalized university recognizes only narrow, specialized, technical problems and is blind to the connections; 2) the practical advice therefore assumes an idealized, functioning polity and economy and recommends only superficial, cosmetic remedies; 3) this sort of education, which hides system dynamics, blinds the educated classes to political reality and therefore serves an ideological function for the system. The relation between science and ideology is a serious problem for the consumer–environmentalist, just as it is for Galbraith. For the Samuelson-type professional the ideologues are to be found only on the right and left fringes of the scientific spectrum; but for the environmentalist professional the dominant professional schools of thought perform an ideological rather than a scientific function.

Nine New Left Marxism

In the United States and Canada, Marxism was beyond the limits of academic respectability until at least the mid-1960's. A few token Marxists such as Baran and Genovese were admitted into the universities to demonstrate academic tolerance and impartiality, but Marxist thought was ignored. The situation in various European countries was complex and varied, but since the main focus of this volume is North American social science I pass by the European experience. Marxism entered the mainstream of North American social science about 1968 as New Left Marxism. Consequently this chapter begins not at the beginning of Marxism but at the point when people began to notice this new phenomenon.

The New Left generational experience of the 1960's was not Marxist; it was left liberal. The student movement began as the student branch of the League for Industrial Democracy, John Dewey's old organization in which the Reuthers were influential, and the Port Huron Manifesto was written in the UAW summer camp on Lake Huron (Sale, 1973). The experience itself was a moral one, a moral revulsion against racism down in the South and mass murder over in Vietnam, and later a moral revulsion against a government that could not be moved to stop these injustices. The appeal was first to the government to pass and enforce civil rights laws, and from 1965 on to the American people to replace a particular government that was implicated in racism and war crimes. This appeal found expression in the McCarthy presidential campaign of 1967-1968. Those New Lefters

249

who remained faithful to this generational experience became the left liberals of Chapter Eight.

Others came to believe that the "whole system" was at fault, not just a particular government, and these became the first New Left Marxists. The problem was to find out how the "whole system" worked so one could change it, and this called for intensive study of the Marxist literature and extensive empirical research.

One important focus of research was the theory of the capitalist state. This was an area in which the discrepancy between received beliefs and the experience of the 1960's was the most glaring and disillusioning, and the need for new theoretical understanding therefore the most acute. Received beliefs were pretty well summed up for us by Lipset (1960): our government was trying to protect and expand democracy abroad and at home. Abroad the enemies of democracy were Communist totalitarianism and military dictatorships, and at home the enemies of civil rights were the intolerant masses and the reactionary Southern politicians. But actually, as it seemed to us, in the Dominican Republic the US intervened to save a military regime against an attempt to restore democracy and the legally elected government. In the South, the Kennedy family foundation offered financial support to SNCC on the condition that it confine its efforts to voter registration, while the Kennedy government did nothing to remove the barriers to registration (Piven and Cloward, 1979, pp. 231-235). In Fayette County, Tennessee, according to a civil rights worker at the scene, Robert Kennedy flatly refused to prosecute a white government that kept a black voting majority away from polling booths with drawn guns. In the 1964 Democratic convention Johnson and the liberals doublecrossed the Mississippi Freedom Democrats and supported the reactionary Southern politicians, to keep them in the party (Zinn, 1965, pp. 251-254). And so on. The reality was the opposite of the theory.

Other research interests were imperialism, stimulated by US activities in Vietnam, Brazil, and elsewhere; the cold war, where the official theory that the US was doing all this to stop Communist aggression was becoming increasingly ludicrous; and the university power structure, which was blocking the student efforts at self-determination.

I begin with the theory of the capitalist state, in which the most important works are O'Connor (1973) and Offe (1972). The purpose here will be to locate the New Left Marxist standpoint and relate it to those presented in earlier chapters. Then I go on to other areas of research to locate the comparative strengths and weaknesses of this standpoint. There will also be a short discussion of Orthodox Marxism, by way of comparison and contrast.

I. O'Connor and the Capitalist State

O'Connor begins with a functionalist conception of the state as the subsystem responsible for maintaining the whole social system including itself. The capitalist state must perform two functions: it must maintain the economic conditions that facilitate capital accumulation, and it must maintain the voluntary support of the population (O'Connor, 1973, p. 6). In Parsons' terminology, these are the A and the G functions of the G subsystem and are performed by the administrative system and the support system.

The accumulation function is a specific version of the general A-function of maintaining the health of any A-subsystem. A capitalist economy is healthy insofar as there are opportunities for profitable investment; given such opportunities, there will be production, employment, demand, sales, and more production; the system will run. Schumpeter's entrepreneur, performing the A_I function, is now institutionalized in the corporations and is no problem.

The state performs the accumulation function, first, by maintaining the physical infrastructure needed for profitable production: the transportation system, utilities, education and R & D facilities, improved land, garbage dumps, and the urban environment in which production occurs. It must also staff these systems and facilities. O'Connor calls investment in the infrastructure "social investment" or in Marx's terminology "social constant capital." Specific parts of the infrastructure may be maintained at a profit, in which case they can be left to private enterprise aided by occasional subsidies. Examples are railroads, urban public transit, utilities, and mining. Other parts such as roads, airports, harbors, hydroelectric dams cannot be run at a profit because of the high initial investment and long-term widespread benefits (cf. also Offe, 1972, pp. 52ff.). As the economy grows more complex and the capital/labor ratio increases, more and more of the infrastructure becomes unprofitable and must be directly maintained by the State. Railroads, airlines, urban transit go bankrupt and are nationalized or heavily subsidized; utilities and coal mining gradually follow. One reason is the increased investment costs of ever more complex infrastructure facilities; another is the ability of powerful corporations such as the auto lobby to get special infrastructure benefits.

Second, the state facilitates private accumulation by reducing the costs of producing labor, thereby making labor available more cheaply and reducing the employers' wage bill. O'Connor calls such expenditures "social consumption" or in Marx's terms "social variable capital"; they include transportation to work, schools and recreation, housing, hospitals, and insurance. Some of these services may be directly profitable for a time, others are subsidized, and still others provided directly by government.

The state performs the legitimation function by providing welfare benefits for the dissatisfied surplus population—and police if the dissatisfaction is expressed too openly. These benefits in turn serve to use up some of the surplus product and thus indirectly perform an accumulation function.

The two functions conflict, as functional prerequisites always do. Welfare benefits, unemployment compensation, minimum-wage laws contribute to legitimation, but by increasing the cost of labor they make accumulation more difficult. Subsidies to business and diplomatic pressure to protect foreign investment advantages are good for business but bad for legitimacy. In general, the accumulation function requires a partiality for profit opportunities, since this is the incentive which makes the economy run (and thereby provides government revenue); but the legitimation function requires an impartial concern for citizen welfare. The state must therefore hide its partiality behind a rhetoric of impartiality, arguing that business profits are good for everybody, calling corporate tax credits "job development credits," and expressing its concern for full employment, welfare, civil rights, and other citizen concerns (O'Connor, 1973, p. 6; Offe, 1972, pp. 91-102; Kidron, 1974, p. 15). This rhetoric is what Parsons calls "leadership responsibility" (1969b, pp. 375, 390) and Edelman (1964) more aptly calls "symbolic politics."

More generally, the ruling elite have managed the contradiction by developing a dual state (Wolfe, 1977, Chapter 6), or in Parsons' terminology two specialized political subsystems. The visible state (Parsons' "support system"), centered in Congress and the judiciary, serves the legitimation function by an elaborate show of legality, due process, impartiality, elections, and services to constituents. The "invisible government," centered in the CIA and the Executive branch, provides a favorable investment climate at home and abroad, among other things.

Offe (1972) and Habermas (1975) expand O'Connor's list by considering structural as well as functional prerequisites, basing their theory on Luhmann's functionalism. If the state is to fulfill the accumulation and legitimation prerequisites it must also maintain an administratively rational structure: a flow of impartial information about the state of the economy (and the support system) and an internal power distribution that enables it to make and carry out impartial budget and fiscal decisions. It must be concerned about the health of the whole economy, not the profits of an individual corporation (and similarly the whole spectrum of citizen discontent, not merely that of influential groups). But the economic contradiction between the interests of capital in general and that of particular capitalists—Marx's "one capital" and "many capitals"—is reproduced within the political structure. "One capital" is represented in government by the relatively class-conscious capitalists—the National Civic Federation (Weinstein, 1968), the Committee for Economic Development, the Council on Foreign Relations, the Business Council—but individual corporations and groups of corporations develop close contacts with specific government departments, providing biased information and mutual assistance (Habermas, 1975, pp. 61-68; Offe 1972, Chapter 3). This is Galbraith's "bureaucratic symbiosis." The resulting administrative irrationality skews the performance of the accumulation function, for instance in the transportation system (O'Connor, 1973, pp. 105-110).

Habermas also discusses the breakdown of the cultural system, which produces the motivations and cognitive orientations needed for the maintenance of the economy and political system (1975, pp. 75-92). The breakdown is induced by the development of the economy, which depends for its maintenance on a cultural tradition it cannot itself replace. In Parsonian terms, the culture acts on society via the L-subsystem but cannot itself be controlled by the polity because it exists at a cybernetically higher level.

The details of the accumulation function are determined by the dynamics of the economy. That is, in order to maintain the health of the economy the state must counteract the economy's own destabilizing tendencies and supplement its self-corrective tendencies. O'Connor divides the economy into three approximately equal sectors: the competitive sector, the monopoly sector, and the state sector (1973, Chapter 1). Actually the three sectors are quite unequal by various measures; the competitive sector is the largest in manpower (Hodson, 1978). It corresponds to Galbraith's "market sector" and the other two to his "planning sector." To briefly summarize O'Connor's model: the competitive sector follows the neoclassical economists' model; the monopoly sector runs by administered prices with wages set by pattern bargaining and COLA in a context of good working relations. The survival and profits of the corporation depend on its relative market power as well as its efficiency; both are advanced by growth. Consequently the monopoly sector is characterized by continuous growth, in productivity, size of firm, surplus capacity, surplus labor and capitalists, and by an inflationary spiral.

The inflationary dynamic of the monopoly sector, plus inflation management by the state, squeezes competitive sector profits, and in general the competitive sector is slowly absorbed by the monopoly sector. However, the competitive sector continually recreates itself by the small businessman's self-exploitation (Galbraith, 1973, Chapter 8), that is by converting family life into capital which then gradually drains into the monopoly sector. Surplus labor goes partly to the competitive sector, depressing wages there, and partly to the state sector as employees and welfare clients. Monopoly profits are supported by the ever growing state-supported infrastructure, and wages in the state sector tend to follow the pattern set in the monopoly sector. Thus capital accumulates in the monopoly sector and drains away from the state and competitive sectors. The state must pay for the monopoly sector infrastructure, for the welfare and military expenses of protecting the economy, and for the rising wages of its own employees. It cannot recover these costs in taxes because that would eat into monopoly sector profits or cause a tax revolt by other groups. Consequently the state budget is chronically in deficit and provides additional inflationary pressure.

O'Connor analyzes several policies designed to manage the accumulation problem and shows that each can produce only a temporary solution. For instance, attempts to get state employees to work harder for less pay provokes resistance, deterioration of output, and protests by state clients. While the state struggles with the accumulation problem, the legitimation problem also grows more serious as welfare clients and unemployed protest and taxpayers revolt. Consequently the state is forced to shift expenditures from accumulation to legitimation as soon as the most immediate profitability problems are temporarily managed. Here we have an example of Parsons' "phase movement" in which a system manages functional contradictions by cycling around the functional prerequisites in sequence. Other examples are the welfare cycle described by Piven and Cloward (1971) which cycles between legitimation and accumulation, and a similar cycle in government treatment of labor (Hurd, 1976).[6]

Though the state must eventually fail and go bankrupt (O'Connor, 1973, Chapter 7), its efforts at system management have important effects on the political alignment of groups, that is on the forms of the class struggle. The state does not have enough resources to manage all accumulation and legitimation problems, so it must choose some problems and neglect others. It also has some range of choice in apportioning the costs. Those groups that get benefits become allies of the state or at least quiescent, while the groups that lose out or have to pay are alienated. Since 1945 in the US the Executive Branch has been in alliance with the monopoly sector by providing infrastructure benefits, military spending, assistance to corporations' overseas operations, etc. As a consequence it has had to skimp in assistance to local government, which is mainly dominated by competitive capital (cf. also Weinstein, 1968, Chapter 4). The result is the bankruptcy of local government and decay of the cities, and a political coalition of state-monopoly capital and labor against the competitive sector, with state employees in an ambiguous position. Wage and price controls would shift the two sides to labor vs. the state and monopoly capital, an explosive situation (pp. 48–40), because labor would lose and the corporations benefit in practice. Efforts to increase state sector productivity would shift the coalition to state-monopoly capital-competitive labor vs. competitive capital-monopoly and state labor (pp. 51–58). This shift, which is now occurring in part, is also dangerous, and in particular it leads to some radicalization of state employees (Chapter 9). But the alternative, to skimp on legitimation demands, produces radicalization of the welfare clientele and other strains; and the attempt to prevent both induces a middle-class taxpayers' revolt (Chapter 8). There is no long-run solution.

Wright (1978, Chapter 3) extends O'Connor's argument back in time and thereby connects it to traditional Marxist theory. The primary obstacles to capital accumulation have changed systematically over time, and each partial solution to an accumulation problem has produced a new accumulation problem. In the nineteenth century when mechanization was the source of increased profits capital accumulated in the form of machinery and physical plant. The accumulation problem consisted of the tendency of the rate of profit to fall as production became ever more capital intensive. This was the problem that Marx analyzed in his *Capital*. The solution consisted of an intensive search for cheap raw materials as a way of reducing capital costs, which led to classical imperialism. The solution was fairly successful: the rate of profit seems to have gradually stopped falling in the late nineteenth century, reaching bottom about 1920 (Hodgson, 1974). However, as a result production increased rapidly, resulting in overproduction crises and Keynes-type business cycles. Overproduction meant that the technical rate of profit could not be realized in fact as goods remained unsold. The solution to over-production consisted of Keynesian policies to increase demand and state spending, including military spending; these measures strengthened the labor movement, and helped produce steadily rising wages, profit squeezes, productivity decline in military production, and stagflation (Boddy and Crotty, 1974, 1976; Sherman, 1976, 1979). One solution to declining productivity and the profit squeeze is government investment in the infrastructure and the other social investments that O'Connor describes. These measures involve the state directly in managing one part of the economy and intensify legitimation problems in the way that O'Connor describes.

The above summary shows that the primary concern of the O'Connor school is with the dynamics of the Object. Marxist science is primarily a science of the Object, in the Keynesian-functionalist-Galbraithian style. The Object is the whole political economy including the state, as for Galbraith and the functionalists. The Object is driven by its inner contradictions and conflicts to continually take new shapes, each with its own contradictions and dynamics. Science is necessarily historical, since each stage in the system's development grows out of the contradictions and the policies of the previous stage. And since policies vary in different countries, capitalism takes somewhat different historical paths in different parts of the world. The only equilibrium in this system is the Keynes-Kalecki-Parsons and Bales type, a point around which the output figures oscillate. Even this point is a moving equilibrium, since each business cycle is different (Sherman, 1979) and the Phillips curve is continually moving (Wright, 1978, pp. 160-162).

To understand the Object, therefore, it is necessary to locate the contradictions that drive it during its present stage. O'Connor focuses on the contradiction at the state level between the accumulation and legitimation requirements, in the period since 1945. Underlying this contradiction is a long run social conflict between the classes that benefit most from the accumulation of capital and the classes that are the target of legitimation policies. Underlying class conflict is the fundamental contradiction of the system: production is social but profits and capital are accumulated by one class, the ruling class.

As long as capital accumulates in the hands of a few there is danger that the many will object and resist; hence the need for legitimating policies, socialization, and repression to maintain mass quiescence. As long as wealth must drain steadily toward one class in society there is a danger of blockages and irregularities in the circular flow of resources; hence the need for a variety of policies to assist accumulation—even though these policies produce mass protest.

In short, the system transforms and ultimately destroys itself by activating and maintaining class conflict. Each ruling-class policy directed to some functional or structural problem tends to activate the resistance of some sector of the oppressed or exploited classes, or the resistance of some segment of business. Each success at solving some functional problem brings a new problem and new forms of class conflict with it, and each failure produces loss of legitimacy and intensified conflict, until eventually the system will break down.

If we look for the Marxist Subject by asking "Who is free?" the most plausible answer is, "the ruling class." This class controls most of the government, has plenty of power, information, and ideas, has room to maneuver and engage in crisis management, selects the dominant form of class struggle and thereby determines the transformation of the economic structure, and has stayed in power for several centuries.

If we look more carefully we find a second Subject, labor. O'Connor discusses particularly state employees and welfare clients, but his argument can be generalized. Labor, like Galbraith's Subject, the public, is at present not free, so freedom consists of emancipation. At present labor is a factor of production, part of the Object, but it is a conscious part. Its consciousness is determined (selected) mainly by its experience at work. When it experiences fair treatment it accepts its station in life. When it experiences exploitation—speed-up, arbitrary regulation and interference, low wages—it resists. First it resists the particular speed-up and the particular employer, but in some circumstances the resistance becomes generalized to a radical rejection of the whole system of wage labor.

The requirements of competition force employers to exploit their labor and to provoke resistance and radicalization. Similarly the accumulation requirement forces the state to attempt speed-up and arbitrary interferences with its employees, thereby provoking their resistance and radicalization. Thus the dynamic of the system produces its own opposition from within itself. Labor, originally part of the Object, becomes the Subject that acts to change the system.

In Marxist science the sharp distinction between Subject and Object characteristic of nearly all liberal science disappears. Subjectivity is always derivative from the Object, exactly the opposite of neoclassic science where the system is the total set of consequences of all subjective decisions. For the Marxist, subjectivity or consciousness is derived from one's place in the system of production and reproduction, that is the place which one identifies as "mine" or "where I belong." Class consciousness is a product of the recognition by some group that it shares a common enemy and a common fate. The emancipation of the Subject, that is the experience of radicalization, is a product of a certain kind of recognized oppression. The struggle between classes is derivative from some opposition of interests in the economy. Thus the dynamics of the Object determine the forms of consciousness and class struggle, and these are in fact part of the dynamics of the Object (Burawoy, 1978, pp. 274–275).

To be sure, the derivation of consciousness from the objective system is never mechanical, but is always mediated by subjectivity, by the processes of empathy, recognition, interpretation, and identification.

In summary, the Marxist standpoint is labor, the working class. The Object is the whole self-maintaining and self-destroying social system including labor. There are two opposed Subjects, the working class and the ruling class. Science is primarily objective, but there is a secondary science of the Subject, a study of the various derivative forms of consciousness.

The Marxist perspective shares some characteristics with all the liberal perspectives from Chapter Four on. The closest affinity is with the Galbraithian-institutionalists. For both perspectives science is an objective study of objective system dynamics, including government. The system dynamics are also roughly similar. Both Galbraith and O'Connor divide the economy into the planning sector and the market sector, and they substantially agree on the short-run dynamics of each sector and on their interactions. Both treat government as responsible but fairly helpless, dependent on the planning sector for its power. Both argue that government cannot apply Keynesian countercyclical policy or wage and price controls but must necessarily expand its budget without limit and live with permanent inflation. Both emphasize the bureaucratic symbiosis between the bureaucracy and the planning sector and regard it as a source of structural irrationality. O'Connor goes into more detail on the dynamics of production in the state sector, but his argument is based on William Baumol and is not incompatible with Galbraith.

The difference occurs in the dynamics of the whole system. For Galbraith and the institutionalists there is no internal check on the system, so it grows without limit. Disaster must eventually come for such a system, but it must come from outside as the system exceeds some environmental limit such as available raw materials. In Melman's version disaster comes to the US from Japanese and German competition, as their economies expand.

Since the system is not self-regulating as it is for the functionalists and system theorists, regulation must come from outside the objective system, namely from the power of ideas. The separation of material conditions and ideas, fact and value, is necessary for Galbraith because of themselves material conditions move blindly on to disaster. They produce many evils along the way, but these evils are only recognizable from a distance, by the moral sensitivity of an emancipated public. The evils—poverty, racism, imperialism, pollution, poor ghetto schools—do not affect the suburban public directly, so of themselves they do nothing to check the system's growth.

For the O'Connor school the system is both driven and checked by its inner contradictions, rather than by ideas coming from outside. The force of the contradictions rests ultimately on the ability of labor to recognize and resist its own oppression. Labor is the part of the Object that becomes a Subject (Lukacs). Emancipation or radicalization of labor is a result of experienced oppression rather than a result of reading Galbraith or Marx. However, the experience must be recognized and interpreted, and that requires ideas; and conversely for Galbraith ideas are given force by experience. It is a mistake to distinguish too sharply Galbraith's emancipation by true ideas and the Marxist emancipation by experience; it is more a difference of emphasis. The two perspectives are quite similar, though the Subject is different.

The similarity with the mass perspective of Chapter Seven is in the treatment of the Subject. Both perspectives recognize two Subjects, the ruling class and the oppressed classes, engaged in very unequal struggle. The "masses" of Chapter Seven overlap with the Marxist "working class," though there are differences.

The principal difference between the two perspectives is that from the subjectivist mass perspective the class struggle is fundamental in society, while for the Marxists the class struggle is a derivative part of objective system dynamics.

If the class struggle is all there is, then its outcome must depend on relative power, so the ruling class always wins. Throughout history the ruling classes have always won, for instance in Piven and Cloward's 1971 history. Revolutions have only brought in new ruling classes and new forms of oppression, and future revolutions will follow the same pattern. The only hope is for small, temporary relief from the worst forms of oppression.

But if, as Marxists assert, the power of the opposed classes depends on changing system dynamics, including changes of consciousness, then the ruling class need not always be the most powerful. In system breakdowns, lost wars, economic collapse, the elite loses both power and legitimacy. And if labor is educated by its work it could possibly become capable of self-government and need not always replace the old oppressor with a new one. However, this requires an alternative technology, since capitalist technology stupefies labor.

The same contrast between the subjectivist mass perspective and the primarily objectivist Marxist perspective comes out in treatments of the state. The Domhoff-type power-elite theorists of Chapter Seven conceive of the capitalist state in terms of its personnel, and try to show that the US government is staffed by members of the ruling class (which it is). The state then is one of the organizations by which the ruling class oppresses and manages the masses. But for O'Connor the capitalist state is itself dominated by objective functional necessities, and its personnel and their motivations are a secondary issue (cf. also Offe, 1972, Chapter 3). If the departments of government represent the conflicting interests of many capitals the state becomes structurally irrational, constantly stalemated, and will fail all the sooner; if the more class conscious capitalists control government, then it may last a long time. But even a capitalist state completely staffed by workers would be oppressive, though the particular forms of oppression would vary in the three cases.

The social democratic governments of Western Europe are an example. The objective function of the British Labor Party is to preserve capitalism in Britain. Three times now it has come to power in an accumulation crisis, when falling profits and investment produced unemployment and a leftward shift of the electorate. Each time it has resolved the crisis by imposing austerity on the working class, the most recent time by a series of wage freezes. A Tory government could not have done that. By the time investment opportunities have improved, enough Labor supporters have become disillusioned to produce a Tory comeback, and the system moves on through the cycle. Labor is uniquely qualified for this task because it has no legitimation problem; since its leaders are ex-workers they must have the interests of labor at heart (cf. Miliband, 1972).

Does this mean that the Laborites are traitors to the working class? Not at all; this would shift the argument to subjective terms again. The social democratic governments *must* deal with the accumulation problem to avoid capital flight, mass unemployment, currency devaluation, government bankruptcy. Even if they have nationalized particular industries, steel or auto, these industries must compete in the world market and are thus dominated by the dynamics of monopoly capitalism. Socialism in one country is impossible.

The subjectivism of the mass perspective produces another important contrast with Marxism. Since for the critical intellectuals present mass consciousness is all there is, they are very attentive to the actual structure of this consciousness. The participant observer studies discussed in Chapter Seven constitute a highly developed science of the Subject, in my opinion one of the most methodologically advanced achievements of the social sciences. In contrast, for Marxists present working class consciousness is always in transition to something else, because the relations of production which shape it are always changing. And in any case it is "false," not yet fully emancipated, still dominated by bourgeois ways of thinking and capitalist illusions. Marxists prefer to look ahead to the truer consciousness that may some day exist and is already beginning to appear (for example Lukacs, 1971, Chapter 3). And they tend wishfully to read the future true consciousness into the present, ignoring or overlooking the temporary present characteristics that the participant observers bring out. In other words, the Marxist approach to consciousness is usually long run, and like all long-run theories it has trouble dealing with short-run fluctuations; the mass perspective is strictly short run.

The similarity of Marxism and Parsonian structural-functionalism comes out if we focus only on the state and treat labor as part of the Object, that is if we leave off the long-run part of Marxism. The part of the ruling class located in the executive branch of government becomes the Subject. Marxism becomes a kind of functionalism in which the executive must try to maintain the system by satisfying the various structural and functional requirements. However, the contradictions in the capitalist economy and between the functional requirements doom it to ultimate failure, just as Eisenstadt's imperial governments eventually failed to manage their functional contradictions (1963). In this case Marxist science becomes a policy science in which the scientist must locate and analyze the various system problems, describe possible strategies and the likely consequences of each, and describe and evaluate actual strategies (O'Connor, 1973, Chapters 2, 8, 9, for example). Marxism is more than this—for instance it also studies government objectively—and so is functionalism, but the overlap is considerable.

Finally, the similarity with Schumpeterian science has already been discussed in Chapter Six. Schumpeter was influenced by Marxists, for instance in his use of the subject-object dialectic to explain the creative activity of entrepreneurs. Throughout history the creative individuals have derived their consciousness, their mentality, from the values and the socialization process of their particular subclass. Then they have objectified these values in the institutional changes they have made.

Given this similarity, there are two differences with Marxist science. There is obviously a different Subject, workers rather than the elite. This brings with it a different time orientation: for Marxists the workers are just becoming emancipated and the period of conscious creativity is in its early stages, while for Schumpeter creativity and history are finished, and for his followers elite creativity is now at its peak. Second, for the Schumpeterians the Object has no dynamics of its own; it simply stagnates. This makes Schumpeterian science primarily an empirical-historical science of the Subject. History is the story of the creative destruction wrought by the elite, and of the battle between elite and counterelite over the shaping of society. In contrast, the Marxist Object is dynamic, and the activity of the two Subjects is a derivative part of objective system dynamics. Marxist science is primarily a historical science of the Object.

The recognition of labor as the Subject created difficulties for New Left Marxists. Most of us identified ourselves as middle class; how then could we understand the working-class outlook on the world, the working-class experience of oppression, working-class modes of organization and resistance? How could we construct a theory of a Subject we did not understand? Some New Lefters like Aronowitz and Braverman are ex-industrial workers and can draw on that experience in their theorizing; they have no problem. Others tried to join the working class by getting jobs in steel mills or auto plants, or at least by wearing overalls, or Nehru jackets like the Chinese, or smoking a pipe like Stalin.

Events solved the problem for some of us teachers. We used to think of ourselves as free professionals or detached intellectuals, gathered together voluntarily to advance knowledge and running the university collectively, accepting new members into our community—our Abbey of Theleme—after impartial investigation of their professional or intellectual abilities. We cherished the memory of the Columbia faculty's putdown of Chancellor Eisenhower: "You are not the University; WE are!" We thought of administrators as our appointees, and students and secretaries as transient visitors who benefited from their temporary proximity to us.

Then we found faculty resolutions ignored by the university administration and tenure recommendations overruled; library budgets cut and class sizes increased; tenured professors fired with three months' notice or less; educational policy and resources shifted without consulting us. Where was our power? The only power we had was our union, which at least negotiated salary and working conditions and provided a grievance procedure for the most arbitrary administrative edicts. Our illusions crumbled; we began soberly to face our real conditions of life, and our relations with our fellow-employees.

We are employees of the State. Those of us employed at private universities are employees of the corporations, as recent studies of the university power structure have shown (Smith, 1974, Chapters 1, 2; Gintis and Bowles, 1976). O'Connor's Chapter 9 speaks directly to our experience; the efforts of various state governments to "increase efficiency" and cut budgets, while simultaneously increasing expenditures designed to "attract investment capital" have damaged our own working conditions. The University budgets tell the story: teaching and research funds are continually squeezed, while lavish physical plant expenditures are enthusiastically and successfully promoted by the construction industry, local bankers, and other friends of the University. Nor are we the only employees affected by State budget-cutting. Within the University the graduate student employees are always the most exploited, lowest paid, and first to be fired in budget cuts; the secretaries come next. Elsewhere, the mental hospitals are now being systematically closed down and the patients dumped into old rooming houses in slum neighborhoods, where they make the preservation of an ethnic community life even more difficult (Scull, 1976). The outrageous rhetoric of efficiency known as the "community mental health movement" that covers over this budget-cutting is similar to the rhetoric of efficiency accompanying our budget cuts. The City of Buffalo continually cuts the school budget, making teaching ever more difficult, but constructs a Convention Center to protect the investment of downtown businessmen and attract new investment capital. The social workers' budget cuts came decades ago, giving them case loads of hundreds, transient case contacts, strict rules and long lists of regulations (Edelman, 1974). Their working conditions taught them that they were not "helping professionals" but custodial and disciplinary employees, and they have been learning to adapt to these conditions (Cloward, 1976).

As employees of the state, we no longer need to search for the working class; we are becoming part of it. Our direct experience of conflict with our employer enables us to appreciate the far more serious struggles of other workers. Organizationally, our union cooperates with other public employee unions such as the policemen and firemen, and we find in conversation that their working experience with their employer is similar to ours. We share a common fate.

II. Other Topics

Radicalization

Our own experience of radicalization provides evidence that such a process exists; it also sensitizes us to the occurrence of radicalization elsewhere, for instance in the Cuban working class (Zeitlin, 1970). Others have noticed the same process from the outside, such as Moynihan (1969, p. 112, referring to Cloward). Usually radicalization is conceived by elitist intellectuals as a kind of mass hysteria or individual psychoneurosis, in which the normally quiescent mass rises up and excitedly demands crude, extremist (Left or Right), immediate solutions to some complex social problem. It is a kind of crowd behavior whose basis is the simplistic and emotional mentality of the masses plus the irrational frustrations and aggressions of the counter-elite (Dye and Zeigler, 1975, pp. 14-17; Kornhauser, 1959).

The Marxist standpoint suggests a second hypothesis: radicalization is an awakening from illusions, a liberation, and therefore a basis for active participation in transforming one's own society. Cuban workers expressed again and again their conviction that they were now taking part in running their own factory, were working freely, and were an important and equal part of society (M. Zeitlin, 1970, preface). Zeitlin also notes that their actions matched their words (pp. xxxii–xxxiii).

Conversely, the elitist intellectuals' own change of consciousness in the 1950's may be interpreted from the inside as an awakening from the illusions of Socialist ideology, or from the outside as elite hysteria over an exaggerated Communist menace.

How do we test these two hypotheses comparatively? What is needed is a standpoint that allows one to interpret both hypotheses in such a way as to make them comparable, and a reliable empirical method that is neutral between the two. Or are they two ways of saying the same thing, so there is nothing to test?

For a Marxist the crucial test is objective. The difference between hysteria and liberation is not located in characteristics of the two forms of consciousness, but in whether consciousness is appropriate to objective conditions of work. If it is, it will be expressed in actions at work that interact with working conditions, and will be shaped by this interaction. If consciousness is unrelated to work it remains subjective, private, and can be called hysteria in retrospect. For instance the radical student who starts a managerial career will find his private attitudes continually disciplined by reality, so that the attitudes become pleasant fantasy or nostalgia, and gradually disappear.

The elitist intellectual will not accept this test, because for him working conditions are the inevitable consequence of industrial civilization, and the appropriate attitude is one of acceptance. The issue between elitists and Marxists, then, is one of possibility, not actuality: what changes in society are objectively possible? A neutral test is not easy to devise here.

Meanwhile, the phenomenon of hysteria-radicalization throws serious doubt on all elitist survey research on the masses. If survey research is used to discover empirical regularities and correlations, rather than the day's public opinion, it presupposes some basis for response stability. But we see that the process of radicalization can completely alter the responses of a population. What then is left of the correlations? They are nothing more than descriptions of a particular state of affairs which may change at any time. Zeitlin's study (1970), for instance, comes out of the elitist survey research tradition via his teacher Lipset. It is in part standard survey research which locates a few significant correlations, the kind from which mass theory is built, and which incidentally disconfirm Lipset's hypothesis of working-class authoritarianism at least for Cuba (ibid., Chapter 10). But running through the tables is the tremendous effect of the Revolution, ten times as strong as the correlations themselves. Is this a real change or only a temporary mass hysteria? Survey research cannot answer this question, because it deals only with consciousness. It can only describe the present scene and, by panel studies, report its continuation or change.

The other half of the radicalization process is deradicalization, a topic that the elitists (Tucker, for instance) have found more congenial to their own experience. It will not do to treat radicalization as an objectively determined process and deradicalization as an immoral action, as Marxists have sometimes done. If the dynamics of the system produce one they also produce the other. An empirical method that studies one side of this process must also study the other side.

Alienation and Exploitation

The employee standpoint brings an awareness of the reality of alienation and exploitation. "Alienation" has been defined by non-Marxists in all sorts of ways best not mentioned here (Diesing and Piccone, 1967), but for us it is the fact that our work is controlled from afar. In the university we are a line number in the State Budget, the plaything of finance committees, and our tools, the libraries and laboratories, are objects of struggle between the construction interests and the banking interests. Our protection is our own solidarity and the union which has its finger in the various political maneuvers and protects us from at least the worst abuses.

For exploitation we turn to the industrial worker Braverman (1974) who shows historically and in detail that "increasing efficiency" means "getting more work out of the worker"—in Marxist terms, increasing surplus value. The task of the efficiency expert is to tighten control over the worker's movements, to take control away from the worker, so that those movements can be speeded up. The task of the chemical and industrial engineers has been to develop technology that would objectify, measure, and control worker movements and then speed them up (Noble, 1977). The task of the industrial psychologist has been to reduce labor unrest and find ways to instill loyalty and dedication to work (Noble, 1977, Chapter 9). In all these cases the measure of efficiency has been simply profit. O'Connor (1975) expresses the same point by arguing that efficiency for management is quite different from efficiency for the employee, and often the opposite. For example, the state measures our productivity by the amount of research money we bring in to the university—with overhead fees going to the central administration—the number of credit hours taught, the number of degrees granted, while for us productivity is measured by what we learn about our society and ourselves.

Braverman reports an amusing instance of elitist misremembering (1974. pp. 102–108). The original was Frederick Taylor's report on how he increased the efficiency of steelworkers carrying pig iron. He began by locating the strongest man in the group, then through detailed carrying instructions got him to work to the limit of his capacity, carrying nearly four times as much iron as before. Only one man in eight was strong enough to maintain this rate; the rest were assigned to other work at lower pay, while the men doing quadruple work received a 60% pay increase. Daniel Bell misremembers this incident as a technical study of shovel size, angles and arcs, that is as a study of the efficient transformation of energy (Bell, 1960, p. 227). But no shovels or wheelbarrows were used, and the increase in efficiency was simply a matter of working harder and faster. Here we see the mental process in the elitist intellectual by which exploitation becomes invisible and is transformed into a neutral "efficiency."

Exploitation is also made invisible by the neoclassical partial equilibrium method, in which one deduces from Walrasian assumptions that at equilibrium each factor of production including labor is paid the exact amount that it contributes to the value of the product. Thus exploitation is assumed away, and attention is focused on the theoretical long run consequences of changes in rates of pay, etc. But empirically, "There is practically no direct information on whether or not labor is paid its marginal product. Economists take it as an article of faith or else claim that it is the best null hypothesis . . . Without this assumption, much of economic analysis falls apart" (Lester Thurow, 1970, pp. 20–21, quoted in David Gordon, 1972).

Once exploitation has been made invisible, econometricians can write about "production functions" and "production possibility curves" and industrial engineers can discuss techniques for increasing efficiency as though the issue were simply one of rearranging factors of production. But the development of capitalist technology is not an increase in neutral efficiency; it is a separation between the mental and muscular aspects of work and a gathering of the mental aspects into the control of management (Braverman, 1974, Chapter 3). This facilitates the control and speed-up of labor mentioned above; it also systematically destroys labor skills and reduces the level of skill needed. Thereby it also reduces the ratio of living labor in production and the levels of pay. The process of skill reduction is hidden by tricky data, which economists misinterpret to show that skill levels have increased (Chapter 20).

In Marxist terms, the forces of production are not neutral technology but embody capitalist social relations of production—capitalist domination and exploitation of labor. "Technical imperatives define only what is *possible*, not what is *necessary* . . . the latter decisions are social in nature" (Noble, 1977, p. 258).

Braverman does not claim that all increases of efficiency are actually increases in exploitation. Some technological improvements may increase efficiency by reducing waste motion or energy, such as the improvements described by Churchman in his operations research text (1957)—reducing unnecessary paper work and unused information storage depots, calculating optimum inventory levels. Marxist experience enables us to distinguish genuine increases in efficiency from techniques that merely increase labor exploitation. It enables us to conceive of alternative technologies that would actually reduce exploitation while increasing or maintaining efficiency levels for nonhuman factors of production. The frequent assertion by elitist intellectuals that the discontents of work arise from industrialism rather than capitalism and therefore are unavoidable shows an insensitivity to the possibility of alternative technologies (for an exception see Bell, 1960, pp. 242ff.). The "industrialism" argument is supported by the observation that Soviet industrialization has produced the same working conditions as capitalist industrialization; to this the Flerons (1972) answer that when the Soviet Union imported capitalist technology it also imported capitalist relations of production, including exploitation, and became to that extent capitalist (cf. also Braverman, 1974, pp. 11ff.).

Is the Soviet Union socialist?

One comes across a variety of terms for the Soviet Union—bureaucratic socialism, bureaucratic collectivism, state capitalism, primitive accumulation, pseudosocialism—but the common meaning is that the Soviet Union is not socialist in any sense relevant to us, however appropriate its development may have been in a Russian context. Socialism is defined for us by the quality of work. Is the capitalist-induced division between mental and physical components of work being reduced? Do workers participate collectively in planning and controlling their own work, as they are reported to do in Cuba and Yugoslavia? Or does management retain the right to specify piece rates and job speeds, tightening them regularly, as in Hungary (Haraszti, 1977)? The Soviet emphasis on ever-increasing armament levels is intelligible in terms of bureaucratic politics and US military power, but has nothing to do with socialism. Whether the surplus from work goes to the corporations or to the government makes no difference in the life of the worker.

Here is another difference between the Marxist and the left-liberal perspective. When the left liberal has a favorable conception of socialism it is expressed in terms of power and organization. Socialism consists of the people controlling the economy. This involves, first, destroying corporation control over the consumer—by eliminating advertising, planned obsolescence, and the capitalist propaganda disguised as social science. Insofar as the consumer frees herself from the endless treadmill of alienated consumption she can devote herself to discussing government policy and formulating the public purpose. Second, it involves destroying the profit-making growth dynamic of the monopoly sector, by nationalization or mixed ownership or price controls or socialized investment. Once the corporations come under government control they can be subordinated to whatever public purpose the voters formulate.

The New Left Marxist thinks of socialism rather as a different way of living, one centered on work rather than on alienated consumption. Work can be the focus of life, the source of self-respect and center of activity, when it is controlled collectively by those who work together. For state employees this involves organizational and budgetary changes; for industrial workers it involves a radically redirected technology in which mental and manual operations are reunited and craft skills reconstituted. Unless some such change occurs in daily life, changes in ownership and control of the economy are unimportant. Bureaucratic socialism, in which the growth imperative of the government departments is substituted for the growth imperative of the large corporations, is not socialism for the worker. In the worker's daily life, his work and his consumption, it is another form of capitalism.

This does not mean that the revolution has been betrayed; that would be a Schumpeterian subjective explanation, in which the party leaders are treated as Subject, as a modernizing elite with the responsibility for creating socialism. An objective explanation is that socialism in one country is impossible because even a "workers' state" must compete economically and militarily in the capitalist world market, where it is bound by the functional necessities of accumulation and legitimation (Hopkins and Wallerstein, eds. 1980, pp. 181-183, 175-177). The Soviet Union cannot secede from the world capitalist economy and the world military system. However, it can on rare occasions and in some respect play a progressive role by "creating more political space" for other socialist movements (ibid., p. 177). For instance, it did protect Cuba and Vietnam from imperialist domination.

Organization of Science

Marxist science brings with it a different mode of organization of the social sciences. We agree with the consumer-environmental movement that professionalism has by now become an absurdity that trivializes education and blocks the advancement of science. The logic of professionalism consists of ever more detailed specialization, proliferating technical language and technical journals that less and less people read, and a resulting trained incompetence to understand the problems of our society. The professional's stock of esoteric terms in which he locates his superior status turn out to be mystified trivialities, and his knowledge consists of acquaintance with the latest technical disputes in the journals. The absurdity of professionalism comes out even more clearly in elementary education, where it consists of teachers taking courses in the latest educational fad. In the 1970's such courses imparted training in constructing reward schedules for behavior modification, which produces a manipulative, dishonest teacher-pupil relationship if teachers take it seriously.

Rejection of professionalism does not imply rejection of specialized research, or of mathematics and technical concepts; quite the contrary. Mathematical concepts are actually clearer, simpler, and more precise than literary concepts, and are essential for understanding the structure, dynamics, and processes of social systems; the same is true

for the anthropologists' kinship terms and classifications, and so on.
Technical concepts become a barrier to science only when they get
developed to enormous complexity by professional virtuosos who have
lost interest in applying them to empirical problems. Specialized
research, even intense specialization over many years, is essential to
understand complex social systems and processes, complex historical
events, complex thinkers and traditions. But specialization becomes a
barrier to science when it is arbitrarily defined by existing subfields;
what is needed is "interdisciplinary" specialization, as the environmentalists have insisted. Rejection of professionalism does not imply
acceptance of the elitist intellectuals' aversion for mathematics, elaborate theoretical constructions, and specialized empirical study. Intel-
lectualism at the extreme becomes a superficial commentary on the
passing scene or a broad superficial survey of theories and theorists,
and is as bad as extreme professionalism.

All this has been recognized by the consumer–environmental
movement.

The triumph of professionalism is institutionalized in the departmental structure of the universities, plus the accompanying professional associations, journals, theories, and controversies. Within and
around this dominant liberal social science, however, are elements of a
developing Marxist organization of science. For instance, I have for
some years participated in three nonspecialized entities: a *center* for
international conflict studies, a *group* for applied psychoanalysis, and
a *college* of ethnic community studies and New Left politics. From
these and similar organizations around the country, like the *Kapitalistate* and *Telos* collectives, we can derive principles for a collectivist organization of science.

A) Organization is interdisciplinary, a coming together of people
from different backgrounds to work collectively on a project—and to
learn each other's background specialties in the process.

B) The distinction between students and teachers, also that between teaching and research, is transcended. People take turns leading
discussion and directing research as their specialties come up; courses
are organized around the needs of research, and research grows out of
current political problems.

C) The distinction between University and community, and that
between theory and action, is broken down. Action research reveals the
hidden structures of the city in the process of opposing them,
publicizing them, and trying to change them. Community members
participate in teaching and research, and university students live and
organize in the community.

D) Local organization is supplemented at the regional and national level by nonspecialized conferences like the Socialist Scholars' Conferences, new associations and new nonspecialized journals, and discussion groups in jail in New Hampshire after Seabrook protests.

The result of collectivist organization is an intense, exhausting, and wholly absorbing learning-teaching experience, completely different from the impersonal, alienated professionalism of the liberal university. Collectivist organization is, however, continually being blocked and corrupted by the dominant specialized hierarchical organization. Community ties are broken by student occupational mobility; the student-teacher distinction is reestablished by grading and degree requirements; courses are rigidified by curriculum and scheduling requirements; continuous attacks by administration and liberal faculty—in the name of educational quality!—gradually exhausts the energy of the participants; and state budget cutting and arbitrary reorganization sweep away laboriously built organizations. A Marxist organization of science is not viable at present.

In the absence of effective interdisciplinary organization and effective ties to community and political organizations, the Marxist scientist is thrown back into the dominant professional organization of science. He has to profess a specialty to get into academic life, and he has to cultivate and display specialized skills to survive. He is under constant pressure to accept a professional identity, that is, to take pride in his superior mathematical skills and his command of the latest mathematical "reswitching"-type controversy. But a professional identity is incompatible with the Marxist perspective, since it narrows attention to one segment of reality or even away from reality to technical tools. It is also incompatible with the Marxist standpoint, the working class, since it defines a distinct and superior status based on technical skills. It tells the professional that he is beyond the class struggle, and obscures his actual dependence on state budgetary politics and the vocational planning of university management, and his enforced participation in carrying out ruling class strategies. The result is a corrupted Marxism, technically impressive but cut off from its roots.

III. Orthodox Marxisms

Classification of the many kinds of Marxism and quasi-Marxism is a hopeless task; in particular the old left/new left distinction is unclear. There used to be an Orthodox Marxism, also called the theory of dialectical and historical materialism or diamat, which was the official theory of the Soviet Union and of its satellite Communist parties. In this theory Marx and Engels discovered the basic laws of motion of society (dialectical materialism) and applied them in a historical analysis of capitalism (historical materialism). Lenin applied the same laws to imperialism, and Stalin added some theoretical clarifications about the base and the superstructure. The theory was to be used to determine the correct strategy and tactics of the international workers' movement, and its truth would guarantee the eventual triumph of that movement.

The standpoint of Orthodox Marxism has already been discussed in Chapter One; it is a variant of traditionalist conservatism. The Wise Men are Marx and Engels; the Interpreters are Lenin, Stalin, and the current party leadership; the teachers and students are hierarchically organized in the only true vanguard party. Both the Eternal Truths and a paradigm for their historical application are found in the great books. The method of science consists of studying the sacred writings, down to the last letter to Bebel, but always under the guidance of the Interpreters.

As with all traditionalist conservatism this standpoint cannot deal with the Subject. Science is objective, and the method of science is a party discipline in which the individual subject learns to lose himself in the objective eternal truths. As we know, this sort of science was used to justify the foreign policy of the Soviet Union ex post facto, with the actual policy decisions being made on other grounds. It was also used to justify the alienated power of a vanguard party, since the party was in possession of absolute truth and any disagreement with the party line was by definition error and counterrevolutionary treason. The invisibility of the Subject served to hide the whole process from the party faithful.

The transformation of Marx's and Engels' works into a system of eternal truths was the work of the Interpreters, as with all traditionalism. Since truth does not contradict itself, it was necessary to show that every last line that these two geniuses wrote, published and unpublished, was consistent with every other line. Unlike the rest of us, they never made a mistake, never changed their minds, never even were vague in their own minds. Every line written to Kugelmann was as profound and well thought out as the final version of *das Kapital*. One sees this transformation occurring in the writings of Stalin, like *Leninism*, and in the Soviet textbooks. Much more could be and has been written about the Stalinist transformation of Marxism into the stiff, mechanistic absurdity of Diamat, that "antiquated, fossilized legacy" as Coletti calls it. Jesse Schwartz says in a slightly different context,

> Contradiction pervades all human ideas and beliefs. Every system of ideas when isolated and set out as an absolute truth becomes yet another episode in the comedy of human delusions. "Marxian Economics" . . . as often taught in colleges and universities shows signs of assuming the character of its adversaries and degenerating into an inflexible and scientistic excursus (Schwartz, 1977, p. 501).

Marx and Engels' work was in one way suited to such a transformation. Marx was a classical economist, working with a Ricardian model of the economy. Here the economy is a closed system within which commodities including labor circulate. As a closed system it is analogous to the Keynesian economy with important differences, and the similarity facilitates discussion, and misunderstandings, between Marxian and Keynesian economists. The neoclassical system with its open horizon is quite different. But classical, Marxian, and neoclassical systems share one characteristic: the deductions assume long run competitive equilibrium—for the classicals, a moving equilibrium as the system grows. Marx's concept of the cost of reproduction of labor is a long run equilibrium concept; so also is his concept of class consciousness (Lukacs, 1971, Chapter 3) and false consciousness. Long run laws includes the tendency of the average rate of profit to fall, the tendency of the rate of profit to equalize throughout the economy, and the tendency of the class struggle to polarize into two classes. There are also short-run analyses in Marx, particularly his theory of business cycles; but the basic analysis, Volume 1 of *Capital*, is long run.

When a long-run equilibrium theory is applied to an immediate situation a good deal of interpretation is necessary. This is called "making a concrete analysis." The long run concepts must somehow be exemplified by specific entities in the immediate chaos, while other, counteracting components must be handled ad hoc. The actual class structure must be simplified into two or three classes, the petit bourgeoisie being the third; actual data must be corrected to allow for historical accidents like the Vietnam war; actual consciousness must be brushed off as false consciousness or bad leadership.

A concrete analysis using Marx's long-run concepts can in principle be enlightening and complex, especially if supplementary ad hoc ideas are picked up from here and there, as in Mandel (1975). The result is illuminating description but nothing new in the way of theory. More often it simply provides an exemplification for each concept and then

draws the practical implication, much as Homans and other neoclassicists did with their long-run theory.

Consider for example Linder's direct application of long-run concepts to an immediate situation, his argument that the US Social
Security Act was a victory for the working class (1977, Vol. 1, p. 164).
Linder's assertion suggests that there was a specific battle over
insurance, a specific episode in the centuries-old class struggle, which
labor won. But if the Business Council wrote the Act (Domhoff, 1974,
p. 99), if the tax is highly regressive and involves a subsidy of the rich
by the poor, if the actuarial basis is unsound and the Fund threatened
by bankruptcy, if the main pressure for social security came from the
Townsend Clubs of California, and the act was written in such a way
as to split the Townsend Clubs off from their supporters (Piven and
Cloward, 1979, p. 31; "The Social Security Act effectively dampened
public support for the Townsend Plan while yielding the old people
nothing."), and if labor was highly divided on the issue, with many
union leaders opposing Social Security as likely to weaken unions and
make workers dependent on government (R. Horowitz, 1978) it is not
clear what "victory" means. Thurman Arnold (1937) might have
commented that the proletariat won a great victory *without anybody
knowing it*. In other words, the long run class struggle is ascribed to
historical events post hoc by the analyst, and the actual opinions and
political positions of the participants are brushed aside as false
consciousness and bad leadership.

The political position of the Interpreter expresses itself in the way
the exemplifications of long-run concepts are chosen. If the Interpreter
is a friend of the Soviet Union the class line-up will be drawn one
way; if he is a friend of China the line-up will be different. Every shift
in Stalin's foreign and domestic policies could be justified post hoc by
his propagandists by a reinterpretation of the immediate situation in
terms of the same long-run concepts. For instance, the Soviet sup-
pression of the workers' uprisings of 1953, 1956, and 1968 could be
justified by "false consciousness" plus the elitists' ubiquitous "outside
agitator."

Stalin's Orthodox Marxism or Diamat is now rightly rejected as a
perversion of Marxism, a propaganda use of the theory to justify
Soviet foreign and domestic policies, an attempt to pretend that the
bureaucratic and degenerate USSR was actually socialist and deserved
the allegiance of radicals all over the world. What we have instead
today is a multiplicity of Orthodox Marxisms, each led by its own
hierarchy of Interpreters, each claiming to be the one true interpretation of Marx's eternal truths. There are the DDR Orthodox (Heyden,

1968), the Trotskyites (Mandel, 1968, 1975) the various British Trotskyites (Kidron, 1974), the French structuralists (Althusser, 1970), the US Labor Party (Marcus, 1974)[7] and so on. These new orthodoxies are far superior in quality to Diamat, but the method is the same. The truth of the sacred texts is assumed, and the problem is entirely one of interpreting that truth correctly. This involves textual exegesis: interpreting a passage in *Capital* in the light of a letter to Kugelmann or an 1866 speech, or vice versa; qualifying one passage by reference to a different one; and in Althusser's case, removing certain portions of the sacred texts as inauthentic. Once the text has been properly interpreted it is only necessary to contrast it with the interpretation or theory being criticized to show the falsehood of the latter. In all cases one finds that a) the person being criticized has no understanding of Marxism; b) his position is bourgeois and therefore counterrevolutionary, and c) he is an idealist.

As for non-Marxist social science, it is of course all bourgeois and worthless. Taking any of it seriously involves "abandoning a large part of the theoretical field to the class enemy" (Linder, 1977, Volume I, p. 383) as though the world had already divided irrevocably into two sides—had reached long-run equilibrium—and the battle was on. Linder's own scholarly critique of Samuelson (Linder, 1977) exemplifies this attitude. This issue as Linder sees it is one of Marx's truth versus Samuelson's error; his strategy is simply to juxtapose the two. Samuelson is simply wrong; his whole work is a crude heap of irrationality and blindness. Again and again Linder asserts, "S cannot see," "S does not realize," as if to say that if Samuelson had studied reality as intensely and steadily as Marx did he would have seen the same truth. But there are also suggestions that Samuelson was not trying very hard, and in fact that he was trying to avoid seeing the truth of Marxism (Volume I, p. 5) by half closing his eyes to reality. This attitude is consistent with the epistemology of traditionalist conservatism: if the Wise Men, Marx and Engels, could discover the eternal truths simply by studying reality intensely, then Samuelson should be able to also, given proper assistance by the Interpreters.

The esssential difference between New Left Marxism and the Orthodox Marxisms is that the New Lefters treat Marx's writings as suggestive theories, guides to thinking and method, models to imitate, rather than as revealed truth. Also they combine Marx's long-run models with various short-run models, some adapted from recent social science and some newly devised. O'Conner uses an institutionalist model of the monopoly sector and its relations to the competitive sector, a functionalist model of the state and its relations to society, and a neoclassical model of the competitive sector; he also makes extensive use of theoretical work in public finance and budgetary politics. Baran and Sweezy (1966) make extensive use of Keynesian concepts and models in their short-run analysis of monopoly sector dynamics.

The difference comes out nicely if we compare O'Connor (1973) with Gough (1975) on the same topic. Gough uses two negative concepts as substitutes for short-run concepts: 1) Mandel's law of uneven development, which says that the long-run dynamics of capitalism work unevenly in different sectors in the short run, and that there is much interaction between these various sectors. 2) The concept of "historical accidents" which says that in the short run all sorts of things happen that are scientifically unknowable. False consciousness is another such negative concept, which says that short-run consciousness is different from long-run equilibrium consciousness. These negative concepts free Gough to use his ingenuity in his ad hoc concrete analysis.

In place of "uneven development" O'Connor discusses the interactions among the three sectors systematically. In place of Gough's long-run concept of the unitary working class O'Connor differentiates the labor force of the three sectors and shows how their different levels and types of unionization result from their economic circumstances and from shifting governmental strategies. In place of "false consciousness" O'Connor shows how the actual consciousness and the temporary alliances of the three sectors vary according to economic circumstance and government strategy. In place of "historical accident" he shows how historically varied governmental policies are all governed by the same functional requirements and thereby become theoretically intelligible. In place of the concepts of underconsumption and immiseration for all labor, which Gough mistakenly finds in his work, O'Connor analyzes, and provides empirical evidence for, demand deficiency in the monopoly sector and immiseration for surplus labor.

The additional stock of concepts enables New Left Marxists to engage in empirical investigations which produce new theory, rather than the "concrete analysis" which merely applies old doctrine to new circumstances.

IV. Imperialism

New Left Marxism provides yet another perspective on imperialism, conceiving it as a regionally organized system of labor exploitation. To evaluate the contribution to science of this perspective on imperialism, let us compare it with the conceptualizations available from the other perspectives.

From the neoclassic perspective imperialism is a negative phenomenon, however one chooses to define it; it is some sort of interference with the international free market. For instance one might define it as a system of imperial preference, a certain kind of tariff, covered by tariff theory. Or it might be an arrangement for preferential investment, an interference with the capital market. All such phenomena must be understood negatively, in terms of how they cause prices and quantities to deviate from the free market equilibrium level. Also they fall into the category of short-run phenomena, which for some neoclassicists can not be dealt with scientifically in any case. They are the result of arbitrary or irrational government activities and therefore not subject to rational analysis. As a short-run phenomenon and as a deviation from equilibrium, imperialism is continually tending to die out of itself, though short-sighted government interference can delay its passing indefinitely.

From the objective-systems perspective in which government is the responsible actor, all cybernetic systems have a boundary which marks the limit of governmental responsibility. Imperialism must therefore be defined in terms of its unique kind of boundary and internal subsystem boundaries. The simplest way is to define an empire as a system composed of territorially distinct and semi-autonomous subsystems. The subsystems may differ from each other in language, culture, and political or social organization; they may have a separate history, having been unified by conquest, and therefore have aspirations for independence. Eisenstadt's concept (1963) is more complex, and emphasizes the difference in mode of organization between system and territorial subsystem. The subsystems were organized according to traditional particularist-ascriptive values, including local immobility of labor and capital. The central administration was organized bureaucratically according to universalist-achievement values, including mobility of labor and capital. The emperor had to combine these contradictory modes of organization and legitimation in his own person and prevent either one from dominating the other. Eisenstadt's work provides a whole functionalist theory of imperialism, rather than simply a definition.

From this perspective the age of imperialism ended about 1960 when most of the African colonies achieved independence. Then began the era of "old societies and new states," with new governments taking responsibility for the modernization of their territories. The subject matter of political science and of comparative sociology had tripled in quantity in a few years. If the old imperial governments desired to interfere in the internal affairs of the new states, this would constitute "intervention," meddling, rather than a continuation of empire, because the old government no longer had responsibility for the maintenance of the new state.

For the Schumpeterian elitists national boundaries are irrelevant, since elite responsibility is worldwide, and imperialism cannot therefore be defined in terms of boundaries. Schumpeter's 1951 treatise on imperialism is the most systematic account available for this standpoint so we will follow its argument.

Imperialism, for Schumpeter, is a survival from the barbaric times before capitalism. In those days military conquest was one of the few outlets for brilliant, vigorous, creative persons, the other outlets being religion and philosophy, so these people went into military careers and formed empires. Imperialism is thus essentially a military phenomenon. Once the empires were formed, they tended to persist; for Schumpeterians the basic dynamic of society is inertia. An aristocratic-military class appeared in the empires, benefited from them, and protected them. Autocratic rulers like Louis XIV allied with the aristocrats to maintain their own power; the rising bourgeoisie did the same, and in the process absorbed the old imperialist mentality. Tariffs, colonies, and cartels are survivals of empire, modified and protected by this bourgeois-imperialist mentality. However this mentality is incongruous with a developed capitalist economy and must eventually die out, along with the military aristocracy, nationalism, prestige needs, and male supremacy.

Schumpeter's followers locate imperialism in the main surviving center of barbarism as they see it, the Soviet Union. They see there an inherent tendency to military expansion, expressing the barbaric urge for conquest. Similarly, the Kremlinologists long interpreted Soviet internal politics as a pure barbaric struggle for power. As for the capitalist countries, one can understand the surviving remnants of imperialism in such backward countries as Portugal; but in the advanced countries and most of all the United States the imperialist mentality and reality has long since died out. The US elite are motivated by that capitalist sense of service, responsibility, and duty which Schumpeter extolled (1942, pp. 127–129).

The bureaucratic-institutionalists, freed of illusions about the benevolence of the US elite, are able to perceive military imperialism in US foreign policy: " . . . an empire the United States has become. In thirty nations around the world the United States military is located in 429 major and nearly 3000 minor bases" (Lockard, 1971, p. 270). The Soviet Union has indeed engaged in a small amount of military expansion since 1941, but only into immediately adjacent countries and only in wartime when its own existence had been threatened. Its imperialism, though real enough, can be interpreted as defensive and reactive (though some institutionalists see it as more than defensive, especially since 1979). But the greatest expansion by far has been that of US military forces since 1945 (Welch, 1971). And if we add to the US overseas forces the Latin American military, trained, indoctrinated, and equipped by the US, the true extent of the US empire becomes apparent. US expansion has continued steadily since the late nineteenth century at least, including intermittent military occupation in the Caribbean and occasional annexation (Lockard, 1971, p. 261).

In addition to this objective military-expansion aspect of imperialism the bureaucratic theorist recognizes a subjective conceptual aspect. The US, the SU, and other expansionist powers do not send out their armies out of sheer barbaric vigor, as Schumpeter asserted. Rather, they have elaborate justifications for their murderous policies. These may be divided into the interest and the ideological components, following Schurmann's discussion (1974). The imperialism of interests is familiar as "dollar diplomacy," the use of Marines to protect US overseas investments (Lockard, 1971, pp. 266-267). This kind of imperialism was dominant in the nineteenth century and is still important. However, the imperialism of ideology has been dominant since Roosevelt's 1941 vision of a global New Deal (Schurmann, 1974, pp. 4ff.). Roosevelt's argument was that the US, as the richest nation on earth, had a responsibility to raise the living standards of the poor all over the earth through massive foreign aid programs. Remember that for the bureaucratic theorists ideological politics is the way the President maintains his power against the bureaucracy. After Roosevelt's death "the earth" was changed to "the non-communist part of the earth," and the financial aid plus military expansion was justified as protection against Communist aggression. The military protection was regarded as a temporary measure until these nations became able to protect themselves; the Dulles-inspired regional defense pacts represented a step in that direction. The nineteenth century predecessor of this ideology was the doctrine of the "white man's burden."

In short, for the bureaucratic theorist, Schumpeter and Rostow's conception of elite responsibility for mass wellbeing is reinterpreted as the ideology of imperialism. Rostow himself becomes the chief ideologist of US imperialism, assisted by Brzezinski, Huntington, J. Schlesinger, E. Rostow, and that whole "committee on the present danger."

A third quite recent aspect of imperialism is the economic imperialism of the multinational corporations (Galbraith, 1973, pp. 123–125; Barnet and Müller, 1974). Imperialism is an extension abroad of the planning sector domination of the market sector. Just as the planning sector continually impoverishes the market sector in its drive for endless expansion so the multinational corporation continually extracts profit from the dependent countries through a variety of devices that Barnet and Müuller describe. According to Galbraith, the main imperial interest of the corporations is in protection of future raw material supplies; profits they get through sales in the rich countries.

For the bureaucratic-institutionalist, imperialism is not a disappearing or disappeared phenomenon, but rather a continuing dynamic that has taken new forms since 1945. "It was not until Fidel Castro that Cuba made its final break with colonialism. In much of the rest of Latin America the break is still incomplete" (Galbraith, 1977, p. 121).

The New Left Marxist conception of imperialism is centered on economic structure rather than military expansion and self-deceiving ideology (A.G. Frank, 1967, 1969; Bodenheimer, 1971; Emanuel, 1972; Leys, 1974; O'Connor, 1974, Chapters 7, 8; Amin, 1976, Chapters 3-5; Wallerstein, 1979). An imperial economy has two geographically distinct sectors, the core and the periphery, or metropolitan and satellite areas. The core or metropolis controls and exploits the periphery through an institutionalized system of production and exchange in which the surplus of the periphery is drawn to the core and accumulated as capital; accumulation of wealth at one pole means accumulation of poverty at the other pole. The onesidedness of the system forces it to continually change to new forms of exploitation and of control, though the underlying imperial structure remains the same. There is also a semiperipheral position, exemplified by Brazil and Ivory Coast since 1970, which combines characteristics of both extremes and connects them or mediates between them. Some basic concepts are as follows:

Exploitation. In America and Africa the original conquerors simply took the valuables of the peripheral areas by force—gold and silver from the Americas, slaves from Africa. This kind of system cannot last long since no provision is made for replacement of the loot; besides, the labor power of the slaves must be harnessed somehow. The answer was plantations and mines that put slaves and native labor to work, either forcibly or through taxation and expropriation of native land, as in Kenya. The early plantation owners were exploited in turn by the mercantile trading monopolies; this was the form of imperialism that bothered some American colonists, who had no objection to slaves and plantations.

The capital accumulated by trading monopolies had to be put to work, and the plantations and mines with their cheap labor supply were profitable outlets. Another outlet was the construction of the colonial infrastructure—ports, railroads, urban centers. Still later the capital from the metropolis was invested in industry, producing both local consumers' goods and parts for products to be fabricated elsewhere.

Control. Over the centuries the forms of control have gotten ever more indirect, complex, and refined. The original conquerors controlled by military force; this was soon refined and disguised as legal prerogatives: land grants from the Crown, trading monopolies, areas reserved for settlers. The colonial government used taxation and land ownership restrictions to force natives off their own land and on to the plantations. Later the power of metropolitan capital was used to direct investments and control the economic policy of the colonial governments.

By now the power of metropolitan capital over the satellites takes many forms. First, there are the international lending institutions: the IMF, the World Bank, the Export-Import Bank, and the Agency for International Development, all of whom can impose stringent conditions for loans (Payer, 1974). The large New York banks have also made huge loans. By 1978 the Third World was in debt to these banks for about $175 billion, including $50 billion from US private banks (Dann, 1979, p. 66). The satellite countries must direct their economies to the export trade so they can repay these debts with interest, or they will get no more credit. Second, US foreign aid has resulted in US control of a substantial part of the currency of aided countries such as India (O'Connor, 1974, p. 198; Hayter, 1971). The African and Caribbean currency boards exercise similar controls over local currencies (Amin, 1976, p. 261; O'Connor, 1974, pp. 171-172). The multinational corporations also collect capital from private savings in the satellites for their own investment purposes. US corporate investment abroad is mainly in the basic industries and the capital goods industries, which dominate the satellite economies (Dann, 1979, pp. 67-68). The corporations exercise a pervasive control, both over their own subsidiaries and over seemingly independent firms. Their control over marketing outlets forces even nationalized firms, such as the Bolivian tin mines (O'Connor, 1974, p. 210) to do business with them on their own terms (Leys, 1974, pp. 11-12). Their own subsidiaries are integrated into an international production and distribution network and could not survive independently, for instance as nationalized industries (Martin Landsberg, 1979). Seemingly independent firms are forced to lease the advanced technology of the corporations for substantial fees and royalties (Leys, 1974, pp. 12-17). Remaining in the background are the military forms of control, including CIA subversion, training and equipping of military forces, and if necessary military intervention by the metropolitan power.

Control means exploitation. All the economic forms of control are based on some form of monopoly: trading licenses, capital, marketing outlets, technology. Consequently the metropolitan corporations can use their superior market power to impose favorable trade terms (Emmanuel, 1972; Amin, 1976, pp. 138-145, 187). The neoclassical economists remind us that in a voluntary exchange both parties benefit; but the game theorists remind us that in a bargaining game whose structure is Chicken, or Bully or Protector, the more powerful bargainer can take nearly all the advantage for himself. Consequently even though the satellites desire employment, industrialization, loans and trade, and do get short-run benefits from all of these, they are progressively impoverished over the centuries. Imperialism is a positive feedback system; unequal bargaining power produces unequal exchange, which through capital accumulation increases inequality of bargaining power.

Structure. Metropolitan exploitation of the satellites is systematized as a structure of production and exchange (Amin, 1976, pp. 199-203). This structure was originally set up by force, and involved disrupting existing production and exchange, destroying craft skills and existing cultures. Some of its characteristics are as follows:

1) The satellite economy is export oriented, producing for the metropolitan market. Trade routes, railroads, lead down to the ports, not cross-country.

2) A dual economy (described in detail in Frank, 1967) in which the export sector dominates the native subsistence sector and derives cheap labor and food from it. The subsistence sector is competitive, with surplus labor, low skill and capital; the export sector is monopolistic, capital-intensive, low-wage because of monopoly bargaining power. Income inequality between these two sectors increases over time

(Amin, 1976, pp. 351ff.). Thus the metropolitan-satellite structure of domination is reproduced in the satellite.

3) Low wages mean inadequate purchasing power in the satellite and therefore few investment opportunities in production for the local market. The satellite businessmen, managers, and landowners therefore must spend their income on luxury goods produced in the metropolis; or, more recently, invest them in ventures controlled by the multinational corporations. Luxury goods maintain the elite culture and prestige that legitimates aristocratic domination of the masses (Genovese, in Edwards et al., 1972, p. 78). Here is an alternative, or supplementary, explanation of the cultural values of the Latin American elite. Lipset (1967) explains these values as survivals of a traditionalist culture; the Marxist explains them as part of the structure of imperial domination, induced and maintained by the production and exchange system. Latin American underdevelopment is maintained by export-oriented, debt-crippled economies, and elite values are only a contributory cause, not the primary cause as in the Schumpeterian theory. "The moral basis of a backward society" (Banfield, 1958) is not a basis but a supporting component of a satellite economic system.

4) The export sector is unilaterally dependent on the metropolis. The commercial exchange between satellite and metropolis is a high proportion of the satellite's income and low proportion of the metropolitan income (Amin, 1976, pp. 144, 157-160). Metropolitan investment in the satellite is a high proportion of satellite and a low proportion of total metropolitan investment.

5) This dependence in turn means that production and investment in the satellite is determined by metropolitan needs: originally the need to accumulate capital, then the need for profitable investment outlets as well, more recently the need to control long-term supplies of raw materials; as corporations expand, their horizon into the future lengthens (Dean, in Fann and Hodges, 1971; Bodenheimer, 1971, p. 174). When these needs change the satellite economy collapses.

Northeastern Brazil was, in the seventeenth century, the scene of an "economic miracle" that led nowhere—the moment that the sugar-growing economy lost its importance, the region fell into a state of lethargy, to become later on the famine area that it is today. . . . When the iron ore of Lorraine is eventually worked out, this may create a difficult reconversion problem for the region, but it will be able to overcome these difficulties, for an infrastructure of integrated industries has been formed on the basis of the mineral, which could be imported from elsewhere. But when the iron ore of Mauritania is worked out, that country will go back to the desert (Amin, 1976, pp. 238–239).

The metropolitan-satellite structure can also appear within a metropolitan country; examples are the US south in the nineteenth century and Southern Italy including Banfield's "Montegrano" (Banfield, 1958. See also Holland, 1976). "Each developed country has created within itself its own underdeveloped country . . ." (Amin, 1976, p. 362). Genovese's studies of the US slave society are thus a relevant part of the Marxist theory of imperialism.

The pol 'ical and the economic aspects of imperialism are interdepender . For example, the economic development of Kenya as a British satellite—setting up white-owned plantations and forcing natives to work on them for almost nothing after taxes—was launched by the British government to pay for the Mombasa-Lake Victoria railroad (Leys, 1974, pp. xvi, 28). The railroad was built to provide military access to the headwaters of the Nile, as part of the British program to deny this area to the French. The French were interested in the upper Nile area as a way of getting leverage on Egypt, from which they had been expelled in 1882. Egypt meant the Suez Canal, the lifeline of the British Empire. British-French rivalry was a continuation of political rivalry dating back to the Middle Ages.

The colonial governments were set up in part to keep out rival imperial powers, in part to enforce the exploitation of native labor; later they were also necessary to protect capital investments and ensure debt repayment. The imperial structure produced a native bourgeoisie in the satellites, culturally and economically dependent on the metropolitan economy; when this bourgeoisie was strong enough to control a colony, the colony could be made independent, if politically necessary, without threatening the imperialist economic structure (Amin, 1976, p. 380). In Kenya, for instance, the British prepared for independence by hastily encouraging the development of an African bourgeoisie (Leys, 1974, Chapters 5–7). In addition the many instruments of financial control developed since 1880 and especially since 1945 were strong enough to dominate a would-be socialist or independent government such as Bolivia, 1952. The new Kenya government, for instance, was tied tightly to various financial agreements. And if financial control failed, there was always military action as a last resort—Guatemala, 1954; Brazil, 1964; Chile, 1973.

The difference between the colonial and the neo-colonial period is thus entirely a difference in the methods of control over the satellites.

In both cases there is a hierarchy of control levers, the military being the ultimate one.

The Marxist tends to pay little attention to the ideological justifications for imperialism. The nineteenth century "white man's burden" to civilize and Christianize the natives, the doctrine of free trade, the Rostow doctrine of elite responsibility for economic development, and the anticommunism of Brzezinski and others are all equally imperialist propaganda that disguise reality (for example Frank, 1969, Chapter 2).

Two standpoints are involved in the Marxist conceptualization of imperialism (Bodenheimer, 1971, p. 176). The view "from above," exemplified by Magdoff and O'Connor, sees imperialism as an enormous extension of the domination and exploitation that we ourselves experience, however mildly, in our work. The same state-corporation team that gave us Vietnam and an ever-expanding military budget but continually impoverishes the cities and tightens the education and social services budget is using all that military equipment abroad to oppress other people. The same corporate dynamics of expansion, exploitation, and capital accumulation operates abroad as well as at home; abroad it is the dynamics of US imperialism.

The view "from below," exemplified by Frank, Amin, and Cardoso, looks at imperialism from the standpoint of the Latin American and African people. These writers describe the economic and political and cultural structures of their own countries as a dependent part of a larger system. They trace their own history of ever-growing impoverishment and dependency, of successive attempts at independence that failed, of successive bloody repressions. "Dependency and imperialism are, thus, two names for one and the same system" (Bodenheimer, 1971, p. 176).

Evaluation. The neoclassic standpoint is plainly not suited for dealing with imperialism. Imperialism becomes a negative, short-run, disappearing phenomenon, a *Schein* rather than an *Erscheinung*. The various pronouncements of this school are persistently remote from reality (Emanuel, 1972, introduction). The persistent neoclassic argument for free trade was accepted only by the British for a few decades when they had a trade monopoly—for the neoclassicists almost all politicians are and have been irrational in their rejection of free trade. The neoclassicists' predictions for the terms of trade have persistently turned out to be the opposite of reality—the terms of trade have been irrational for a century. In particular, the assumption of perfect labor mobility assumes imperialism away.

The government and elitist standpoints make possible systematic conceptions of imperialism, but these conceptualizations locate imperialism in the past and in the barbaric Soviet Union. They thus distort the understanding of capitalist imperialism in the period 1880-1914 when imperialism was expanding and developing, not dying out; they blind one to the vigorous growth of US imperialism since 1945. I refer here to US military-economic expansion since 1945, whether or not one chooses to call this "imperialism," and to the systemic continuity of the world system before and after 1945, whether or not one calls this system imperialist. Wallerstein (1979), for instance, summarizes the same theory discussed above without using the terminology of imperialism.

The bureaucratic-institutionalists distinguish and relate three aspects of modern imperialism: the political-military, the ideological, and the political-economic. Of these three, the economic aspect is the least well developed. Galbraith's few sentences are a sketch of a theory, and the Barnet and Müller is a specialized study. The emphasis up to now has been on military and ideological aspects. The Marxist theories of imperialism concentrate on the political-economic aspect and treat military considerations as secondary. Ideology is criticized as pure *Schein*, disguise of reality.

It seems then, at first, that the two standpoints supplement each other. They approach modern imperialism from two opposite ends, and each is strong where the other is weak. From a Marxist standpoint the Marxist theories focus on economic-political reality and deal more sketchily with appearance, while the Galbraithians focus carefully on appearance and scarcely get very far into reality; but since appearance (Erscheinung) and reality, or superstructure and base, are interdependent, the contrast is not important. The Marxist theories have been thoroughly developed in a great number of theoretical and empirical studies since 1957 (a fact apparently unknown to Galbraith), while the bureaucratic institutionalists have produced only a few scattered studies since 1970 and one classic, Schurmann (1974); but this merely means that the potentialities of the Galbraith-Schurmann standpoint remain to be developed.

In particular, the Schurmann-Ellsberg-Melman explanation of the Vietnam war, which focus on bureaucratic politics and on ideology, is superior to the Marxist explanation, both systematically and in detail. Marxists have explained that the US was not involved in Vietnam to protect some particular business interest or some potential oil resources, but to preserve all of southeast Asia for long-run world capitalism, and also to demonstrate the costs of attempted independence to other US satellites. Good enough, but general and sketchy.

Schurmann explains not only the main stages of our involvement since 1950 but also detailed strategic and tactical decisions in terms of the conflicting ideologies and bureaucratic politics in Washington. He (and others) show that ideology is not simply a disguise for reality, but the form in which capitalist reality appears to itself. It is an autonomous causal factor; subjective reality and even self-deception is part of reality.

To be sure, the Vietnam war was a commotion in the superstructure, the special domain of the bureaucratic theorists. It was also a short-run phenomenon, while the strength of the Marxist theories of imperialism is their ability to bring out the continuity in change of the imperialist structure over several centuries, with each new structure growing out of the previous one. The two perspectives again seem to be vaguely supplementary.

Ten Schumacher and Appropriate Technology

The ecological standpoint, which we consider in this chapter, has drawn its adherents from several of the standpoints discussed earlier. Schumacher began as a Keynesian; Leiss, a student of Marcuse, built on a foundation of Marxist categories. The closest connection is to the consumer-environmental movement, some of whose members combine an ecological theory with a populist citizens-lobby practice, for example Rosenbaum (1973). Also, as the ecological standpoint happens to suggest an anarchic organization of society, the anarchist wing of the New Left adopted the standpoint enthusiastically, for instance Bookchin (1970). An anthropological school has also developed around this standpoint since 1965. As a result one does not find a well organized community taking this standpoint, but rather a number of diverse tendencies. One might say that the adherents of this standpoint are as anarchic and heterogeneous as the society they recommend for the future.

The diversity is most marked in practice. Schumacher's disciples travel around the Third World teaching appropriate technology to the peasants in an imitation of Keynesian foreign aid. The environmentalists lobby, testify, and sue, trying to loosen the grip of the corporations on government policy and practice. Marxists, anarchists, and others organize antinuclear demonstrations aimed at hastening mass radicalization and an anticapitalist movement. Anarchists live in rural communes powered by solar energy and develop a technology and

288

social organization appropriate to human survival (Boyle and Harper, 1976; Merrill, 1976; the journal *New Roots*). Thus action runs the gamut from liberal reform through revolutionary mass organizing to the abandonment of a dying society and construction of a new one in the ruins of the old. And all these tactics are compatible.

We consider first the work of Schumacher, Commoner, and others to locate the conceptual scheme and the standpoint.

I. The Ecological Standpoint

The basic ecological concept is that of an *ecosystem*, "by which ecologists mean the community of organisms living in a specific locale, along with the non-biological factors in the environment—air, water, rock, and so on—that support them, as well as the ensemble of interactions among all these components" (Ophuls, 1977, p. 20). An ecosystem is a *community* of living species in a non-living environment. "Community" here means that the various species provide the necessities for each others' continued existence. For example, in an abstract three-species system of predators, prey, and plants: the prey are food for the predators, the plants are food for the prey, the droppings and bodies of predators and prey are food for the plants, the predators limit the prey population to fit the supply of plants, and so on. For a formalization of such a system see Kemeny and Snell (1962, Chapter 2) developing earlier work by Lotka.

Relations between species in an ecosystem are *cyclical*, as in the example above. Each biological cycle contains three functional stages—production, consumption, and decomposition (Ophuls, 1977, pp. 25-26)—in which production is the photosynthesis of organic materials and decomposition is the reduction of organic materials into inorganic compounds. In the predator–prey example the soil micro-organisms which decompose dead bodies, and the soil itself are essential components of the biological cycle. There are also inorganic cycles like the path of water from ocean to sky through the ground and rivers to the ocean.

Each species in an ecosystem has a *niche*; a position and a function in various cycles. The species survives insofar as the other species in the community perform their functions at an appropriate transformation rate and thereby maintain that niche. The ecosystem survives insofar as all the niches are maintained and functions performed at appropriate rates. The appropriate rates are maintained by various negative feedbacks. For instance too-efficient predators deplete their prey, produce a food shortage, reduce their own numbers by starvation, and thereby reduce their aggregate consumption rate to the previous less efficient level (Commoner, 1971, pp. 29ff.).

Here we have the concept of *homeostasis*. An ecosystem survives or *is* a system insofar as negative feedbacks maintain each flow in its component cycles within necessary limits. The limits are set by the needs of all the related niches in the cycle. This implies that the necessary rate of a cycle is set by the slowest link in the cycle, the bottleneck (Commoner, 1971, p. 33). When there is continuing pressure, not controlled by negative feedback, to exceed this rate the ecosystem is damaged or destroyed, and its parts are absorbed into larger ecosystems.

The largest ecosystem is the ecosphere or *biosphere*, the thin skin of the earth that sustains life.

Ecosystems, and the biosphere, have evolved in stages of *ecological succession*, from the beginning of life to the present (Commoner, 1971, pp. 13-17; Ophuls, 1977, pp. 34-39). The general direction of evolution is toward complexity, co-operative symbiosis of species, longer life cycles of more complex organisms with slower reproduction rates, adaptation of the inorganic environment to life, and more efficient use of energy throughput (Ophuls, 1977, p. 36). Localized ecosystems eventually reach a climax state of homeostasis in which the inorganic environment prevents further succession.

Human survival and prosperity depend on man's adaptation to his niche in the biosphere. This is the steady-state society. It involves limiting consumption rates to the slowest decomposition rates of the various cycles involving man; using primarily renewable energy rather than nonrenewable fossil fuels; and adapting natural cyclical processes to human needs. In practice renewable energy means solar energy, including direct solar power, methane, wood, wind, hydroelectric, and hydrothermal power (Commoner, 1979; Ophuls, 1977, Chapter 3). Since most forms of solar energy have no economies of scale but do have transmission costs an efficient solar economy would be mainly decentralized. The appropriate technology would be small scale, adapted both to the economics of solar energy and to the human capacity for creative labor; it would be "technology with a human face" (Schumacher, 1973, pp. 34, 146ff.; Boyle and Harper, 1976).

A steady-state society is not stationary; it can expand in many ways by enlarging cyclical bottlenecks, devising new biological cycles, and adjusting various positive and negative feedbacks (Ophuls, 1977, p. 13). However, there are ultimate limits based on the heat limits of the earth's climatic balance (Commoner, 1979). All energy use gives off waste heat, thereby warming the earth; if the earth gets too warm the biosphere will degenerate.

Note that the thinking underlying all the above concepts is systemic and cyclical. Ecological processes are all cyclical, so an adequate conceptualization of them must also be cyclical. This mode of thinking is embodied in various aphorisms or ecological laws: everything is connected to everything else, everything must go somewhere, and you can never do just one thing (Commoner, 1971, Chapter 2; Ophuls, 1977, p. 22). However, ecosystems are set in an ultimate linear context of the irreversible degradation of energy, as expressed in the second law of thermodynamics.

The opposite sort of thinking is linear. A linear organization of society maintains a flow from a supply of natural resources through production to consumption to waste products to garbage dumps. From an ecological standpoint this sort of society destroys itself, in three ways (Schumacher, 1973, Chapter 1). First, it lives on the earth's capital, its deposits of nonrenewable resources, rather than on circular flows of energy and materials. As that capital is depleted its cost goes up exponentially, producing inflation and exponentially increasing impoverishment (Commoner, 1979). Second, the concentrated garbage dumps exceed the flow limits of the decomposition stage, so the earth is progressively polluted and made unfit for human habitation. Third, linear technology aimed at a maximal rate of production and consumption destroys the creative potential of human labor through automation.

Linear thinking by itself has no destructive effects, nor does cyclical thinking preserve ecological homeostasis. Ophuls observes that China was dominated for thousands of years by Buddhist thinking, which enjoined harmony with nature, respect for natural processes, and the planting of trees; yet there was continuing severe environmental damage such as deforestation and erosion. Maoist China repaired this damage without benefit of Buddhist thinking and in spite of a linear-growth mentality (1977, pp. 153-154).

Most of the world today, with the temporary exception of China and Tanzania, is organized in a linear fashion, oriented to growth in GNP beyond all ecological limits, and therefore in process of self-destruction. The causes of this disastrous situation are not simply linear thinking, but ecologists disagree on what the other causes are. Schumacher blames human greed and envy in the abstract (1973, pp. 38-39). Ophuls (1977), following Garrett Hardin, focuses on the public goods problem—really an n-person Prisoner's Dilemma—inherent in the fact that the biosphere is the common habitat of mankind. It is to each individual's and each country's advantage to exploit, pollute, and destroy, and in fact the individual who tries to preserve the common good is penalized. Note that this structural cause assumes permanent human greed as a given. Commoner (1971) points to the structural compulsion to grow which is inherent in a competitive capitalist economy. In the Soviet Union and other bureaucratic socialist countries the compulsion to grow is built into the dynamics of bureaucracy and strengthened by an ideology of growth. Most of the Third World is similarly growth-oriented and aspires to either the capitalist or the Soviet model.

What is needed for survival is a rapid shift to a steady-state society dependent on solar energy and flow resources. The appropriate technology, labor-intensive and small-scale, is now in process of being devised—for example photovoltaic cells and biological pest controls. The appropriate politics is mainly that of autonomous small communities, with central governments responsible for the maintenance of larger ecosystems (Ophuls) and equalizing local advantages through rents and subsidies (Schumacher). The common-goods problem would be solved partly by community controls at all levels and partly by cultivating the values of frugality, modesty, and a sense of stewardship toward nature.

The conceptual scheme sketched above is plainly a type of systems thinking, explicitly holistic and cybernetic. The closest affinity is with the other types of system theories—functionalism, general system theory, cybernetics, and Marxism. In contrast, the various types of systems analysis and operations research are essentially different from the ecological perspective inasmuch as they assume a goal or goals outside the system and thus become linear. As with the other types of system theories science is the objective study of objective system dynamics. The strong subjective component present in functionalism and Marxism seems to be absent here; instead there seems to be a split between the objective science of ecology and the subjective Buddhist values of frugality, modesty, and stewardship for living things (Schumacher, 1973, p. 220). However, the evidence for the existence of a fact-value dichotomy is fragmentary.

The system is the ecosystem. This is more inclusive than the social systems of functionalism and Marxism since it is a man–nature system. From the ecological standpoint these other system theories are fundamentally deficient because they treat Nature as an external given.

The standpoint is a man-nature standpoint: Man is a part of the biosphere with his own niche. As a part of the system his conditions of survival and growth are determined; he is not free to ignore those conditions. But man is also responsible for the maintenance of the biosphere, and as responsible he is free to invent new techniques that expand the complexity of local ecosystems and improve their quality.

"Nature" is conceived mainly in rural terms. Just as the bourgeois economists have progressively reduced other factors of production to capital, with labor and land nearly disappearing, and the Marxists have reduced other factors to labor, so for the ecologists the emphasis is on land. Land is neither illiquid capital nor objectified labor, nor even a factor of production; it, including the organisms that live in and on it, is the chief part of the biosphere itself (Schumacher, 1973, pp. 102ff.). Agriculture is not properly a form of industry but its opposite; and of the two, agriculture is primary (p. 111). Civilization requires the balancing of these opposites rather than the reduction of agriculture to industry. Agricultural operations represent man's direct interdependence in the cycle of nature and thus reminds man what he is. Agriculture serves "to keep man in touch with living nature, of which he is and remains a highly vulnerable part" (p. 113). Just as the Schumpeterian elitist Michael Novak sets up his own business as a propagandist and thinks of himself as an entrepreneur, one of the creative 2% responsible for the progress of humanity (*Buffalo Courier-Express*, June, 1, 1979), so Barry Commoner returns to his Missouri farm to renew his unity with nature.

In class terms, therefore, one can say that the ecological standpoint is an agrarian standpoint. Subjectively, the standpoint is man-in-nature, with agrarian man the best and most normal type of man. That is, subjectively the agrarian standpoint is universalized, just as for Marxists like Lukacs the proletariat is the universal class and for the neoclassicists we are all of us small businessmen.

II. Conceptions of Nature

The ecological standpoint enables us to see the inadequacy of all previous concepts of nature, by providing us with a more adequate concept. Nature is the biosphere in which we live. It is a living, open, homeostatic, evolving system composed of multiple cyclical processes and maintained by negative feedbacks. The traditionalist conservative reminds us that this is an old concept, found in Plato's *Timaeus*, Whitehead's *Nature and Life*, and probably other places. However, the concept has gained greatly in formal precision and empirical content compared to these early intuitions.

Conception 1

For the neoclassicist, nature appears in three forms: natural resources, cultivated land (not Land, the factor of production, which is location), and externalities of production. Natural resources are free goods, *res nullius*, nothings, having no value until they are "produced" and made available for exchange. This definition is a tautology, since nothing can have exchange value until it is made available for exchange. Resources do have a cost of discovery and production, and the cost curve rises as resources are depleted, according to the *a priori* principle of diminishing returns. This implies that there is an infinity of resources, including substitutes, at a cost of production that approaches infinity.

The concept of free goods with rising production costs obliterates the vital distinction between reproducible and nonreproducible resources, flow and stock, sunshine and oil. This distinction disappears because cost is *present* production cost; the future dissolves into the rate of interest, and any cost differences thirty or more years in the future are negligible when discounted back to the present. Thus resource conservation becomes an arbitrary preference of do-gooders (Alchian and Allen, 1964, pp. 516-519). Here again the neoclassical theory fits the practice of the small businessman better than that of the multinational corporation, for which the availability of resources thirty years from now is an urgent question. Nor does "rising costs" differentiate between an exponentially rising cost curve, which means disaster, and a nearly horizontal curve. Thus the fact that civilizations have been founded on stocks of readily available resources and have declined when the resources were depleted (Brooks, 1973, p. 140) is obscured by the "rising cost" concept. The fact suggests that these resource stocks had some sort of value, great value for the civilizations which rested on them, but this sort of value—the value of free goods— is not readily expressible in neoclassical terms. It can be expressed in terms of "consumer's surplus" or some such indirect concept, if necessary, but the neoclassicist would not devise such a concept himself. It is near the limits of his perspective.

The concept of agricultural land as a form of fixed capital obliterates the distinction between agriculture and industry. It suggests that land should be devoted to its most productive use, and thus encourages the monoculture that has again and again produced ecological disasters (Ophuls, 1977, pp. 27, 37, 56). It also suggests the desirability of increasing the efficiency rate at which land transforms input into crops, and thus encouraged the research that produced the disastrous

"Green Revolution" (Cleaver, 1972; Merrill, 1976, Chapter 8, pp. 264-266). This technology produced a variety of ecological damages ("externalities"), a concentration of wealth and poverty, concentration of land ownership, rural and urban unemployment, and regional conflict.

The concept of external costs is totally inadequate. It is a negative concept, suggesting something outside the normal production and exchange system which economics explains. External costs are accidental, unsystematic byproducts of normal economic activity. As they are accidental there can be no scientific study of them; they are unpredictable and must be discovered from case to case after the fact; and of course they cannot enter into the cost calculations involved in production decisions. The proposal to internalize the externalities through taxes and fines is also inadequate, as Ophuls argues at length (1977, Chapter 5). First, many external costs appear far away from their source in time and space, perhaps through complex causal links. In the case of the thousands of new chemicals these links are not knowable till long after the event, so even the assessment of blame is highly disputable. Second, by definition there is no market in externalities, so pricing must proceed without guidelines. Consequently taxes and fines must be assessed arbitrarily after the fact, in a long drawn out legal process in which the polluting corporations have superior legal and political resources. Finally, if a penalty is imposed the market power of the corporations ensures that it will be passed on to the consumers and will affect the poor the most. Here the neo-classicist's squeamishness about interpersonal comparison of utilities blinds him to the question of who pays and who benefits from pollution.

The pervasiveness of "externalities" also means that a price system which ignores them cannot possibly allocate resources optimally by any social welfare function that includes them. If the official cost of a productive process includes only the money cost of the capital and labor and excludes the external costs (pollution, waste disposal, health) it will seriously misrepresent the cost of the process to society. A different process, more expensive in money terms, might be much cheaper overall. Thus Commoner shows that in agriculture, transportation, energy, and petrochemicals the technology that produces maximum profit is the opposite to the most ecologically and socially efficient technology (1976, Chapters 7, 8). The market, which allocates resources by price, is not merely an imperfect mechanism whose failures can be corrected by vigorous government action; it is a totally wrong mechanism for allocating land and natural resources.

Conception 2

Game theory formalizes nature as a public good, to which the theory of the n-person Prisoner's Dilemma applies. This is a very useful formalization that some ecologists have adopted, as indicated earlier. It states the problem precisely, under the assumption of individuals with independent utility functions. This assumption fits the international scene empirically, so game theory explains the difficulty of reaching international agreement to stop polluting the sea, or cutting down tropical rain forests, or hunting whales, or depleting the ozone, or manufacturing atomic weapons. Unfortunately there is no mathematical solution even to a 2-person Prisoner's Dilemma, so proposed solutions will have to come from other standpoints. Those using the game formalization, such as Ophuls, have proposed world government as a solution, but this begs the question. It says that if there were a power strong enough to solve the problem the problem would be solved. The obvious neoclassical solution to the public goods problem is private appropriation of nature, for instance Milton Friedman's proposal to preserve the national parks by selling them to private enterprise (1962, p. 31). In the case of the oceans, air, and water this solution reduces to the internalization proposal ridiculed above.

Conception 3

For the Keynesians and other government standpoint scientists nature is a public resource that the government is obliged to manage for the general welfare. This was the original conceptualization of the conservation movement from about 1910. The basic management issue always is, which resources should be developed now and which should be preserved for the future. Present use might be development as a public park or development by private industry, or multiple use; preservation includes reserves for future industrial use and perpetual preservation as wilderness or wildlife refuges. Note that this standpoint provides a much longer time-perspective than the neoclassical standpoint by substituting "national heritage" for "estimated future value discounted by the interest rate." It also allows some systemic considerations to occur in the arguments for preservation of some wildlife refuge or national monument, while for the neoclassicist one has to show damage to some individual because only individuals exist for him. Thus for the neoclassicist the extinction of the whooping crane is bad if there are individuals who happen to have a strong liking for whooping cranes, while from the government perspective it is bad because it depletes the national heritage.

For the conservationists government decisions would be rational if the proponents of immediate use and the proponents of preservation could each present their case to the responsible government agency, say the Forest Service, which would then decide impartially. Hence it was necessary to have a lumber industry association, a National Parks Association, a Wilderness Society, a Wildlife Society, and so on.

The inadequacy of this concept of nature has become apparent in the ensuing decades. First, the national heritage is *national*, not for foreigners, so one way to protect it is to keep immigrants out. Consequently the National Parks and Conservation Assn. urges stricter immigration controls to stabilize the US population and thus avert ecological disaster in our parks (National Parks and Conservation Magazine, June, 1979). The boundary of the US ecosystem coincides with the US boundary.

Second, it has become obvious that the government is not a neutral decision-maker balancing the claims of industrial development and of conservation, to say nothing of wilderness. Industrial development has priority. Recognition of this fact threw the conservation movement into turmoil in the 1960's, with splits in old organizations and the founding of new ones. Those environmentalists who focused on the fact that the Bureau of Land Management was tied in with the cattle ranchers, the Forest Service with the timber industry (Kaufman, 1967), the Reclamation Bureau with agribusiness, have turned to Congress for remedy. Those who noticed the symbiosis of Congress and industry have turned to the people, as discussed in Chapter Eight. Out of this experience has come another conception of nature.

Conception 4

These desperate, disillusioned environmentalists now conceive nature as those remnants of the national heritage that have not yet been developed and spoiled by industry and government. They call on us to save the New River, the last wild river in North Carolina; the Great Swamp, the last wild swamp in New Jersey; the last few snail darters, the last caribou herd, and so on. This conception is the obverse side of the New Yorker's conception of nature: that wild, unpaved swamp or jungle out beyond Lake Hopatcong or Coral Gables, inhabited by alligators, rattlesnakes, black widow spiders, and poison ivy. In both cases there is a sharp distinction between society and nature. One lives in society, but it is necessary occasionally for some people to get back to Nature, to the wild, unspoiled places for a few days, to express their primitive impulses.

New Left Marxists have provided a critique of conceptions 3 and 4 in their work on the state. The responsibility of the capitalist state is not to preserve the national heritage; it is to provide conditions for the accumulation of capital. Without favorable prospects for accumulation, investment declines, then employment, then output, and then system legitimacy. The national heritage represents investment opportunities, to be given away if it can be used up profitably; if not, then it is necessary to cultivate it and develop it before giving it away. The long-run outlook of large corporations requires them to set aside reserves for the future, and government is the appropriate agency to protect the reserves until they are needed. The conservationists are normally on the losing side except in prosperous times, when capital can manage without extra state assistance.

Conception 4 is closer to the truth than 3 in that it recognizes government's role in destroying nature; but when type 4 conservationists inconsistently turn to some branch of government to plead or sue for exceptions they are fighting only a delaying action.

The ecological critique of conceptions 3 and 4 is more fundamental because it is an internal critique. 3 leads into 4 from experience with government; but 4 conceives nature as something that is vanishing. But could there be a world without any nature in it, when the Jersey swamp is a trailer camp and the snail darter is safe in the aquariums? Nature does not disappear, it just gets "spoiled." But if one shifts the focus of attention from "vanishing" nature to "spoiled" nature, nature *in the city*, one needs a conception of "spoiled." Since this is a negative concept it must be defined in terms of its opposite, unspoiled. This cannot be wilderness or wildlife refuges in the city; it is the steady-state ecosystem. One sees this shift toward the ecological standpoint in some of the environmental organizations as they shift from merely opposing nuclear power to working out the characteristics of a society based on solar energy.

The elitists and anti-elitists have produced no unique conception of nature. If society is people doing things together, then nature is not part of society and belongs to the natural sciences.

Conception 5

New Left Marxists, and Marxists in general, conceive nature mainly as part of the man/nature dialectic. Mankind survived by adapting its needs to what nature offered, and by adapting nature to its needs. Beginning with cultivation of the soil and taming of animals, man changed nature to fit his needs. This is the humanization of nature—

the development of edible fruits, tools, new sources of energy, new chemicals etc. We are now surrounded by a nature that we have remade thoroughly to suit our needs. Conversely, the humanization of nature develops the potentialities of man—the humanization of man. Man develops himself by work, that is by objectifying his ideas in matter. Nature is the material with which man works, so its characteristics provide the possibilities and limitations of work. A humanized nature offers greatly expanded possibilities for creative and productive work; it expands man's creative and productive powers. Thus over the centuries man has made himself via the humanization of nature.

Capitalism breaks through this dialectic, this spiral, and substitutes a linear production-consumption dynamic. Both nature and labor are treated as means to the endless accumulation of capital. As a result both are impoverished. Nature is transformed into capital plus waste, its own inherent dynamics and regenerative powers ignored and destroyed. Labor skills are destroyed, work becomes meaningless drudgery, and man becomes a passive consumer or surplus labor.

From the ecological standpoint the Marxist has the priorities backwards. The Marxist regards man, the worker, as Subject and nature as the Object to be transformed. This relation is expressed in Marx's interpretation of nature as man's inorganic body, and also in the labor theory of value, which says that nature takes on human value as it is transformed by labor. Such a conception is incorrect because nature is not passive matter waiting to be shaped to man's needs, but an active system with its own rhythms, needs, and limits. Man is a dependent part of this system, not its lord and master; the outcome of work is determined by system dynamics, not by human plans and desires. The needs of nature, of other living things, take precedence over the needs of man (Leiss, 1976, pp. 113ff.) since man, the part, is dependent for survival on the well-being of the whole. In the past mankind survived by adapting to nature; but this means occupying a niche in cycles of production-consumption-decomposition. Mankind's original niche was that of a hunter-gatherer, and since he moved beyond this niche he has been putting a strain on the ecosystem at an increasing rate. The "humanization of nature" has been a large part a domination and destruction of nature (Leiss, 1972), a using up of nature's savings. It is not a growth spiral but a spending spree, in large part, and the day of reckoning has arrived. To survive, mankind must again adapt itself to nature's cycles. This does not mean hunting and gathering or an end to growth; it means that growth must consist of the enrichment of ecosystems rather than their simplification. Humanization of nature is possible in the long run only insofar as man adapts himself to nature's rhythms and cycles.

This criticism applies particularly to that tendency in Marxism that criticizes capitalism for retarding economic growth and conceives socialism as a time of more rapid economic growth—Soviet Marxism, for instance. The vision of an economy of abundance is an illusion based on ignorance of the limits set by natural processes (Ophuls, 1977, p. 8). Abundance can be had only by limiting human desires sharply, not by expanding production to meet ever expanding needs (Schumacher, 1973, p. 33 and passim). The whole advantage of socialism is that it brings the goals and standards of the economy under working-class control; but if the capitalist goals of profit, growth, accumulation of capital are chosen then socialism is pointless (Schumacher, 1973, pp. 254-261). However, there are also opposing tendencies in Marxism that define socialism much as Schumacher defines it: dealienated work and consumption, self-governing communities, equalization of income rather than endless growth. For these tendencies the ecological criticism is mainly an insistence that in the man-nature dialectic it is nature's rhythms and needs that are dominant, not man's.

III. Evaluation

This standpoint has provided a powerful critique of all the growth-oriented traditions in the sciences, and also a critique of their associated societies. The societies are moving toward disaster, and the scientific traditions are either blind to the problem or they actively encourage and participate in the movement. This criticism applies to all current social science standpoints except the anti-elitists, who have never had any illusions that elite-directed growth would benefit the masses, and the traditionalists, who can find an anticipation of any new idea in the great tradition.

The standpoint also provides a critique of technology, the immediate cause of approaching disaster. Einsteinian physics laid the basis for nuclear weapons, which could make the earth uninhabitable. Chemistry and nuclear technology are introducing thousands of new substances into the biosphere against which there is no biological defense. The internal combustion engine has been a disaster for cities and for the atmosphere.

The critique is of the linear thinking that treats a technique merely as a means to an end and ignores all its other systemic effects. You can never do just one thing, says the ecologist, and ignorance of the systemic effects of new chemicals should be a reason for extreme caution in introducing new techniques. Instead, our engineers and technologists have been rushing new techniques and substances into production. They are guilty not only of linear thinking but of a technocratic faith, the belief that unlimited technological development will solve all mankind's problems. This faith encourages the engineer to rush a new technique into production in the belief that if any problems result, more technology will solve them. Hence the building of nuclear power plants when there is no adequate technique of waste disposal and of decommissioning old power plants.

What is needed is a systemic technology that is appropriate both to the needs and limits of the biosphere and to the human potential for creative work, in that order of priority. That sort of technology cannot be devised by specialists, but requires broad biophysical knowledge of systemic processes. Here the ecologist is in agreement with those Marxists who have criticized capitalist technology as a device for destroying labor skills and increasing management control. Both want an alternative technology; both reject the technological determinism that treats technological growth as an autonomous, self-generated force in history.

But if technology does not develop by its own inner logic, one must look beyond it for the social causes of ecological destruction. One cannot simply blame the mad scientist who invents new poisons and weapons of destruction; one must look for his employer. Here the ecological people have not yet done much substantial work. Mainly they have made vague suggestions—it's industrialism, it's human greed and envy, it's a wrong paradigm. Naturally I believe Commoner's work is the outstanding exception; he has shown how private enterprise aimed at private profit sustains the destructive momentum of linear technology, in many ways (Commoner, 1971, Chapter 12; 1976, Chapters 7-9). However, much work along this line remains to be done.

Nor has much work been done on the strategy and tactics of a shift to a steady-state society, other than Commoner (1979). Most important, the ecological thinkers have not located a potentially progressive class that would in its own interests push toward a steady-state society. The ecologists have no Subject, no one to advise. But without a creative Subject, the resistance of corporations–government–consumers to change guarantees disaster.

In short, the potentialities of this standpoint have only begun to be developed. Until recently the ecologists have mainly developed their central concept of the biosphere and their critique of linear technology; they are about as far along as the New Left Marxists were in

1968, when they had a concept of the capitalist system and little else. Consequently it is also far too soon to discern the eventual limitations of this standpoint.

As long as the concept of the biosphere and its associated critique of technology stands alone, it is too easily absorbed into other standpoints. New Left Marxists can use it to enrich their critique of capitalism, and imagine that a socialist revolution will solve all ecological problems, since of course we will avoid all the mistakes made in the Soviet Union. Environmentalists and conservationists can use it to support their latest lawsuit or lobbying effort, supposing that some new regulatory agency or revised budget priorities, or a pipeline through Canada rather than through Alaska will begin moving us toward an ecologically sound society. Heilbroner can argue that the coming ecological crisis requires more control by the elite—presumably the same benevolent, responsible elite that has guided us into the crisis (Heilbroner, 1974). Even a neoclassicist like Boulding can incorporate some caricatures of ecological concepts (1978). For instance Boulding defines "niche" as equilibrium population—which in the argument becomes simply population—and asserts that mankind has been expanding its niche through modern high-output technology (pp. 62-63, 17-18). Consistent with this reversal of ecological thinking, he argues that further expansion of this *same* technology to invent substitute materials, and our free market to allocate them, will move us to the ecological steady-state. See also Boulding's atrocious review (1976) of Commoner, 1976.[8] The fact that some ecologists treat Boulding as a spokesman for the ecological standpoint is further evidence for the immaturity of the approach.

The effect of these borrowings is to change the meaning of ecological concepts more or less to fit into other conceptual schemes, and to lose the unique potential contribution to science of the ecological standpoint.

Eleven Summary of Part I

Part I is a historical description of the standpoints taken in the policy sciences from about 1930 to 1975. The subject matter is mainly US-British-Canadian social science, but some continental European work from the 1970's is also included. During the period 1935-1960 English-language social science was largely isolated from the Continent, but since then the isolation has broken down.

A standpoint is the location in society that a scientist sees as active, free, creative, responsible. Sometimes it is where the scientists locates himself; his standpoint is where he is in society. At other times the scientist is not at the location but relates himself closely to it; he empathizes with it, advises it, defends it, interprets it for outsiders. The standpoint is also the location of the scientist's faith and hope, the location that he glorifies and idealizes. The neoclassical conception of the rational individual comparing utilities at the margin and planning consumption far into the future is an idealization, and so is the Keynesian-functionalist-social problems treatment of government as the benevolent universal problem-solver. Schumpeter ridiculed "the unscientific habit of economists of using a clearly ideological theory of the state that raises the latter into a superhuman agency for the public good and neglects all the facts about the realities of public administration" (1954, p. 37) but he and his followers did exactly the same with the entrepreneur and the modernizing elite. The Galbraithians soberly study the realities of public administration and bureaucratic routine but place their faith in an aroused public that will be devoted purely to the public interest. Critical intellectuals and

Marxists place their faith in the masses and in the humanizing effect of self-managed work, respectively; once oppression is ended these people will demonstrate their potential intelligence and goodness and class-consciousness. It is easy to see the mote in the other person's eye.

I have characterized each standpoint in the concepts of those who take it; I have described it from the inside, subjectively. There has also been some interpretation of the standpoint from the outside, that is from a different standpoint. All such interpretations are secondary and questionable, because they are relative to some other standpoint. The self-interpretations may also suffer from self-delusion.

Each standpoint affords a conceptual "view" of society spread around it. This view is the perspective. A perspective is embodied in a conceptual scheme that classifies the main interrelated components of society. The conceptual scheme channels the scientist's creativity: it is the source of his hypotheses and concepts, it determines his choice and understanding of method, and it guides his production and recognition of facts. It also limits his understanding of ideas and facts coming from other perspectives, since he has to translate everything into his own conceptual scheme to make sense of it. The process of translation distorts the products of nearby perspectives, but it reduces the products of far-off perspectives to weird, perverse nonsense.

Each conceptual scheme has three or four main categories: 1) The standpoint itself, the Subject, where free, rational responsible action occurs. 2) The rest of society, the Object. In one case, the critical intellectuals, there is no Object; society is composed of subjects. Both Subject and Object can be subdivided in secondary categories. 3) If the scientist does not locate himself at the standpoint, then his location in society is a third main category. 4) Those phenomena that are inherently unknowable and beyond the scope of science, like random fluctuations and historical accidents. There are also phenomena that ought not be studied. The items in this category provide the excuses scientists give for the shortcomings of their conceptual scheme.

The task of social science is to study both Subject and Object and their relations. If the Object is the primary focus of study, science is the study of an external, objective reality. If the Subject is the primary focus of study, science is the study of subjectivity, of free, creative, rational action, and must use methods that afford access to subjectivity. In the former case social science is seen as continuous with natural science; in the latter case social science is seen as sharply distinct from natural science.

Each standpoint and perspective exists in the writings and communication of a school or tradition of social scientists. In most cases two or more schools have taken the same or nearly the same stand-point and have been studied together. The study of a school or tradi-tion is a sociological-historical study, while the study of a conceptual scheme embodying a perspective is a kind of conceptual analysis. One cannot study ideas adequately without also studying their social embodiment and historical context, but the two can be distinguished.

The conceptual potential of a perspective has to be developed over time by a school of scientists, who may do the job well or poorly. Those traditions that have been in existence for thirty or more years have by now developed their conceptual schemes and empirical studies rather thor-oughly, while the new schools of the 1970's are in the middle of the task. The newest school, the Schumacher ecologists, is just getting started, and has hardly coalesced into a school yet. However, one can assume that no school can ever exhaust the conceptual potential of the perspective it embodies. As society changes, the standpoints included in it also change their relative centrality in society and the conceptual potential of each standpoint therefore also grows or diminishes.

A school or tradition grows through a series of fairly typical stages. First, there is an incubation period in which new ideas appear in an article or suggestive book or in discussion and research. These ideas relate to some important and puzzling phenomenon that requires scientific explanation and urgently demands social action. This is the "anomaly." It is played down by existing schools, declared to be unimportant or temporary, perhaps the accidental result of some mistaken policy, perhaps not a proper subject of scientific study until enough data are available a decade or so in the future. There are variations here, and in some cases the anomaly is rather technical and is less important than the invention of a new concept such as feedback or game theory.

Second, the school bursts on the scene in one or two major works, for instance Malinowski (1922) and Radcliffe-Brown (1922) announc-ing the birth of functionalism. This is a time of tremendous excite-ment, of the rapid accumulation of disciples, of broad manifestos, (Lakatos' "research program") rapid circulation of unpublished mate-rials and verbal reports, founding of new journals and organizations. This period lasts about two years.

The next ten years are a period in which several major works appear, the classics of the school that embody its main categories, arguments, and conclusions. They are also a period of energetic data gathering and interpretation. However, in some cases a classic or classics can appear decades later, summarizing the data and arguments of two decades and making a new departure in another direction.

Table 11.1. Summary of Part I

School	Period of development	Causal focus	Period of Prominence	Subject	Social status of the scientist	Object	Organization of science
Traditionalist conservative	—	—	400 BC–	The wise man	Interpreter	Eternal truth	Hierarchical
Neoclassical	—	—	1870–1951	The individual; the small businessman	The individual; the small businessman	The market	Free market?
Game theory	1928–1944	Oligopoly	1947–	The individual player	[undetermined]	The game	[undetermined]
Keynesian	1920–1935	Unemployment	1936–1966	Government, treasury department	Professional advisor	The national economy	Professional and specialized
Functionalist	1907–1922	Colonial societies	1922–1970	Government	Professional advisor	The national social system	Professional and specialized
Systems analysis, cybernetics	1943–1950	[undetermined]	1950– 1958– (H. Simon)	Government, management	Professional advisor	Any managed system	Professional and specialized

Table 11.1. Summary of Part I (continued)

School	Period of development	Causal focus	Period of Prominence	Subject	Social status of the scientist	Object	Organization of science
Social problems	[undetermined]	Some social problem	ca. 1900	Government	Professional advisor	The subsystem	Professional and specialized
Schumpeterian elitists	1946–1960	Preservation of democracy	1960–	The elite; the big businessman	Intellectual	The masses	Unspecialized
Critical intellectuals	ca. 1929–1956	Poverty, discrimination	1956–	The masses; the underclass; the deviant	Intellectual	None	[undetermined]
Bureaucratic-institutionalists	1960–1970	Vietnam war	1970–	The people; the consumer	Professional advisor	The bureaucracy; political economy	Professional and antispecialist
New Left Marxism	1966–1973	Vietnam war, civil rights	1973–	The government employee; the worker	The government employee; the worker	A capitalist world system	Collective
Ecological	1963–1970	Ecological crisis	1971–	Man-in-nature; the farmer	Professional advisor	The ecosystem, the biosphere	Collective

After a school is well established there is time to divide into branches, to point out the substantial dependence on ideas from earlier schools and to attempt to reduce that dependence, or conversely to incorporate the ideas of competing schools, and to work on the difficult technical details and controversies that have appeared. It is a time of accumulating techniques, indices, definitions, controversies, of Kuhn's "normal science." It is also a time to criticize some brash new movement, point out its unscientific character, its lack of data and lack of confirmation of its bold pronouncements, its apparent ignorance of established knowledge in the field; see, for example, Solow's criticism of New Left Marxism (Solow, 1971). As persistent criticisms or technical difficulties appear—these are the limits of the perspective making themselves known—there will be methodological discussions that prove that such difficulties are inherent in all science and that the criticisms are unscientific.

Finally, in its old age a school lives on by incorporating ideas from other schools, suitably translated into its own categories. Empirical findings from other schools will be reinterpreted or deduced from its own categories to provide further confirmation of the old truths. Empirically inclined scientists will use the familiar categories as a framework around which they build rich empirical observations and generalizations, but no new general theory. The rigidity and absoluteness of the categorical scheme at this stage, its immunity to further modification or disconfirmation, is a sign that the theory is dead while the school lives on.

Many scientists do not belong to any particular school. They may be partial to one school without rejecting the teachings of one or more other schools. Thus the schools themselves rest on a foundation of eclectics and uncommitted supporters. Most of these eclectics and supporters will share the standpoint of the dominant school, and their eclecticism will extend to the various schools sharing the same standpoint. Some may waver ambiguously between two standpoints, and a few are able to combine two or more standpoints. Then there are also the self-conscious travelers, who move between two schools and try to interpret them to each other, or who gradually abandon one school for another. Finally there are the sudden shifts of standpoint and school when a person's eyes are opened and his identity changes. Most of these shifts occur at the birth of a new school or shortly thereafter.

Within a school one can distinguish the strongly committed partisans from the more tolerant. The partisans are the ones who engage in polemics to show that other schools are unscientific or produce trivial conclusions, who insist that their students learn the one and only truth.

There are also degrees of commitment to a standpoint in society. The strongly committed see their location in society as the source of all goodness, battling against evil and inertia on all sides. For these people social science ought to be heavily engaged in the social struggle against evil. Some Marxists are like this, but the clearest example is those committed to the US government during the Cold War. These people include some deterrence theorists taking a game-theory perspective and some elitists. In both cases the US government was seen as the defender of democracy and civilization against the evil forces of world communism without and within. The result was a black and white picture in which US acts were interpreted as motivated solely by noble ideals while Soviet acts were motivated solely by a desire for power. I can give thirty references like this, starting with the *Orbis* group of the 1950's and 1960's. At the extreme this has led to the bitter diatribes and distortions of Lewis Feuer, a once intelligent man crippled by his own anger, and to the apparently deliberate distortions and caricatures of opposing views by Moynihan in his recent works. As a reviewer remarks of a recent Moynihan book, "Perhaps the saddest part of his career is that a man so two-fisted should be so one-eyed, that the ideal of liberty should be defended by so much intolerance" (Manchester Guardian, June 10, 1979). For these partisans social science is a weapon in the battle against evil, and as a result has ceased to be science in its distortions, hallucinations (Sartre as the typical New Left Marxist, according to Feuer), and tricky arguments.

I have tried to rely on the works of the more tolerant, rather than the works of the standpoint-partisans and fighters for democracy, in estimating the conceptual potential of each perspective. The potential of a perspective appears most clearly in the work of those who use its categories undogmatically and tentatively, and who perhaps can even reinterpret these categories somewhat from other perspectives. Those elitists who can even look at the US government a little from a Soviet perspective, and those deterrence theorists who can conceive of aggressive or dishonest US acts, are better scientists than those who see all the aggression coming from our enemies.

Part II

Part II of this book is intended to be practical and constructive. If we assume that Part I provides a biased, distorted, selected history of some developments in social science since 1930, then Part II asks, 1. How can we organize our own scientific research to achieve greater objective truth? (Chapter Fourteen) 2. Who are "we?" Whom do we include in the scientific enterprise? For instance, is NSF part of "we?" ONR? IDA? The Hudson Institute? (Chapter Fourteen) 3. What do we mean by "objectivity" and "truth" (Chapter Twelve)? 4. In particular what positive contribution, if any, do the various standpoints and perspectives make to the pursuit of objectivity? (Chapter Fourteen) The preliminary evaluations in Part I contribute to answering question 4.

The philosophic method is Deweyan-instrumentalist. It moves from fact to value in several steps:

1. What have we been doing in the recent past, and how did we come to be doing that (Part I)? The historical approach is essential to understanding the present, because the present is the many-layered continuation of the successive waves of growth in the past. A history spreads out the layers of the present in time, relating each present community of scientists to its own past and tracing its development into the present, thereby relating present communities to each other via their respective origins. For example Meade (1972) and Ellsberg (1972), both published in the same year, come out of problem contexts thirty years apart—the Keynesian circular flow concept of the econ-

omy with government as control point, and an objectification of government in which "the President was part of the problem" (Ellsberg, 1972, p. 34). Meade's work is the ripe completion of one tradition; Ellsberg's, part of the beginning of another tradition.

2. What problems have we been having? There is an inescapable personal element in the selection of problems for study. One problem underlying the present work is the failure of communication among different groups of scientists, expressing itself in interminable polemics, absurd refutation of straw men, dismissal of whole research traditions as totally worthless or even unscientific, persecution of dissenters and their students. A second problem is onesidedness: every scientific tradition seems to have only a biased, distorted, partial grasp of reality; how can we put together the whole truth out of these parts? Improved communication is an obvious part of the remedy, so that the two problems are closely related.

3. What short-term goals are implicit in what we have been doing? What have we been trying to do, perhaps without knowing it? In other words, if the goal of science is objective truth, what have we meant by objectivity and truth in the recent past? This question treats the goals of science as imperfectly embodied in present activity. If a goal has been mostly achieved, I can find the goal implicit in a line of development over the decades. If a goal is demanded rather than achieved, I can find it implicit in the criticisms scientists make of each other's theories. That is, if a theory looks onesided from some different perspective, I can estimate what a two-sided theory would look like.

4. Are these goals still pursuable, perhaps with some revision, or are they themselves part of the problem? A goal is questionable if attempts to achieve it always fail and cause trouble, or if there is no way of measuring achievement. I argue below that these goals are being gradually achieved, so that they remain valid targets.

5. How do we solve the problem, by reference to current or modified or new goals?

Question 1 is answered in Part I. Question 2 has just been answered: the problems are bias, distortion, and poor communication. Analysis of the problems has been implicit in Part I, and further analysis will occur in Chapters Thirteen and Fourteen. Questions 3 and 4, what have our objectives been and are they still worth pursuing, will be dealt with in Chapter Twelve. Chapter Fourteen will finally take up the original questions: how can we improve the organization of our research and who are "we."

Twelve Some Historical Patterns

This chapter moves a short distance beyond description to locate some persistent patterns that have taken shape over a period of five decades. These patterns point to implicit objectives that scientists have been struggling to achieve in a variety of ways. They also bring out further differences among the various standpoints, intense differences that contribute to the extreme difficulty of intelligent communication.

I. Long and Short Run Theories

We begin with Keynes, the father of modern social science, as some would assert. The Keynesian revolution was in part a shift from a long run to a short-run theory. What does this mean? Neoclassical theory before 1930 had both long-run and short-run models. The difference depended on how many of the variables in the model were allowed to vary; the greater the number of variables that were held constant, the shorter the run.

In part this array of models resulted from the inadequate mathematical techniques available in those days; deductive reasoning was mainly verbal, and mathematical diagrams were used as aids to clarity of thinking. Consequently, to avoid error one had to approach the long-run models a step at a time. One began with a one-day model in which Q, D, S, N, and in fact everything except P was held constant, and deduced equilibrium P. (A crucial error, according to Leijonhufvud.) Then one allowed Q to vary, then D and S, and so on until everything was changing simultaneously. In part the array resulted from the belief that everything in the real world economy did change simultaneously, but some things changed rapidly, like prices, and others more slowly, like the labor supply, tastes, and technology.

What happened in the 1940's and 1950's was that the short-run models were shown to depend on long-run assumptions, the chief one being the assumption of individual rationality. To defend their theory against empirical studies that suggested that individuals do not maximize expected utility in observable short-run circumstances, some neoclassicists retreated to the assertion that rationality was itself a product of long-run market dynamics and hence need not be observable in the short run. A second assumption was that of perfect information, which no one asserted was available in the short run. A third assumption was resource mobility. To simplify, the short-run models became partial versions of the long-run general equilibrium model, which alone gave a true description of reality but was not directly observable.

What characterizes a long-run model? First, there are no time subscripts. The model does not predict how many years a particular change will take, nor does it plot a curve over time which approaches the 100% mark of the change. Instead, it asserts that there is now a continuing tendency in a direction, the asymptote of which can be specified. Second, the model does not assert that the asymptote will ever be approached to any specified degree. Machlup in particular has emphasized this point (1958). Disturbances could occur at any time to either counteract the change temporarily or to shift the asymptote itself. In other words, the model claims only to be valid *ceteris paribus*. Third, the model ignores all short-run fluctuations, using the *ceteris paribus* clause to exclude them. Some of these fluctuations are due to factors outside the model; others result from interaction among the model's variables. The partial equilibrium method does not allow one to study such interactions. Fourth, what the model does assert is that the tendencies it describes will continue, inexorably, in spite of all temporary counteracting tendencies, as long as the specified initial conditions exist.

If we take the Keynes-type short-run model as example, it focuses precisely on the short-run fluctuations and cycles excluded by the neoclassical model. That is, it deals with the interdependence over time of simultaneous changes in several or many variables. Ideally there should be time subscripts and time lags, as in Kalecki's version, based on empirical observation. Such models are built up empirically out of actual variables and time lags. They tend to become more complex over time as more and more empirical factors are included, in the attempt to copy the actual fluctuations and cycles more accurately. The problem in constructing such models is to specify the correct interconnections among the many empirically observable variables.

Short-run models assume an unchanging institutional framework of some sort. The distinction between short and long here is a matter of degree, but specific contrasts can be made clearly enough. A model which assumes two or more different kinds of labor and of capital, specialized to different sectors of the economy, is short run; a model with homogeneous labor and capital is long run. A model with international mobility of capital and labor is long run; a model assuming a national boundary is short run.

Keynes also made various remarks about the long run, such as "euthanasia of the rentier" and "abundance of capital," and these remarks are a paradigm of what a long-run model is not. One does not get a long-run model by extrapolation, that is by letting a short-run model run for two generations. One gets only fiction or fantasy (Chase, 1975). For a long-run model, it is necessary to vary some institutional constants, or to bring in some long-run processes that have no detectable effects in only a few years. An example is the Marxist "accumulation of surplus value," which has negligible effects in one year but becomes quite important in a fifty-year model. The Keynesian growth models are also not long run, since they merely extrapolate required annual rates of investment that will maintain fluctuations around a moving short-run equilibrium.

A third kind of theory must be distinguished from both long- and short-run models, namely a historical or evolutionary theory. The term "model" is inappropriate here. A theory is evolutionary if it distinguishes at least two different historical stages, each with rather different institutional conditions and dynamics, each describable with rather different long and short-run models. It should also have some theory about the transition from one stage to the next, and it may also specify some unchanging nonhistorical factors such as human nature or steady technological progress. Schumpeter's theory of imperialism is evolutionary, because it specifies the precapitalist stage in enough detail so that it has its own variables and its own dynamics. In contrast, Frank Knight's characterization of precapitalist times—a long night of ignorance, intolerance, barbarism, and religion—assigns no unique dynamic to this period. Even back then men maximized expected utility, on the rare occasions that they thought rationally at all.

Once can also distinguish evolutionary theories that stop at the present, declaring that history is now over, and those that provide for a possible future stage. Schumpeter's theory predicts a future stage, while the Parsons–Eisenstadt theory does not.

The period before 1920 was the heyday of evolutionary theories, culminating in the magnificent 1915 synthesis of Hobhouse, Wheeler, and Ginsberg. By 1930 evolutionary theories were out of fashion, and the few survivals like Schumpeter, the Marxists, and the fading diffusionists were a public scandal. In the 1950's evolutionary theories were making a comeback, beginning with Julian Steward's circle in anthropology and including a revival of diffusionism by Naroll.

If we run through the period from 1930 with the preceding paradigms in mind we get something like the results shown in Table 12-1.

The neoclassicist models of Chapter Three are illegitimate short-run models based on the long-run assumption of maximizing-rationality. Functionalist short-run theory appears in the Parsons et al. *Working Papers* of 1953—phase movement, leadership differentiation—and in many case studies of short-run self-maintenance or disintegration. The

Table 12.1 Short-run (S), long-run (L), and evolutionary (E) theories.

Standpoint or tradition	S	L	E
Traditionalist conservatism		X	X
Neoclassicism, gold economists		X	
Game theory	X		
Neoclassicist diffusions	X		
Keynesian	X		
Functionalist	X	X	X
Systems analysis, social problems	X		
Cybernetics	X		
Schumpeterian	X	X	X
Anti-elitist	X		
Galbraithian-bureaucratic	X		X
New Left Marxist	X	X	X
Schumacher		X	

basic theories of Parsons, Radcliffe-Brown, Malinowski, Levi-Strauss, etc., but not Merton are long run in that they discuss the functions, structures, and processes necessary to self-maintenance but give no time subscripts or detailed dynamics; nor is the steady state of self-maintenance ever achieved. Some large historical case studies like the Leach study of Highland Burma are long run. Evolutionary theory, in 1920 the opposite of functionalism, reappeared in Parsons' work of the 1960's and in the case studies of the 1960's developmental functionalists like Eisenstadt. The Schumpterian evolutionary theory includes Schumpeter's *Imperialism* and Rostow's five stages; the general theory of development by creative destruction might imaginatively be called long run; and the many statistical studies of the masses, the cross-polity surveys, and the elite-perspective comments on the passing scene are short run, as their data base changes even in ten years. The elite-perspective futurology consists of short-run observations extrapolated into the future, like the Keynesian development models. The fragments of evolutionary theory provided by the Galbraithian-institutionalists come from the C.E. Ayres wing of the institutionalists' Society For Evolutionary Economics. New Left Marxism is an uneasy, sometimes jerry-built combination of Marx's long-run and evolutionary theory with short-run models derived from Keynesians, functionalists, institutionalists, and other liberal social science, plus new short-run models and empirical studies.

If we half close our critical faculties and look at Table 12.1 we can imagine a certain regularity in it. Liberal social science, with one important exception, is short run. It deals with contemporary society, the problems we are having these days, and possible immediate remedies. The conservatives including Schumpeter are long run except for the Chapter Three types. Schumpeter's liberal disciples are short run. Conservatives are disdainful of short-run liberal tinkering and feel that the task of social science is to disclose the underlying, permanent dynamics of society. The liberal remedies can create temporary commotion and apparent improvement, but are gradually undermined by the inexorable slow-working fundamental processes. Radical social science is mainly long run; it too regards liberal reforms as temporary, certain to be eventually undermined by the fundamental systemic contradictions. However, it needs short-run theory to relate Marxism to the present both in theory and in practice, and its own liberal past provides handy, sometimes incongruous short-run components (like Deweyan instrumentalism) which at least provide a start in developing better short-run theories. Also both the mass and the bureaucratic-institutionalist perspectives are compatible with a radical rejection of capitalism, and the result is radical short-run theories.

Failure to recognize the difference between long-run and short-run theory is one source of fruitless controversy. One example is the Friedman–Heller–Samuelson debate (1968) and in general arguments between neoclassicists and Keynesians or organization theorists of the Simon–March–Cyert school. Another example is the long controversy over the Marxist theory of the falling rate of profit. Robinson's critique of this theory begins by translating it into Keynesian terms, which transforms it into a short-run theory. Then she points out that empirically several counteracting tendencies exist. Marx has arbitrarily selected one of several conflicting tendencies and called it a law, which is illegitimate. Moreover the data refute Marx's hypothesis. Rosdolsky replies that the law is long run and the counteracting tendencies are short run (Rosdolsky, 1968, pp. 467–483). The data show the temporary effectiveness of some capitalist policy, but the long-run tendency is always present and is bound to triumph eventually. The argument is fair enough, a typical long-run argument. But as long run it rejects the information in the short-run data, and it reduces the short-run tendencies to arbitrary, merely empirical happenings. After much confused argument and data gathering (Parijs, 1980), Erik Wright has provided a New Left synthesis (1978, Chapter 3). The falling rate of profit was a long-run tendency in the nineteenth century, with short-run counteracting policies; tendency and counteraction together produced a structural shift to a different accumulation problem (under-consumption), whose partial solution produced another structural shift, and so on. The long-run tendency is recognized, the short-run data fit the theory, and the short-run counteracting policies take their place in a systematic long-short theory.

On the basis of Table 12.1 we can induce that one current objective of the social sciences is the development of a combined long-run short-run evolutionary theory, such as Wright (1978). The evidence suggests that the objective is not easy to achieve; indeed it suggests that achievement is very difficult, even apart from questions of validity. The objective draws attention to itself mainly by its absence.

Why is this a desirable objective? A short-run theory tends to lose sight of the institutions whose fixity it assumes, if indeed it was ever aware of them at all. Or, if it does refer to them in its concepts, it tends to refer to them as permanent in reality rather than simply as assumed constants in the theory. As a result, twenty years later when conditions have changed, the old short-run theory is seen to be erroneous and a new one put in its place. Science progresses; or does it?

1. The economic development theory of the 1950's, which stressed rapid infusion of investment capital into underdeveloped economies, was seen to be erroneous in the 1960's as initial increases in productivity were maintained in some countries but not in others. The mistake was in applying the successful Marshall Plan experience to countries with a quite different institutional structure, it seemed. Well then, some economists hypothesized, the missing institutional constant is political stability, present in Western Europe but not in the new countries; either a stable democracy like India under Nehru or a stable military regime like Brazil will do the trick. By the 1970's this assumption too had collapsed, as India and other stable regimes got into ever deeper trouble. The political development theory of the 1950's went through similar transformations, as Apter sadly notes: ". . . the political aspects of development are far more complex than they appeared to observers a decade or so ago. It seemed at that time that the description of developing areas would . . . bring us back to 'fundamentals.' . . . Now even the new "fundamentals" are lost in the bewildering array of political problems which succeed one another in Latin America, Asia, and Africa" (Apter, 1968, p. 331).

2. World War II, various Keynesians asserted, was the first successful application of Keynesian countercyclical principles. For the first time government engaged in massive deficit spending—never mind on what; as Keynes observed, even pyramid-building is better than nothing, just so people are put to work—and the economy responded with prolonged growth. Twenty years later it is obvious, asserts Melman (1974), that military spending is ruining the civilian economy in the long run. Civilian technology stagnates, and the Pentagon style of management, with cost-plus contracts and continuous subsidies via cost overruns is ruinous to efficiency and price stability. The missing institutional constant assumed by the Keynesians was technological progress, Melman asserts; the solution is massive investment in civilian R & D so we can outdistance the Japanese and the Germans in the consumption goods race, and a new cost-conscious management willing to eliminate redundant labor and speed up lazy production processes. Not so, says Lester Thurow (1980, Chapter 4). US productivity is down, but not because of declining R & D; "As the decline in productivity is examined more closely, simplicity disappears" (p. 89). Japanese productivity depends partly on management's unwillingness to eliminate redundant labor (p. 84) and on "the absence of a sharp dividing line between public and private" (p. 95), just the opposite of Melman's recommendations. What we need, then, is not R & D but some way to imitate Japanese culture, labor-management relations, or something.

3. Much of liberal political science was founded on the 1954 account of the American voter as traditionally bound to one of the two parties and relatively uninterested in issues. Theorizing about voter apathy, functional rationality, etc. was founded on these data and confirmed in subsequent elections. Now the data have changed as of the 1972 elections (A. Miller et al., 1976), and the theorists can start over.

4. Lipset's 1960 empirically confirmed theory about the relation of economic development to political democracy is already out of date fifteen years later, as the democratic countries in his table get military governments and vice versa.

In general, liberal social science with its short-run outlook tends to be superficial and changeable, running after the latest data and discarding old theories one after the other. Each new institutional situation is tacitly assumed to be permanent, even as the mistaken institutional assumptions of the discarded theories are pointed out. Plainly a long-run theory is needed to explain and predict those institutional changes that can be ignored in the short run.

Conversely, long-run theories have difficulty relating to present reality. These theories allow for endless short-run fluctuations and disturbances that can counteract the long-run dynamics, and thus they can survive long periods of apparent refutation. Yet theory must eventually somehow be applicable to the present. In the absence of a short-run theory that deals systematically with fluctuations and disturbances, they tend to rely on one of three tactics: a) either ignoring the fluctuations, eliminating them from the data, or declaring them unknowable, as Friedman does; or b) blaming ad hoc interferences, as Rosdolsky does; or c) trying somehow to see present factors as instances of long-run concepts. Thus Marxists have hailed every temporary downturn or protest as the start of the long-awaited final collapse of capitalism, and see the imperialistic hand of Wall Street in every US foreign policy move. When the final collapse is postponed they can afterwards point to the particular government policy, trade union error, or raw material bonanza that once more saved capitalism. Similarly, when monetary policy fails to control inflation as predicted Friedman can simply explain that it took longer than he expected: "I must confess that I made overly optimistic predictions in 1969 about how soon inflation could be expected to respond to the monetary slowdown" (Friedman, 1972, p. 14). And since inflation rates do fluctuate, he can always find some eventual downturn in the data and claim success. "The sizeable error simply reflects the limitations of our quantitative knowledge" (1972, p. 17), but it does not disconfirm the long run prediction that inflation will eventually subside.

In the meantime there are always interfering factors that can be blamed. In 1975 Friedman was hedging that the Chilean experiment with monetary policy was not conclusive because of the abnormal political situation. The ineffective Israel monetary policy was not a good test either, as Israel is a quite atypical country. In 1979 Britain was to be the test case that demonstrated the truth of monetarism; but in 1980, with both inflation and unemployment rising in Britain, Friedman hedged again. Monetarist policy has not been properly applied: "The Civil Service and the Bank of England have been unbelievably incompetent" (*Manchester Guardian*, Oct. 26, 1980). A purely long-run theory can always be saved from refutation by this sort of ad hoc trickery, in which the theorist finds some short-run factor that interfered with the experiment. Consequently the politician who takes policy advice from a long-run theory, for instance advice that a subminimum wage will eventually reduce teenage unemployment, is likely to find that the next election arrives long before the predicted results.

The closest approximations to the desirable short-long-evolutionary theory have been some currents of functionalism including Parsons and Luhmann; Schumpeter; and New Left Marxist works such as Baran and Sweezy (1966), O'Connor (1973), and Wright (1978). Whether any of these are empirically valid is a different question; the rarity of the achievement makes these theories important in any case.

II. Ideology and Utopia

In this section we classify the various perspectives by means of Mannheim's conceptions of ideology and utopia (Mannheim, 1936, Chapters 2, 4). The reader might expect me to begin with Mannheim's definition of these terms, but this is not possible. Mannheim's hermeneutic-dialectical method involves a continuous redefinition of concepts as he interprets their current uses, moves through successive perspectives in the history of thought, and moves through successive stages of self-analysis and self-criticism. The meaning of these concepts is their whole history, and Mannheim's whole work is their definition, as of 1930.

Mannheim begins with the ordinary conception of an ideology as a set of ideas advanced by our opponent, which disguise a present situation, the true recognition of which would not be in accord with his interests (p. 55). The schema here is: we are scientific, they are ideological. This position is the normal one in the social sciences. But the opponents are also "we" and find that they can make the same charge in reverse. For Samuelson science is located in the great synthesis of the middle positions, with extremists of left and right like Galbraith and Friedman constituting the purveyors of ideology. For Galbraith and Melman the conventional wisdom, including Samuelson's traditional Keynesian doctrine, serves to disguise reality in the interests of the corporations and the military. Consequently the location of ideology shifts according to one's standpoint. We need a more general conception of ideology, and the obvious next one is that all positions are ideological in contrast with the real experience of the practical politician (Mannheim, p. 72). This conception of the ideologue shows up in Halperin (1974) and other foreign policy analysts, but rapidly runs into difficulties as we discover that politicians share the short-sighted ideologies of the in-and-outers. Then everybody is ideological except the pragmatic national security managers, and we move on to a new definition.

The concept of utopia undergoes similar changes. It is first defined as a state of mind that is incongruous with the reality in which it occurs, in such a way that if acted on it would shatter the order of things prevailing at the time (p. 192). Ideological states of mind, then, are those which are effective in the realization and maintenance of the existing order of things. In short, ideology vs. utopia = maintenance vs. change in the status quo. This definition focuses attention on the concept "prevailing order of things," which is specified differently from different standpoints. All political positions wish to change something and thereby preserve something else. Consequently, Mannheim observes, to concretely distinguish the ideological from the utopian is extremely difficult (p. 196). The contemporary concept of the utopian as the unrealizable is itself ideological because it erases the distinction between possible changes and absolutely impossible changes, suggesting that all desires for change are personal wishes unrelated to science, which merely describes what is (p. 196). But the utopian thinker is interested only in possible changes, not in fantasies, and the purpose of science for him is to distinguish the two.

If all political positions wish to change the present order of things toward a better one, then each position has its own utopia, or imagined better society (pp. 205ff.). A utopia may be located in the past (p. 230) or even paradoxically in the present as contrasted with past and future (pp. 233-235). In the latter case the present is divided into the good society we now essentially have and the tasks and problems, the bad elements, which remain to be mastered in it (p. 233).

We need not follow Mannheim's argument further at this time, because we now have a preliminary basis for classifying the perspectives of Part I. Each perspective has produced its own history in which better states of society are preceded or followed by worse states. If we collect the histories *provided by the standpoints themselves* we get Table 12.2.

Comments: For traditionalist conservatives there is a decay of knowledge from the time of the Wise Men to the present. In addition, most kinds of traditionalism have a conception of the Wise Man as a cultured gentleman–scholar, remote from worldly concerns, delving into knowledge for its own sake. The preferred hierarchical organization of science completes the picture of an idealized aristocratic society familiar to US Southerners. For the gold economists the collapse of the gold standard in 1931-1933 was the final consequence of decades of irresponsible currency meddling and government deficits. For the neoclassicists the high tide of capitalism began to subside well before

Table 12.2 Ideology and Utopia, as of 1975.

Standpoint	Location of Utopia
Traditionalist conservatism	Distant past
Gold economists	Past well before 1930
Neoclassicists	19th century
Keynesians	1960-1966 (U.S.); 1945-60 (U.K.); 1969- (Germany, Austria)
Functionalists	various past, present, future
systems analysts-operations researchers	present
social problems	1964-1970 (U.S.)
Elitist intellectuals	present
critical intellectuals	various; sometimes no utopia
Galbraith-bureaucratic	twenty years or so in the future
New Left Marxists	30-150 years in the future
Schumacher anarchists	indefinite future

1900, with governments beginning to regulate working conditions and hours, imposing tariffs, etc.; with business getting involved in government out of self-defense; and with the more power-hungry businessmen using government to gain advantages and start the ruinous march toward cartels and monopolies. For the US Keynesians the Kennedy–Johnson countercyclical policy finally showed what scientific fiscal policy could do to produce steady growth and full employment, but the crucial error in 1966 of failing to damp down a booming war economy produced the beginnings of inflation, and things have gone wrong ever since. In Britain, Keynesian planning by the 1945-1951 Labor government produced growing GNP and full employment which continued until balance of payments difficulties somehow intensified by 1955, and the shortsighted stop-go policies of the 1960's could never get things started again. In West Germany and Austria, I gather that the Keynesian policies of the Social Democrats since 1969 are still regarded as a political golden age.

There are all sorts of functionalists. For example, Radcliffe-Brown-type functionalists including Warner in his Yankee City series tended to look back to the well-integrated simpler societies that have now vanished. Parsons in the early 1960's was hailing the Kennedy–Johnson civil-rights policies as a shining example of social growth through wise leadership, and his evolutionary theory pointed to the present US as the culmination of history. Some Almond-type developmental functionalists look to the future of the developing societies when the specialized structures for maintaining functional unity will, they hope, have been set up.

For the systems analysts and operations researchers the present kit of mathematical techniques is the best ever, and steady incremental improvement can be expected. The social problems theorists regard the poverty program and many other welfare measures of the Johnson era as the golden age of the experimental welfare state, "the experimenting society" (Campbell, 1969) which was dimmed by the Nixon cutbacks. They look forward with hope to expanded 1960's-type programs in which we can apply what we learned from the successes and failures of the 1960's. For Rostow the present stage of high mass-consumption is the culmination of history, though there are signs of an even better stage of more cultivated tastes in prospect. Other elitists celebrate the present period since 1945 when the US began to assume its global responsibilities for the maintenance and expansion of elitist democracy. For the critical intellectuals, the small intensive case-studies celebrate the vividness of life in the present, of people coping amid poverty and oppression. One cannot call the present a golden age for the masses. But the past was no better, nor is there hope for the future. Piven and Cloward's 1971 history, for instance, portrays the past as static; the elite have always oppressed the masses since at least 1400. The history is cyclical, with mass uprising or unrest at the low points producing slight temporary reduction of oppression but with no real improvement. In contrast, the women's movement sees a steady reduction of oppression by the elite (men) during the last century from perfectly horrible to barely tolerable. This improvement was due to the steady efforts of the feminist movement, which has increased in strength in recent years. As a result we can look forward to substantial success in the next few years, when the ERA will have been passed, more occupations opened to women, and the new styles of family life more firmly established.

The bureaucratic-institutionalists look forward to the time when people will rise up and take responsibility for establishing a people's government that will take power from the corporations, shut down the military economy, stop oppressing other countries, and protect the little remaining environment. For the Marxists the good times begin when capitalism loses legitimacy and working people organize to build their own society. This process is well advanced today but will continue through ups and downs for a century at least. In other countries it has developed explosive momentum—Cuba, 1959; Czechoslovakia, 1968; Chile, 1970; Portugal, 1974; Poland, 1980; but these movements have been frustrated or even destroyed by the US or the SU. Consequently the revolution in the US is the crucial one, and the time estimates for this event range from 30 to 150 years. The category "New Left Marxist" does not include the chiliastic utopianism of those student activists who wanted to complete the revolution in the next few years, and when that failed, turned inward toward religious ecstacy (cf. Mannheim, 1936, p. 237). For the Schumacher anarchists the good society begins—if we survive—beyond capitalism and growth-oriented socialism; it will be based on solar, water, and wind power and on technologies that do not yet exist.

The result is something of a curve, with the two ends arching away into the past and future, and the midpoint tangent to the present with the systems analysts and elitist intellectuals. If we move our reference point from 1975 into the past, we find fragments of another regularity: those standpoints whose utopias now are in the past used to locate them in the future. In the 1930's the Keynesian utopia was located in the near future when government will have learned the techniques of fiscal management, and the social problems sociologists of the 1920's and 1930's were future-oriented. Way back in 1848 even the classical economist, Mill, located his utopia of profit-sharing co-operatives in the future. Conversely, as we move toward 1975 we find a few instances of the elitist intellectuals looking nostalgically to the recent past: Huntington's 1974 report to the Trilateral Commission about the new ungovernability of some democracies due to mass activism, Heilbroner's pessimism of 1974, and Bell's 1976 call for a new public philosophy to restore the declining legitimacy of elitist democracy. Nothing can be induced from these fragments of data.

So far we have considered utopias; where are the ideologies? *Those perspectives whose utopias are located in the past perform an ideological function.* They do this by hiding the actual exercise of power and by idealizing some existing institution projected into the past. Our purpose in this book, however, is not to discuss the propaganda uses of social science, so we drop this argument of Mannheim.

We have now classified the various perspectives in terms of one stage in Mannheim's concepts of ideology and utopia. The classification enables us to make explicit one aspect of what we mean by "truth" these days.

The goal of science is to describe and explain (understand) what is; but "what is" includes both what is actual and what is possible. Present-oriented traditions, including non-utopians, are specialists in the actual; future oriented traditions are specialists in the possible (Mannheim, 1936, pp. 260-263).

"Possible" here means "real, objective possibility" as distinguished from fantasy. It refers to changes that are actually now occurring, that have some continuing support in objective system dynamics or even human nature, and that therefore could continue or even intensify. A utopia provides a touchstone that enables one to recognize such changes, which would otherwise be dismissed as ephemeral fluctuations or surface manifestations of other things. It enables one to interpret the changes, to find meaning in them as a movement toward a better society, and to look for supporting or hindering processes. To be sure, it also enables one to exaggerate the importance of the changes or to wishfully construct imaginary changes out of real ephemera. Here the present-oriented traditions can provide a necessary corrective. If a participant–observer in Gary, Newark, or Ocean Hill–Brownswille finds evidence that the underclass is moving toward self-government via community associations, we have Piven and Cloward to remind us that the elite are wily, tenacious scoundrels with enormous reserves of power, whose humanitarian and democratic principles are immediately discarded at any threat to their position, and that the poor have no economic staying power. We also have

Gouldner's sobering reminder, after a survey of class struggles throughout history: *"The lowliest class never came to power.* Nor does it seem
likely to now" (1979, p. 93).

To be sure, either or both of the above interpretations might prove
to be mistaken; that issue is to be determined by empirical testing. But
testing cannot occur unless two opposed hypotheses have first been
formulated as plausibly as possible, and that is the function of the
utopian and the present-oriented traditions. In addition, as Mannheim
emphasizes, the testing of a perceived possibility must be done in
action, by trying to help it along, and this requires a partisan attitude.

If the goal of science is to describe and interpret both the actual and
the possible, what scientific perspectives contribute to this goal? In
general, we seem to need some future-oriented and some present-
oriented perspectives. The present-oriented perspectives are essential to
remind us of the staying power of the actual, which utopians always
underestimate. Among the future-oriented perspectives the Galbraithian–bureaucratic perspective would seem to be the most obviously
valuable one, because its utopia is located in the near future and thus
is the most open to empirical test. That is, when a Galbraithian
discovers some alleged movement toward a true people's government,
the interpretation could in principle be confirmed or disconfirmed in
twenty years; and in either case we would learn something. For the
Marxist or anarchist, it is always possible to allege short-run interferences and to modify the short-run part of the theory while keeping the
long-run part intact. Similarly, those perspectives whose utopia is in
the very recent past do not specify any date for the return of utopia
and so can always postpone their hopes until the next election.

The perspectives whose utopias are in the distant past are in a
different predicament. One can hardly expect the world ever to return
to the gold standard, with all that implies about the role of government. Nor will the simpler societies ever return. Nor will the corporations, unions, military establishments, national boundaries, computer-
ized information systems, credit, and government bureaus ever disappear as the neoclassicists would prefer. (This last statement would be
disputed by the James Buchanan group, which drew up a philosophy
and a constitution for such a society; Buchanan, 1975). Consequently,
the distant-past utopias cannot be used to discover real possibilities of
movement toward them. Instead they are used negatively to interpret
movements away from them. This is the "Road to Serfdom" mentality, or "Ideas for the Ice Age." Whether such an undifferentiated,
blanket condemnation of reality is scientifically useful is doubtful. If
the whole world except Switzerland has long since gone crazy, there is

not much point in investigating the many varied dynamics of madness; and if the good society is irretrievably gone, then there are few real possibilities left worth investigating. One turns instead to philosophy, like Buchanan.

In summary, one goal of science is to understand both the actual and the possible. The relevant organization of science is centered on the bureaucratic-institutionalists, and includes some of the future-oriented and the present-oriented perspectives. The past-oriented perspectives, now including the Keynesians, are of diminishing value as their utopia recedes further into the past.

III. Subject and Object

The goal under this heading is already well-known: to understand ourselves both as subject and as object, both as free and as determined. A science of man, a science of ourselves, must necessarily move toward this goal. In earlier times the full implication of the goal remained hidden because scientists tacitly distinguished themselves from society, the object; but now that the social studies of science have treated scientists too as objects of study the full recognition is unavoidable: in social science we study ourselves.

The goal has presented itself to social scientists as a contradiction between freedom and determinism, and earlier traditions have tried to overcome the contradiction by locating themselves on one or the other side of it. Those traditions whose standpoint required management or control or responsibility for society chose the determinism side, since an object can be managed only if one knows its dynamics, knows how it is determined. Those traditions whose standpoint involved resistance to control chose the freedom side, and their science was an affirmation and interpretation of human freedom—an affirmation of freedom for one class, interpreted as a universal human freedom.

Consequently, the contradiction has expressed itself in science as a disagreement between different traditions and different methods, intensified by the conviction on each side that it is defending science or human freedom.

The same disagreement has occurred in the philosophy of science. The hermeneutic tradition and the Wittgenstein–Winch school emphasize human freedom, arguing that the proper way to study human beings is to interpret and understand their reasons, goals, and perceptions. The positivist tradition has emphasized determinism, arguing that the only proper scientific treatment of objects is to explain and predict their behavior, and this requires knowledge of their causes, in some sense of "cause." The hermeneutic tradition implicitly asserts that all of society is Subject, and the positivist tradition implicitly asserts that all of society is Object—*except the scientist*! Even positivists are hermeneutic when they study Einstein and Galileo, and Popper positively abhors any study of scientists as objects. Scientists are always subjects.

Whether because of this argument or for other reasons, there has been cumulative progress in the last fifty years, and in my opinion the goal has been achieved in the 1970's. The progress has not been linear and has never involved any consensus, but has come about through the simultaneous attempts at quite different solutions by different traditions. The difficulties experienced in these diverse attempts have contributed to the solution as much as the partial successes. Consequently an account of the movement toward the solution, even a highly simplified and biased account, must also jump around somewhat.

There are many varieties of traditionalist conservatism, and Table 12.3 represents only one of these, exemplified by Popper's work since about 1965 and by Plato. This position is plainly unsatisfactory; it consigns all activity of S, and particularly the whole scientific process, to a lower, changeable, unknowable world. Science itself does not deal with this subjective world, nor with objective history, but with the Third World of eternal truth (Popper, 1972). As against this position, the neoclassicists had a firm grasp on the fundamental *a priori* truth of human freedom. Man is free by nature; each of us knows this about himself, and by extension knows it about all other beings who have the same nature. A science of man, a science of our own world, must be a science of free choice and action; its subject-matter is subjectivity. Generic human subjectivity is knowable because each of us knows it in ourselves. As for society, since O is created by S it must be understood as the consequence of decisions by S.

The difficulty with a science of free choice is that any determining influences on human decisions must be outside of science because they are incompatible with freedom. Determinism runs only from S to O. The origins of preference schedules or tastes are unknowable. Consequently also the utilities of different individuals cannot be compared. The variable resources possessed by individuals are irrelevant to their generic freedom and therefore must be ignored by science. Freedom, in fact, becomes a pretty empty thing, being reduced to the bare fact of choosing the better. Since it is universal, it has no content: ". . . everyone 'wants' to do whatever he is doing at the moment; otherwise he

Table 12.3. Subject and Object

Standpoint	Conception of science	Subject-Object relation (S-O)
Traditionalist Conservatism	Objective	Various. One answer: Subjectivity is error; should disappear by absorption into O. S is finite, O is infinite. Ex: Late Popper; Stalinism; Leo Strauss
Neoclassic	Subjective; many subjects	O is totality of unanticipated consequences of myriads of decisions by subjects. S determines O.
Keynesian	Objective	S-O, value-fact dichotomy. O has independent dynamics, unsatisfactory to S. S manages O.
Schumpeterian	Subjective and Objective	a) for elite and intellectuals: S-O dialectic. O shapes S; S remakes O. b) for mass: Mass is O. S manages and transforms O.
Underclass	Subjective: two subjects	O is reified S, either in an alienating society or in an objectivist social science. S-S relation: a) mutual exclusion, class or gender struggle. b) mutual inclusion of self and other. Self-definition by introjecting the role of the other.
Bureaucratic-Institutionalist	Objective	a) O determines S, leaving S a small range of freedom. O dynamics work through S, though irregularly because of S's freedom. b) S can become emancipated by the power of ideas. c) O has independent, unsatisfactory dynamics; will be managed by emancipated S. Free society returns.
New Left Marxist	Objective; two determined subjects	a) O determines S_1, S_2, leaving S_1 a small range of freedom. O dynamics work irregularly, because of S_1's freedom. b) Both O and S (class struggle) transform each other in successive stages, during which S_2 gradually becomes emancipated. S_2 creates a new society; history of freedom begins.

Table 12.3. Subject and Object (Continued)

Standpoint	Conception of science	Subject-Object relation (S-O)
Schumacher	Objective	Man-nature dialectic. S is free to enrich or impoverish O and thereby S, within limits set by O.

would not do it" (Patinkin, 1956, p. 211). The content of choices, being determined by tastes and resources, falls outside of science. Consequently the actual determination of O by S cannot be known either, because much of this depends on the content of S's choices; and therefore most of the short-run dynamics of O are unknowable.

A science of freedom ends by telling us we are helpless to do anything about the problems of our society, because they are caused by unknowable objective factors prior to choice—a taste for discrimination, a taste for leisure, money illusion, the actual distribution of human abilities, etc.

Keynes and his contemporaries were intensely concerned about the problems of our society—cyclical unemployment, urban disorganization, the gold coast and the slum. If these problems are caused by objective factors, as the neoclassicists assert, a science that deals with them must be objective and empirical. We have to observe and measure the actual processes of society: the actual flows of population and resources, the actual spending habits and employment history and family life of the slum dwellers, the actual investment decisions of businessmen. We do not assume generic rationality, but observe how businessmen do act, and we find crowd phenomena, bullish and bearish propensities, and also some calculation. Empirical studies of business decisions found rules of thumb, cost-plus pricing rather than marginal utility pricing, levels of aspiration, satisficing, and so on. So much for the *a priori* neoclassic truths.

The consequence of making science objective is dualism—economics and sociology become objective, political science must necessarily be subjective. Economics and sociology deal with the objective empirical processes of which our social problems are composed. Sociologists construct flow models and compile population and income statistics block by block in the city, describing the actual dynamics of current problems. But the point of studying social problems objectively is to do something about them; that is government's responsibility. Responsiblity implies subjectivity, freedom. Government, the subject matter of political science, is free. The task of political science, then, is to understand and interpret government policies, evaluate them, and advise improvements. So we get a subjectivist case study tradition in foreign politics, which picked up some of the subjectivist neoclassic models in the 1950's; a case study legal tradition analyzing the decisions of the Warren court; and a Keynesian economic policy tradition at Brookings and elsewhere analyzing and evaluating government fiscal and monetary policies. Corresponding to the two kinds of science are two causal schemes: O determines O, that is O has its own dynamics, and S manages O, that is S redirects the dynamics toward target levels.

The dualism is unstable, however. Not all of political science need be subjective. Having objectified the economy, one can also study the administrative apparatus as an objective instrument of policy decisions and implementation—a very imperfect instrument, as Wildavsky has been pointing out since 1962. The Cabinet, the White House staff, the Budget Bureau are also part of the apparatus, and their behavior is determined by their location in the communication and influence structure, which can be improved by its creator, S, the President. S now has responsibility not only for managing the economy, but also for managing the apparatus of management. He becomes also the last refuge and symbol of freedom in a determined world. But the President too is part of this same apparatus and is likewise determined by his location in it. The Keynesian objectification of society reaches its limit in the bureaucratic politics theory of the 1970's, when all of society is determined and freedom has disappeared.

Subjectivity is still present, but its character has changed. It has gotten content by being determined. Instead of the generic human propensity to choose the better rather than the worse we now have a multitude of particular mentalities or consciousnesses corresponding to the various positions in an organization. Each position determines the mentality of its occupant, by selective recruitment, socialization, experience on the job, and organizational group dynamics. The only generic human properties contributed by the individual are conscientiousness and loyalty, the desire to do a good job, the desire for approval and promotion. The mentality of consumers is determined by urban geography and the socioeconomic institutions through which consumers must move daily. The organization-member's mentality, in turn, determines what problems and resources he will recognize, what objectives he will have, and what strategies he will follow. Some freedom or operating space exists, especially at the higher levels of organization, but its limits are set by organizational structure and imperatives. For the consumer, freedom is limited by what the organization chooses to produce. The scheme throughout is, O determines S; O determines O via S. The neoclassicist "free" choice is real but trivial; determinism works through the mediation of choices.

Now that all of society is determined, freedom reappears—for Galbraith, Lockard, Ellsberg, etc.—by a leap of faith outside society to the realm of ideas. The power of ideas will free some people from determination by O. Or, for Kharasch, it is the power of human nature freeing itself: human decency and common sense will break through, sometimes, despite the enormous conditioning power of the organization (1973, p. 70). This is a reasoned faith, based on experience; these people have experienced their own emancipation (or have experienced decent treatment) and therefore can hope to spread it to others. Freedom now is not a generic human property or a little space for maneuver; it is emancipation from O. Emancipation will effect a reversal of determination with S managing O as in the Keynesian scheme. The dualism is now between present and future. At present O determines S; in the future S will manage O.

We drop this line of development now and turn to Schumpeter, who comes out of a neoclassic background combined with a sociological tradition represented by Marx and Weber. Here O and S are mutually determining, an obvious improvement over the two one-way determinisms. The mentality of S, the entrepreneur (the spirit of capitalism, for instance) comes from his Protestant cultural background, and he in turn transforms that background indirectly, in the long run, by changing society. Freedom here means creativity, the transformation of society. But the entrepreneur can be free only if he has determinate material to work with and transform. He needs the masses to fight in his armies, staff his organizations, consume his products. Freedom for the elite means determinism for the masses. The mass perspective enables us to correct this new dualism by understanding the masses also as S.

We now have two S's, elite and masses. The elitist "S transforms O" scheme is reinterpreted from the mass perspective as "S_1 oppresses S_2," and since S_2 are also free, they fight back. The reality is class struggle. The remaining O component, namely the institutional transformations by the creative entrepreneur or modernizing elite, is reinterpreted as an instrument of oppression of S_2. O essentially disappears, and determinism with it. That is, all social changes are interpreted as schemes initiated by the ruling class to further oppress the masses. Only freedom is left, the freedom of class struggle in which

S₁ always wins. Why always? There is some unexamined determinism in the background somewhere. Why do elite welfare measures and even revolutions that are sincerely intended to help the masses somehow end up oppressing them?

New Left Marxists investigate this background determinism. As a consequence they combine the class struggle scheme with the bureau-cratic-institutionalist scheme. There are three polar class tendencies: elite, small businessmen, and workers, whose mentality is shaped by their position in economic and political organizations. But since two of these tendencies are present in most occupations and persons, nearly everyone has some choice of which tendency to claim as his own. Two people in the same objective occupation can subjectively belong to opposite classes. Thus occupation determines mentality, but only through the mediation of subjective identification (Wright, 1978, Chapter 2).

The elite, located at the higher occupational levels, bear responsi-bility for organizational maintenance, and therefore are constrained by the functional imperatives of system maintenance, and especially the imperative to accumulate capital unceasingly. The imperatives force them to extract more work out of the working class, and this is sooner or later felt as oppression and resisted. Thus the class struggle is a subjective manifestation of objective system dynamics. The class struggle is determined; but it in turn transforms the economic-political structure and sets new system maintenance problems for the elite. Their new maintenance policies produce new forms of class struggle, which once again change the structure, and so on.

Freedom and determinism are now intertwined. The Subject-Object dialectic is the basic scheme with two opposed Subjects. The objective system determines its own changes through subjectivity and class struggle, and the working class frees itself by changing the system which determines its mentality. The subjectivist view of history as class struggle is correct; but the struggle itself is determined, and the objectivist view is also correct.

The reconciliation of freedom and determinism was made possible by changing the meaning of both terms several times. By now at least seven senses of "determine" have appeared in the literature from functionalism through Marxism, and several corresponding senses of "free." I have used several terms to suggest these changes of meaning in the preceding summary: manage, mediate, constrain, transform, select. Other terms in the literature include structural incompatibility and system maintenance. The Marxist Erik Wright (1978, Chapter 1) has systematized six of these senses of "determine," based on the work of Poulantzas. One task of Marxists now is to further systematize and clarify the various structural, functional, processual, and productive causes that we have learned to distinguish over the decades.

No doubt the Marxist solution to the problem of subjectivity and objectivity, freedom and determinism, will be improved on in future decades. Every solution, even the dualistic ones, has seemed adequate to its own proponents at the time, and its weaknesses have appeared only gradually or from different perspectives.

IV. The Two Roads

Any attentive observer of the social sciences will have noticed the occasional shifts of position of prominent scientists, both gradual and sudden. Sometimes the shift is explained away as due to individual weakness; "failure of nerve" was once the standard absurd explanation. Thus Ellsberg's sudden shift in 1968 has been explained as due to the desire for fame of an otherwise unimpressive hack. Or the scientist himself will assert "It is not I, but the world that has changed. I believe as I always have." To be sure, there is always continuity in change and change in continuity, and social and individual changes are always correlative.

The changes go in both directions, radical and conservative, and in other directions on other dimensions as well. One can even imagine a zigzag change—left in the 1940's, right in the 1950's and early 1960's, then left again. They may apparently start anywhere and go anywhere—a leftist may move right or farther left, a rightist may move left or farther right. Even the far right Hayek, describing himself as an eighteenth-century Whig in 1960 (Hayek, 1960, Epilogue), has managed in his old age to move still farther right, embracing the nostrums of the gold economists—in a speech delivered in Switzerland, to be sure (Hayek, 1976).

According to some scientists the normal movement is rightward, and leftward movement is a sign of personal neurosis or bad training (Stigler, 1959; the Schumpeterian intellectuals). For others, such as the sociologists of deviance, the normal movement is leftward as one delves into the oppressions of our society.

These phenomena suggest the "two roads" or left-right polarization hypothesis. If one searches for polarization one finds a great deal of it; the left and right Keynesians, whose differences were embedded in the two opposite possibilities of countercyclical policy (cf. Chapter Four, Section IV), are the most prominent. Then there is the polarization of responses to the student movement, the polarization in attitudes toward the Vietnam war, the polarization of thought and politics in the two Germanys, and in the 1950's a polarization over the Cold War, with such people as Mills and Melman and Rapoport moving left in opposition to US militarization. In the late 1960's and early 1970's there has been some polarization over the experience of the poverty program and the welfare state in Western Europe; people such as Moynihan and the *Public Interest* regulars have moved right to a more limited conception of government responsibility and power, and others such as Cloward have moved left to a criticism of the welfare state on quite different grounds.

If we treat these shifts as individual phenomena and try to explain them by correlation with something, we are in difficulty. With an N of about 50,000 we need statistical techniques; and then, as Lazarsfeld reminds us, "It's not evidence unless you have a count." Our evidence has disappeared; it was only illustrations, discovered by search. We can find anything if we search hard enough. The same point applies to the explanations of shifts as due to individual neuroses; we can always find personality defects.

If we treat these shifts as group phenomena our N goes down to around fifteen and we no longer need a random sample and a count. However, we can no longer explain why individuals move with one or another theory group.

We notice first that the shifts are not evenly balanced at all. Nearly all the Keynesians were right Keynesians; nearly all responses to the Cold War were rightward. As for the Vietnam war, if we exclude those groups who were already in vigorous rightward movement due to the Cold War, the main response was leftward. The student movement was part of this leftward response. The rapid spread of Keynesianism in the late 1930's was a leftward movement, with very few moving right in disgust. The data on movements since the late 1960's are not in yet.

We notice next that the dominant shifts, right or left, are responses to dramatic events that lasted several years or more. Further, when groups are set in motion by some dramatic event they continue to move in the same direction for a time. This is the "generational experience" concept, except that each generation is accompanied by a minority opposition movement.

These directions are summarized in Table 12.4. There is some overlap when a generational experience pushes in the same direction as the previous one. The Keynesians interpreted the planning of World War II as further evidence that government is now able to take

Table 12.4. The Two Roads.

Experience	Main Move	Prominent Exponents
Mass unemployment 1920-1940	Left	Keynesians Social problems sociologists
World War II	Expansionist	Operations researchers Cybernetic-systems analysts International development economists
Cold War	Right	Elitist intellectuals Deterrence theorists
Postwar prosperity	Right	Right Keynesians Elitist intellectuals
Civil Rights movement; Vietnam War	Left	Bureaucratic Politics New Left Marxism

on and manage the major problems of our society. Postwar prosperity further convinced the Cold War intellectuals of the superiority of elitist democracy and the mixed economy. The fiscal crisis of the 1970's reinforced New Left Marxists in our belief that capitalism is in decline.

The expansionist impetus of World War II consisted of the experience that the US could use the newest mathematical techniques developed during the war to do good abroad by defeating Fascism. Here were powerful scientific tools that could be used at home to manage social and economic problems and abroad to assist other countries in economic development. As far as I know, the operations researchers and cybernetics people confined their attention at first to domestic problems, mainly problems of industrial efficiency, but remained convinced that their tools could be applied in principle to any social problem. Their postwar enthusiasm continued into the 1950's in the Simon–March–Cyert group and the computer simulation people, but became more of a professional enthusiasm for the new techniques. Later the systems analysts and the like moved abroad as well, using their techniques to assist modernizing governments. The international development economists like Hirschman, coming out of a generally Keynesian background, were the ones who shared Roosevelt's vision of a global New Deal (Schurmann, 1974, Chapter 1) which

would extend the wartime planning techniques and wartime US generosity to the poor countries. The Marshall Plan was the first success in this project, and the economists studied ways to repeat that success elsewhere. They recommended broad social reforms, particularly land reform along the lines of postwar Japan and 1950-1954 Guatemala (T.W. Schultz, 1953) and cultural integrity combined with economic and political modernization (M. Mead, 1955). The main journal of this movement was *Economic Development and Cultural Change*, beginning in 1953. Schultz later recommended mass technical education, that is, investment in human capital (Schultz, 1971). This was a liberal, reforming internationalism whose origin in the Roosevelt era gave it a quite different mentality from the Cold War internationalism of the anti-Communists. The one was optimistic and expansionist; the other was defensive, combative, even paranoid. The two came into direct opposition in one country after another, such as Guatemala 1954.

The remaining movements have already been discussed in Part I.

Our problem has now changed. We are no longer considering the left-right shifts of individual scientists; this phenomenon is common enough, but requires statistical surveys or intensive case studies even for the development of plausible hypotheses, to say nothing of testing. Instead we are dealing with the origins of the various theory groups discussed in Part I. Nor are there always only two roads; this concept is a political simplification.

The events associated with the various generational experiences of Table 12.4 all had important effects on system legitimation. Extended mass unemployment reduces system legitimacy; so also does fiscal crisis and bankruptcy, a lost war, and a failure to end racial oppression and poverty. Prosperity, full employment, and growth increase system legitimacy; so also does a successful war and an external threat. The perceived moral character of the war also makes a difference, apart from its outcome. World War II was perceived as highly justified because the Fascist enemy was bad, so it had a strong legitimating effect, except for the pacifists. In Europe the prewar collusion of various right parties with the Nazis had a delegitimating effect after the war. The Vietnam war was perceived in two opposite ways. The elitist intellectuals and the deterrence theorists, whose generational experience was the perceived Soviet threat, interpreted the war in terms of that experience as defensive, anti-Communist, and therefore highly moral; others interpreted it as a big country bullying a little one and therefore immoral.

The delegitimating events produced a demand for change and therefore a leftward movement in social science. The legitimating events had two different effects: the threatening Cold War experience produced a rightward movement, a desire to use science to defend our system, while the exhilarating, successful war effort produced a generous desire to share our goodness with the less fortunate.

The ambiguity of these events, which allowed them to be perceived in two opposite ways, is a plausible explanation of the "two roads" phenomenon. Mass unemployment could be and was interpreted by some as a consequence of government bungling, in particular in the Federal Reserve failure to expand the money supply from 1929-1931, and this interpretation produced a minority right tendency rededicated to reducing government responsibility for social problems. As for the Cold War, there was something implausible about the idea of a ruined, nearly defeated Soviet Union threatening victorious, nuclear armed America, and those few who felt this implausibility moved left in opposition to US militarism and aggressiveness. Postwar prosperity looked impressive to most, but there were groups like the share-croppers who were being severely damaged—as became apparent in the 1960's—and those few who noticed this moved left in opposition to domestic policy. The ambiguity of the Vietnam War was experienced directly by some, who interpreted it first as a defense against Communist aggression and only later as immoral. The poverty program and the fiscal crisis are also ambiguous.

The careful reader will have noticed the negative evidence, namely all the theory groups of Part I who do not appear in Table 12-4. Of these missing groups, the critical intellectuals and the functionalists are really a variety of groups of different origin, which may or may not have had a unifying generational experience. In addition many other groups have not even been discussed in Part I. The fantastic complexity of the social sciences defeats any simple interpretation of their development such as the generational experience hypothesis.

Nevertheless it is clear that a generational experience has been important in the origins and motivation of some important social science traditions. To that extent the development of the social sciences has not been an autonomous phenomenon, but has reflected developments in society. The periods of national triumph and expansion have been accompanied by rightward currents in science, with small left counter-currents; the periods of crisis and failure have produced left currents and right countercurrents. This means that our original question, How can we reorganize our own scientific research to achieve greater objectivity? is misguided. It assumes freedom; but as I argued in Secton III, we are both free and determined. The reorganization of science is in large part a consequence of changes in society; we ourselves are a product of two of those changes, the Vietnam war and the civil rights movement. If the 1980's are a period of consolidation of capitalism, of full employment and prosperity, social science will experience one or more rightward movements—and we ourselves may be included in them. It may be that we can see our own dismal future in the history of the Schumpeterian intellectuals, and to some extent this reversal is already occurring. On the other hand, if the 1980's are a time of legitimation crisis and failure, as we fervently hope, parts of social science will move leftward. The outcome is in the main not of our doing.

Thirteen Science and Morality

The above title reflects the current status of the topic discussed in this chapter. In earlier years it would have been "science and values" or in a philosophical tradition, "fact and value." A history of social science traditions is also a history of their associated ethical theories, and the scientific disagreement between different traditions is also an ethical disagreement. As a result the purely cognitive barriers to rational discussion examined in Part I are supplemented by moral outrage, and the polemicist finds himself obliged to criticize not only nonsense but vicious nonsense as well.

I. Ethical Beliefs Of Social Scientists

For the neoclassicists the topic was called "science and values," or the relation between positive and normative economics. Hutchison has provided a history of this relation in economic thought from 1835 on (1964, Chapter 1). The neoclassicists were value-relativists, believing that each person's value preferences are his own business. Deciding one's own preferences was in fact of the essence of freedom; it was what distinguished humans from animals. Consequently, the investigation of the causes of tastes was immoral as well as conceptually impossible within the neoclassical scheme. If such causes could be found, they could be used to control preferences and thus destroy human freedom. Here was a moral reason for objecting to the Keynesian objectification of society: even a small success at this scientifically impossible enterprise would play into the hands of the liberal-socialist-communist planner, the expert who thought he was God and could decide what was good for other people. The neo-classicist standpoint was the little man whose freedom was threatened by big government and the big corporations; and the Keynesian-systems analyst-social problems professional—the "expert"—was a servant of government and corporations and an enemy of freedom—as well as a poor scientist.

Those who seek specific descriptions of the good society will not find them here. A listing of my own private preferences would be both unproductive and uninteresting. I claim no rights to impose these preferences on others. . . . In these introductory sentences, I have by implication expressed my disagreement with those who retain a Platonic faith that there is 'truth' in politics, remaining only to be discovered and, once discovered, capable of being explained to reason-able men. We live together because social organization provides the efficient means of achieving our individual objectives and not because society offers us a means of arriving at some transcendental common bliss. Politics is a process of compromising our differences. . . . When we view politics as process . . . any attempt to lay down standards becomes effort largely wasted at best and pernicious at worst, even for the man who qualifies himself as expert." (Buchanan, 1975, p. 1.) Frank Knight put it more succinctly: "I don't mind your claiming there is an absolute truth, as long as you don't claim to know what it is."

Here the opponent is not only the expert who claims to know what is good for other people, but also the traditionalist conservative who finds eternal truth in Plato, Aristotle, Aquinas, or some other Wise Man.

Relativism, of course, implies absolutism, just as the absolutism of the traditionalist conservatives implies relativism. That is, the tradi-tionalist finds enduring wisdom in the philosophic tradition, but different interpreters define that tradition differently. For the Leo Straussians, the tradition comes down from Plato, and Aristotle and Aquinas are hardly ever mentioned; for the Great Books people, Aquinas and Aristotle are it; for Nisbet, Tocqueville is the high point of the tradition. Enduring wisdom thus is relative to the interpreter.

For the neoclassicists the relativism of preferences implied the absolute truth of Benthamite utilitarianism. If everyone's preferences are his own business, and if more of any good is better than less, then social welfare, the subject of normative economics, must consist of the most for everybody. This is the only ethics compatible with human freedom.

Over the years of the neoclassicist area (1870–1950) a number of philosophic problems of utilitarian ethics were discussed by the welfare economists. There was the question of whether normative economics deals with all values or only those measurable by money, with Marshall and Pigou arguing for the money limitation. There was the problem that a through-going relativism makes interpersonal comparison of values impossible, which Pareto solved in principle by the Pareto-optimal criterion, later embodied in the Bergson social welfare function. There was the dispute in the 1930's and 1940's over cardinal vs. ordinal measurement of utility. Old-timers such as D.H. Robertson remained skeptical about these quibbles and preferred to rely on our common sense knowledge of the obvious truth of cardinal, non-Pareto, non-money utilitarianism (Robertson, 1951).

The period of respectability of Benthamite act-utilitarianism ended that same year with the publication of Arrow's paradox (Arrow, 1951). Arrow proved that if one assumes randomness of preferences between individuals, then it is logically impossible to guarantee the existence of a social welfare function. That is, in a purely individualist society "the most for everybody" or "the greatest good for the greatest number" is indeterminate. However, the real world is not purely individualist, with randomly varying preferences. There is a sharing of preferences; there is community. By "community" we do not mean Buchanan's "transcendental common bliss" or anything that transcends individual preferences, but merely a similarity of preference orderings among individuals. What Arrow's Paradox shows is that act-utilitarianism depends on the existence of community for its usefulness. It presupposes a community of interests that it itself cannot account for, given its conception of freedom. Or, in Schumpeterian terms, the small businessman appears and flourishes in a society that he did not create and cannot maintain.

What we need, therefore, is a systematic concept of community, in which utilitarianism is interpreted as the ethics appropriate to one aspect of community, the economic aspect. The concept was developed by the early functionalists who celebrated the integrity of the simpler societies and analyzed the ways in which these societies maintained their integrity against stresses and strains. Malinowski analyzed Trobriand society as a complex system of social relations in which production and exchange were organized by the reciprocal obligations inherent in social relations. The economy, the political system, and social relations were maintained in equilibrium insofar as everyone carried out the duties inherent in his or her social role. Conflicts and strains were managed and reduced by legal processes and by ceremonies. Radcliffe-Brown's 1922 study, building on ideas of the Durkheim school, showed how Andamanese ceremonies, myths, and legends all had the effect of maintaining social relations at points of potential stress or strain. He also described how the ceremonies changed, or varied in different localities, as the pattern of economic stresses changed or varied.

The ethical theory implicit in the early functionalist conception of the self-maintaining society is the right-Hegelian ethics of community. The standard version is Bradley's *Ethical Studies* (1876), especially Chapter 5, "My Station and Its Duties." The theory was further developed by the British Hegelian MacBeath (1952), who applied the Bradley–Bosanquet conception of community to the case studies of the British functionalists.

The right-Hegelian ethics of community is often called self-realization ethics. The good for man is life, action, including thinking, feeling, loving, working. Through action we develop our human creative potentialities, become more fully human, and enrich our experiences and capacity for experience. But action requires community, first as the source of training in culturally accumulated skills, and then as the cooperation that complex actions (like raising children) require. Community consists first of shared concepts and values that enable us to communicate and coordinate our actions. This is Durkheim's "collective conscience" and Hegel's "conscience" (*Philosophy of Right*, par. 137–141). It includes the shared preferences pointed to by Arrow's Paradox. Community consists also of a system of coordinated roles that make task specialization in complex activities possible; a process of socializing new members; a system of production and distribution of the instruments of action; and a control subsystem which ensures that the whole system keeps running (Malinowski, 1944, p. 125).

See, in contrast, what one elitist intellectual does with the concept of community: ". . . another part of the explanation . . . must be found in the sense of community and obligation, and further in an acceptance of authority—the authority of doctors, government officials, experts, of those who are put above one to govern . . . Altruism, yes. But also

community, and where one says community one says accepted authority" (Glazer, 1971, p. 94). Here the functionalist's objective, systemic
concept of community is first subjectivised as "a sense of community"
and then turned into a respect for the authority of the elite. For the
elitist a community exists insofar as the masses respect elite authority.

When we shift our attention from the well integrated simpler
societies to modern society we find that a great deal of co-ordination
and repair is required. Government has a lot to do. Here is the ethical
justification for Keynesian interest in maintenance of the economy,
and the social problems theorist's interest in maintenance of socialization. Not only the national society but also smaller organizations and
subsystems require maintenance and repair; this is the task of the
operations researchers and systems analysts. All these systems, small
and large, have a similar structural differentiation, because all are self-
maintaining systems. Each one must have a control subsystem, a
socialization or personnel subsystem, a technical or production subsystem, a communication subsystem, and so on. Consequently the repair
man, the systems analyst, can carry a set of standardized mathematical
models in his kit. But since the subsystems are themselves specialized
in the larger society, they will have different kinds of structures and
repair problems. A subsystem that produces shoes cannot have the
same communication and role structure as a subsystem that produces
people or educates them or resocializes juvenile delinquents. Consequently, the models will have different detailed applications in
different kinds of subsystems. Or, more likely, professionals will be
specialized to the problems of different kinds of subsystems, with the
overall government coordinating the various research and repair
activities. Here is the ethical justification for NIH, NIMH, and NSF;
also ONR, RAND, and IDA.

The left shift of the Galbraithian–institutionalist comes with the
recognition that actual governments do not work that way. Actual
governments are not neutral control subsystems by which a society
repairs and maintains itself; they are large organizations in symbiosis
with other large organizations—corporations and "enemy" governments—running by their own dynamics. Just as the young Marx
ridiculed the Hegelian idealization of the bureaucracy, the universal
class, pointing out that the bureaucratic mentality was self-sustaining
and treated society as an excuse for its own indefinitely continued
activity (Marx, 1970, pp. 45-48), so the bureaucratic-institutionalist
ridicules the idea that government is a rational problem-solver that
keeps a society running. Its interest is rather in keeping itself running.
"The bureaucracy has the being of the state, the spiritual being of

society, in its possession; it is its private property. . . . The bureaucrat has the world as a mere object of his action." (Marx, 1970, pp. 46–48).

The positive ethical theory of the bureaucratic–institutionalists is implicit in their call to the people, the public, to rise up and take control of their own government away from the corporations and the Pentagon bureaucracy. So also the young left-Hegelian Marx called for a true people's democracy that would sweep away the selfish monarchy, aristocracy, and bureaucracy (1970, p. 48). So also another ex-right Hegelian, Dewey, who turned sharply left and absorbed the institutionalist ideas of Veblen into his political theory.

Dewey develops the concept of a people's government most fully in *The Public and Its Problems* (1927). A public or political community is an organization devoted to maintaining the common good or public interest, the community life that all share. Today, this public is eclipsed by the organized special interests that are a natural outcome of a capitalist economy, since a capitalist economy organizes production in terms of private interests. The result is a fragmentation of communication and community into warring special interests. The goal of the social scientist must be to construct a political community that does not now exist, and with it the construction of a socialist economy that produces for the common good. "Production for use, not for profit" was the slogan of the old League for Industrial Democracy to which Dewey belonged. Today this goal is pursued by the Public Interest Research Groups, the People's Business Commission, Common Cause, and the consumer-environmentalist organizations. In short, the right-Hegelian conception of community is ridiculed by the bureaucratic-institutionalist as an ideological mask for a special-interest government; but the same conception is shifted to the future as a utopian goal.

"Wherever there is conjoint activity whose consequences are appreciated as good by all singular persons who take part in it, and where the realization of the good is such as to effect an energetic desire and effort to sustain it in being just because it is a good shared by all, there is insofar a community. The clear consciousness of a communal life . . . constitutes the idea of democracy" (Dewey, 1927, p. 149). "The prime condition of a democratically organized public is a kind of knowledge and insight which does not yet exist" (p. 166). Compare this with Galbraith's "The first step in reform is to win emancipation of belief."

We turn now to another line of development that begins with the elitist intellectuals.

Bell discusses Weber's distinction between an ethics of responsibility and an ethics of ultimate ends (1960, Epilogue). This is a Kantian approach to ethics, part of Weber's generally Kantian epistemology. The ethics of responsibility is the correct one. In it, actions are governed by duty rather than desire, by impersonal rules rather than personal goals. The type of duty varies according to one's position in society: a member of an organization has assigned duties, and the head of the organization has overall responsibility for the well-being of the organization. There is also a universal component of duty, based on the Kantian respect for human beings as ends in themselves. This respect expresses itself as a voluntary self-limitation, a refusal to take actions that would degrade other people to the status of objects to be manipulated.

The extreme form of manipulation is killing, since it sacrifices the other's whole life to one's end. Lying is another form of manipulation, which terminates rational communication; also abusing a trust, stealing, and using terror to subject others to arbitrary commands. Self-limitation is built into the duties assigned regular members of an organization, at least an organization structured like Weber's ideal-typical bureaucracy. Organization rules ought to be impersonal and impartial, assigning tasks and rewards according to universal criteria of merit and ability. But organization heads ought to limit themselves voluntarily, governing themselves in Kantian fashion by universalizable rules they lay down for themselves.

In the other kind of ethics, actions are treated as means to some goal, which in turn is a means to another goal, and so on to some ultimate all-justifying end. Actions are chosen and evaluated in terms of how well they contribute to the achievement of the ultimate end. Utilitarianism in all its forms, but especially act-utilitarianism, is an example of an ethics of ends, in which the end is the happiness of all human beings, or for Bentham the happiness of all sentient beings. An ethics of ends is bad because it allows and even requires one to treat human beings as pure means, and this is immoral. Bell's example of an ethics of ultimate ends is Stalin's policies in the 1930's, when millions of peasants and party members were sacrificed by starvation and execution, to the ultimate end of Communism. The example shows that the most horrible crimes against humanity can be justified by an ethics of ultimate ends.

Here we have a contrast between the ethics of the elite and the ethics of the counterelite. The elite are chosen, because of their merit, to a position of leadership in society. Leadership means responsibility for the continued well-being of their society, and a responsibility to respect the dignity of all human beings. The counterelite seek to achieve an ultimate end, world Communism, interpreted as a society in which all human beings will be happy; they are utilitarians. In pursuit of this absolute good they are willing to sacrifice a whole present generation of human beings, in their own country by enslaving them and working them to death, in other countries by threatening war in order to expand their power.

The concept of elite responsibility gains content from the third form of Kant's categorical imperative, the kingdom of ends. This is a regulative ideal of a society in which each person limits himself by universalizable rules and thereby respects the dignity of all other members. Individuals can pursue private ends, but only within the limits set by respect for others. The name for this ideal is democracy. It includes self-government by discussion, in which people relate to one another by rational discussion rather than force, threats, verbal trickery, or appeals to emotions. Rational discussion respects the free rationality of the other, but the nonrational tactics are tactics of manipulation that degrade the other to a means, an object. The counterelite use tactics of manipulation; their preferred form of government is totalitarianism, in which a society is treated as a means to some grand social goal, some utopian vision.

Kantian democracy is not the same as the neoclassical democracy of Hayek (1960), or Buchanan (1975), in which individuals come together in order to pursue their individual ends more efficiently, and treat society as a means to their private ends. Rule-utilitarianism is the ethics of such a society, and people make rules in such a way as to ensure themselves a maximum of freedom to pursue their own ends. In a Kantian democracy the rules of mutual tolerance are self-imposed out of respect for human dignity, and they are compatible with democratic planning, welfare measures, education, and other public activities. Kantian democracy is also vastly different from Dewey's conception of democracy, in which ordinary people organize themselves to protect the public interest against the special interests. Popular participation is essential to Dewey's democracy, while for Kant the universalizable rules of merit, tolerance, and rational discussion are the essence or formal structure of democracy.

Elite responsibility for the continued well-being of their society includes promoting the well-being of the masses by welfare measures and social insurance. It also includes protecting and preserving democracy, internally against the authoritarianism and intolerance of the masses and externally against totalitarian aggression. There is no responsibility to extend democracy to other countries; that would make democracy a goal to be achieved, if necessary by force against recalcitrants. Consequently it is not immoral, irresponsible, to cooperate with authoritarian governments in resisting the aggressive moves of the counterelite.

Elitist science is an instrument for carrying out these responsibilities. It is not value-free, but controlled throughout by the moral responsibilities of the scientific intellectual. The title of this chapter, "Science and Morality" refers to the problem of the moral responsibility of the scientist, the issue which has been important in the 1960's and 1970's. Responsibility for mass welfare requires studies of poverty, the discontents of work, race relations, education, and all forms of mass behavior. Responsibility for preserving democracy requires investigation of the social conditions which preserve or endanger democracy; it also requires us to publicize how democracy works, in case studies such as Dahl (1961), so that people will appreciate what they have and join in protecting it.

Among those publicizing how democracy works is Sidney Hook, who has written and spoken extensively on democracy as a system of mutual tolerance and respect. He has also concerned himself with the problem of protecting democracy against totalitarianism. A totalitarian country (namely the SU) is one that is governed by a counterelite that seeks to promote an ultimate end, world Communism. These people do not, by definition, recognize any limitation on the means they are willing to use in promoting their ultimate end. They are willing to use force and threats of force to impose their end on other people, and have already done so in a long list of countries. Consequently rational discussion is useless as a means of stopping them, and one must be prepared to resist their threats with one's own force. This means that one must be prepared to risk war, nuclear war, when Communists threaten war to gain their own ends. The alternative to risking nuclear war, Hook argues, is surrender to totalitarian aggression. But a totalitarian world would be one in which all human dignity was completely lost; human life would be degraded to the status of a means. This would be a fate worse than death, since it would be subhuman in a Kantian sense; consequently nuclear war, even if it wipes out the human race, would be preferable to a total victory of Communism (Hook, 1958). I have been told that he did not mean it, that he merely wanted the US to *pretend* such a stance, to bluff, so the SU would back down over Laos, or Berlin, or some such place. But war would not be necessary, because Communists are all bluffers.

At this point a reversal has occurred. The committed intellectuals began with the responsibility of the elite to protect US democracy

against specific aggressive moves. Aggression then becomes generalized into a worldwide program of the world counterelite, which must
be countered by an equally general world strategy. This strategy has
an ultimate end, the negative end of preventing a victory of world
Communism, and Hook is willing to sacrifice all of humanity to this
end. Hook represents the extreme case, the paradigm case, of an ethic
of ultimate ends, which Bell rightly condemns and to whom he
dedicates his book (Bell, 1960).

Rostow expresses the same conception of elite responsibility in his
various writings. The US, as the most advanced nation economically,
has the responsibility of sharing its wealth (loaned at interest) with the
poorer countries so they can achieve the takeoff to self-sustained
growth. It also has the responsibility of protecting them against Communism during this transition period, because Communism would
permanently prevent the coming of a free society. Rostow's chance to
act on these ideas came in the Vietnam war. Unlike the deterrence
theorists, who were continually calculating costs and returns and who
one by one calculated that the costs of war had gotten higher than the
return of deterrence against future wars (Brodie, 1971, pp. 159–160), the
war was an absolute obligation for Rostow. It was not a means to
anything, it was a responsibility we had freely assumed.

The scene now shifts to Ellsberg, who also acted on an ethic of
responsibility. He agreed that the US government was acting re-
sponsibly; it was responsible for mass murder, destruction of a whole
society, and continuous lying to the American people (Ellsberg, 1972,
Chapter 6). His responsibility was to expose these crimes, for which he
shared guilt, and the responsibility of the people was to stop them.
Ellsberg's ethical basis did not seem to be Kant or Weber; it seemed to
be Intuitionism, in which we just know that killing and lying are
wrong.

Ellsberg's actions horrified government officials and progovernment
scientists. He had betrayed the trust of those who had let him see the
Pentagon Papers, he had stolen government documents, and he had
revealed a secret. But if all government employees acted like that, they
reasoned in Kantian fashion, if any employee could reveal secret
documents any time he felt like it, then government would become
impossible. Society in fact was founded on trust.

One notices here a replay of *Antigone*.

Government officials took two measures to prevent a recurrence of
leaks and the destruction of government. One was administrative, the
plumbers' unit which checked the reliability of other government
officials and their newspaper and university contacts; the other was

legal, the well-known S.1 bill to outlaw publication of secret documents and to prevent other interferences with the conduct of government. Democracy must be protected, even if necessary by establishing a
police state.

Another form of aggression is guerrilla warfare, according to
Rostow (1971, pp. 283–286). Guerrillas act on an ethic of ends; they
murder and terrorize as a means to achieving some ultimate end like
world communism. Rostow does not discuss CIA guerrillas in China;
presumably they were trying to destabilize a totalitarian government
that threatened democracy, so they were not engaged in aggression. If
we consult a guerrilla leader, however, the picture looks different.
Take for instance Menachem Begin, the guerrilla leader of 1947; in his
view he was carrying out the responsibility entrusted him by his
organization to free his homeland from a foreign occupying army, the
British. Thirty years later, again entrusted with responsibility for the
defense of his country, Begin fails to recognize himself in the guerrilla
leader Yasser Arafat, who also has been entrusted with the responsibility of freeing his homeland from a foreign occupying army. In fact
he does not even recognize Arafat as human in the Kantian sense, since
he refuses to talk to Arafat. His position now has become that of
Rostow.

Some readers may be outraged at any comparison between Begin
and Arafat. They are opposites, it may be asserted; one was a terrorist
and the other a freedom fighter. This attitude illustrates my point.

The schema throughout, from Bell (1960) on, is: I am responsible,
you have ends. You engage in immoral acts to further your ends; I
have the responsibility of stopping you.

What went wrong here? The Kantian ethic tells us we ought to
recognize and respect the generically human in all men, and to govern
ourselves by rules that we could consistently will all men to follow in
relation to us as well. But in a society divided by class or ethnicity or
sex the divisions prevent us from recognizing ourselves in the other. So
the rules we make up for ourselves take on a partiality that justifies
our action but condemns the actions of the other. And since we are
now acting conscientiously we have a responsibility to continue our
actions or to punish the other. So an ethic of responsibility intensifies
intolerance, conflict, and violence.

The same reversal occurs in the social science community. A
Kantian conception of science treats it as a community of rational
truth-seekers, another case of Kant's kingdom of ends. The mark of
membership is respect for all other members in the sense of toleration
of their views, and willingness to submit one's own views to the same

tests of truth that one applies to the views of others. Science is an endless process of criticism and self-criticism in which no theory can claim exemption from critical examination. Popper in particular has developed this conception of science, parallel to his Kantian conception of democracy, in his work on the Open Society (1945). But this criterion excludes Freudian and Marxian theories from science, because these two theories refuse to submit themselves to possible empirical falsification (Popper, 1963, Chapter 1, esp. pp. 34–39). In particular, according to Hans Albert, one of Popper's followers, it excludes the Frankfurt School critical Marxists like Marcuse, because these people refuse to be self-critical about their own Utopian proposals (Spinner, 1974, pp. 231–233). They are willing to criticize everybody but themselves. But as Spinner observes, what is utopian and what is realizable is of the essence of political controversy; it may be that Popper's own liberal proposal to set up political controls over economic power is utopian. Is Popper willing to criticize his own views? Anybody could be excluded from science by that criterion.

The schema here is: I am tolerant, you are dogmatic. You refuse to submit your theory to my falsifying evidence and give up your theory. Therefore I have the obligation to exclude you from science, the system of toleration, because you refuse to follow the rules. This scheme has especially been applied to Communists in recent years. The argument is: Communists are under party discipline, or in some other way dedicated to their goal of world Communism. They do not participate in science to arrive at a common truth through discussion, but in order to propagandize. Therefore they are not scientists. Most especially they ought to be prevented from teaching, because their purpose is indoctrination, not socialization into the scientific community. Sidney Hook has especially stressed the importance of preventing Communists from teaching. As for propaganda for democracy, one of the purposes of social science, that is different because democracy is the system of tolerance itself.

The elitist intellectuals have a second ethical theory which takes us in a still different direction. They are not just interested in the responsibility of the elite; they also have a conception of the good life. This conception is best expressed in Chapter 3 of Mill's *On Liberty*: "Of Individuality as an element in wellbeing," and finds its recent expression in Riesman, et al. (1950), in the conception of the autonomous person. The individualist, or autonomous person, has as his life goal the development of his own unique capacities of thinking, feeling, and acting. He learns to do things his own way, not because it is better but because it is his, because it uses his particular talents. He becomes sensitive to what he wants to do, what makes him feel comfortable and fulfilled, rather than what others expect of him. He tries to be open, free, expansive, to act in a big way rather than being cramped and confined by worries over what people will think. The result, says Mill, is creativity in thought, action, and feeling. Not all can be creative geniuses, the ideal; but all can be original or at least eccentric, and even eccentricity is valuable as a stimulus to others to develop their individuality.

The opposite of individuality is conformity or other-directedness. The conformist, or sheep as Mill calls her, is sensitive to the expectations of others and afraid of criticism. She does not want to stand out and be noticed as different in any way, so she imitates the crowd in appearance, behavior, and tastes. She seeks to please others by doing what is expected of her and by being polite, cheerful, and helpful. As a result she is nothing in herself, but exists only by reference to others.

The ideal individualist is Schumpeter's entrepreneur, who ignores the accepted ways of industry and boldly develops new techniques— the assembly line—new industries, and new markets. Schumpeter's contrast between the creativity of the entrepreneur and the routine of ordinary life is another version of the individuality–conformity contrast. Schumpeter's followers celebrate the creativity of the modernizing elite, who shape and drag whole societies into the modern world. Or they celebrate the creative innovator in the Washington bureaucracy, a Kennedy or Rickover, who breaks through routines and establishes a new policy, technique, or agency to deal with new problems. The elitist intellectuals also value creative originality highly in their own writings; unlike the professionals patiently accumulating data or models or techniques in their special field, they try to create a bold new characterization of a whole era that will revitalize thinking. Or at least bold new terminology: technetronic, organizality, mobiletic.

The elitist intellectuals, from Schumpeter and Weber on, differ from Mill in one important respect, their emphasis on responsibility. For Mill the only responsibility of the creative genius seemed to be to set an example, so others would try to begin thinking for themselves too. But for Schumpeter and his followers it is unrealistic to suppose that the masses will ever become individualists. A few of them will, and we should try to encourage this in every way, picking out potential achievers and helping and rewarding them. This is the concept of the meritocratic society: not just equality of opportunity, but positive encouragement and help for any disadvantaged person who shows promise of originality. But realistically most of the mass will remain as they are, stupid conformists. Consequently, the elite have the responsibility of caring for and protecting the mass, as well as the responsibility of picking out and training the potential leaders that appear among the masses. These responsibilities are not imposed but are freely undertaken as part of the self-development of the creative individualist.

The conception of elite responsibility provides the justification for elitist democracy; it also connects the Kantian ethic of responsibility with the ethic of individuality and the meritocratic society.

The women's movement has taught us what elitist individualism means in practice: machismo. One individualist in a family, sensitive to his own needs and abilities, acting to develop his own talents, moving always to where new career opportunities appear, means a conformist wife and children sensitive to his needs, rearranging their life around his career and his search for new opportunities. Or it means a succession of wives, discarded when they become a hindrance to further achievement. Similarly, the entrepreneur, who seeks creative achievement on a grand scale, produces drastic life changes in the masses who work in his new industry. Their careers do not develop according to their abilities but according to the production requirements of the industry he has created. The great modern innovation of the assembly line enforces conformity to the line on millions, and produces the discontents of work that Bell recounts so sympathetically (1960). In the developing countries like Iran the modernizing autocrat imposes his new society by terror.

Even the radical student movement was sometimes a vehicle for macho males to display bold, vigorous, assertive actions and to develop leadership skills, while the women did the typing, dishwashing, and lovemaking on demand (E. Langer, in Alberston, 1975). In some cases the movement became a vehicle for launching men into a professional career or into leadership of some new political party. The result was a proliferation of radical parties, each led by a vigorous assertive macho leadership and each quarreling with all the others (O'Brien, 1978).

This critique by the mass-perspective theorists takes us back to Aristotle—not to the virtuous man of the *Ethics*, who is a remote predecessor of Mill's individualist, but to the oligarchic and democratic justice of the *Politics*. The oligarchic conception of justice is that if a person is better in some respects—say, verbal glibness, self-esteem, and ambition—then he is better absolutely. He is part of the elite. This is one-sided, says Aristotle, but the democratic conception is equally one-sided. It is that all people are equal in merit. This seems to be the implicit ethic of the Black and the women's movement, or of anti-elitist movements in general.

The democratic ethic begins as the abstract negation of the oligarchic ethic. If people are equal in all respects, then the respects in which they are equal are those in which the elite claim superiority. Thus one tendency in the women's movement has been to assert that women can be just as individualistic and creative as men; liberation consists of becoming just like the oppressor. Women, too, can have a career that develops their unique talents; they too can move where career opportunities beckon, taking husband and children along. They too can treat their family as an instrument of creative self-assertion, molding it according to their needs and demanding conformity from the others. Or they can discard husband, children, or lover when these are no longer conducive to personal growth. Or they can forsake the company of men almost entirely just as men used to congregate in their own clubs and bars for friendship and sociability. The pursuit of individuality is an exhilarating experience.

Other anti-elitists have focused on higher education. If admission to universities has been by merit, that is by biased achievement tests or parental wealth or other criteria that favor upper over lower classes, then this is unjust and all should be admitted equally. And since grading is biased all should receive passing grades, or at least should evaluate their own progress by their own standards. But what does such an education mean? What is it for? Does it mean that entry into the higher-paying professions should be by lot?

What it seems to mean is that all should become part of the elite. But one cannot construct a society on such a principle. To say that all should receive equal pay is indeed a beginning of a good society, but then one must still distribute work.

The Marxist ethic provides a basis for constructing a society that goes beyond abstract equality. For the Marxist, and for Schumacher, the good life is self-realization through work. Various aspects of work may be emphasized in different circumstances: creativity in design, skill in execution, pride in achievement, the sociability of shared activity, a feeling of being useful to others, a sense of responsibility for bringing home the paycheck, a continuity with past and future by living with or in what one has made. But since human beings are being produced in work, not just material products, we need a kind of work that develops a wide range of human potential. A stunted, mechanical work produced stunted, mechanical human beings; work that calls for both intelligent planning and skilful execution produces intelligent, skilled human beings.

Work is also the source of community, both as process and as product. Work is inherently a collective activity in which there must be a differentiation of function within a common task; thus it unites people in action. This does not mean permanent task specialization, and job rotation is desirable so people can appreciate each other's tasks and broaden their own skills. The product of work, whether a family, a city, fertile land, a nation, is an objective world which we have made and in which we are at home.

According to this ethic a capitalist society is bad, not only because it produces unsafe cars, pollution, and weapons of death, but because it continually destroys the meaning of work, in many ways. I will mention two. One is capitalist technological progress, which continually fragments work to increase control and profit, which reduces the fragments to mechanical motions and finally substitutes machines for human beings (Braverman, 1974). A second is the fact that one's product is owned by the boss, who sells it for profit. This means that the harder and more skillfully one works, the better off the boss is. But in a capitalist union-management structure, the boss is the enemy who seeks to control one's actions, speed them up, change them according to profit or budget requirements or just out of ignorance, rather than according to the requirements of the task. The product itself becomes a mere commodity, and one's labor therefore also becomes a commodity of no intrinsic value. Consequently one's desire to work well and produce something good is a mere private fantasy or even a free gift to the boss, who makes money from it. It must be suppressed and replaced by apathy, "working to rule."

The problem then is not primarily one of providing work, as it is for the Keynesians, but of humanizing work. We need a human technology and worker control over our own work. This is the main difference between the Marxist and the Keynesian and functionalist self-realization ethic. For functionalists and Keynesians the function of labor is to produce and consume at a rapid enough rate to maintain the circular flow near a growing equilibrium rate. Unemployment compensation is nearly as good as employment for this purpose, and the nature of the work makes no difference at all. The right Keynesians and Parsonians are concerned with the maintenance and growth of the whole system and with the effectiveness of the control mechanisms, not with the quality of work. Even the left Keynesian is concerned only that the whole working class receive enough education and income to produce and consume at the necessary rate. Joan

Robinson asks in all seriousness, "If Marx really believed that trade unions could raise the share of wages in the value of output merely by raising money-wage rates, why did he think it necessary to have a revolution?" (Kregel, 1973, p. xi). Lynn Turgeon, less seriously, expresses Left Keynesian disdain for actual work: "I think most any job—except the economist's—can be learned in a week" (1980, p. 43). Capitalism cannot destroy craft skills because there is no such thing; work is simply a commodity that people sell so they can consume. For the Marxist such an attitude is a mark of a rotten society, and a good society would put work, not consumption, in a central place.

The material with which we work is, in general, nature. Work is ultimately a humanizing of nature, the construction of a human world in which we can live and work. This world, which our ancestors made and to which we contribute, in which our children will live, connects us to past and future as well as providing a shared present experience. The Marxist ideal is embodied in Faust, who tamed sea and land to provide a setting in which future generations could work together.

What does Nature have to say about this? This question is meaningless for a Marxist. Nature does not talk. Nature is the sea, the rocks, the soil that lies around and is meaningless until it is organized by man into a livable world.

Not so, says the Schumacher anarchist. Nature is the biosphere, the ecosystem in which we live. We are part of nature, not master of nature. We can indeed conquer nature, weaken and even destroy it; but in so doing we weaken and destroy ourselves. Our work, if we are to survive, ought not be a conquest of nature but a completion and fulfillment of nature. We ought not adapt nature to our needs, but rather adapt ourselves to nature.

The proper ethics, in other words, is Buddhist ethics (Schumacher, 1973, Chapter 4). Our obligation is to control and reduce our desires until we again become part of the great cycle of life which evolved us and sustains us. Our desires are not the criterion of the good life, as in utilitarianism; nor are our potentialities for grand, creative self-expression, as for the individualistic elitists; nor even the technical requirements for collective fulfillment in work, as for the Marxists. All these conceptions of the good have in the past justified an ever-expanding society which ignored the limits of the biosphere; this error must now be corrected by a reduction of desire. In principle, expansion need not be wrong, if it is an expansion of the cycles of life rather than a merely human expansion. Reclaiming fertile land from the sea may well be justified as an expansion of the biosphere, if a self-sustaining agricultural cycle can then be built on it. The criterion, however, is in nature, not in man.

An ethics of obligation, such as Buddhist or Kantian ethics, need not guarantee the ability of people to act according to it. One could argue that a capitalist society or a bureaucratic socialist society is not free to stop expanding. Buddhist ethics then condemns such societies, condemns them to extinction. It may be that Buddhist ethics is too good for us, and that we must first develop a society that is free to control its own technology before we can begin to follow its precepts. In our present expansionist world Buddhism becomes a morality that teaches workers and peasants to live on less and less while the corporations and the military bureaucracies live on more and more (Leiss, 1976, p. 112).

II. Science and Morality

We turn now to the main topic of this chapter, the moral barriers to scientific communication. The cognitive barriers discussed in Part I are serious and sometimes very serious, but they are not insurmountable. It is possible to overcome them by imaginatively taking the standpoint of the other and learning to think in the categories of the other. This takes time and normally requires a continuing association with the other so one can practice using the categories in daily interaction, but learning is also possible through intensive reading. There are also personality barriers; the aggressive macho-masculine personality, for one, is not used to taking the standpoint of the victim or the enemy. And most of all there are social barriers to identifying with the outgroup. All these barriers, not in themselves insurmountable, are reinforced by morality.

One might suppose that the value relativism of the neoclassicist would make him tolerant of other standpoints. However, the underlying absolutism is the governing principle in this case. The neoclassicist is the defender of individual freedom against anyone who wishes to impose authoritative preferences on him, and value relativism is part of that defense. The enemy includes all social scientists who look to government to play a more active role in society—Keynesians, theorists of the welfare state, Galbraithian institutionalists, and Marxists. All these types, whatever their internal differences, are advocates of the road to serfdom. The more moderate ones are just as dangerous as the full totalitarians because their doctrines sound generous and humanitarian and are therefore more likely to dupe the innocent. The neoclassicist defender of freedom is therefore responsible for unmasking these insidious doctrines and revealing what they really are: attempts to interfere with the free market. This involves translating them into "economic" categories, that is neoclassical categories, thereby brushing aside the ideological mask and revealing the coercive essence.

The neoclassicist is more tolerant toward the elitist intellectuals, since 1960 when this standpoint become prominent.[9] He appreciates the elitists' support for Millian individualism and especially the individualism of the upwardly mobile individual. Writers who value individual creativity are not likely to be advocates of serfdom, and their ideas are therefore deserving of serious and sympathetic study. But he does not approve of the liberal elitist's advocacy of welfare measures. He sees the elitist intellectual as the spokesman for upper-class liberals who want to take from the working and lower middle class and give to the shiftless ghetto rioters (J.Q. Wilson, 1969). Welfare measures, even price controls, may be justified as temporary measures in extreme emergencies (Frank Knight), but if continued they produce the very evils they are supposed to prevent—poverty, family breakup, shiftlessness, dishonesty and crime (Banfield, 1969). Consequently the elitist's theories (Moynihan's theory in Banfield, 1969) and the welfare measures must also be unmasked as interferences with the free labor market.

The Keynesians-system theorists–functionalists are the most tolerant of social scientists, in my impression. Samuelson and Parsons are typical: generous, friendly, optimistic, willing to admit that even the most bizarre theory could have some truth in it and willing to work carefully to find that truth. Even Marxists are taken seriously. For these people a grand scientific synthesis and a nearly all-inclusive scientific community is a practical vision toward which they are ready to work. The unifying principle of the synthesis is the overall goal of social science, the application of knowledge to the problems of society. Each subcommunity of scientists can specialize in one problem or one aspect of a larger problem, and others can synthesize. The actual problem-solving agent is normally the government.

Tolerance applies only to professional social scientists, however; the dilettantes and superficial intellectuals, who verbalize about a variety of fields without having achieved technical mastery of any of them, are not to be taken seriously. But even among the professionals, it turns out that some scientists are slackers in the common enterprise. They criticize, but not constructively; they point to problems, but offer no solutions or even deny that solutions are possible (for example

Banfield, 1969). Or they quixotically call for revolution. Such lapses from scientific decorum are ignored or gently rebuked.

For example: "It is unfortunate that Baran's brilliant intellectual powers could not be employed more constructively in persuading his countrymen what they ought to do about the underdeveloped countries, instead of telling them that whatever they do is bound to be wrong" (Kaldor, 1958, p. 169).

The limits of tolerance here are set by the practical aim of making science useful to society. Theories that assert the impossibility of effective government action—and that means most long-run theories— are not to be taken seriously. To give them practical meaning they are translated into short-run terms. It may even be asserted that long-run theories are untestable, since we cannot act on them and since no short-run contrary evidence can refute them.

The ethic of elite responsibility is a much more serious barrier to tolerance, when it is taken seriously. If one has the responsibility of defending the Free World against both internal and external aggression then science becomes a weapon in the struggle against the counterelite. It is necessary to use science to demonstrate the evils of communism, and to use every opportunity to remind people how bad the Soviet Union is. Conversely it is necessary to remind people how good our democratic society is, to expose all the attempts to weaken it and defame it, and to invent a new public philosophy that will justify it (Bell, 1976). In short, one function of social science is to carry out the program of the Hoover Institution at Stanford.

This program divides the social science community into the defenders and wreckers of elitist democracy, plus neutral bystanders. But it would be immoral, irresponsible, to try to take the standpoint of the wreckers. It is an evil standpoint, or in the case of the New Left a neurotic standpoint. Besides, nothing would be learned by doing so. In the struggle between democracy and totalitarianism, science is on the side of democracy. Social science cannot flourish in a closed, totalitarian society, so the totalitarian has no ideas to contribute to the scientific community.

This intolerance is reciprocated by some of the opponents of the Vietnam war. For those whose "eyes were opened" by the war, it would be immoral to consort with war criminals like Rostow. Besides, a standpoint which produces justification for mass murder, wholesale pollution of water and soil in Vietnam, overthrow of democratic governments and support of oppressive military governments all over the world, is a morally perverted standpoint that cannot have much of value to contribute to social science.

The ecologist, with his Buddhist responsibility for the biosphere, feels a similar but broader kind of moral condemnation. The researchers in atomic, biological, and chemical warfare, declares Ravetz, work on weapons whose use lie beyond the pale of civilized practice and morality (1971, p. 57). These weapons would make the planet unlivable for man and other living things. Therefore research on them constitutes a perversion of science, since the aim of science is to support life. The old stereotype of the mad scientist who invents a doomsday weapon becomes a reality in the secret military research laboratories. The guilt Ellsberg felt for his participation in the war was matched by Oppenheimer's Buddhist guilt as he watched the first atomic explosion, for which he was responsible. "I have become Death, the destroyer of worlds." And, by extension, the strategic thinkers who write scenarios for "World War VIII" to develop strategies by which the US could win, though the biosphere be destroyed, are also mad. It would be immoral even to communicate with these moral idiots as Walter Lippman once called them, let alone try to sympathetically see the world from their perspective.

Present social science is fragmented by the demands of these three kinds of morality: the moral responsibility of social scientists to combat the totalitarians, or to shun the war criminals and servants of the imperialist war system, or to shun the mad worshippers of Kali, the goddess of death. The policy scientist's dream of a benevolent and rich government that takes responsibility for managing the problems of society is a utopia from the past; today social scientists are themselves called on to take responsibility for the direction of science. This demand can be evaded only by escaping into a dream of the past, or a dream of the future.

Fourteen The
Organization of Science

We turn now to our original question: How can we organize our own scientific research, our pattern of collaboration, so as to improve the quality of our knowledge? The question has become: What existing perspective or combination of perspectives has the greatest potential for truth, and how can that potential be developed? We will first examine several well-known answers to this question as a way of surveying possible answers and of narrowing the range of plausible answers. Then we will combine the conclusions of the preceding chapters to arrive at a plausible answer.

I. A Theory of Data

The obvious starting point is the null hypothesis that perspectives are all neutral with respect to truth. A perspective is a source of hypotheses which may or may not be true. The study of standpoints and perspectives is a study of the backgrounds from which hypotheses originate, so it belongs to the context of discovery. Truth, however, belongs to the context of justification. A hypothesis is provisionally true if the empirical evidence justifies it, to a criterion; or if the evidence continually fails to falsify it. The source of a hypothesis in some perspective is irrelevant to its truth; what counts is the evidence.

363

In recent philosophy of science this view is identified with Karl Popper and his followers. Popper argues for a sharp distinction between discovery and justification. Discovery is a private act of creation; justification is a public act of appraisal and criticism carried on by the scientific community (1945, Volume 2, pp. 217–218; 1963; 1972). There is no logic of discovery; there is a logic of appraisal and criticism. The circumstances and background of discoveries are subject matter for psychology and sociology, two infant sciences riddled with fashions and errors (1970, pp. 57–58); the logic of justification is subject matter for philosophy of science, a well-established discipline. Popper asserts the further claim that because the logic of science is rational and the psychology of science is nonrational, the former is inherently more knowable; consequently everything true in logic is also true in psychology, but not the reverse (1972, pp. 6, 112). In other words the psychology of science is dependent on the logic of science. This means that even the background and circumstances of discovery must be studied by reference to the logic of justification.

In his criticism of Kuhn, Popper recognizes the possibility that the sociological fact of membership in a particular school will limit and direct the thought of a particular scientist. However, he asserts that logically a scientist is free at any time to drop his membership and join another school, or found his own school. "I do admit that at any moment we are prisoners caught in the framework of our theories; our expectations; our past experiences; our language. But we are prisoners in a Pickwickian sense: if we try, we can break out of our framework at any time" (1970, p. 56). In terms of standpoints, this implies that even if a scientist's standpoint limits his creativity, he is free at any time to shift to a different standpoint.

There are three relevant assertions here. First, Popper asserts that the standpoint from which a hypothesis arises is logically irrelevant to its truth. Second, he asserts that the testing of hypotheses is logically a public process, engaged in by the whole scientific community, a process that logically has nothing to do with any standpoint. Third, he asserts that if a particular scientist is committed to any school, paradigm, standpoint, etc., he is logically free at any time to discard this hindrance to rational scientific activity.

One cannot refute logic with fact. Actually I agree with the above assertions, as logic, and have no wish to refute them. But one can question their relevance to a body of facts. In particular, one can argue that Popper's Kantian idea of a community of rational individuals is so remote from the real practice of the social sciences that it cannot direct the improvement of that practice. It is an abstract counsel of perfection rather than a chart of particular difficulties and ways to overcome them.

To begin with the third assertion, that a scientist is free at any time to discard his own presuppositions, his own perspective: it is a fact, documented in Part I, that most policy scientists of the sample studied keep the same perspective throughout their career. They pick up a perspective during the period of socialization in school and retain it as a member of some school or tradition thereafter. A few do shift perspective once or twice, but these shifts result from the impact of some overwhelming social experience, some "anomaly," rather than from rational reflection on one's own conceptual limitations. A very few may shift for other reasons or combine two perspectives.

We can understand this persistence from our experience with scientists. A standpoint is not like a coat that one can take off when the weather changes. It is a part of one's professional and personal identity, and changing it means becoming a different person. In most cases it also symbolizes one's continuity with the ancestors and one's fellows, and changing it means rejecting friends and relatives and becoming an outcast. Consequently the logical freedom to change at any time has no practical significance.

The first assertion, that the perspective from which a hypothesis arises is logically irrelevant to its truth, is acceptable as logic. But if in fact some perspectives are more likely to produce true or fruitful hypotheses than others, if some standpoints and perspectives are more attuned to our society or contain fewer blind spots than others, then it would be good practice to encourage those perspectives—to teach them, to collaborate with them, to give them research grants. We take up this possibility in section 3.

The second assertion, that hypothesis testing is logically independent of standpoints, is the crucial one. It constitutes the null hypothesis that perspectives are irrelevant to hypothesis testing and therefore irrelevant to truth.

Against the relevance of the null hypothesis, I assert:

1. To test a hypothesis at all, one must understand it. But one's perspective sets limits on what can be understood. Consequently hypotheses deriving from radically different perspectives cannot be understood and cannot be tested. Most of the "refutations" occurring in the policy sciences, say 1/2-2/3, are of this sort. What happens is that the researcher translates a hypothesis into the categories of his own perspective in order to understand it. Consequently what he falsifies or refutes is not the original hypothesis but some perversion of

it. For example the neoclassicist or Keynesian, confronted with the ecological arguments of a Schumacher type, interprets the opponent as arguing for a no-growth society, the logical alternative to his own position. He then rehearses the disastrous predicted consequences of stationary GNP and ends with assorted name-calling, such as "eco-freaks" (Olson and Landsberg, 1973; Thurow, 1980, Chapter 5). Nothing has been falsified because nothing has been understood.

2. One cannot assert that a hypothesis is confirmed by given data unless one can show that it fits the data better than alternative available hypotheses (Feyerabend, 1965). If three hypotheses fit or explain given data equally well the data do not decide between them. If a fourth hypothesis fits or explains the data still better, none of the three are confirmed. A person who is aware of only one of the three hypotheses cannot know this, and will erroneously believe that his hypothesis is confirmed (see for example Herbert Simon, 1957, Chapter 16). Consequently hypothesis testing requires an understanding of alternative hypotheses, and one's perspective limits the alternatives that can be understood.

3. When data and hypothesis do not fit well, one must always make a judgment among five possible interpretations: a) the data are bad, unrepresentative, contaminated, poorly measured, and should be discarded. The practice of discarding bad data is normally unreported and belongs to the underworld of science. b) The data need interpretation, refinement, qualification, after which the fit is much improved. Of the many ways of reinterpreting data I will mention a few common ones:

  i. Pick out one segment of a fluctuating series that fits the hypothesis and explain away the rest as deviations.
  ii. Assume the deviations away in advance by uttering the magic words "ceteris paribus": then correct the statistical data or control the experimental data accordingly.
  iii. Pick out the best case, call it typical and locate traces of it in the other cases.
  iv. Stigmatize the data with a bad name like "irrational" or "paradoxical" to express one's puzzlement.
  v. Admit that the data look bad, then focus on very recent evidence to show the beginning of a trend in the expected direction.

c) The data are suggestive but inconclusive and more data are needed. This interpretation can be chosen when none of the reinterpretations mentioned above are possible and when data and hypothesis are flatly opposed. d) The hypothesis is erroneous in some detail, which needs to be corrected. e) The hypothesis is totally disconfirmed.

The choice among these five interpretations is a variant of the common problem of deciding on the desired proportion of Type I and Type II errors, where Type I is the error of preserving hypotheses that are in fact false, and Type II is the error of discarding hypotheses that are in fact true. There is no decision rule that will eliminate all errors of both types in a large number of trials, and it is difficult to decide on an optimum proportion of the two types of errors. To do so one must have some sort of cost–benefit measure of the two types of errors.

One of the findings of cognitive psychology is that we tend to resist abandonment of our own hypotheses, preferring to distrust the data or if necessary abandoning a small part of the hypothesis rather than the whole thing (Jervis, 1976, pp. 156-162). That is, we try to minimize Type II errors with our own hypotheses. Conversely, we try to minimize Type I errors with the hypotheses of opponents. This double standard, very common in my experience, is rational for the individual and the school. It is rational to avoid prematurely discarding hypotheses and models in which one has invested great research effort. What one desires from data are disconfirmation of details, so that one may correct and improve one's theory. Conversely, the hypotheses of opponents are available free of charge, to say the least, and bring few benefits or negative benefits if adopted, so it is rational to pick and choose carefully among them. Presumably these cost-benefit differences vanish for science as a whole, so there is a conflict between the interests of a school and the general interests of science. Consequently the division of scientists into schools does affect the testing process, producing differences of judgment that are based on rational self-interest and that cannot be resolved by any impersonal logic of justification.

4. The previous points dealt with the use of given data to test given hypotheses. But data are not given, they are produced or collected, and one's perspective influences the production and collection of data. Consequently the perspectives that exist at any time will affect the stock of data that is recognized to exist at that time, and thereby will affect the validity status of existing hypotheses. A historical study of standpoints and perspectives is not merely a study of concepts and theories, as in Part I; it is also a study of data. The present work could therefore also be titled "a theory of data."

Perspectives influence the production of data in two ways. *First*, each perspective demands use of a certain method, and this method will produce or collect certain kinds of data. A perspective or conceptual scheme tells us what our subject matter is like and therefore what method or methods are most appropriate for studying it. If society is composed of rational individuals making allocation and exchange decisions, an *a priori* deductive method is needed to work out the necessary consequences of aggregate decisions. If society is a bounded system within which resources and exchange media circulate, one needs aggregate and disaggregated stock and flow data for numerous locations, and a model of the flow channels. If the Object is the inert masses, one needs opinion and attitude surveys and census data to describe the statistical characteristics of the mass; and so on.

Each method produces or uses its own kind of data. An econometric-statistical method produces quantitative stock and flow data, and nonquantifiable factors are either mutilated into numbers or dropped. Opinion surveys and censuses produce masses of discrete individuals, each with a long, atomized list of abstract characteristics. Participant-observation discloses an active, creative, self-maintaining community that copes more or less adequately with multiple stresses and strains. Controlled experiments produce passive reactors to stimuli—or individuals who try to play that role.

Conversely, each perspective also provides good reasons for rejecting other methods and the data they produce or collect. From a neo-classical long-run perspective the Keynesian stock and flow data measure those endless short-run fluctuations which are essentially unknowable; they can be described empirically after the fact but not predicted or made theoretically intelligible. Also they fail to distinguish between short-run irrational behavior, money illusion etc. and long-run rational behavior—"you can't fool all the people all the time" (Friedman, 1975). Conversely for the Keynesian the neoclassicist seems to select and manipulate data arbitrarily to fit his hypothetical constructs; for example Friedman smooths out the data on business cycles by adjusting for his imaginary "permanent income" and "permanent prices" (1969, p. 179n.).

For the mass-perspective participant–observer with his subjective subject-matter, the Parsonian system models with their multiple flows and boxes within boxes are grotesque reifications. First the system theorist invents an abstract scheme and then he forces living reality into the rigid categories, the flows and stocks. But for the system theorist, the small case studies, though vivid, have not been theorized; the underlying objective systemic reality has not been brought out, and one gets only the flux of appearance. Note that in this case the two methods are supplementary rather than incompatible: the functionalist and system theorist can use participant-observer studies as material for theoretical analysis, and the participant observer can use functional categories, cautiously, as an aid to observation.

For the elite-perspective researcher the survey data on mass attitudes and opinions show that the masses are and continue to be passive, apathetic, authoritarian, etc. The Marxist cannot deny these facts, which refute Marxism conclusively; instead he uses dialectical hocus-pocus to twist the facts around to their opposite, asserting that freedom is really oppression, the Soviet Union is really a workers' democracy, the masses are really revolutionary deep down, etc. But for the Marxist with his mutual determination of Subject and Object, the survey data describe mass consciousness in abstraction from the objective social conditions which sustain it. Consequently the data acquire a false appearance of permanence. They describe what is actual as of 1964 in the interview context, but not what is possible (Mann, in Lindberg, 1975). Changing social conditions do produce changes of consciousness—as in Cuba—and such possible changes cannot be picked up by attitude surveys until after the fact, particularly when the interviewer represents the elite oppressor. The elitist surveys, which universalize a particular historical situation, become legitimations of the status quo, just as Michels' falsely universalized data became a legitimation of Fascism (Beetham, 1977).

Once the method and the data of a different perspective have been rejected as unscientific, it is an easy matter to disconfirm the hypotheses coming out of that perspective—with one's own objective data, of course. Let us eschew examples here, since I am sure every reader is familiar with some. And finally it is an easy step to surmise that the whole source of the trouble is ideology. What makes those people—psychoanalysts, survey researchers, Marxists, behaviorists, systems analysts, econometricians—cling to pseudoscientific methods that produce bad, misleading data? Perhaps because only bad data will support their thoroughly falsified theories. The reason for this stubbornness must be ideological fervor (Friedman, 1977, pp. 29-35). So at the level of data we come again to the standard schema: we are scientific, they are ideological.

The *second* way in which perspectives influence data production is as follows: A scientist's particular hypothesis, or his desire to refute a particular hypothesis, will unconsciously affect his production or collection of data in the desired direction. This is a more technical process which can in part be corrected by technical means within each method. It occurs throughout the sciences (Rosenthal, 1966, pp. 3-7) but takes different forms in different methods. It also occurs in the natural sciences: see Bruno Latour's meticulous participant observations of the social construction of facts in a biology laboratory (Latour and Woolgar, 1979).

1. The study of experimenter effects has shown that experimentation is a more complex process than the positivist philosophers of science imagined (Rosenthal, 1966; N. Friedman, 1967; Wuebben, 1974). Standardization is a myth (Friedman, 1967, Chapter 5); the quality of replications is poor, and there is a serious publication bias (Rosenthal, 1966, Chapter 18). Results are affected by the laboratory situation, various experimenter characteristics, and experimenter-subject interaction (ibid., Chapters 4-8); and errors of observation, recording, and calculation are common (ibid., Chapters 1-3). Experiments are in fact a form of social interaction exhibiting all the complexity of dyadic and small-group interaction (N. Friedman, 1967, Chapters 7-9).

In particular, experimenter expectations have been shown experimentally to influence the behavior of subjects in the desired direction (Rosenthal, 1966, p. 307), can be reversed (pp. 218-219), and are even communicated through assistants who are not consciously aware of the expectations. Communication is through subtle kinesic signals, particularly leg movements (Rosenthal, 1966, p. 258 and Chapter 15), handling of animals before the experiment perhaps (ibid., p. 178), paralinguistic communication such as the tone of the experimenter's voice at the start of the experiment or on particular words (Friedman, 1967, pp. 98-100), and probably other channels as well. It is possible to control these channels once one has discovered them; but it is also possible that expectations will then be communicated through different channels.

The implication is that to some extent experimental hypotheses produce the data that confirm them. Consequently hypotheses and refutations coming out of different perspectives will to some extent produce different data.

A second well-known experimental problem is control. One can control only variables which one can conceive; consequently experimenters from different theoretical traditions will be aware of different variables, institute different controls, and get different results.

2. Opinion and attitude surveys display surveyor-expectancy effects analogous to experimenter-expectancy effects (Sudman and Bradburn, 1974). In addition there are literally dozens of sources of bias in the sampling procedure, interviewer characteristics, interview situation, interviewer-respondent relation, differences of concepts between interviewer and respondent, internal situation of respondent (response uncertainty), questionnaire construction, and data process-

ing. Spurious precision is produced by forcing the respondent or judge to pick a particular rating and discarding responses from those who refuse. Data processing can compound the above errors or reduce them. These problems have been studied for decades and progressively brought under control; but new errors are still being discovered.

3. Statistical and census data suffer from most of the above errors plus reporting error for hard-to-find people such as migrants, plus deliberate falsification of reports on income, voting, employment, and the like. The problems of income tax, unemployment, and census data are well known; but how are we to assess the data reported by the multinational corporations, who, we read, keep up to five sets of books for different readers, each with different profit and cost figures? Should we accept the reports made for tax purposes at face value—innocent until proven guilty; or with Barnet and Müller, 1974, treat them all as suspect and systematically misleading; or take a moderate position and suspect half of them? Plainly our perspective on the corporations will affect our assessment of their official reports.

When we turn to data analysis, the many ways to manipulate statistics to unconsciously get the desired results are too well known to require detailed listing here. Recently Beardsley (1980) has listed the many ways in which pluralists and antipluralists can differ in their manipulation of the same data—selecting variables, selecting indicators, locating intervening variables, controlling for feedback among the variables and intervening variables, subtracting the influence of counteracting variables, interpreting causality as "magnetic" (the value of B approaches the value of A) or as "covariational" (B changes in the same direction as A), assigning weights to subsets of data, varying the lags, and setting zero points. Does one measure the effectiveness of a policy by comparing results with conditions at t_0, or with past trends extrapolated to the present, or with results of a different policy in some other country? In comparing socialist and capitalist imperialism, does one take the Soviet Union as the zero point of a completely socialist country, or does one take Tanzania, or an imaginary socialist country? Does one exclude Cuba from a Latin American data base because of its atypical characteristics (pp. 168–170)? In each case the democratic elitist perspective suggests one treatment of the data and the mass or antielitist perspective suggests a different treatment.

Consider the well-known multicollinearity problem, which occurs in multivariate analysis. In this analysis the statistician simultaneously correlates many independent variables against the dependent variable to see how much each contributes to its variation. When several independent variables are similar they reduce each others' correlation coefficient, while a highly unique variable collects a higher coefficient. Thus the nature of the variables tested affects the results; and one's hypothesis determines the variables that are tested. At the extreme, if the statistician tests his own variable against five versions of the opponent's theory, he is bound to win—unintentionally of course. A competent statistician would not commit such an obvious error; but how evenly must the variables be spaced to eliminate the error, and what does "even" mean? Here again recognition of the problem can lead to its partial control (Lemieux, 1978) but scientists with different perspectives can still disagree on whether a particular set of variables biases the results.

Simple correlations, with other variables held constant, are even more theory-dependent because they require the researcher to arbitrarily cut through the many interdependencies of variables in society. For example the attempt to test the comparative effects of fiscal and monetary policy is practically hopeless because the two variables cannot be separated by holding one constant (David Fand, Chapter 15 in Havrilesky and Boorman, 1976). A fiscal deficit almost automatically changes the money supply, so the results will be attributed by the monetarist to the monetary change. But a change in money with fiscal policy held constant changes interest rates, which for a Keynesian obscures the effect of any policy and must be held constant. Similarly, Friedman's comparative test of the Keynesian investment multiplier would not convince any Keynesian (Friedman, 1969, p. 212). For Friedman the issue is whether changed investment or changed money supply causes changes in consumption, and he tests the two theories by correlating $\dot{I}$ with $\dot{C}$ when M is held constant and correlating $\dot{M}$ with $\dot{C}$ when I is held constant. He finds that *for a given stock of money* there is no correlation between investment and consumption; the Keynesian multiplier does not exist. But for a Keynesian the effect of investment operates through changes in the stock of money and/or credit, just as for Friedman change of money works through investment, and Friedman has missed the point of the multiplier.

More generally,

It is not possible to discriminate between competing macro models simply on the basis of in-sample fit. Given the highly serially and cross-correlated nature of economic time series, the range of choice of variables for use in any model, and the flexibility in the specification of lags, marvelous fits of historic data can be obtained by models with

widely different implications for the behavior of the economy and its
response to policy (Brainard and Cooper, 1975, pp. 169-170).

Consequently the economist whose perspective urges one hypothesis
on him and closes off understanding of others will regularly be
encouraged by good fits with the data. Conversely the economist with
a broader perspective will find it terribly hard to conclude anything
from econometric data, as Robert Eisner (1969) and Charles Wilber
(1979) observe.

4. The participant-observer and clinician come to their subject
matter in a relatively passive and receptive manner, as compared with
the definite expectations of the experimenter and survey researcher and
econometrician. They try to pick up the concerns and categories of
their hosts, rather than imposing their own categories. Nevertheless
their previous theorizing will sensitize them to certain events rather
than others and will shape the way they conceptualize these events.
The "third ear" of Reik and the "free-floating attention" of Freud
pick up some things easier than others. Here the control is continuing
immersion in the subject matter, during which the host's way of
thinking and acting should more or less displace the observer's
original predispositions. However, socialization is always a two-way
process, most especially in a one-to-one clinical situation, so the
observer's categories also get absorbed by the host to some extent. As a
result the scientist's own concerns and categories come back to her
from the data to some extent.

But conversely, if the participant-observer could succeed in completely immersing herself in the data, an opposite weakness would
appear. By completely absorbing the host's categories, the observer
loses the ability to take a critical stance toward those categories, to
notice self-deception and wishful thinking. And worse, a completely
receptive observer may not even penetrate behind the official front to
the private view of the world. A good participant-observer is not only
receptive and accepting, but also critical and detached. However, the
line between critical penetration of disguise and deception on the one
hand, and reading one's own categories into the data on the other
hand, is extremely difficult to draw.

There are also the usual accidental sources of biased data: scientists
with different personalities will bring out different aspects of their
hosts' lifestyle, and the participant-observer's explanatory hypotheses
will be most strongly influenced by her earliest observations or some
striking event and less by later observations.

5. In historical case studies the problem is the enormous masses of

potential data that could be collected for any historical event. The
source of the problem is the historian's interest in a particular event,
in contrast with the participant-observer's interest in the typical, the
regular, the institutionalized. Any event, say a meeting between three
people in Berlin on July 6, 1914 (the Kaiser, Bethman-Hollweg, and
Falkenhayn), is of infinite complexity, since it includes the intentions,
strategies, world view, memories, and decision rules of each participant; the shared understandings, relations, and history of the three;
their relations to their subordinates down through the bureaucracy
and to their Austrian allies; and the successive reinterpretations of the
event. This complexity is also apparent in the Bales-type small-group
"experiments," where multiple recording apparatuses are used to
capture the event.

The usual historical case studies in the policy sciences are of events
within the last twenty or thirty years. Potential data include interviews, official documents, news reports, memoirs and diaries, private
documents, biographies, statistics. These data must be searched out, in
libraries, archives, cellars, and the interviews must be taken. Some are
readily available, some can be dug up with great ingenuity, and some
are apparently nonexistent after exhaustive search. Time and money
limitations force the researcher to limit his search. He must decide
which data are most important and collect at least those. For instance
he must decide which people should be interviewed because they are
likely participants, which archives are likely to contain a relevant
memo, how wide the net of influences on his event is likely to be. But
the criterion of relevance is set by his hypothesis or expectations, his
other beliefs, and possible alternative hypotheses; so the researcher's
hypotheses necessarily limit what data are produced.

A second problem is data interpretation. *No* historical data can be
accepted at face value; *all* must be evaluated or interpreted. Memoirs
and interviews are self-serving; official documents and press releases
give an official version of what happened; private letters and conversations can exaggerate or give a selective interpretation; there may
be differing understandings of what was said and what was agreed on;
some participants may not be aware of private understandings among
other participants, and may have a quite distorted understanding of
what happened. Data interpretation and evaluation is done by cross-
checking and by coherence. When several data sources agree, they
validate each other—unless they all come from the same faction; and
when several partial accounts fit coherently they partially validate and
interpret each other. Historical explanation follows the pattern model
of explanation (Kaplan, 1964, Chapter 9; Stretton, 1969, Chapter 3).

It follows that multiple types of data are absolutely essential to historical case studies, to allow for cross-checking. Those studies which use only one source, say newspaper reports or refugee interviews, are simply unscientific. They have no data. An example is Tanter (1974), which has only the flimsiest of contacts with historical reality.

The researcher's expectations affect each step of the interpretation process. Data that agree with expectations are highly visible and will be noticed immediately, while negative data may not even be noticed, or, if noticed, may make no impression. Of the data that the researcher focuses on, those that agree with expectations will be accepted eagerly, while ones that disagree will be greeted skeptically and checked thoroughly. When two clusters of data do not fit each other, the one agreeing with expectations will unconsciously be given precedence. Expectations will suggest possible patterns that produce a coherent picture, and will point to questionable spots. The search for negative data, if time permits, is guided by recognized alternative hypotheses.

As a result, two researchers with different perspectives will necessarily produce quite different accounts of the same historical event. Usually, moreover, researchers choose events for study that happen to fit their perspective (Gilbert, 1971). Here is a third problem in historical case studies; one's perspective unconsciously influences the choice of cases for study.

An example of different accounts of the same event is the pair of studies by Dahl (1961) and Domhoff (1978) of New Haven urban redevelopment from 1945–1957.

From Dahl's pluralist perspective, politics is a scene of conflict and alliance among multiple interest groups. Each group is a coalition of individuals with similar interests. Groups differ in size, power, cohesion, and leadership; some win more of what they want, some less or very little or none, but no group wins all the time, contrary to the ideological claims of the elitists (mass perspective in my terminology). The politician is the entrepreneur; he brings groups into coalitions, works out compromises, distributes rewards, thereby collecting power for himself and his allies against other politicians.

To test the competing pluralist and elitist hypotheses it is necessary to study several political conflicts, reasoned Dahl, to see whether the same interest group won them all. So he picked three quite different issue areas, one of which was urban redevelopment. As it happened, the Mayor was involved more or less in all three areas, so he placed an observer in the Mayor's office and interviewed the other participants himself with assistants.

The results were a confirmation of the pluralist hypothesis: different groups were involved in each of the three issues, with the Mayor serving as political entrepreneur in all three and building up his own power in the process.

From Domhoff's mass perspective, there is a national ruling class with local branches which runs politics in its own long-run interest. It does not have absolute power and does not always get its way, nor does it bother about minor local issues. It is definitely not an interest group, though it includes groups with differences of interest on some issues; also there are continuing policy differences between NAM-type and CED-type businessmen within a basic consensus.

Given this perspective the way to locate New Haven politics is to first find the members of the ruling class by studying membership lists in key organizations and by tracing the network of connections among positions of power in the economy. Domhoff found Yale officials, the New Haven National Bank, and the Chamber of Commerce at the center of this network. Then one goes to the archives to study the pattern of decisions made by this power network—decisions about urban redevelopment, since Dahl's two other issues, school budgets and political nominations, do not interest the New Haven ruling class and thus are irrelevant to the pluralist-elitist controversy. Domhoff found that urban redevelopment was planned by Yale architects and Chamber members in the early 1940's and activated in the late 1940's by businessmen and by Yale's President Griswold and Yale development committee chairman Senator Bush. Dahl's hero, Mayor Lee, was drawn into the action in 1953 well after negotiations with federal and state officials were underway and became a front man and administrator, carrying out plans made a decade earlier. Dahl's interviewees in 1957 gave him the official cover story which gave Mayor Lee all the credit, and Dahl believed this story because it fit his pluralist bias. As for Yale involvement, Dahl—thinking of Yale as faculty—argued that it would be impossible to get the Yale people to agree on anything (1961, p. 138), and found only peripheral Yale involvement.

Polsby, one of the original researchers for Dahl's study, has commented in turn on Domhoff's case history (Polsby, 1980, pp. 172–188). He begins by questioning the quality of Domhoff's data. Domhoff spent eleven days in New Haven after twenty years had elapsed, while Dahl and his students spent several years there while the events were happening. This comment begs the question by assuming that the main events were occurring in 1957–1960, while according to Domhoff the plans and decisions were made between 1942 and 1949, long before Dahl and Mayor Lee got involved. Nor is it necessary for a historian to be an eyewitness; in fact, distance in time from the events chronicled is an advantage, since additional documents—memoirs, archives, letters—become available only decades after an event. For instance the Munich agreement of 1938 could not be adequately studied by historians until 1968 when the British archives were opened, and the resulting history (Middlemas, 1972) is far superior to eyewitness accounts. In Domhoff's case the Yale archives remained closed for twenty years, so Dahl could not have had access to them.

The rest of Polsby's comments (1980, pp. 172–188) are absolutely appalling: continual misrepresentation of Domhoff's position, sarcastic remarks, irrelevant arguments, dogmatic assertions, and evasions—until one realizes that Polsby still has no conception of Domhoff's hypotheses. He cannot conceive what "rule by a power elite" would mean in practice in New Haven; his vision is pluralist through and through. Consequently he also does not understand the "nondecisions" approach (1980, Chapter 11). He has no concept of a power network; the words remind him of Milgram's "small world" findings, which are entirely different.

Since Polsby cannot conceive of Domhoff's hypotheses, Domhoff's new data seem irrelevant to him, and he can find no evidence leading him to correct Dahl's history. In other words, Domhoff's power-elite perspective is necessary not only to find the relevant facts, but also to see the significance of facts after they have been found. For instance, Dahl does not mention the fact that Yale President Griswold was head of the state CED. Domhoff mentions this fact as evidence of Yale's involvement in the state power network. The fact apparently is meaningless to Polsby, because it does not tell of any participation in any official decision. Similarly, Domhoff points to a number of statements in Dahl's interview data that fit into a power-elite history; Dahl ignored these statements.

The pluralist–elitist-system theorist case studies of urban politics are interesting because they are an instance of researchers with three different perspectives using the same method, case study, and producing three different kinds of data. Here data differences reflect differences of perspective directly, without the mediation of methodological differences. Pluralists, elitists, and system theorists cannot accuse each other of using an unscientific method, since they all use the same method. Instead, the assertion "they are ideological, we are scientific" is based directly on differences of data.

Hunter (1954, Chapter 4), thinking of pluralist speculations about conflicting interest groups, declares that he is going to report the facts "unobscured by abstract value descriptions which do not fit reality." Polsby (1963), noting with dismay that community power studies seem to agree on propositions which are obviously wrong, explains this error by observer bias (pp. 45-56, 67-68, Chapter 5). The elitist researchers, all of them sociologists, simply assumed that power, like status, was stratified in a pyramid distribution and read this into the data, explaining away negative evidence by a variety of devices. Hunter, for instance, asked people "Who are the top leaders in this town?" thus guaranteeing that a ruling elite would appear in the data. Pluralists, in contrast, make no assumptions about power distribution (Polsby, 1963, or 1980, p. 113) and are therefore able to see the facts as they are.

Wirt, in turn dismisses both pluralists and elitists as ideologues:

> There is a final caution against relying on the "independent" observer's evaluation of "who wins" and "who loses" rather than on the judgment of the actors. . . . This is the likelihood that the outside observer will apply his own values to observed behavior. The danger here is not that the observer evaluates what he thinks he sees. Rather it is that what he thinks he sees has been preordained by what . . . his values have taught him to see. It is this fallacy which seems to underlie some, if not much, of the "elitist–pluralist" argument. In some cases, ideology provided the assumptions about reality, which shaped the methods employed, which in turn generated the "reality" the analysts thereupon perceived. This is not merely ideologues arguing about the results of empirical analysis; it is ideologues divining results they expect to find (Wirt, 1974, p. 365).

Wirt then adds that the advantage of his concepts and method is that it brings out what is really there. What is there, it turns out, is problems in the urban system: "It is time, too, to abandon those community studies whose aim is to strengthen the ideological conception of the current health or infirmity of American society. The search for community power has the potential to provide new insights which can help us with the many problems of our increasingly urban society; it is this potential above all other attractions which justifies further inquiry" (Hawley and Wirt, 1974, p. 263).

In summary, standpoints and perspectives influence the public process of hypothesis testing, first by dictating one's choice of method and by influencing the production and collection of data; second, by limiting the awareness and the understanding of the hypotheses to be tested; and third, by activating a cognitive double standard in relating data to hypotheses. This means that the context of discovery cannot be empirically separated from the context of justification; standpoints are deeply involved in both. It does not mean that reliable data and reliable hypothesis testing are illusory goals; the errors of data production and interpretation can be reduced. Indeed, "reduction in errors of data production and hypothesis testing" is another way of expressing the goal of this book.

Reduction of error does not involve "eliminating ideology" so that the researcher can see the facts as they really are. Perspectives provide guidelines for the discovery of possible data as well as hindrances to seeing what is there, and without any guidelines the researcher would not know what to look for or to report. For example Domhoff's anti-elitist perspective guided him in finding data that Dahl did not look for and could not see even in his interviews. The problem is to maximize the productive use of perspectives in empirical research while gradually reducing the many errors and blind spots.

Nothing in the above argument has at all refuted Popper's proposed logic of research. Hypothesis testing can still be regarded, logically, as a process of public criticism of hypotheses by reference to evidence. One must add that evidence must also be criticized and corrected; but Popperians have recognized this. The major correction I wish to make in Popper's logic is to assert that multiple perspectives are *necessarily* involved in the critical process. They are needed to produce the data that will test a hypothesis, and are also needed to interpret the data and to criticize other interpretations. This correction makes Popper's logic less abstract by giving content to the concept of "criticism." It is the same correction that Feyerabend made long ago (1965).

If multiple perspectives are necessarily involved in the public criticism of theory and evidence, I have one corollary to suggest. The critical process is more effective when scientists are partly aware of their own perspectives, including their limitations, and when they recognize that the opponent's perspective may have positive as well as negative contributions to make to science. Such a recognition would make them more receptive to criticism and perhaps less defensive and intolerant.

As long as scientists believe that they look at the facts directly without preconceptions and see only what is there (for example Polsby, 1980, p. 233) they can hardly avoid bafflement when they are confronted with the irrelevant data and weird interpretations of opposing schools. The obvious explanation is the schema, "we are scientific, they are ideological." or in Polsby's version "we are scientific, they are religious" (ibid., p. 234). The obvious solution is to eliminate ideology, at least from the scientific community, and this becomes in practice the elimination of the "ideological" opponent. One eliminates opposing schools from science by teaching absurd distortions of their positions and absurd refutations; by ignoring their

writings and rejecting their requests for research grants; by refusing to
publish their articles because of the bad data and implausible arguments; finally by refusing them tenure because they do not publish in
the reputable journals and attend the reputable conventions. The
editor of the most reputable journal in political science is Nelson
Polsby; how many "power-elite" articles would be scientifically
acceptable to him (cf. Beardsley, 1980, p. 41)?

Popper himself was guilty of this intolerance, which contradicts his
own principle of eliminating prejudice by intersubjective criticism,
when he attempted to logically eliminate Freudians and Marxists from
the scientific community. His excuse was that Freudian and Marxist
hypotheses are immune to empirical falsification; but this empirical
judgment of Popper's simply expresses a difference of perspective, or
an overgeneralization from a few early encounters in Vienna. It is the
same judgment that pluralists and elitists make of each other in
frustration as they see their opponents refusing to accept the clear and
persistent refutations of their doctrines. Fortunately, Popper's personal
bias against Freudians and Marxists is not a necesssary part of his
philosophy.

Here again I have no objection to Popper's logic. I agree with the
rule that any theory that is completely immune to empirical falsification is not part of science, since science is the empirical search for
truth. However, I have met no one so free of bias that he is able to
apply this logical rule unerringly to an actual theory.

Althusser provides a null hypothesis that is the opposite of Popper's
(Althusser and Balibar, 1970). For Popper the origin of a hypothesis is
irrelevant to its scientific status, and science is defined solely by the
intention to submit one's own hypotheses to public test; for Althusser
the origin of a hypothesis completely determines its status. All
hypotheses that derive from any perspective are ideological in the
sense that they express some socially determined consciousness, the
consciousness appropriate to some class standpoint. Consequently all
the ideas discussed in this book are ideological since they all derive
from some location in society. Science appears only when some
thinker transcends society; that is, only a Wise Man can be scientific.
In Althusser's version there was only one Wise Man, Marx, and only
one Interpreter, Althusser; indeed even Marx did not realize that he
was inventing science, and this fact remained unknown until
Althusser revealed it with his corrections of the texts.

I cannot deal with a hypothesis that rejects all of social science since
1930 as uniformly unscientific. There may be an entirely different kind
of knowledge somewhere, so different that we cannot get from here to

there. However, Althusser's followers-and-critics have already toned down his flamboyant manifesto, so that we can interpret it as a typical founding manifesto of a new school. Hindess argues that Althusser's corrections of *Capital* are arbitrary ("teleological"); Althusser decided to eliminate all marks of "ideology" in *Capital* because he had decided beforehand that *Capital* was science, not ideology (1977, pp. 204-211). As with all orthodox Marxisms, the Interpreter reads his own ideas into the sacred texts, hiding his subjective concerns behind a mask of objectivity. For Althusser's concerns, see Liebich, 1979. Resnick and Wolff (1979, p. 4) assure us that they mean nothing invidious by the term "ideological": "... to designate the other social sciences as ideologies is in no way to label them as false or inadequate to the facts. ... An 'ideological science' is a concept within Marxist science which defines the connection between itself and the sciences against which it struggles." In other words, *they are ideological, we are scientific*. Nothing new here.

There are social scientists who think like Althusser. They tell me, "Some social scientists do express their class background or sympathies in their work; they are ideological. I, however, have risen above my background and see things objectively; I am scientific." I cannot correct such delusions by argument. Instead, I have described the conceptual schemes that actually exist, the blind spots of each scheme, and the self-concepts or identities that actually accompany each scheme (from my perspective) Those scientists who have risen above society still define themselves as professionals or as intellectuals, whether detached, committed, or critical, and these are locations in society.

II. Mannheim and the Free-Floating Intellectuals

If the argument of section I is accepted one comes naturally to the hypothesis that scientific objectivity is a product of the collaboration and mutual criticism of many perspectives. Each perspective is able to bring out the blind spots and limits of some other perspective, while remaining imperfectly aware of its own blind spots. Each perspective is able to suggest hypotheses and produce data that cannot readily be produced from other perspectives. Each perspective is able to reveal errors of data interpretation and theoretical argument that are hardly recognizable from some other perspective. One need not assume that all perspectives are equally valid; some may be vastly better than others—broader, more self-critical, more open to alien ideas, or whatever. However, even the poorest, narrowest perspective may have some little bit to contribute to science. Thus Mannheim (1936, pp. 150-151) argues that even the Fascist standpoint, for all its narrowness, sensitizes its bearers to one important fact: the possibility of a putsch at certain moments of instability. This possibility is part of reality, and a science that overlooks it is incomplete, however slightly.

The above position is what Mannheim calls "bourgeois liberalism," and is fairly common among current social scientists. It is sometimes identified with Mannheim; but Mannheim's own democratic socialist view differs in two respects. Mannheim regards the utopian mentality, that is the standpoints with future-oriented utopias, as the core of social science, and has scant respect for the ideological mentality, the present- and past-oriented standpoints. Social science ought to be oriented primarily to the study of possible changes in society. Second, the testing of possibilities must be done in political practice, by trying to actualize them; science should be closely related to socialist political action. The bourgeois social scientists indulgently overlook these radical aberrations of Mannheim in their interpretation of his views.

Bourgeois liberalism founders on the central problem discussed in this book: communication failure. The partial incommensurability of perspectives means that communications must be translated from one set of categories into another and back again, and this requires thorough familiarity with at least two perspectives for even limited communication. Cognitive difficulties are intensified by the varied moral commitments of social scientists—to defend individual freedom, to contribute to solution of social problems, to defend democracy, to induce emancipation of beliefs, etc.—which oblige them to push their own perspective at every opportunity. The liberals have failed to recognize the moral barriers to communication because of their own belief in the autonomy of science, the separation of fact and value. As I have argued in Chapter Thirteen, this belief is part of the ethic of the professional specialist and advisor, and is quite compatible with a commitment to government and to social problem-solving as the aim of science. When liberals universalize their belief in the autonomy of science they also tacitly universalize their own moral commitment to government, which prevents them from being interested in some aspects of radical and conservative perspectives.

Three kinds of cognitive barriers have appear in Part I. *First*, two perspectives may have partly incommensurable categories, so that obvious and plausible propositions in one make no sense in the other. The clearest case of incommensurability is that between neoclassical and Keynesian perspectives, or in sociology between Homans and

Parsons. The neoclassical system has an open horizon, bounded only by diminishing returns and rising costs; empirically this means an international economy with freely moving capital and labor and products. The Keynesian system is closed by a national boundary. Since national boundaries and other hindrances to mobility indisputably do exist in the short run, the neoclassical perspective which overlooks such hindrances is necessarily long run, while the Keynesian perspective which takes them into account is short run. Neoclassic science is subjective; each of us has direct *a priori* access to its subject matter in ourselves. Each of us knows how decisions are made. Keynesian science is objective and empirical; this means that we do not know, prior to empirical investigation, how decisions in various sectors of the economy, polity, and society are made.

The many fruitless disputes about rationality, including bounded rationality, deterrence, permanent income, and lifetime income, have foundered on the subjective-objective difference. For the Keynesians and the Lester–Simon–Cyert–March people we do not know *a priori* the extent and circumstances in which people are rational, nor do we know what forms rationality takes in various circumstances. For the neoclassicists maximizing-rationality is a certain truth and empirical investigation deals only with details like the number of years included in our planning for the future, or in other words the shape of the time-discount curve.

The Keynesian short-run closed system focuses attention on issues outside the scope of neoclassic economic theory: relation between GNP growth and unemployment rates, Phillips curve phenomena (relation between inflation and unemployment rates), and credit fluctuations. It also focuses attention on the systemic media, money and information, which act differently from ordinary resources and require systemic treatment. The neoclassical Walrasian model cannot deal with money and information. In Parsons' models, power, influence, and commitment are additional systemic media. But conversely the long-run laws of the neoclassicist may be invisible in the Keynesian short run, since the slope of the cost and return curves may be nearly horizontal in the short run. In particular, international movements of money, capital, and labor, theoretically knowable for the neoclassicist, become illegal and therefore arbitrary evasions of government policy for the Keynesian: smuggling, currency speculation, illegal immigration, brain drain; to be handled by ad hoc controls.

The incommensurability of conceptual schemes has been hidden by the historical continuity between the two traditions. In sociology these continuities are absent, and the Homans-Parsons differences have been open and obvious.

A *second* kind of cognitive barrier exists when the categories of one perspective are included in the more inclusive set of categories of another perspective. In this case communication can move from the included to the inclusive perspective but not back again. Some return statements will seem puzzling, perverse, ideological, or uninteresting, or will be misunderstood. As a result the adherents of the narrower perspective will simply ignore the parts of the wider theory that do not fit into their perspective, and the communication that does occur will reassure them that all is well.

The best example is the Keynesian-functionalist perspective on the one hand and the Galbraithian-institutionalists and New Left Marxists on the other. For all these perspectives science is the empirical study of objective system dynamics, but the Galbraithian-Marxist system is more inclusive than the Keynesian-functionalist system. The latter system has a national boundary, while for both Galbraithians and Marxists the imperialist or world system has its own dynamics which condition the dynamics of the national sub-system. Also for Keynesians, functionalists, and social problems professionals some part of the government always escapes the system dynamics and is treated as rational and free, while for Galbraithians and Marxists government is an integral part of the "old system" (Raskin, 1974).

Another example of inclusiveness is the absorption of neoclassical system dynamics into Keynesian, institutionalist, and Marxist system dynamics. For the neoclassicist the dynamics of perfect competition were the economy's basic and ultimate dynamics, except for the troublesome problem of oligopoly. Keynes objectivized these same dynamics as the dynamics of resource allocation, subject to the more inclusive dynamics of investment, savings, growth, and employment. For Galbraithians and Marxists they are the dynamics of the competitive sector only, very much subject to the expansionist dynamics of the planning sector and the fiscal policies of the state.

An inclusiveness relation also exists when a primarily objective science includes subjective processes as part of the dynamics of the Object. Schurmann (1974) includes Schumpeterian concepts of entrepreneurial creativity and bureaucratic inertia in his theory of bureaucratic politics, O'Connor (1973) includes government fiscal policy as part of the dynamics of the capitalist state, and other Marxists include elite-mass conflict as part of the dynamics of capitalist society. Schumpeter incorporporated neoclassic equilibrium analysis as an account of the diffusion-inertia phase that succeeded the creative destruction phase, in his theory of the growth of capitalism. Thus the neoclassics could treat him as one of themselves, by ignoring his theory of entrepreneurial creativity which for them was outside the scope of deductive science.

A *third* kind of cognitive barrier to communication consists of the incompatible practical concerns of different schools. One principle of cognitive psychology is that we interpret information in terms of our current practical problems (Jervis, 1976, pp. 211-216). A corollary is that when we search for information the search is guided by our practical needs, not by idle curiosity. Consequently when a scientist of school A reads or hears theoretical output from school B, he interprets it to throw light on the practical problems of school A, and ignores or forgets material that does not relate to those problems. When members of school B read the results in terms of their problems, they find selective distortion of the B theories, while they in turn must also select and distort the A theories.

Consider for example the sociology of deviance. When this topic is approached from the "social problems" perspective the aim of sociology, the practical concern, is to cure the deviant in some sense and reintegrate him or her into society. For this purpose it is necessary to find the objective causes that can be corrected, whether they be job opportunities, psychological inadequacies, social disorganization, or subculture conflict with the dominant culture. These causes are necessarily located in the deviants or their social circumstances; the deviants and their milieu constitute the Object. The helping agency, usually a part of government, has responsibility for the deviant; it is the Subject and is therefore studied by different professionals in a different field, policy evaluation.

When deviance is studied from the mass perspective the problem is the deviants' own problem as they understand it, and this is usually the problem of survival with dignity in an oppressive society. The helping agency represents that society and is therefore part of the problem, one of the oppressors. From this perspective one finds that deviance is a stigma, a spoiled identity, imposed from without (Rubington and Weinberg, 1968; Goffman, 1963). No one chooses to become a "deviant"; he is given that label by others.

The social problems professionals can interpret mass-perspective work on deviance as criticisms of normal professional procedures or as revelations of shocking local inadequacies in policy implementation. It can be read as advice on how better to "cure" the deviant. So the stigmatizing procedures are corrected: retarded children are renamed

"educable mentally handicapped" or "trainable mentally handicapped" and the problem is solved. Thus the participant-observer
studies which were intended as hermeneutic means of encouraging understanding, tolerance, and sympathy are interpreted as means to improve control over deviants and the officials dealing with them (Gouldner, 1970,
p. 445). Conversely, the social-problems literature can be misinterpreted
from the deviants' perspective as "blaming the victim" (Ryan, 1976).
For the deviant, this is unfair. There is nothing wrong with me; the
problem is out there, and I am coping as well as I can.

The clearest example of communication barriers due to differing
problems is between the elitists and the anti-elitists or critical intellectuals. The two perspectives are practically identical; one could
say that the two standpoints are located at opposite ends of the same
perspective, the same set of categories. But because of the differences of
standpoint the practical concerns are very different. The elitist concern
is with the preservation of elitist democracy, and welfare measures
which pacify the masses are a means to this end. The critical, anti-
elitist concern is with oppression and injustice.

Consequently the data offered by each school seem irrelevant and
misleading to the other school. When anti-elitists offer evidence of
predominant elite participation in decisions, this is of no interest to
the elitists. Of course the elite participate; that is their responsibility,
and occurs in all societies. The question is, is the participation
effective? Has democracy been preserved, or are the masses being
stirred up and legitimate viewpoints excluded? For the anti-elitists the
demonstration that the possibility of participation is still legally open
to any potential legitimate interest group is of little importance, given
the enormous actual difference of power between elite and mass. The
important question is one of distributive justice: Who benefits? And
who loses (Hayes, 1972)? The masses lose. For the elitists the question
of who benefits is irrelevant and misleading, since "we" all benefit
from democracy, and since the questions of fair distribution and how
to achieve it are complex (Polsby, 1963, Chapter 7). As for power, in a
democracy its distribution keeps shifting, and nothing can be inferred
from a local concentration of power.

Communication problems resulting from differences of practical
concern are not insurmountable. The trick is to read the writings of a
school by reference to that school's practical concerns. But perhaps not
all concerns are morally acceptable? The fact is that empathetic
interpretation of the work of opposed schools in the light of their
concerns, not ours, is much less common than it could be in social
science.

Mannheim was aware of the cognitive barriers to communication, but supposed that they could be overcome. Social scientists, like everyone else, occupied a position in society, and their particular position produced a mentality that is empathetic to opposing standpoints and that naturally strives for a synthesis of perspectives. Scientists belong to the intellectual stratum, which is not directly a part of any class but floats somewhere between rulers and ruled. This stratum is not numerous and powerful enough to engage in independent political action and so has to attach itself to other classes to achieve its interests. Consequently particular groups of intellectuals tend to voluntarily identify with some class and become its spokesmen. The various perspectives in science result. These express the vicarious class experience of intellectuals, but also express their partial detachment from classes in the separation of theory (the intellectual element) from practice (the class element) and in the systematization of theory (1936, pp. 173–174).

Intellectuals are also influenced by their common experience in education. In educational institutions a multiplicity of perspectives is always present, so people become accustomed to heterogeneity and learn to absorb other perspectives into their own thinking. Consequently the tendency to a synthesis of perspectives is always present (pp. 155–157).

Mannheim's account of the free-floating intellectual stratum sounds strange to American experience. The professionalization of social science since 1940 has produced specialists who are not accustomed to working with other perspectives but rather with other specialists like themselves. Moreover the professional and also the public employee have their own positions in society which define their experience and appropriate modes of political action. They have no need to become spokesmen for other classes.

Mannheim's account does fit the mass-perspective and elite-perspective intellectuals, and also students. Most of the mass-perspective scientists define themselves as intellectuals in Mannheim's sense; they empathize with an oppressed class and act as its spokesmen; and they preserve a distance between their own identity and that of the masses, the poor, the deviants, with whom they empathize. Some of the elitists empathize with the elite in similar fashion. However, in recent years a good number of elitists have gone beyond mere spokesmanship and identified themselves as an actual part of the meritocratic elite. They have gone into government in pursuit of the power to carry out the elite program of mass welfare, economic development, and anti-Soviet foreign policy. These people are no longer interested in a larger truth transcending their own standpoint; they have work to do. Other elitists, particularly in political science, have become professional data crunchers, not interested in loose dialogue.

It would seem that the intellectual dialogue for which Mannheim hoped is most likel˙ to occur between anti-elitists and the more detached elitists. As happens, these two groups have a practically identical perspective, so the usual cognitive barriers to communication are not present in this case. Also the ambivalent identification discussed in Chapter Seven enables anti-elitists to empathize with the elite standpoint, and vice versa. Examples of such dialogue are Horowitz and Lipset (1978) though no real discussion occurs in this dialogue, and also the Dye and Zeigler collaboration (1975, p. xiii). My impression is that such dialogue is rare.

˙ This is by no means the total dialogue that Mannheim and the liberals have called for. Given the cognitive barriers discussed above and the moral barriers discussed in Chapter Thirteen, there can be no such dialogue.

How then can we achieve objective truth? If the ideal of a comprehensive dialogue and ultimate synthesis of all perspectives must be given up, perhaps there is one perspective so comprehensive that it includes most of the categories of the other perspectives within its categories. Scientists who took this perspective would have a uniquely broad understanding of the work of other scientists; they could appreciate the best achievements of each narrower perspective as well as its weaknesses. Each narrower perspective might afford its practitioners a more vivid, precise, and detailed view of some restricted aspect of reality, but the adherents of the comprehensive perspective could combine and correct these partial theories in a grand synthesis.

Or there may be a perspective which, if not comprehensive, is at least more adequate to our times than any other perspective. It may not afford us the whole truth but would allow us to understand the essential characteristics of our society and miss only the marginal or superficial aspects. This suggestion is associated with Lukacs (1923), who argued that the proletarian standpoint is the one most adequate to our society. Or there may be two or three fairly adequate standpoints, each making possible a limited or partial synthesis. We turn therefore to a search for the most comprehensive or at least adequate perspective.

III. The Comprehensive or at Least Adequate Perspective

The problem with the criterion of comprehensiveness is that each perspective seems, to those who take it, to be the most comprehensive. The other perspectives, or those which make any sense at all, are located within its horizon and therefore can be classified within its categories. In the process they are adapted to its categories in such a way that they all become partial or inadequate.

In Chapter Four I observed that Keynesians and neoclassicists each treated the other as a special case of their own more general theory, and each produced a synthesis of the two on that basis. Similarly, to me the New Left Marxist perspective seems the most comprehensive. It includes short-run, long-run, and evolutionary theories, one of the few perspectives to do so, and it provides a synthesis of subjective and objective approaches. It includes the class struggle concepts of the critical intellectuals as the subjective pole of social dynamics. It includes the Keynesian, functionalist, and Galbraithian categories and dynamics as the objective pole. It includes Schumpeter's subject-object dialectic as the unity of the two poles. It includes the elitists' struggle of good (the US) and evil (the SU) in its theory of bureaucratic conflict and symbiosis, picked up from the bureaucratic politics theorists. It includes game-theory categories within Wallerstein's larger model of the world system. It includes the neoclassical model as the dynamics of the competitive small business sector. It supplements the Keynesian-Galbraithian short-run dynamics with long-run system dynamics derived from its close relations with one or another Orthodox Marxist such as Mandel. Unlike the functionalist long-run dynamics, the Marxist dynamics point to the future (though vaguely and uncertainly) as well as to the past. The only possibility of a more comprehensive perspective is the ecological perspective, but its categories have not yet been worked out.

I imagine that representatives of other perspectives could make a similar case for the comprehensiveness of their perspective.

Conversely, each comprehensive synthesis seems, from other perspectives, to be a pitifully narrow failure. For example, Boulding's *Ecodynamics* (1978), hailed by some as a triumphant achievement, seems to me just another narrow playing out of neoclassic categories. The synthesis is of the sort described in Chapter Four, in which a few Keynesian short-run concepts are added to the neoclassic equilibrium system, plus in this case a few game models and misinterpreted ecological concepts. Schumpeterian and Marxist categories are grotesquely distorted and dismissed (ibid., Chapter 12); the mass perspective is ignored, as its adherents suffer from the disease of infracaninophilia, and the individualist political theory of Chapter Three above is assumed to be correct. The bureaucratic-institutionalists and functionalists are also ignored. Boulding's synthesis was already out of date in 1960.

Apparently the search for a comprehensive perspective reproduces at a higher level the conflict of perspectives described in Part I. This does not mean that all perspectives are equally comprehensive; it merely means that none of us are able to objectively determine which perspectives are more comprehensive. Nor does it mean that we should stop trying to make our own perspective more comprehensive. It merely means that we should abandon claims to have *achieved* a comprehensive synthesis.

Nor can any perspective claim to be so comprehensive that it no longer needs other perspectives as supplements or critics. The blind spots of each perspective discussed in Part I were brought out by taking a different perspective, usually a later one. Only by studying the criticisms coming from other perspectives can one become aware of one's own blind spots and attempt to overcome them or allow for them.

The same arguments apply to any search for the most adequate or relevant perspective. Whatever criterion of adequacy one proposes will come from one's own perspective and thus will enable that perspective to validate itself.

For example, Lukacs (1923) argued that only the proletarian standpoint could overcome the various subject–object dualisms that tormented the nineteenth century philosophers and drove them to construct one failed synthesis after another. His argument is similar to the one presented in Chapter Twelve, Section 3; I believe this is a strength of Marxism. But if one were to demand of a perspective that it afford a synthesis of the actual and the possible, ideology and utopia, Marxism would score poorly because it is skewed to the possible, that which is becoming rather than that which has been and still is.

The ideal of a comprehensive truth, either through a general dialogue and synthesis of all partial truths or by adoption of a comprehensive or adequate perspective, must therefore be given up. Even if such a truth or perspective were to exist among us, we would be unable to agree in recognizing it because of our partial vision.

We are faced therefore with the prospect of accepting multiple truths, each from a different perspective. In this case partial objectivity would be approached through the mutual criticism of different standpoints without synthesis and without agreement. This sort of organization of science is represented by Churchman's "Hegelian Inquirer," which we examine next. It is also the type of organization recommended by Feyerabend in a much maligned book, *Against Method* (1975, 1976).

IV. Churchman, Feyerabend, and the Hegelian Inquirer

The Hegelian Inquirer is discussed and exemplified in Churchman, *Design of Inquiring Systems* (1971, Chapters 7, 8) and in Mitroff, *The Subjective Side of Science* (1974, Chapters 3, 4, 7). The model is Hegelian in the sense that it uses the Kantian thesis-antithesis-synthesis triad plus the Hegelian emphasis on conflict; but it omits the essential restlessness of the Hegelian dialectic, the restlessness of life, that finds in every partial achievement a source of new dissatisfaction.

Churchman develops the model as a set of rules for designing an inquiring system or, in our terms, for organizing scientific inquiry. One begins with a position of some kind, a theory or policy or method or point of view to be asserted. Next one produces and organizes data in support, marshals arguments in support, and from data and argument constructs a case for the position. Next one selects an opposing position, the contrary or "deadliest enemy" of the first position, and constructs a case for this position. Then the two positions argue it out *without ever reaching agreement*. Then there is a third group that observes the other two and tries to make sense of the conflict. The third group is not antagonistic to either of the other two, but tries to work out a position that includes ideas from the other two, or that explains or explains away the conflict.

Feyerabend's position is more pluralistic than Churchman's. Feyerabend argues that at the present time, when the natural sciences are dominated by rigid methods and narrowly limited thinking, they need to be loosened up and opened to broader ranges of possibilities. This requires a plurality of positions, as many as possible differing as completely as possible. The holders of each position ought to argue with all the others, each holding to his own position tenaciously. Feyerabend goes farther and argues that if a position becomes implausible and loses supporters it ought to be strengthened, if necessary by deceptive rhetoric and tricky analogies or by government support. "He must try to improve rather than discard the views that have failed in the competition." "The task of the scientist . . . is 'to make the weaker case the stronger . . . and thereby to sustain the motion of the whole" (1975, p. 30). If weaker positions are allowed to lose out the richness of imagination needed for scientific progress will gradually be reduced and we may in the end return to the present narrow orthodoxy.

This prescription, however, only holds at the present time for the natural sciences. It is not clear what Feyerabend would prescribe for the social sciences. He might declare that the present absurd chaos is just right, and that this organization should be preserved by channeling government grants to the gold economists, parapsychologists, and other weaker positions to strengthen them. Or he might conclude that things have gotten too wild and more methodological discipline and rigorous thinking is called for (1975, p. 22). If he took the latter track he would be mistaken, because the pluralism in the policy sciences does not result from loose thinking but from the multiplicity of standpoints provided by our society.

What sort of truth is a Hegelian Inquirer or an anarchic organization of science supposed to yield? The criticism of a position by its "deadliest enemy" is supposed to reveal its empirical, formal, and methodological weaknesses. Empirically, any position tends to produce or collect data to its own specifications and thus confirm itself in general, though not in details. The reasons are partly cognitive, as I argued briefly in Chapter Fourteen, Section I, and partly socio-emotional: each school is trying to promote its own position and thereby affirm its own identity. Consequently, it is up to an opposing school to produce or collect the strongest possible disconfirming data. For instance, political scientists formerly regarded Dahl's 1961 study of New Haven politics as empirical confirmation of the pluralist thesis; Domhoff's 1978 study should reopen the issue for some of them. Formally, the opposing school can also be expected to scrutinize the arguments, looking for errors and hidden assumptions; methodologically, they will point out the errors that led to the production of self-confirming data (Mitroff, 1974, pp. 240-242; Feyerabend, 1975, pp. 29-32).

Such criticism is supposed to alert the criticized position so it improves its arguments, methods, and data. For example pluralist criticisms of Hunter's (1954) method led to several reformulations of the power-elite method and theory by Domhoff. Conversely, some pluralists will presumably learn from Domhoff's criticisms and produce methodologically improved pluralist case studies. In this way each position is induced to make its most plausible possible case. The benefits of this "struggle" accrue to the later third position—in this example the urban system theorists—who can build on the achievements of the other two.

Criticism is also supposed to reveal the theoretical assumptions and intellectual commitments which underlie each position and thereby increase the self-awareness of those taking the position (Mitroff, 1974, p. 240). Increased self-awareness in turn is supposed to enable a school to examine its own presuppositions, perhaps correct them or control them or carry them out more effectively.

In short, the Hegelian Inquiring System is supposed to produce a plurality of biased truths in which each position is stimulated to its best efforts by conflict with an opposite position. Over time the list of positions changes somewhat but the plurality of truths is never reduced.

When we apply this model to the present inquiry, "position" becomes "standpoint." As a result the positions are no longer arbitrary, as they are in the formal model (Churchman, 1971, p. 171). Instead, they are the standpoints produced by the historical development of capitalist society: rentier, small businessman, big businessman, etc. The oppositions are not merely the logical opposition of contrary theses but also the actual opposition of strivings and experiences. Consequently the oppositions are not complete, but vary greatly in degree and kind. Between elite and mass the opposition of standpoint is complete, but the perspectives, the categorial schemes, are very similar. Conversely between Schumpeterian elitist and functionalist or social problems theorists the standpoints are close—both groups will focus on similar social problems and have similar solution criteria—but the conceptual schemes are very different.

There are in fact at least six independently varying sources of conflict in the policy sciences.

1. *Standpoint*: this determines the aims of science, location of its utopia in time, subject-matter and method(s) of science.
2. *Perspective*: this is the intellectual component that determines the amount of logical compatibility.
3. *Moral* (Chapter Thirteen): this determines the pattern of moral tolerance of other standpoints.
4. *Method*: this, like perspective, is an intellectual component. Differences of method intensify problems of communication and disputes over data resulting from differences of perspective.
5. *Psychological*: this cuts across the other four. It consists of the transferred conflicts and methods of handling conflict that a person has developed in early childhood, particularly in relations with siblings; masculine-feminine differences in ways of relating to people; modes of identification and rebellion; and cognitive styles in organizing data, of the sort that appear in the

Rorschach test. Mitroff and Kilman, 1978, have described the
various cognitive styles that occur in the social sciences.
6. One may also find characteristic national or sub-cultural styles
of thought, which baffle or infuriate scientists from other
national backgrounds. For example I believe the fruitless
Miliband-Poulantzas interchanges of the early 1970's mainly
reflect national differences between British and French
Marxists.

When we apply the "Hegelian Inquirer" model to the controversies
of the last several decades we come immediately to a distinction. Some
controversies are within a standpoint and some are across standpoints.
In terms of categories, some conflicts are between the categories of a
conceptual scheme, such as creativity and inertia in Schumpeter and
in Schumpeterian bureaucratic politics; internal integration and external goal achievement in Parsonian functionalism; the legitimation
function and the capital accumulation function in the Marxist theory
of the state. These conflicts enable the scientific school to conceptualize and study actual conflicts in society. Other conceptual conflicts
are across perspectives, such as neoclassical internationalism and
Keynesian nationalism, or the elitist and social problems objectification of the masses and the anti-elitist subjective treatment of the
same people.

As it happens, all the examples offered by Churchman and Mitroff
to illustrate the Hegelian Inquirer are conflicts within a perspective,
in fact conflicts within one theory. Churchman's first example is
unfortunate: "The deadliest enemy of democracy is not nondemocracy,
but a very explicit and detailed political design called the Communist
Party" (1971, p. 172). This piece of manure is an instance of familiar
Cold War categories of the elitist perspective, the struggle between US
(good) and SU (evil). Churchman's second example (1971, Chapter 8)
is a foreign policy debate between two poles of Rostow's theory: As the
elite responsible for world welfare—"We the United States, being the
most affluent nation," 1971, p. 182—should we give first priority to
protecting the Free World against Communism, or should we help the
developing nations achieve self-sustained growth and thereby render
them immune to Communist temptation? Rostow argued the second
position in Millikan and Rostow (1957) and the first position while in
government from 1964–1968. Churchman's third example (pp. 184–
185) is of an operations researcher devising an alternative policy for
achieving market expansion for a company. I see nothing dialectical
in any sense in this example.

Mitroff (1974) draws up two contrary lists of norms for scientific inquiry and uses them to analyze and interpret his interview and test data. He uses them to describe and classify individual scientists' self-concepts, ideals, and conceptions of other scientists. The first list includes norms like emotional neutrality, disinterestedness, impartiality, absence of bias, suspension of judgment till all the facts are in. The second, opposite list includes emotional commitment, interestedness, partiality for one's own theories, bias, and exercise of judgment on incomplete data (p. 79). The two lists are "deadly enemies" but both are found in Merton's sociology of science with its characteristic functionalist dialectic of opposite prerequisites for social systems. Mitroff has corrected the overemphasis on the first list of characteristics in Merton's early work. Merton's later work is more balanced, but still needs Mitroff's correction.

The use of polar opposite categories to understand society is rather common, especially in the functionalist tradition and among the Schumpeterians. It is commended also by Mannheim: "What formerly appeared merely to be an unintelligible margin, which could not be subsumed under a given concept, has today given rise to a supplementary and sometimes opposite concept, through which a more inclusive knowledge of the object can be gained" (1936, p. 103). Redfield also advises the use of a "pair of lenses" to get a more comprehensive view of any human community, and gives examples (1960, Chapter 9). But again all the concepts are part of Redfield's own third world peasant perspective, the predecessor of the mass perspective of Howard Becker and Erving Goffman.

Perhaps the difficulty here is that when one *designs* a Hegelian Inquirer there is a designer, and the oppositions designed into the system must all be within the perspective of the designer. The designer always is in the third position, the synthesis that transcends conflict, so the conflict has already been transcended in principle *before* the system is set up.

But one cannot design the organization of the policy sciences. The standpoints are already there, given by the self-development of capitalist society, the conflicts between them reflect the actual conflicts in our own society, and no synthesis is available. Nor can we invent a synthesis or other new standpoint as Feyerabend advises "We must invent a new conceptual system" (1975, p. 32), though this may be possible in the natural sciences. New standpoints have been thrown up by crises and by the growing self-consciousness of some formerly submerged stratum or class. The experience of this class is the indispensable social source of scientists' concepts and problems. The policy scientists of the 1970's, for instance, build on the real experience of policymakers and implementers in government; without such experience the perspective would be mere speculation.

Conversely, the decay or quiescence of a class removes the experience that speaks out through the categories of a perspective and reduces them to quaint, arbitrary constructions. For instance the world-view that would validate the Hopi rain dance, one of Feyerabend's examples (1976, p. 77) cannot be revived even by living Hopi because the culture that produced it has been encapsulated and rigidified by Western influence. Without that cultural background the dance is a tourist attraction, not a meaningful experience.

Nor can we eliminate a standpoint that seems to us to have outlived its scientific usefulness; it will persist as long as the social basis for it persists. Any designing we do has to work with existing standpoints, by collaborating with their partisans or ignoring them.

With this qualification, we can apply the principles of the Hegelian Inquirer and of Feyerabend's pluralism to the policy sciences. As I interpret them, the principles are:

1. Do not expect to achieve a comprehensive truth; that is, do not try to persuade everyone else of the correctness of your own perspective. It won't work. Learn to live with differences of perspective.
2. Develop your own partisan truth by working with those who share your standpoint.
3. Criticize the work of opposing schools; criticize their data, their methods, their assumptions, their reasoning, their blind spots— but do not expect to convince them.
4. Try to learn from the criticisms coming from opposing schools; look for possible inadequacies in one's own data, methods, reasoning, and correct them without giving up fundamental principles.

Points 1 and 2 agree with the conclusions of previous sections; points 3 and 4 are new. The purpose of criticism is presumably to induce greater self-awareness and to stimulate attempts at self-improvement.

Here again we come up against the central problem of this study, the problem of communication. If the critic does not understand the position he is criticizing, his criticism will be worthless shadow-boxing. If the school being criticized does not understand the critic it will not be stimulated to self-awareness or self-improvement. Communication can be a problem even among people sharing a perspective, due to social, psychological, or national barriers, as in the Miliband-Poulantzas exchange. But when there are differences of perspective as well, intellectual and moral barriers add to the difficulty. Churchman did not have to face this problem because all his examples of conflict were within one perspective.

Feyerabend or Mitroff might reply that even complete failure of communication might be useful to a later third position, because the failures clarify the assumptions and limits of the earlier perspectives. Thus Marxists and Schumpeterians will learn nothing from Boulding's absurd criticism of what he calls "dialectic" (1978, Chapter 12) since they already know how narrow the neoclassical categorial scheme is, but a later observer might learn something about the limits of the neoclassical perspective from it. On this principle, however, anything that any scientist does might be useful to a later historian. To take an extreme example, even the reviews of Feyerabend, 1975, might be good for something, perhaps as a stimulus to Feyerabend's reply (1978) or as further evidence of the incredible narrowness of some philosophers.

But Churchman of all people has most emphasized the importance of cost-benefit considerations in science. Anything a scientist does can have *some* value, but life and government grants are short and we must concentrate our resources on effective activities. This means, in the present context, that one should not waste time trying to communicate when communication is nearly impossible. One should avoid criticizing schools which will not understand the criticism, and ignore criticism coming from such sources.

In other words we should concentrate our critical and self-critical efforts on schools whose perspective is close to our own, or who share some other basis of understanding with us. For example, Lipsky examines the objective dynamics of relations between "street-level bureaucrats" (social workers, teachers, judges, policemen) and their clients, from a bureaucratic politics perspective (1976, 1980). He describes how we appear to others, and he describes objectively the dynamics we experience subjectively and onesidedly. This is a very useful study, made from a perspective close to that of the New Left Marxist and supplementary to it. Sztompka (1974) argues for the mutual usefulness of functionalists and Marxists, both of them objective system theorists. The functionalists study, and overemphasize, the bases of a social system's stability; Marxists concentrate too narrowly on the possibilities of system breakdown and self-transcendence. In these examples the perspectives overlap enough to make possible intelligible mutual criticism.

Where mutual criticism is cognitively possible, the point of criticism is to supplement a perspective at its weak points, by providing data it could not produce or focus on, alternative interpretations of data, alternative explanations; by revealing wishful thinking, reading of preconceptions into the data, and so on. Criticism therefore is most useful when it comes from a perspective that is opposite in some respect, though not a "deadly enemy." The opposition must be moderate enough to allow for communication, since otherwise most of the available polemical energy will be used in correcting misconceptions and fighting straw men, as with neoclassicists and Keynesians. In any case, the "deadly enemy" concept is a rhetorical exaggeration, as we see from Churchman's and Mitroff's examples.

In summary, if we give up the goal of a single comprehensive truth we are left with a plurality of slanted truths that conflict in varying degrees and ways. These truths are advanced by mutual criticism of moderately opposed perspectives, as well as by internal development ("normal science"). Criticism of extremely different perspectives is pointless because of the communication problem. Nor is it possible to invent a comprehensive synthesis of perspectives or a new critical perspective; we must work with the perspectives that are given by history.

V. The Royal Road to Objective Truth

We now have all the components needed to answer our original question, How can we revise the organization of perspectives in the policy sciences so as to improve the quality of our knowledge? And who are "we"? All that remains is to assemble the parts.

I argued in Chapter Twelve that the truth we seek in the policy sciences has at least three characteristics. 1) Since the society we seek to understand is our own, we seek to understand ourselves. We have been doing this in two opposite ways: from the inside, we understand ourselves as free, rational, creative, intentional. From the outside, we understand ourselves as determined or conditioned in various ways. Both sides are part of the same truth; we are both free and determined. 2) As free, we perceive the future as open; as determined, we are something actual in the present, and what we now are limits what changes are possible in the future. 3) The processes and dynamics that determine us have different periodicities. Some have rather short irregular cycles of three or four years and large, easily visible amplitude. Some build up over a ten-year period, then peter out.

Others continue, imperceptibly but inexorably, over a thirty to fifty year cycle or period. Still others take several centuries. Each requires conceptual and measuring instruments of a different magnifying power to bring into focus. Consequently to understand the dynamics of society we must separate the shorter and longer processes for individual study and then put them all together again. They are all part of the same truth.

No organization of science is adequate today unless it makes room for both freedom and determinism, the actual and the possible, the long run and the short run, and combines each pair effectively.

I argued in Part I that these characteristics of the truth have emerged out of the successive efforts of many schools of social scientists. Each school, impressed (because of its perspective) with some aspects of the truth, has striven to comprehend them and has neglected other, opposite aspects, gradually getting into difficulties as a result. A later school, impressed with the importance of what was omitted, has concentrated on the omitted portion with perhaps better but also partial results. For instance, the neoclassicists tried to treat us all as small businessmen, buying and selling our goods and services and trying to increase our net worth. Schumpeter and his followers, impressed with the narrowness of this attempt, exaggerated the differences between elite and mass, elite and counterelite, good and bad intellectuals.

The result has been a massive failure of communication and furious polemics, as each school defended its own partial truth and attacked the partial truths of other schools.

The succession of schools and their successive failure to carry out their own research programs has gradually brought the conflicting aspects of truth into awareness (Mannheim). The awareness first took the form of recognizing that an opposing school had made a few good points, which ought to be incorporated into one's own theory. The result was the one-sided neoclassical and Keynesian syntheses of the 1940's and 1950's. The research programs of the 1970's have come to recognize the need for a more comprehensive truth and a more comprehensive perspective that builds on and incorporates earlier perspectives. However, our achievement and even our recognition of the problems are still partial; the result is the conflicting syntheses of the 1970's.

At the present time, our more comprehensive perspectives, which build on and incorporate past perspectives, provide a basis for engaging in "normal science" with those who share our perspective. However, we know that we are still one-sided in some respects. In addition, when we survey the appalling history of past scientific blindness, how can we deny the possibility of our own blind spots? Consequently we still need the critical efforts of opposing perspectives, and we also should criticize opposing perspectives at their weak points (Churchman).

This is by no means a criticism of all against all, as Feyerabend may have temporarily favored for the natural sciences; such a principle is unhistorical. Criticism from one-sided perspectives that we have transcended is of no use to us. But criticisms from more comprehensive recent perspectives may be useful.

The need for criticism between opposed perspectives brings us back to the problem of communication. Criticism is useless unless it is both understanding and understood. Part I and Chapter Thirteen have brought out several bases for limited communication across standpoints and perspectives.

1. A similarity of standpoint, which produces similarity in the aims of science, type of problems recognized, and location of the utopia in time. The government-oriented professionals and the elite intellectuals have a similar standpoint; both can be called "technocrats" in that they are concerned with solving social problems from the top down, whether for reform or for mass quiescence. Both are concerned with immediate, practical, particularized problems. Conversely the anti-elitist, consumer-environmentalist, and Marxist standpoints are located in various parts of the bottom looking up, and are concerned with short- and long-run problems of oppression and exploitation. Similarities of standpoint produce empathy and a framework for communication but not necessarily mutual understanding.

2. A similarity of perspective, which provides the commensurable categories essential to communication. The best examples of similar perspectives are elitists and anti-elitists; also the Galbraithian-institutionalists and Marxists.

3. Moral similarity, which produces tolerance of intellectual differences. Tolerance is the essential prerequisite for the attempt to communicate across puzzling and untranslatable cognitive barriers. There are several instances. a) Neoclassicists and elitists vaguely share the values of individual freedom, upward mobility, and self-development, though the content of individuality differs. b) The various liberal standpoints of Chapters Four through Eight vaguely share the value of social reform with the goal of producing a more democratic and just societal community, but the meaning of "reform" varies. c) The Vietnam war produced shared moral opposition to US imperialism, to domestic and foreign oppression, among anti-elitists, bureaucratic-

institutionalists, Marxists, and ecologists, though the content of "oppression" varies.

Given these varied and overlapping bases of communication, a variety of communication patterns across standpoints are possible. From the various combinations that occur I single out four prominent research communities that have been active in the last twenty years. By "research community" I mean a set of schools from at least two standpoints who work together both critically and constructively. As it happens, the primary basis of unity for three of these four communities is moral, not intellectual. Such unity as exists across standpoints today rests mainly on a moral foundation; science is unified as well as fragmented by morality.

1. The individualist community includes mainly neoclassicists and elitists, with the elitists dominating. The two standpoints share the overriding value of individual freedom. Their categories, appropriately, are both subjectivist; they both see social institutions and history as the product of individual decisions or individual creativity. They both have an internationalist outlook. Each of these concepts or values has different meaning for the two standpoints.

One main area of debate is welfare measures and in general the role of government in promoting the public interest. This debate appears in the pages of the *Public Interest*. The journal, and the elitists, are concerned with finding effective solutions to the mass discontents and rising expectations that threaten elitist democracy. The neoclassicists—Solow, Banfield, J. Wilson, Feldstein, Laffer, Weidenbaum—insist that basic solutions are not possible, that brief superficial remedies are the most we can hope for, and that government is inherently incompetent at such tasks. Occasionally they defend the "little man" who is pushed around by elite welfare measures. A few social problems professionals join the debate and are welcomed by the elitists.

A second area of debate is how to protect the Free World against Communist aggression. One finds this debate in the pages of *Foreign Policy* and *Orbis*, though bureaucratic politics dissenters also appear in the former journal. The military-oriented organizations like RAND also join the debate. Here the theory—deterrence theory and game theory—is provided by the neoclassicists, and the hallucination—the Soviet Union or China as a scheming aggressive monster—has been provided by the elitists' case studies. See for example Possony, 1967.

This community overemphasizes the actual and neglects the possible; its utopias are mainly in the past.

2. By far the largest community is the liberal reformers. This group

is defined and controlled by the government-oriented professionals. It is a very tolerant group. All social scientists are welcome to join—that is, all professionals with some expertise in a specialty who are willing to be practical and constructive reformers. To many of its members this group seems to be coextensive with the policy sciences; "policy science," after all, refers to all knowledge that may be useful for improving government policy. The only people left outside are the extremists, dilettante intellectuals, Cold Warriors, and impractical utopians.

The policy science of this community is short run, objective, oriented to the actual with its utopia in the present or very near the present, nationalistic, and dualistic in the sense that subjectivity, freedom, and value are located in government. Its foci are the proliferating specialized Sage journals; the whole institutional complex surrounding the government and private research foundations from NSF down, except for the military-oriented foundations; and the older professional journals.

This community neglects the long run and is limited by its fact-value, freedom-determinism dualism.

3. Mannheim's discussion of the intellectuals alerts one to the possibility of an unspecialized community united around the elite-intellectual-mass categories, where discussion ranges freely and loosely over the changes taking place in mass society. Opposition would center on one's attitude toward these changes, and on hopes and expectations for the future; these oppositions come from differences of standpoint. A focus for such discussion is unspecialized journals like *Society*. This community focuses on the short run and the actual.

4. We are all of us members of the fourth community. I say "all" because I believe that anyone who has read this far with understanding or at least sympathy belongs in the fourth community. The others, I fear, will by now have given up in disgust or incomprehension. We are the people who have been awakened (or perhaps misled and blinded) by the Vietnam war, by the failed poverty program, by Third World impoverishment, and by the ecological crisis. The perspectives included are those of Chapters Seven through Ten, plus some left Keynesians on some limited issues (for example the Keynesian contributors to Schwartz, 1977).

The basis of unity is moral—revulsion against a system that promotes mass killing and military rule around the world, that systematically draws in and destroys the world's resources in pursuit of endless, meaningless growth, that treats worker and community as

resources to be exploited and then discarded, that has even learned to
exploit future generations by piling up nuclear and chemical wastes.
There are, however, also considerable cognitive similarities to facilitate communication, which have been described earlier.

Moral unity is maintained for many of us by participation in the
antinuclear movement. Here ecological activists, Marxists, and
consumer-environmentalists experience a community of action that
transcends difference of standpoint.

The institutional foci of this community are, first, a broad spectrum
of newer journals like *Politics and Society, Working Papers, Theory
and Society, The Insurgent Sociologist, Telos,* and *Antipode.* These
journals are radical but are not controlled by any one perspective or
specialty. Second, the new left organizations like URPE and CNPS,
each with its own journal. These journals and organizations all grew
out of the antiwar movement and preserve the moral unity of that
movement. They are also developing connections with the multiperspective antinuclear movement. Third, there are almost monthly
conferences on specialized topics like radical education, energy, the
Soviet Union, which draw together scholars from various perspectives.

In addition each school maintains its own distinctness with its own
journals and its own conferences. The institutionalists have the
Journal of Economic Issues; the environmentalists have a multitude of
journals like *Environmental Action*, where one can see the shift to an
ecological perspective taking place; Marxists have *Kapitalistate, New
Left Review, Socialist Review, Monthly Review,* and others; the
anarchists have *New Roots.* Thus participation in a multiperspective
community does not mean submerging or losing one's own
perspective.

The fourth community includes the short-run theory of the critical
intellectuals, the Cambridge left Keynesians, and the Galbraithian-
bureaucratic-institutionalists; the mainly long-run theory of the Marxists and ecologists; a synthesis of subjective and objective components,
with the subjectivist mass perspective balancing the primarily objective emphasis of the other three perspectives; and a predominently
utopian mentality balanced by the present orientation of the mass
perspective. The breadth of the community enables us to incorporate
the achievements of the older perspectives: the neoclassical and
Keynesian models, game theory and cybernetics, functionalist and
system theories. For many of us these schools are our direct ancestors
and deserve our filial respect for their historic past achievements. The
work of Keynes, Parsons, Schumpeter, Redfield belongs to the

foundations of modern social science and as such still repays continuing study. Our own traditionalists like Mandel and Rosdolsky maintain our connection with the wisdom of the ancients, the Wise Men like Marx, Engels, and Veblen, and are an essential part of our community.

The main weakness of the fourth community is its predominantly utopian orientation. Our utopias are in the future, and we are much more sensitive to the possible that is coming to be than to the actual that stubbornly persists. Mannheim's critique of the utopian mentality (1936, Chapter 4) applies to us. The main spokesmen for the persistence of the actual are critical intellectuals like Gouldner and Piven, participant-observers of underdog life like Howard Becker, anti-elitists like Domhoff, and bureaucratic politics theorists like Schurmann, and we should take their work very seriously. Most of these spokesmen belong to the mass perspective of Chapter Seven, so this perspective is an essential part of the fourth community. I am convinced by Prewitt and Stone's argument (1973) that the anti-elitist perspective is one necessary ingredient of an adequate social science, and books like theirs and Prewitt, 1970, show the usefulness of the perspective.

As for the older perspectives, we can ignore their current work. They have little new to contribute to our practical concerns. Criticism of this work is pointless; they would not understand. In particular we should avoid getting caught up in the tolerant, friendly professionalism of the government advisers. These people may well want an occasional radical critic in their research projects, but only on the condition that he abandon his utopian fantasies and concentrate on the practical question of improving government policy or organization. Instead we should concentrate our efforts at dialogue on the nearby perspectives of the fourth community, where the prospects of effective communication are much better and the practical concerns are very similar.

The four research communities embody four different sets of practical concerns. For the first community science is an instrument committed to the defense of individual freedom, in various senses including elitist democracy and freedom of contract and discussion. For the second community science is an instrument of control of society, as epitomized in Meade's *The Controlled Economy* (1972), and an instrument of social reform. This sort of science requires objectivized subject matter and much attention to measurement, since measurement is a prerequisite of control. For the third community science is a process of broad observation, reflection, and criticism. This process requires unspecialized, detached, but critical observers. For the fourth community science is a means of emancipation; its long-range goal is a freedom for the many that does not yet exist, in contrast to the first community's freedom for the few that already exists.

The main problem for the fourth community, as for the social sciences in general, is still communication across perspectives. Too many people have still not learned to live with differences of perspective even among those with a common cause. The overt message of this book is that diversity of perspective will continue to exist among us in the foreseeable future, and we have to learn to communicate even though we speak different languages. When a reviewer writes, "Sherman has modernized the traditional Marxist tract by paying homage to a modicum of twentieth century economic theory" (S. Gordon, 1973, p. 688) of a book that is anything but traditional, he is really expressing his intolerance of Sherman's Marxist standpoint.

The basis of communication is tolerance of differences. But active tolerance consists in learning to think in the categories of the other perspective, even if one wishes later to criticize the perspective. Several rules will help.

1. Locate the standpoint by seeing where the author and his school place their subjectivity and their objectivity. Notice whether the theory is mainly long run or short run, etc. Notice the difference from your own standpoint, and respect that difference.

2. Locate the problems and basic categories.

3. Interpret the theory in terms of *its* concerns and categories, not your own; interpret concepts in terms of the categorial set. As I indicated earlier, this should not be impossible because of the various similarities of perspective.

4. Don't pick on one proposition or conclusion or interpretation as evidence that the whole theory ought to be discarded. Living theories do not stand or fall as a unit; they can be corrected, shifted around, broadened or narrowed. Weak points are grounds for criticism, not wholesale dismissal. One example is Poulantzas' wholesale dismissal of functionalism because it cannot recognize a separate political subsystem (1973). His evidence is Parsons, 1951, a particular stage in a particular branch of functionalism. As it happens, Parsons corrected this error in his next major work but one, Parsons and Smelser, 1956, and since then he has written a great deal on the political subsystem (Parsons, 1969b). Is Poulantzas' error a reason for wholesale dismissal of Poulantzas' ideas? Certainly not.

5. Don't pick out an extreme version of a theory as representative of a whole tradition. This tactic does not permit the tradition to display its full potentialities. In fact the opposite tactic is preferable: pick out the version closest to your own position. The differences that remain are the ones worth criticizing.

6. In providing empirical refutation of a theory, don't assume that your own data are perfect. Data are very tricky, slippery things. In particular, don't enthusiastically report the latest still unpublished findings as conclusive disproof of a theory. Too many people have fooled themselves like that.

7. Don't assume that because you have followed the above rules you have eliminated all bias. Bias persists through our attempts to eliminate it, just as, Freud taught us, the Unconscious gets its way even around and through our attempts to repress it.

In summary, I have now answered the original question of this book. We are all part of a multiperspective community, one of several overlapping research communities in the social sciences. We can improve the work of this community, externally, by attentively studying the work of those who emphasize the persistence of the actual, who insist that things will never change except for more of what we already have—when they present some evidence. The other schools and traditions outside our community we should respect as our ancestors, part of the cumulative history of science which we have absorbed into our own thinking. We look to these traditions for ideas, not for truth; they are blind to large and important aspects of society and we must go beyond them to find truth. Still, we can check occasionally to make sure.

Internally, we can work within our own perspective to develop its possibilities. All of our separate research programs are new, and much remains to be done. We can be sensitized to our own weaknesses by attending to criticisms from opposite standpoints or perspectives within the community. External criticism we can ignore. Finally, we can criticize the weak points of other perspectives, but only after we have learned to think in their terms and absorbed their positive contributions.

Fifteen The Growth of Science

How does science progress? The evidence in Part I should provide some suggestions for an answer. If the goal of science is truth, then we should expect to see some progress toward it in the last fifty years.

Probably fifty years is too short a span to provide a general answer, since we do not know how representative this period is. A longer history might reveal a repetitive cyclical pattern, or long waves of alternating progress and stagnation, or irregularity. The pattern of growth in the policy sciences may also be quite different from the patterns in other areas of science.

Also the evidence in Part I is by no means definitive. Part I is history as experienced, but any such history must be corrected by a long series of reflective histories which reinterpret and rewrite. Perhaps fifty years from now the progress that seems so evident now will be reinterpreted as an illusion; can we deny the possibility? There are individuals, say Levi-Strauss, who are convinced that their own work over forty years represents progress, even spectacular progress, but others may want to assert the contrary. The following propositions are therefore meant only as inductive generalizations.

1. It is no longer necessary to discuss the proposition that science grows by the linear accumulation of verified truths to be collected in a Berelson–Steiner inventory. Anyone who still takes that idea seriously should study the experimental work of Clark Hull and his students in the 1930's, culminating in his *Mathematico-Deductive*

Theory of Rote Learning (1940) and *Principles of Behavior* (1943). These works were packed full of verified truths. Logical empiricists like Bergmann hailed Hull's work as a shining example of how science progresses; but by the time Hull died in 1952 the whole program had been abandoned. Some experimentalists went into statistical learning theory; others picked up an entirely different concept of the nervous system involving feedback, reverberating nets, TOTE units, and the like, and started constructing electric turtles and talking typewriters. Nor can one say with the Popperians that science progressed when Hull's hypotheses were refuted; they were not refuted, they were abandoned. The idea that they had been verified was also abandoned. It turned out that Hull's data were no good; they were not adequately controlled.

2. Another proposition that is no longer tenable is the idea that science progresses by professional specialization. The theory goes as follows: originally there were philosophers who speculated about everything but investigated nothing in particular. Then physicists separated off a small domain and studied it intensively enough to learn something. As their knowledge grew they had to subdivide the domain so that each part could be studied more intensively. Similarly, the social sciences split off from philosophy one by one, then subdivided again and again. Sociology divided into urban, rural, demography, criminology, social psychology . . . ; the latter divided into leadership, communication nets, cooperation and conflict, etc. One could trace this process by noting the ever more specialized journals and the new specialties appearing in national convention programs.

The crucial difficulty with this program is that society is not divided into compartments that are intelligible in isolation. Specialized research that ignores the larger dynamics of society produces partial and superficial explanations at best. What is needed is specialized research that builds on some understanding of overall dynamics, that is, an antispecialist or collective-nondisciplinary organization of science.

3. The growth pattern that Kuhn found in the natural sciences does not occur in the policy sciences. My students have recognized this and uneasily described themselves as being in a pre-paradigm state, following Kuhn, without knowing exactly what they ought to do about that. But this is nonsense. "Pre-paradigm" is nothing more than a negative term indicating that Kuhn's pattern has not occurred. For economics at least, "post-paradigm" would be more accurate. In 1930 there was one almost universal paradigm, or disciplinary matrix as

Kuhn now calls it, the neoclassical, with several schools and branches. Members of the Swedish school were doing interesting things and seemed to be in the forefront of economics. There was also a small, diffuse institutionalist trend—Veblen, Commons, Mitchell—that reacted against the neoclassical paradigm even while using its concepts. Since 1930 new "paradigms" have proliferated. The same proliferation has occurred throughout the policy sciences; for instance, Mullins' careful delineation of theory groups in sociology shows how variety has increased in the 1960's (Mullins, 1973). Garson's history of Bentleyan group theory traces its rise to a position of being a unifying conceptual framework for much of political science in the 1950's and then its decline to one among many research areas in the 1970's (Garson, 1978). Baumberger (1977) argues that even in the nineteenth century the advent of the neoclassicists did not follow Kuhn's pattern; it was a proliferation of paradigms, not a revolutionary replacement of a failed paradigm by a new one. To be sure, this proliferation of "paradigms" in economics seems like regression to Hayek, who has written (1976) of a "lost generation" of economists since 1935.

Nor can one say that the whole period since 1930 has been a "revolutionary" period with the end nowhere in sight. This is too broad a generalization to convey any positive meaning. In addition most of the research fits the pattern of Kuhn's "normal science"; most communication is within a community.

The concept "multiple paradigms" or better still "multiplying paradigms" at least starts us in the right direction. However, this concept cannot even be expressed in Kuhn's revised terminology (Kuhn, 1977)! The pattern is the one favored by Feyerabend rather than by Kuhn; by Feyerabend's principles progress has been spectacular.

I turn now to positive assertions.

4. The policy sciences grow by the establishment of new perspectives alongside the old. The new perspectives reflect changes in society; they are primarily a product of society, not of science. The precipitating event is some spectacular crisis whose standard interpretation is obviously unsatisfactory—unemployment, Cold War, poverty, war, environmental degradation. The standard interpretation is unsatisfactory both because it describes the crisis as an unpredictable accident (according to Keynesian Arthur Okun, 1972, the Vietnam war was a unique event) and because it provides no remotely adequate way to deal with the crisis. One could say that the crisis is an "anomaly" which reveals the limitations of previous perspectives—to some people only.

The precipitating event produces excitement and confusion, as well as appeals for calmness and order. A new perspective emerges as concepts for interpreting the crisis are systematized *in opposition* to some prevailing system of concepts. The new concepts define an Object within which the crisis is located and which enables one to interpret the crisis. Or they reinterpret a respected Subject as oppressive, for example, Mills' *Power Elite* (1956).

The Subject or standpoint is also provided by society; it is either a stratum or class that is coming to self-consciousness and organized activity, or some growing, active branch of government.

Finally the new perspective has to provide a location for the scientists themselves. The location defines their identity, relates them to the Subject in some way, and somehow justifies their intellectual competence to understand the crisis. Here again the available identities are provided by society, not invented by scientists. They are provided by the existing occupations or statuses that are open to thinkers.

The two basic identities available since 1930 have been "professional" and "intellectual." The problem for both Old and New Left has been that both of these identities were contaminated by association, first with capitalism and later with the Vietnam war and imperialist oppression. The main Old Left response was to take the identity of "bourgeois intellectual who has gone over to the side of the proletariat." However, this identity denied the intellectual's competence to understand society adequately because of his ineradicable middle-class origin or training. The truth had to come from outside, namely from the Party of the Proletariat. The Old Leftist's career had to be a continuous guilt-ridden practice of self-denial, eradication of his own ineradicable bourgeois impulses, and slavish submission to the Party line. "I live; yet not I, but Christ lives in me." This degrading spectacle (or noble spectacle) was at least intelligible, because society had provided no other acceptable identity.

The New Left faced the same problem and responded by frantically searching for a way to relate to the working class—wearing overalls, drinking beer, working in the steel mills. The problem was solved for some of us when we realized that we ourselves were paying dues to a union and had our own arrogant employer. Our own experience connected us to the dynamics of capitalism. For instance, we notice Lenin's "trade union consciousness" as a bureaucratic phenomenon in our union officials, not as an occupational phenomenon. Others solved the problem by rehabilitating the intellectual or professional roles or by joining communes. In any case we need no Party to bring

us the truth from Moscow. The Maoists revived the Old Left identity
when it was no longer needed, playing out the old farce of personal
redemption and missionary work.

Once a new perspective has come into existence, the development of
its potentialities—the research program—requires decades of empirical
research. Society provides the perspectives, but scientists have to
develop the potentialities and produce the actual theories and data.
The structure of science, its standpoints and perspectives, is a product
and reflection of society. Scientific knowledge, however, feeds back on
society and changes it. Knowledge is praxis, as Markovic has argued
(1968, Chapter 2), not reflection of society.

5. The evaluations in Part I suggest that new perspectives have
been more comprehensive and complex than their predecessors, partly
because they originate as remedies for glaring inadequacies of their
predecessors and partly because they incorporate some of the older
concepts in a subordinate position. For instance, both Keynes and
Schumpeter reacted against obvious inadequacies of the neoclassical
perspective but both also incorporated neoclassical models. The reverse incorporation of the newer by the older, with distortions and
some loss of meaning, also occurs to some extent. Thus the policy
sciences grow by increasing complexity of theoretical frameworks and
increasing variety of data.

Perhaps some older concepts are lost for the new perspectives due to
incompatibility, and some older data are forgotten or made unintelligible. It is possible that some future new perspective will be narrower
than its predecessors and will lose more than it contributes by the
correction of older blind spots.

6. The policy sciences also grow by the gradual elimination of
antiquated perspectives. Antiquation results from changes in society,
which throw up institutions, processes, and problems that cannot be
adequately conceptualized from the old perspectives. The crisis that
precipitates a new perspective is only the most spectacular indication
that silent changes have gradually accumulated in a transformation of
society. Processes and institutions that once were typical—for instance
the Austrian wine industry, the typical process of production for
Böhm-Bawerk—become peripheral, and formerly marginal processes
expand and develop into central institutions with their own marginal
offshoots. The assumptions and models built to explain the old
processes do not fit the new ones as well, if at all; this incongruity
calls for either a modification of the old models or a denunciation of
the new processes and institutions as a threat to a free society. The
categories of the old perspectives limit the changes that are possible in

the old models and limit the imagination needed to construct new models.

At the same time the assumptions and models that were more or less adequate to explain the old processes are being incorporated to some extent into newer perspectives, perhaps with losses. Thus the old perspectives gradually become useless to science and remain useful only for propaganda. However, they continue in existence on the fringes of science as long as the class whose experience they express is still active.

The best example of this process in recent experience is the long, gradual decay of the neoclassical perspective. Its antiquation resulted from changes in society under way long before 1930. The main change was the rise of the large corporation. This produced oligopolistic market structures in which market power and financial strategies determined the outcome of industrial conflict, not the neoclassicist's supply and demand curves. It also produced the new phenomena of organizational politics and decision-making for which there was no neoclassic political theory. The large corporation also gained control over technology in its R & D departments, its foundations and research institutes, and its captive university departments (Noble, 1977); henceforth changes in technology were determined neither by unpredictable human inventiveness nor by consumer demand, but by corporate strategy decisions and science policy.

Accompanying the corporations were the financiers, who produced a set of new financial-legal instruments and developed systems of credit that made the older concept of money obsolete. Gradually a whole portfolio of credit instruments replaced paper money and gold certificates as the principal medium of circulation, just as the latter had earlier replaced actual gold coins and bars; the quantity theory of money followed the gold theory into irrelevance.

A parallel rise in government organization produced the phenomena of bureaucratic politics and bureaucratic symbiosis. These are forms of nonelectoral politics that burst the bounds of the old theory of rational–individualist electoral politics. They also constitute nonmarket decision-making, to which the neoclassic categories are poorly adapted.

Another manifestation of bureaucratic politics was the proliferation of administrative agencies and regulatory boards, both public and private. These produced a whole field of quasilegal decisions, new forms of power and influence, new modes of bargaining and politicking. The neoclassic concept of a permanent legal framework kept in repair by rational debate and electoral politics became completely irrelevant to reality.

The rise of government and private corporations also meant that economic fluctuations could now be influenced by government and corporate action. Consequently a demand appeared for scientific interpretation of short-run economic and social trends, a demand which the neoclassic categories could not satisfy.

At the international level new forms of imperialism appeared that could not even be described within the old political categories. New forms of international organization appeared, such as multinational corporations, that bypassed or transcended the old anarchic organization of independent, self-contained states.

The retreat of the neoclassicists before these new phenomena was long and gradual. Already in 1885 Marshall was warning economists that not all men act like City bankers, and they had best be cautious in applying their models to non-monetary phenomena. The accumulating reports of preliterate economies gave support to the institutionalist argument that the neoclassic models applied only to a particular, and changing, economic system. In the 1930's economists were recognizing one exception after another, even in the civilized monetary world, of people who did not act "rationally." However, they saved their models by calling these exceptions a name—"irrational." They were deviations from the models, and could be ignored. Thus the models gradually turned into tautologies, impervious to negative evidence. The corporations were denounced as a threat to a free society, and the new oligopolistic markets, mergers, and holding companies were dismissed as infringements of the antitrust laws. If government would only do its job of law enforcement the corporations would disappear as Standard Oil had disappeared, and neoclassic theory would be relevant again.

The appearance of Keynesian models after 1935 made it more difficult to ignore phenomena that did not fit the neoclassic models. Phenomena like mass unemployment, "irrationality," and uncertainty were being studied and modelled by Keynesians, however bizarre and misguided the models may have seemed, so it became implausible to exclude such phenomena from the scope of science. It was necessary, rather, to give a better explanation of them than the Keynesians were able to do.

To this end a whole series of concepts was invented that seemed to deal with the obstinate phenomena but that on closer inspection actually assumed them away. An example from the 1940's was "certainty equivalent." This seemed to incorporate Keynesian uncertainty by treating the "risks" associated with an investment as a cost; but the assignment of probability numbers to risks actually assumed uncertainty away. If one could know the exact probability of an event's occurrence there would be no uncertainty about it. Or the importance of uncertainty could be recognized by postulating a "precautionary" motive for saving; but in practice this meant that one added an unknown amount "Pr" to S in the model and then proceeded as before. Friedman's distinction between money and credit, which seems like an exercise in clarification, is actually a device to assume away the troublesome credit system. The concept of a natural rate of unemployment seems to admit that unemployment indeed continues to exist; but in the model the "natural" rate is functionally equivalent to "full employment." That is, the system automatically returns to the natural rate after any disturbance. Unemployment does exist, but nothing can be done about it. And since there are many natural rates (Lucas, 1978), any actual rate can be called natural with a little effort. Moreover, all unemployment is voluntary: 1) There is always some job at some wage available somewhere, but the unemployed choose not to accept it (Lucas, 1978). 2) The reason might be a preference for leisure, either intermittently or at some wage rate; some people have a "taste for leisure." It turns out that women and blacks are the ones who have a taste for intermittent employment; thus the concept disposes of racism and sexism instantly by blaming the victim. Or 3) The unemployed are really searching for a better job, and continue to search until the value of the new information is no longer worth the cost (Alchian, in Phelps, 1970). Unlike the earlier concepts, the "search" explanation for unemployment can actually be tested, and the evidence is dead against it (Tobin, 1972a). Administered prices and the wage-price spiral can also be translated into "natural rate of unemployment" and thus rendered invisible (Wachter, 1976). Keynesian expectations seem to be incorporated into Muth's concept of "rational expectations," which says that people can accurately forecast the effects of government policy, apart from random errors. However, this concept tacitly assumes away uncertainty emanating from the economy, by focusing on government policy as the source of uncertainty.

The "natural rate of investment" concept assumes away the Keynesian phenomena of liquidity preference and animal spirits as unknowable short-run deviations, and thereby eliminates Keynesian explanations of business cycles by definition. The "crowding out" concept, which assumes that a natural rate of employment and of investment are now occurring, asserts that government fiscal policy is pointless because government must compete with private industry for the fixed quantity of investment money available. Thus the concept of countercyclical fiscal policy disappears.[10] In international economics the "small country" assumption, that each country is a price taker, assumes away all large-country and multinational corporate influence on international investment and trade, i.e., the whole politics of international finance.

Recent neoclassicists no longer denounce corporations as illegal, power-mad, and inefficient, like their predecessors did in the 1930's; instead they observe that corporations, too, must compete in the market. This looks like a concession to reality until one notices the tacit assumption that corporations compete *in the same way* that small businessmen do. Thus market power and game strategies are assumed away, and the planning sector of the economy disappears from view.

Finally, the concept of "external costs" seems to recognize the existence of ecological effects and open a whole new area for cost-benefit analysis. However, the concept gives the analyst no clues as to how to locate the costs, so he has to fall back on his standard concept of "effects on individual utilities." The external cost of totally polluting a lake consists of the transportation costs to the nearest unpolluted lake, for all former users of the lake (example cited by Bruce McFarlane, in Lindbeck, 1977, p. 189). In other words the concept actually serves to assume away ecological effects by reducing them to individual preferences. The related concepts of "neighborhood effects" and "spillover effects" further suggest that the effects are trivial and involve only a few unlucky bystanders who get spilled on by accident.

The other half of the neoclassicist-monetarist defense action is a set of techniques to produce data that fit these increasingly absurd concepts. Friedman devised a series of hypothetical constructs that enabled monetarists to produce the desired data: permanent income, permanent velocity, permanent prices (Friedman, 1959), and temporary stock of purchasing power. These are all subjective constructs, entirely appropriate for a subjective–individualist perspective. That is, if individual decisions are the causes of all social change, scientists need to work with the categories that individuals actually use in making decisions, and these are subjective categories. However, the monetarist does not get at these categories directly, by participant observation or experimentation, since his Subject is the individual in general; he estimates their value from statistical data. There is no valid or reliable way to get an objective measure of subjective magnitudes from statistical data, so in practice the monetarist estimates whatever values produce regularities in the raw data (Laumas and Mohabbat,

1972). For instance, Friedman in 1957 estimated permanent income as a weighted average of three years' objective income; others in the 1960's used different weights and time spans. Friedman found that M_2 correlated best with his monetary postulates, so he called that "money," but others used M_1 or M_{1B}. Critics could be charged with "a very narrow interpretation of the data" (Wachter, 1976, p. 69) and refuted by re-estimations of the subjective magnitudes. In addition some data could be simply discarded as tainted by external disturbances which are excluded by the *ceteris paribus* clause. As a result "... the 'testing of hypotheses' is frequently merely a euphemism for obtaining plausible numbers to provide ceremonial adequacy for a theory chosen and defended on *a priori* grounds" (Harry Johnson, 1971a).

What future now remains for the adherents of the neoclassical perspective? They can continue to construct ever more arbitrary models supported by ever more complex data juggling; for instance a theory of the firm as a multiplicity of implicit contracts that are continuously and simultaneously being renegotiated (Alchian and Demsetz, 1972). The Walrasian auctioneer lives! Or they can do normative work. Since the real world, with its corporations, credit system, labor unions, etc. no longer conforms to the neoclassic perspective, they can make up dreams of a pure neoclassic world (Hayek, 1960; Buchanan, 1962, 1975). There would be a permanent simple legal framework constructed by rational discussion, no unions, a tax and tariff structure that eliminate big business, minimal government, strict limits on majority rule, and no non-electoral politics. They can even try to bring this pure neoclassic world into existence, like Harberger and his students in Chile after 1973, with the kind assistance of some soldier-statesmen.

Such developments move ever further from science and deeper into fantasy. The one remaining useful route for the neoclassicists is to recognize the very limited validity of their perspective, and to treat it as a supplement to other, broader perspectives. Machlup is an example of this possibility. After decades of work with marginalist models, he came to admit that these models are very limited in scope, dealing only with the direction of changes in a certain class of decisions (Machlup, 1967). *Homo oeconomicus* is only one of many possible ideal types useful to science (Machlup, 1970). Similarly, James Q. Wilson is now admitting that cost–benefit calculation is a very limited aspect of behavior (Wilson, 1975, pp. 203-204). Consequently, the cost–benefit approach to crime is no panacea; increasing the opportunity cost of crime will at most have some deterrent effect on some people for some crimes some of the time—a very hard proposition to disagree with (1975, Chapter 8; 1977).

Once the neoclassicist recognizes the limited validity of his perspective, he can participate in a multiperspective research community as specialist in the subjective-individualist aspect of society. The rational choice theorists, except for the Virginia school, have developed such a community around the mathematical modeling method. Others have gravitated into the first two research communities where they collaborate with elitists or social problems specialists.

7. The same changes in society that present problems to old perspectives and reduce their relevance provide opportunities for newer perspectives. Adherents of the old perspectives must necessarily regard these changes as accidents, chance intrusions into normal trends, and therefore sources of confusion rather than enlightenment. However from the newer perspectives the changes are not accidental; they represent the further working out of the developmental potentialities of our society. Large corporations grew out of small ones under the pressure of market forces and opportunities; they therefore reveal what market forces can produce. Large government grew out of small government. International trade, multinational corporations, and neocolonialism grew out of market pressures and bureaucratic dynamics; and so on. These developments brought into the open the hidden potentialities of our society and therefore made it possible for us to understand ourselves better. As Aristotle taught, in order to understand the inherent characteristics of some system one should study the mature form in which those characteristics are fully developed. Our society is more mature than it was a century ago and therefore more knowable in itself (in the Aristotelian, not the Hegelian sense). Some structures that once seemed to be part of the nature of things, like sex roles, turn out to be changeable (as anthropologists observed long ago); some stocks that once seemed infinite and free, like air, raw materials, and garbage dumps, turn out to be systemically interdependent. Our ancestors could not have understood these things, because the society they studied was more undeveloped and enigmatic in itself than the society we study.

8. Up to this point I have described how changes in society cause growth in science by replacing older perspectives with newer perspectives, and by providing more knowable subject-matter for these perspectives. There are also internal aspects of growth. Perspectives grow old and die, but they leave behind their mathematical models.[11] Models can be reinterpreted, modified, and incorporated in larger models or systems of models. Over the decades our stock of models and

model construction techniques has grown steadily, and this has made possible much greater flexibility in interpreting social structures and dynamics. We no longer need to depend on the crude partial equilibrium method, which misleadingly isolates individual changes from their social context by assuming that all other factors are in equilibrium. This technique is useful today only as a propaganda device for hiding reality behind its *ceteris paribus* clause.

9. There is a similar accumulation of techniques of data gathering and processing. Participant observation and historical case studies have been enriched by sampling techniques and techniques for manipulation of statistics. Statistical techniques in turn have grown enormously.

10. Finally, the accumulating knowledge of perception, decision processes, socialization, identification and identity maintenance, feeds back to improve the practice of science research. As we learn more about ourselves we become more aware of the nonrational and unconscious processes involved in research, and become able to control them in part. The naive experimenters and questionnaire constructors of the 1930's and 1940's thought they were discovering the real, objective facts, not knowing the many ways in which they participated in constructing those facts. The rationalist model-builders thought they could capture the truth by infallible reasoning based on obvious or self-evident or generally valid assumptions—and could discover the obvious errors in others' reasoning and assumptions. In these and other ways we of the fourth research community have become more cautious in our claims and careful in our procedures.

The accumulation of models, and of empirical techniques, and of caution and error control, and of experience with capitalism, and of vigorous neighboring perspectives that can bring out each other's blind spots, and the increased awareness of the characteristics of the truth we seek, give us the opportunity to produce better theories and data than our predecessors. If we use this opportunity, science will progress. Unless—the present crisis of capitalism simmers down, the rising dissatisfied classes again become quiescent and lose their own self-respect, and the newer perspectives consequently become isolated from the social process, become scholastic and stagnant like Orthodox Marxism. In that case the old perspectives will reassert themselves and science will regress. It has happened before. The growth of science is primarily a reflection of the growth of society.

Notes

1. The social sciences are presumably partly similar and partly different from the natural sciences; and there are also large differences among various natural and biological sciences. These circumstances have enabled philosophers of science to sustain a dispute over whether social science is the same or different from natural science. The various arguments have been all the more dogmatic when they have been based on only sketchy acquaintance with the social sciences: casual reading of a few bestsellers or some collection of articles, sustained observation of one group at the Center for Advanced Study in the Behavioral Sciences, conversations with two or three economist friends, selective attention to a few critical commentaries or book reviews taken out of context. I intend the present work to be completely neutral on questions of how similar to the natural sciences the social sciences are, have been, could be, or ought to be. I do not have the empirical knowledge needed to deal with any of these questions; nor do I know of anyone who has or ever had such knowledge.
2. By Braithwaite's calculation Matthew's optimum strategy is to play his trumpet 26 out of every 43 nights; by Raiffa's calculation Matthew's optimum strategy is to play on 16 of every 23 nights. Most trumpet players would not be able to perform either calculation.
3. The episode lasted only a few years. "Since about the mid-1960's strategic deterrence has been primarily a technical specialty for systems analysts and operations researchers associated with the services and the Office of the Secretary of Defense . . . rather than an active area of inquiry by political and other social scientists" (George and Smoke, 1974, p. 40). However, the pseudoscience of the military analysts continues to appear. Wohlstetter (1974) uses elaborate data displays and newly declassified excerpts from secret documents to lend hocus-pocus plausibility to an argument that there is no armaments race, and besides the US is falling behind the SU and needs a bigger military budget to catch up.

4. No achievement at all, comments Schumpeter (1954, p. 1179). Anyone could construct such a model if he were willing to make bizarre enough assumptions, and in the freakish conditions of deep depression one could even find empirical support for such models.
5. Those cynics who doubt the compatibility of science with hope and faith should consider the following statement by two scientific proponents of nuclear power:

> The number of shipments of nuclear wastes expected to 1995 are shown in Table 8.1. However, no shipments will occur before 1983 because spent fuel will not be reprocessed before 1977 and then the wastes will probably be cooled for 5 to 10 years before shipment. Shipments will originate at the reprocessing plants (West Valley, New York; Barnwell, South Carolina; and possibly Morris, Illinois plus an unnamed site for a new plant) and go to the location of a federal repository whose site has not yet been selected (Campana and Langer, 1976, p. 41). Start up of reprocessing plants has been delayed (p. 45).

The West Valley plant has been closed since 1972, written off and abandoned by the company owning it; the Barnwell plant construction had been stopped before 1976, when the authors were listing it as a plant; the Morris plant, as the authors note on p. 45, has technical problems and requires extensive modifications if it is to be made operational; the unnamed site was never selected. The underlying problem is that there is as yet no economically feasible reprocessing technology and no economically feasible method of permanent storage.

This is an example of faith in technology and industry rather than in the consumer. The authors knew that they were writing about plants that were not operating, and technology that did not exist, but they had faith that the technology would develop on schedule. And of course they assure us that they are completely objective in their judgments, and their mentality has not been influenced in any way by their occupation as nuclear consultants. The issue between pro-nuclear and anti-nuclear scientists is not one of science vs. faith, but one of faith in technology vs. faith in the public. Or rather faith in a profit-oriented technology vs. faith in an appropriate human technology.

6. Harrington criticizes Piven and Cloward's interpretation of the poverty program as a legitimation tactic by pointing out that the urban riots occurred after the program had started (1976, pp. 303–306). However, the architects of the poverty program were quite aware even before 1960 of the serious urban problems associated with the black migrants, as Marris and Rein (1967) and Moynihan (1969) indicate. It did not take riots to awaken the administration to the existence of a legitimation problem; rising crime, juvenile delinquency, and unemployment rates were sufficient. In addition Jennings (1978) finds a strong state-by-state correlation between occurrence of urban riots and increase in welfare rolls, holding other factors like unemployment rates constant; welfare is another legitimation tactic discussed by Piven and Cloward.

7. Marcus–LaRouche's US Labor Party is a sad case of a party moving from a promising beginning in 1968 to collective psychosis by 1973. They see

the world as run by CIA agents: Mao and Chou, Assad and Ben-Gurion, Brandt and Berlinguer, Avakian and Marcy. The political struggles among these agents are CIA plots; another US plot to start World War III in early 1976 was foiled by its timely exposure to the party faithful (see *New Solidarity*). Marxist friends have invariably protested that my characterization of the Labor Party as insane is far too charitable. They prefer to not even mention this repulsive organization (for example O'Brien, 1978, ignores them). But I see no difference in organization or tactics between the Labor Party and the Maoist parties. Each claims to be the only authentic vanguard party possessing the whole Marxist truth, and condemns all other parties and individuals as counterrevolutionary traitors. Such exclusivism naturally leads to paranoid schizophrenia.

8. "The brute fact is that, with presently visible techniques and at present energy prices, the solar energy that falls on the average square meter of the earth is at the moment not worth picking up. If it is to be worth picking up prices must rise sharply . . ." (Boulding, 1976, p. 89). Here is the straight neoclassical conceptual scheme, in which market price measures social value, whereas Commoner has labored to demonstrate that price and social value are very different things. Boulding ignores external costs, while Commoner points to the high external costs of oil, coal, and nuclear energy not reflected in their prices. Boulding assumes technology as an autonomous given, while Commoner points to corporate government funding for nuclear and petrochemical research rather than solar research; consequently the potential economies of solar energy are not yet available. Boulding assumes that price reflects consumer demand, which is based on autonomous preferences, while Commoner shows that present agriculture, transportation, and petrochemical technology resulted not from consumer demand but from market-expansion tactics of corporations using market power. Boulding's review simply ignores Commoner's whole argument and dogmatically asserts the neoclassical concepts.

9. My evidence is the content of the articles by neoclassical writers in the *Public Interest* since 1966, plus citations and discussions in neoclassic writings.

10. For a recent example of "crowding out" see Milton Friedman's column in *Newsweek*, August 2, 1976. Friedman is criticizing the Humphrey-Hawkins bill, a mild Keynesian commitment to full employment via countercyclical policy. He comments: "Government employment would replace employment in building homes or factories. . . . Is anyone so naive as to suppose that the government jobs created will be more productive than the private jobs destroyed?"

Lawrence Klein comments: "Keynes' opponents contended that employment on public works schemes would merely divert employment from jobs in private industry. They were clearly operating with the classical assumption of full employment. . . . It is amazing, in the light of British experience, that people would argue this way" (Klein, 1947, pp. 14–15).

Robinson comments, "Looking back now, it seems almost incredible that such views should have been taken seriously" (Robinson, 1951, p. 106, referring to the Treasury assumption of a fixed investment fund). If such views were almost incredible in 1951, what should we call them when Friedman asserts them dogmatically in 1976, with 8% unemployment? Friedman is assuming crowding out, a natural rate of investment, a natural rate of unemployment, and therefore he is assuming that the economy is in long-run equilibrium in 1976. Substantively his views are identical with those of the 1929 Treasury officials. Friedman's "science" was obsolete in 1929; his elaborate battery of concepts and his data trickery and fraudulent tests should not disguise that fact.

11. I was persuaded of this point by Fred Betz.

References

Ackley, Gardner, 1961. *Macroeconomic Theory*. New York: Macmillan.

Aharoni, Yair, 1966. *The Foreign Investment Decision Process*. Cambridge: Harvard.

Alberston, Dean, ed., 1975. *Students Movements of the 1960's*. New York: Simon and Schuster.

Albritten, Robert, 1979. Social amelioration through mass insurgency? A re-examination of the Piven and Cloward thesis. *American Political Science Review*, 73: 1003–1011. Reply by Piven and Cloward, pp. 1012–1019 and rejoinder.

Alcaly, Roger, and D. Mermelstein, eds., 1977. *The Fiscal Crisis of American Cities*. New York: Random House, Vintage Edition.

Alchian, Armen, and Wm. Allen, 1964. *University Economics*. Belmont, Calif.: Wadsworth.

Alchian, Armen, and Harold Demsetz, 1972. Production, information costs, and economic organization. *American Economic Review*, 62 (no. 5): 777–795.

Alker, Hayward, and Roger Hurwitz, 1979. *Resolving Prisoner's Dilemmas*. MIT Center for International Studies, Project Working Paper No. 12.

Allen, R.G.D., 1960. The structure of macroeconomic models. *Economic Journal*, 70: 38–52.

Allison, Graham, 1971. *The Essence of Decision*. Boston: Little, Brown.

Almond, Gabriel, 1970. *Political Development*. Boston: Little, Brown.

———, and James S. Coleman, eds., 1960. *The Politics of the Developing Areas*. Princeton: Princeton University Press.

Althusser, Louis, 1970. *For Marx*. New York: Random House.

——— and Etienne Balibar, 1970. *Reading Capital*. London: New Left Books.

Amin, Samir, 1976. *Unequal Development*. New York: Monthly Review Press.

Apter, David, 1968. *Some Conceptual Approaches to the Study of Modernization*. Englewood Cliffs, NJ: Prentice-Hall.

Arnold, Thurman, 1937. *The Folklore of Capitalism*. New Haven: Yale University Press.

Arrow, Kenneth, 1951. *Social Choice and Individual Values*. New York: Wiley.

Aspaturian, Vernon, 1966. Internal politics and foreign policy in the Soviet system. In R.B. Farrell, ed., *Approaches to Comparative and International Politics*. Evanston, Ill.: Northwestern University Press.

Bachrach, Peter, 1967. *The Theory of Democratic Elitism*. Boston: Little, Brown.

_____ , ed., 1971. *Political Elites in a Democracy*. Chicago: Adline.

_____ and Morton Baratz, 1970. *Power and Poverty*. New York: Oxford University Press.

Banfield, Edward C., 1958. *The Moral Basis of a Backward Society*. New York: Free Press.

_____ , 1961. *Political Influence*. New York: Free Press.

_____ , 1969. Welfare: a crisis without solutions. *The Public Interest*, 16: 89-101.

Baran, Paul, and Paul Sweezy, 1966. *Monopoly Capital*. New York: Monthly Review Press.

Barnet, Richard, 1972. *Roots of War*. New York: Penguin Books.

_____ , and R. Müller, 1974. *Global Reach*. New York: Simon and Schuster.

Baumberger, Jörg, 1977. No Kuhnian revolution in economics. *Journal of Economic Issues*, 11 (no. 1): 1-20.

Baumol, William, 1967. Macroeconomics of unbalanced growth: the anatomy of urban crisis. *American Economic Review*, 57: 415-426.

Beardsley, Philip, 1980. *Redefining Rigor: Ideology and Statistics in Political Inquiry*. Beverly Hills, Calif.: Sage.

Becker, Gary, 1957. *The Economics of Discrimination*. Chicago: University of Chicago Press.

_____ , 1976. *The Economic Approach to Human Behavior*. Chicago: University of Chicago Press.

_____ and William Baumol, 1952. The classical monetary theory: the outcome of the discussion. *Economica*, 19: 355-376.

Becker, Howard S., ed. 1964. *The Other Side: Perspectives on Deviance*. New York: Free Press.

_____ , 1970. *Sociological Work, Method and Substance*. Chicago: Aldine.

_____ and Blanche Geer, 1958. *Boys in White*. Chicago: University of Chicago Press.

Beetham, David, 1977. From socialism to fascism: the relation between theory and practice in the work of Robert Michels. *Political Studies*, 25 (no. 1): 3-24; (no. 2): 161-181.

Bell, Carolyn S., 1977. Expanding human resources. *Society*, 14 (no. 3): 46-50.

Bell, Daniel, 1960. *The End of Ideology*. New York: Free Press.

_____ , 1976. *Cultural Contradictions of Capitalism*. New York: Basic Books.

_____ and Irving Kristol, eds., 1969. *Confrontation: the Student Rebellion and the Universities*. New York: Basic Books.

Berger, Peter, and T. Luckman, 1966. *The Social Construction of Reality*. Garden City, NY: Doubleday.

Bergsten, C. Fred, 1975. *Dilemmas of the Dollar*. New York: New York University Press.

————, et al. 1978. *American Multinationals and American Interests*. Washington, D.C.: Brookings Institution.

Black, Duncan, 1958. *Theory of Committees and Elections*. Cambridge: Cambridge University Press.

Blau, Peter, 1964. *Exchange and Power in Social Life*. New York: Wiley.

Block, Fred, 1978. *The Origins of International Economic Disorder*. Berkeley: University of California Press.

Boddy, R.A., and J. Crotty, 1974. Class conflict, Keynesian policies, and the business cycle. *Monthly Review*, 26 (no. 5): 1-17.

————, 1976. Stagnation, instability, and international competition. *American Economic Review*, 66 (no. 2): 27-33.

Bodenheimer, Susanne, 1971. Dependency and imperialism: the roots of Latin American underdevelopment. In K.T. Fann and D.C. Hodges, eds., *Readings in U.S. Imperialism*. Boston: Porter Sargent.

Boesel, David, and Peter Rossi, eds., 1971. *Cities Under Siege*. New York: Basic Books.

Bonacich, Philip, et al., 1976. Cooperation and group size in the n-person Prisoner's Dilemma. *Journal of Conflict Resolution*, 20 (no. 4): 687-706.

Bond, John R., and W.E. Vinacke, 1961. Coalitions in mixed-sex triads. *Sociometry*, 24: 61-75.

Bookchin, Murray, 1970. *Post-Scarcity Anarchism*. San Francisco: Ramparts Press.

Borch, Karl, 1968. *The Economics of Uncertainty*. Princeton: Princeton University Press.

Boulding, Kenneth, 1953. Economic progress as a goal of economic life. In A.D. Ward, ed., *Goals of Economic Life*. New York: Harper.

————, 1966. *Economic Analysis, Volume II: Macroeconomics*. 4th ed. New York: Harper.

————, 1976. Review of Commoner's *The Poverty of Power*. *Society*, 14 (no. 1): 87-90.

————, 1978. *Ecodynamics*. Beverly Hills, Calif.: Sage.

Boyle, Godfrey, and Peter Harper, eds., 1976. *Radical Technology*. New York: Random House.

Brainard, W.C., and R.N. Cooper, 1975. Empirical monetary macroeconomics: what have we learned in the last 25 years? *American Economic Review*, 65 (no. 2): 167-175.

Braithwaite, Richard, 1955. *Theory of Games as a Tool for the Moral Philosopher*. Cambridge: Cambridge University Press.

Brams, Steven, 1976. *Paradoxes in Politics*. New York: Free Press.

Bramson, William, and A.K. Klevornick, 1969. Money illusion and the aggregate consumption function. *American Economic Review*, 59 (no. 5): 832-849.

Brandis, Royall, 1968. *Principles of Economics*. Homewood, Illinois: Irwin.

Braverman, Harry, 1974. *Labor and Monopoly Capital*. New York: Monthly Review Press.

Brodie, Bernard, 1971. Why were we so (strategically) wrong? *Foreign Policy*, no. 5: 151–162.

Bronfenbrenner, Martin, 1954. Some neglected implications of secular inflation. In Kenneth Kurihara, ed., *Post-Keynesian Economics*. New Brunswick, N.J.: Rutgers University Press, pp. 31–58.

Brooks, Harvey, 1973. The technology of zero growth. In Mancur Olson and Hans Landsberg, eds., *The No-Growth Society*. New York: W.W. Norton, pp. 139–152.

Brunner, Karl, and Allan Meltzer, 1977. The explanation of inflation: some international evidence. *American Economic Review*, 67 (no. 1): 148–154.

Brzezinski, Zbigniew, 1968. Revolution and counter-revolution. *New Republic* (June 1).

————, 1970. *Between Two Ages*. New York: Viking.

———— and Samuel P. Huntington, 1965. *Political Power: USA/USSR*. New York: Viking.

Buchanan, James, 1975. *The Limits of Liberty*. Chicago: University of Chicago Press.

———— and Gordon Tullock, 1962. *The Calculus of Consent*. Ann Arbor: University of Michigan Press.

————, and Robert Tollison, eds., 1972. *Theory of Public Choice*. Ann Arbor: University of Michigan Press.

Burawoy, Michael, 1978. Toward a Marxist theory of the labor process. *Politics and Society*, 8 (no. 3): 247–312.

Burns, Arthur Lee, 1968. *Of Powers and Their Politics*. Englewood Cliffs, N.J.: Prentice-Hall.

Campana, Robert, and S. Langer, 1976. *Nuclear Power and the Environment*. Hinsdale, Ill.: American Nuclear Society.

Campbell, Don, 1969. The experimenting society. mimeo.

Campbell, John Franklin, 1971. *The Foreign Affairs Fudge Factory*. New York: Basic Books.

Carlo, Antonio, 1974. The socio-economic nature of the USSR. *Telos* (no. 21): 2–86.

Cartwright, Dorwin, and Alvin Zander, eds., 1953. *Group Dynamics*. Evanston, Ill.: Row, Peterson.

Chase, Richard X., 1975. Keynes and U.S. Keynesianism. *Journal of Economic Issues*, 9 (no. 3): 441–470.

Christie, Richard, and Marie Jahoda, eds., 1954. *Studies in the Scope and Method of "The Authoritarian Personality"*. New York: Free Press.

Churchman, C. West, 1968. *The Systems Approach*. New York. Dell.

————, 1971. *The Design of Inquiring Systems*. New York: Basic Books.

————, et al., 1957. *Introduction to Operations Research*. New York: Wiley.

Cicourel, Aaron, 1964. *Method and Measurement in Sociology*. New York: Free Press.

Cleaver, Harry, 1972. Contradictions of the green revolution. *American Economic Review*, 62 (no. 2): 177-186.

Cloward, Richard, and F.F. Piven, 1975. *The Politics of Turmoil*. New York: Random House.

—————, 1976. The acquiescence of social work. In Roy Bailey and M. Brake, eds., *Radical Social Work*. New York: Random House.

Clower, Robert, 1960. Keynes and the classics: a dynamical perspective. *Quarterly Journal of Economics*, 74: 318-323.

—————, 1965. The Keynesian counterrevolution. In F. Hahn and F. Brechling, eds., *The Theory of Interest Rates*. London: Macmillan.

Coddington, Alan, 1968. *Theories of the Bargaining Process*. Chicago: Aldine.

Coleman, James S., 1964. *Introduction to Mathematical Sociology*. New York: Free Press.

Commoner, Barry, 1971. *The Closing Circle*. New York: Alfred A. Knopf.

—————, 1976. *The Poverty of Power*. New York: Alfred A. Knopf.

—————, 1979. *The Politics of Energy*. New York: Alfred A. Knopf.

Crenson, Matthew, 1971. *The Un-politics of Air Pollution*. Baltimore: Johns Hopkins University Press.

Cross, John, 1965. A theory of the bargaining process. *American Economic Review*, 56: 522-530.

—————, 1969. *The Economics of Bargaining*. New York: Basic Books.

Crozier, Michel, S.P. Huntington, and J. Watanuki, 1975. *The Crisis of Democracy*. New York: New York University Press.

Cyert, Richard, and J.G. March, 1963. *A Behavioral Theory of the Firm*. Englewood Cliffs, N.J.: Prentice-Hall.

Dahl, Robert, 1956. *A Preface to Democratic Theory*. Chicago: University of Chicago Press.

—————, 1961. *Who Governs?* New Haven: Yale University Press.

—————, and C.E. Lindblom, 1951. *Politics, Economics, and Welfare*. New York: Harper & Row.

Dann, James, 1979. U.S. hegemony over the three worlds. *Review of Radical Political Economics*, 11 (no. 4): 64-77.

Davidson, Donald, S. Siegel, and P. Suppes, 1957. *Decision-making, an Experimental Approach*. Stanford: Stanford University Press.

Davidson, Paul, 1972. A Keynesian view of Friedman's theoretical framework for monetary analysis. *Journal of Political Economy*, 80: 864-882.

—————, 1978. *Money and the Real World*. New York: Wiley.

Destler, I.M., 1972. *Presidents, Bureaucrats, and Foreign Policy*. Princeton: Princeton University Press.

Deutsch, Morton, 1964. Homans in the Skinner Box. *Sociological Inquiry*, 34 (no. 2): 156-165.

Dewey, John, 1927. *The Public and Its Problems*. Chicago: Gateway reprint.

Diesing, E., 1952. The Social Studies Textbook in the Lower Class School. Unpublished MA Thesis, Department of Education, University of Chicago.

Diesing, P., 1962. *Reason in Society*. Westport: Greenwood Press reprint, 1973.

————, 1971. *Patterns of Discovery in the Social Sciences*. Hawthorne, N.Y.: Aldine.

————, 1972. Subjectivity and objectivity in the social sciences. *Philosophy of the Social Sciences*, 2: 147–166.

————, and Paul Piccone, 1967. Kaufman on alienation. *Inquiry*, 10: 208–210.

Dörnberg, Stefan, 1968. *Kurze Geschichte der DDR*. Berlin: Dietz.

Domar, Evsey, 1957. *Essays in the Theory of Economic Growth*. New York: Oxford University Press.

Domhoff, G. William, 1974. *The Bohemian Grove*. New York: Harper Torchbooks.

————, 1978. *Who Really Rules?* New Brunswick, N.J.: Transaction Books.

Downs, Anthony, 1957. *An Economic Theory of Democracy*. New York: Harper & Row.

————, 1970. *Urban Problems and Prospects*. Chicago: Markham.

Duesenberry, James, 1949. *Income, Saving, and the Theory of Consumer Behavior*. Cambridge: Harvard University Press.

Dye, Thomas H., and Harmon Zeigler, 1975. *The Irony of Democracy*, 3d ed. North Scituate, Mass.: Duxbury Press.

Easton, David, 1965. *A Systems Analysis of Political Life*. New York: Wiley.

Edelman, Murray, 1964. *The Symbolic Uses of Politics*. Urbana: University of Illinois Press.

————, 1974. The political language of the helping professions. *Politics and Society*, 4 (no. 3): 295–310.

Edwards, Richard, et al., 1972. *The Capitalist System*. Englewood Cliffs, N.J.: Prentice-Hall.

Ehrenreich, B. and J., 1977. The professional-managerial class. *Radical America*, 11 (no. 2): 7–32; (no. 3): 7–22.

Eichner, Alfred, ed., 1978. *A Guide to Post-Keynesian Economics*. White Plains, New York: M.E. Sharpe.

Eisenstadt, Shmuel N. 1963. *The Political Systems of Empire*. New York: Free Press.

Eisner, Robert, 1952. Unemployment equilibrium rates of growth. *American Economic Review*, 42: 43–58.

————, 1953. Rejoinder. *American Economic Review*, 43 (June): 385–393.

————, 1969. Investment and the frustrations of econometricians. *American Economic Review*, 59 (no. 2): 50–64.

Ekeh, Peter, 1974. *Social Exchange Theory*. London: Heineman.

Ellsberg, Daniel, 1956. Theory of the reluctant duelist. *American Economic Review*, 46 (no. 2): 909–923.

————, 1964. The crude analysis of strategic choices. In Martin Shubik, ed., *Game Theory and Related Approaches to Social Behavior*. New York: Wiley, pp. 230–239.

————, 1968. *The Theory and Practice of Blackmail*. Santa Monica: RAND.

————, 1972. *Papers on the War*. New York: Simon and Schuster.

Emanuel, Arghiri, 1972. *Unequal Exchange*. New York: Monthly Review Press.

Engler, Robert, 1961. *The Politics of Oil*. Chicago: University of Chicago Press.

————, 1978. *The Brotherhood of Oil*. New York: New American Library.

Fann, K.T., and D.C. Hodges, eds., 1971. *Readings in U.S. Imperialism*. Boston: Porter Sargent.

Fellner, William, 1946. *Monetary Policies and Full Employment*. Hamden, Conn.: Anchor Books Reprint.

————, 1949. *Competition Among the Few*. New York: Alfred A. Knopf.

————, 1957. Keynesian economics after twenty years. What is surviving? *American Economic Review*, 47 (no. 1): 67–76.

————, 1960. Rapid growth as an objective of economic policy. *American Economic Review*, 50 (May): 93–105.

Feuer, Lewis, 1969. *The Conflict of Generations*. New York: Basic Books.

————, 1975. *Ideology and the Ideologists*. New York: Harper & Row.

Feyerabend, Paul, 1965. Problems of empiricism. In J. Colodny, ed., *Beyond the Edge of Certainty*. Englewood Cliffs, N.J.: Prentice-Hall.

————, 1975. *Against Method*. London: New Left Books.

————, 1976. *Wider den Methodenzwang*. Frankfurt: Suhrkamp.

————, 1978. From incompetent professionalism to professionalized incompetence—the rise of a new breed of intellectuals. *Philosophy of the Social Sciences*, 8 (no. 1): 37–53.

Fisch, Rudolph, 1977. Psychology of science. In Ina Spiegel-Rösing and Derek Price, eds., *Science, Technology, and Society*. Beverly Hills, Calif.: Sage.

Fleron, Fred and L.J., 1972. Administrative theory as repressive political theory: the communist experience. *Telos* (no. 12): 63–92.

Fox, John, and Melvin Guyer, 1977. Group size and others' strategy in an n-person game. *Journal of Conflict Resolution*, 21 (no. 2): 323–338.

Frank, Andre Gunder, 1967. *Capitalism and Underdevelopment in Latin America*. New York: Monthly Review Press.

————, 1969. *Latin America: Underdevelopment or Revolution*. New York: Monthly Review Press.

Freeman, C., 1977. Economics of research and development. In Ina Spiegel-Rösing and D. Price, eds., *Science, Technology, and Society*. Beverly Hills, Calif.: Sage.

Frey, Frederick, 1971. Comment: on issues and nonissues in the study of power. *American Political Science Review*, 65 (no. 4): 1081–1101.

Friedman, Milton, 1952. Price, income, and monetary changes in three wartime periods. *American Economic Review*, 62 (May): 612–625.

————, 1953. *Essays in Positive Economics*. Chicago: University of Chicago Press.

————, 1955. Leon Walras and his economic system. *American Economic Review*, 45 (no. 2): 900–909.

————, 1956. The quantity theory of money—a restatement. Reprinted in Richard Thorn, ed., *Monetary Theory and Policy*. New York: Random House. Also reprinted in Friedman, 1969.

————, 1957. *A Theory of the Consumption Function*. Princeton: Princeton University Press.

————, 1959. The demand for money: some theoretical and empirical results. *Journal of Political Economy*, 327–351. Reprinted in Thorn, 1966 and in Friedman, 1969.

————, 1960. *A Program for Monetary Stability*. New York: Fordham University Press.

————, 1962. *Capitalism and Freedom*. Chicago: University of Chicago Press.

————, 1968. The role of monetary policy. *American Economic Review*, 58 (no. 1): 1–17.

————, 1969. *The Quantity Theory of Money and Other Essays*. Hawthorne, New York: Aldine.

————, 1972a. Have monetary policies failed? *American Economic Review*, 62 (no. 2): 11–18.

————, 1972b. Comments on the critics. *Journal of Political Economy*, 80: 906–931.

————, 1973. *Money and Economic Development*. New York: Praeger.

————, 1975. *Unemployment vs. Inflation? An Evaluation of the Phillips Curve*. London: Institute of Economic Affairs.

————, 1977. *From Galbraith to Economic Freedom*. London: Institute of Economic Affairs.

————, and Walter Heller, 1969. *Monetary vs. Fiscal Policy*. New York: W.W. Norton.

————, and L. Savage, 1948. The utility analysis of choices involving risk. *Journal of Political Economy*, 56: 279–304.

————, and Anna Schwartz, 1963. *A Monetary History of the United States*. Princeton: Princeton University Press.

Friedman, Neil, 1967. *The Social Nature of Psychological Research*. New York: Basic Books.

Fromm, Erich, 1947. *Man For Himself*. New York: Rinehart & Co.

Fusfeld, Daniel, 1972. *Economics*. Lexington: Heath.

Galbraith, John, 1952. *American Capitalism*. Boston: Houghton, Mifflin.

————, 1955. *The Great Crash*. Boston: Houghton, Mifflin.

————, 1958. *The Affluent Society*. Boston: Houghton, Mifflin.

————, 1967, 1971. *The New Industrial State*. Boston: Houghton, Mifflin.

————, 1973. *Economics and the Public Purpose*. Boston: Houghton, Mifflin.

————, 1977. *The Age of Uncertainty*. Boston: Houghton, Mifflin.

Gamson, William, and A. Modigliani, 1971. *Untangling the Cold War*. Boston: Houghton, Mifflin.

Garson, G. David, 1978. *Group Theories of Politics*. Beverly Hills, Calif.: Sage.

Gearing, Fred, 1970. *The Face of the Fox*. Chicago: Aldine.

——————, M. Netting, and L. Peattie, eds., 1960. *Documentary History of the Fox Project*. University of Chicago, Department of Anthropology.

Gelb, Leslie, with Richard Betts, 1979. *The Irony of Vietnam: The System Worked*. Washington, D.C.: Brookings Institution.

George, Alexander, D. Hall, and W. Simons, 1971. *The Limits of Coercive Diplomacy*. Boston: Little, Brown.

——————, and R. Smoke, 1974. *Deterrence in American Foreign Policy: Theory and Practice*. New York: Columbia University Press.

Gilbert, Claire, 1971. Communities, power structure, and research bias. *Polity*, 4 (no. 2): 218-235.

Gintis, Herbert, and S. Bowles, 1976. *Schooling in Capitalist America*. New York: Basic Books.

Glazer, Nathan, 1968. Student power in Berkeley. *Public Interest* (no. 13): 3-21.

——————, 1971. Blood. *Public Interest* (no. 24): 86-94.

Goffman, Erving, 1961. *Asylums*. Garden City: Doubleday.

——————, 1963. *Stigma: Notes on the Management of Spoiled Identity*. Englewood Cliffs, N.J.: Prentice-Hall.

——————, 1967. *Interaction Ritual*. Chicago: Aldine.

Gordon, David, 1972. *Theories of Poverty and Unemployment*. Lexington, Mass.: D.C. Heath.

Gordon, Robert A., 1976. Rigor and relevance in a changing institutional setting. *American Economic Review*, 66 (no. 1): 1-14.

Gordon, Sanford, 1973. Review of Howard Sherman, *Radical Political Economy*. *Journal of Economic Issues*, 7: 688-690.

Gough, Ian, 1975. State expenditure in advanced capitalism. *New Left Review* (no. 92): 53-92.

Gouldner, A.W., 1963. Anti-Minotaur. In Maurice Stein and A. Vidich, eds., *Sociology On Trial*. Englewood Cliffs, N.J.: Prentice-Hall.

——————, 1970. *The Coming Crisis of Western Sociology*. New York: Basic Books.

——————, 1974. Marxism and social theory. *Theory and Society*, 1 (no. 1): 17-35.

——————, 1976. Revolutionary intellectuals. *Telos* (no. 26): 3-36.

——————, 1979. *The Future of Intellectuals and the Rise of the New Class*. New York: Seabury.

Green, Mark, et al., 1972. *Who Runs Congress?* New York: Bantam.

Green, Philip, 1966. *Deadly Logic*. Columbus: Ohio State University Press.

Greer, Ed., 1971. The "liberation" of Gary, Indiana. *Transaction*, 8 (no. 3): 30-63.

Gromyko, Anatol A., 1973. *Through Russian Eyes: President Kennedy's 1036 Days*. Washington D.C.: International Library.

Gruchy, Allan, 1974. Government intervention and the social control of business: the neoinstitutionalist position. *Journal of Economic Issues*, 8 (no. 2): 235-249.

Gurley, J.G., and E.S. Shaw, 1955. Financial aspects of economic develop-
    ment. *American Economic Review*, 45 (no. 4): 515–538.
Haberler, Gottfried, 1950. J.A. Schumpeter. *Quarterly Journal of Economics*,
    64 (no. 3): 333–372.
Habermas, Jürgen, 1975. *Legitimation Crisis*. Boston: Beacon Press.
Hahn, Werner, 1972. *The Politics of Soviet Agriculture, 1960–1970*. Baltimore:
    Johns Hopkins.
Halperin, Morton, 1974. *Bureaucratic Politics and Foreign Policy*. Washing-
    ton D.C.: Brookings Institution.
Hamblin, Robert, and John Kunkel, eds., 1977. *Behavioral Theory in
    Sociology*. New Brunswick, N.J.: Transaction Books.
Hamburger, Henry, 1969. Separable games. *Behavioral Science*, 14: 121–132.
Hammond, Phillip, ed., 1964. *Sociologists at Work*. New York: Basic Books.
Hansen, Alvin, 1955. Post-Keynesian economics. *American Economic Review*,
    45 (no. 2): 360–372.
Haraszti, Miklos, 1977. *A Worker in a Worker's State*. London: Penguin.
Haring, Joseph, and G.C. Smith, 1959. Utility theory, decision theory, and
    profit maximization. *American Economic Review*, 49 (no. 4): 566–583.
Harrington, Michael, 1976. *The Twilight of Capitalism*. New York: Simon
    and Schuster.
Harris, Seymour, ed., 1947. *The New Economics*. New York: Alfred A. Knopf.
Harrod, Roy, 1939. An essay in dynamic theory. *Economic Journal*, 49: 14–33.
————— , 1951. Notes on trade cycle theory. *Economic Journal*, 61:
    261–275.
Havrilesky, Thomas, and John Boorman, eds., 1976. *Current Issues in
    Monetary Theory and Policy*. Arlington Heights, Ill.: AHM
    Corporation.
Hawley, Willis, and Fred Wirt, eds., 1974. *The Search for Community
    Power*, 2d ed. Englewood Cliffs, N.J.: Prentice-Hall.
Hayek, Friedrich, 1952. *The Counter-revolution of Science*. New York:
    Free Press.
————— , 1960. *The Constitution of Liberty*. Chicago: University of
    Chicago Press.
————— , 1976. *Choice in Currency: A Way to Stop Inflation*. London:
    Institute of Economic Affairs.
Hayes, Edward C., 1972. *Power Structure and Urban Policy: Who Rules
    in Oakland?* New York: McGraw-Hill.
Hayter, Teresa, 1971. *Aid as Imperialism*. Harmondsworth: Penguin.
Hegel, G.W.F., 1942. *Hegel's Philosophy of Right*, tr. Knox. London:
    Oxford.
Heilbroner, Robert, 1968. *The Economic Problem*. Englewood Cliffs,
    N.J.: Prentice-Hall.
————— , 1970. *Between Capitalism and Socialism*. New York: Random
    House.
————— , 1974. *An Inquiry Into the Human Prospect*. New York: W.W.
    Norton.
————— , 1977. Es war einmal einfach, Sozialist zu sein. *Zukunft* (Okt.):
    35–37.

Heller, Walter, 1967. *New Dimensions in Political Economy*. Cambridge: Harvard University Press.

Heyden, Günter, ed., 1968. *Die Philosophische Lehre von Karl Marx und ihre Aktuelle Bedeutung*. Berlin: Verlag der Wissenschaften.

Hicks, John R., 1937. Mr. Keynes and the classics: a suggested interpretation. *Econometrica*, 5: 147–159.

——————, 1939. *Value and Capital*. London: Oxford University Press.

——————, 1974. *The Crisis in Keynesian Economics*. New York: Basic Books.

Hindess, Barry, 1977. *Philosophy and Methodology in the Social Sciences*. Hassocks: Harvester.

Hodgson, Geoff, 1974. The falling rate of profit. *New Left Review* (no. 84): 55–84.

Hodson, Randy, 1978. Labor in the monopoly, competitive, and state sectors of production. *Politics and Society*, 8 (no. 3): 429-480.

Holland, Stuart, 1976. *Capital Versus the Regions*. London: Macmillan.

Holt, Robert, and J. Turner, 1966. *The Political Basis of Economic Development*. Princeton: Van Nostrand.

Homans, George C., 1961. *Social Behavior: Its Elementary Forms*. New York: Harcourt, Brace.

——————, 1962. *Sentiments and Activities*. New York: Free Press.

——————, 1964a. Bringing men back in. *American Sociological Review*, 29: 809-818.

——————, 1964b. Commentary. *Sociological Inquiry*, 34 (no. 2): 221-231.

——————, 1967. *The Nature of Social Science*. New York: Harcourt, Brace.

——————, and David Schneider, 1955. *Marriage, Authority, and Final Causes*. New York: Free Press.

Hook, Sidney, 1958. A free man's choice. In Raziel Abelson, ed., *Ethics and Metaethics*. New York: St. Martin's, 1963, pp. 162–167.

Hoopes, Townsend, 1969 and 1973. *The Limits of Intervention*. New York: McKay.

Hopkins, Terence, and Immanuel Wallerstein, eds., 1980. *Processes of the World-system*. Beverly Hills, Calif.: Sage.

Horelick, Arnold, and Myron Rush, 1966. *Strategic Power and Soviet Foreign Policy*. Chicago: University of Chicago Press.

Horie, Shigeo, 1960. *The International Monetary Fund*. New York: St. Martin's.

Horowitz, Irving, 1968. *Professing Sociology*. Chicago: Aldine.

——————, 1977. Social science and presidential choices. *Society*, 14 (no. 4): 21-23.

——————, and William Friedland, 1970. *The Knowledge Factory*, Chicago: Aldine.

——————, and Seymour Lipset, 1978. *Dialogues in American Politics*. Oxford: Oxford University Press.

Horowitz, Ruth, 1978. *Political Ideologies of Organized Labor: The New Deal Era*. New Brunswick, N.J.: Transaction Books.

Howard, Nigel, 1971. *Paradoxes of Rationality*. Cambridge, Mass.: MIT Press.

Hull, Clark et al., 1940. *Mathematico-deductive Theory of Rote Learning*. New Haven: Yale University Press.

Hull, Clark, 1943. *Principles of Behavior*. New York: Appleton-Century.

Hunt, E.K., 1977. The ideal foundations of welfare economics. In Jesse Schwartz, ed., *The Subtle Anatomy of Capitalism*. Santa Monica: Goodyear, pp. 22-35.

Hunter, Douglas, 1971. *Aspects of Mathematical Deterrence Theory*. Los Angeles: UCLA Security Studies Paper No. 19.

_____, 1972. The decision-making model in nuclear deterrence theory. *Journal of Peace Research*, 9: 209-222.

Hunter, Floyd, 1954. *Community Power Structure*. Chapel Hill: University of North Carolina Press.

_____, 1959. *Top Leadership, USA*. Chapel Hill: University of North Carolina Press.

Huntington, Samuel P., 1960. *The Common Defense*. New York: Columbia University Press.

_____, 1968. *Political Order in Changing Societies*. New Haven: Yale University Press.

_____, 1975. The democratic distemper. *Public Interest* (no. 41): 9-38.

_____, and Joan Nelson, 1976. *No Easy Choice*. Cambridge, Mass.: Harvard University Press.

Hurd, Rick, 1976. New Deal labor policy and the containment of radical union activity. *Review of Radical Political Economics*, 8 (no. 3): 32-43.

Hutchison, T.W., 1964. *Positive Economics and Policy Objectives*. London: Allen and Unwin.

Jackson, Bruce, 1971. In the valley of the shadows: Kentucky. *Transaction*, 8 (no. 8): 28-39.

_____, 1972. *Wake Up, Dead Man*. Cambridge: Harvard University Press.

Jennings, E., 1978. Urban riots and welfare policy change: a test of the Piven and Cloward theory. In Helen Ingram and Dean Mann, eds., *Why Policies Succeed or Fail*. Beverly Hills, Calif.: Sage.

Jervis, Robert, 1976. *Perception and Misperception in International Politics*. Princeton: Princeton University Press.

Johnson, D. Gale, 1947. *Forward Prices For Agriculture*. Chicago: University of Chicago Press.

Johnson, Harry, 1971a. The Keynesian revolution and the monetarist counterrevolution. *American Economic Review*, 61 (no. 2): 1-14. Reprinted in Johnson, 1973.

_____, 1971b. *Macroeconomics and Monetary Theory*. London: Grey-Mills.

_____, 1973. *Further Essays in Monetary Economics*. Cambridge, Mass.: Harvard University Press.

Kadushin, Charles, 1972. Who are the elite intellectuals? *Public Interest*, (no. 29): 109-125.

Kaldor, N., 1958. Review of Baran's *Political Economy of Growth*. *American Economic Review*, 48 (no. 1): 164-170.

Kalecki, Michal, 1939. *Essays in the Theory of Economic Fluctuations*. New York: Farrar and Rinehart.

————, 1972. *The Last Phase in the Transformation of Capitalism*. New York: Monthly Review Press.

Kaplan, Abraham, 1964. *The Conduct of Inquiry*. San Francisco: Chandler.

Kaplan, Morton, 1957. *System and Process in International Relations*. New York: St. Martin's.

Katona, George, 1951. *Psychological Analysis of Economic Behavior*. New York: McGraw-Hill.

Kaufman, Herbert, 1967. *The Forest Ranger: A Study in Administrative Behavior*. Baltimore, Johns Hopkins University Press.

Kemeny, John, and J.L. Snell, 1962. *Mathematical Models in the Social Sciences*. Boston: Ginn.

Keynes, John M., 1936. *The General Theory of Employment, Interest, and Money*. New York: Harcourt Brace.

————, 1937. The general theory of employment. *Quarterly Journal of Economics*, 51 (Feb.): 209–223.

Keynes, John N. 1904. *The Scope and Method of Political Economy*. London: Macmillan,

Kharasch, Robert, 1973. *The Institutional Imperative: How To Understand the United States Government and Other Bulky Objects*. New York: Charter House.

Kidron, Michael, 1974. *Capitalism and Theory*. London: Pluto Press.

Klein, Lawrence, 1947. *The Keynesian Revolution*. New York: Macmillan.

————, 1950. *Economic Fluctuations in the United States*. New York: Wiley.

————, 1954. Empirical foundations of Keynesian economics. In K. Kurihara, ed., *Post-Keynesian Economics*. New Brunswick, N.J.: Rutgers University Press.

Knight, Frank, 1921. *Risk, Uncertainty and Profit*. New York. Kelley and Millman, 1957 (8th impression).

————, 1935. *The Ethics of Competition*. New York: Harper & Row.

————, 1947. *Freedom and Reform*. New York: Harper & Row.

————, 1952. Institutionalism and empiricism in economics. *American Economic Review*, 42 (May): 45–55.

Kornhauser, William, 1959. *The Politics of Mass Society*. New York: Free Press.

Kramer, Ralph, 1969. *Participation of the Poor: Comparative Case Studies in the War on Poverty*. Englewood Cliffs, N.J.: Prentice-Hall.

Krasner, Stephen, 1972. Are bureaucracies important? *Foreign Policy*, 7: 159–179.

Kregel, J.A., 1973. *The Reconstruction of Political Economy*. New York: Wiley.

Kristol, Irving, 1973a. Capitalism, socialism, and nihilism. *Public Interest*, no. 31: 3–16.

————, 1973b. Is the worker alienated? In P. Samuelson, ed., *Readings in Economics*. New York: McGraw-Hill, pp. 354–356.

Kuhn, Alfred, 1974. *The Logic of Social Action*. San Francisco: JosseyBass.

Kuhn, Thomas, 1962. *The Structure of Scientific Revolutions.* 2d ed., 1970. Chicago: University of Chicago Press.

————, 1977. *The Essential Tension.* Chicago: University of Chicago Press.

Kurihara, Kenneth, ed., 1954. *Post-Keynesian Economics.* New Brunswick, N.J.: Rutgers.

Landsberg, Martin, 1979. Export-led industrialization in the Third World: manufacturing imperialism. *Review of Radical Political Economics,* 11 (no. 4): 50–63.

Landsberger, Michael, 1970. The life-cycle hypothesis: a reinterpretation and empirical test. *American Economic Review,* 60 (No. 1): 175–183.

Lange, Oskar, 1938. The rate of interest and the optimum propensity to consume. *Economica,* 5: 12–32.

Langer, William, and S. Gleason, 1953. *The Undeclared War, 1940–1941.* New York: Harper & Row.

Lasswell, Harold, and Daniel Lerner, 1951. *The Comparative Study of Elites.* Stanford: Stanford University Press.

————, 1965. *World Revolutionary Elites.* Cambridge, Mass.: MIT Press.

Latour, Bruno, and Steve Woolgar, 1979. *Laboratory Life: The Social Construction of Scientific Facts.* Beverly Hills, Calif.: Sage.

Laumas, Prem, and Khan Mohabbat, 1972. The permanent income hypothesis: evidence from time series data. *American Economic Review,* 62 (no. 4): 730–734.

Leijonhufvud, Axel, 1967. Keynes and the Keynesians. *American Economic Review,* 57 (no. 2): 401–410.

————, 1968. *On Keynesian Economics and the Economics of Keynes.* New York: Oxford University Press.

Leiss, William, 1972. *The Domination of Nature.* New York: Braziller.

————, 1976. *The Limits of Satisfaction.* Toronto: University of Toronto Press.

Lekachman, Robert, 1966. *The Age of Keynes.* New York: Random House.

————, 1976. *Economists at Bay.* New York: McGraw-Hill.

Lemieux, Peter, 1978. A note on the detection of collinearity. *American Journal of Political Science,* 22: 183–186.

Leontief, Wassily, 1956. Factor proportions and the structure of American trade. *Review of Economics and Statistics,* 38: 386–407.

————, 1966. *Essays in Economics.* New York: Oxford University Press.

Lerner, Daniel, 1958. *The Passing of Traditional Society.* New York: Free Press.

Lewis, Oscar, 1969. *Six Women: Three Generations in a Puerto Rican Family.* New York: Random House.

Leys, Colin, 1974. *Underdevelopment in Kenya.* Berkeley: University of California Press.

Lieberman, Bernhardt, 1962. Experimental studies of conflict in some two-person and three-person games. In Joan Criswell et al., eds., *Mathematical Models in Small-group Processes*. Stanford: Stanford University Press.

Liebich, Andre, 1979. Hegel, Marx, and Althusser. *Politics and Society*, 9: 89–102.

Lindbeck, Assar et al., 1977. *The Political Economy of the New Left*, 2d ed. New York: New York University Press.

Lindberg, Leon et al., eds., 1975. *Stress and Contradiction in Modern Capitalism*. Lexington, Mass.: D.C. Heath.

Linder, Marc, 1977. *Anti-Samuelson*. 2 volumes. New York: Urizen.

Lindesmith, Alfred, 1968. *Addiction and Opiates*. Chicago: Aldine.

Lipset, Seymour Martin, 1950. *Agrarian Socialism*. Berkeley: University of California Press.

—————— , 1960. *Political Man*. New York: Doubleday. 1963 edition.

—————— , 1963. *The First New Nation*. New York: Basic Books.

—————— , 1972a. *Rebellion in the University*. Boston: Little, Brown.

—————— , 1972b. Ideology and mythology: reply to critics. In A. Effrat, ed., *Perspectives in Political Sociology*. New York: Bobbs-Merrill, pp. 233–265.

—————— , and J. Solari, 1967. *Elites in Latin America*. New York: Oxford University Press.

—————— , and Earl Raab, 1970. *The Politics of Unreason*. New York: Harper & Row.

Lipsky, Michael, 1976. Toward a theory of street-level bureaucracy. In Willis Hawley et al., *Theoretical Perspectives in Urban Politics*. Englewood Cliffs, N.J.: Prentice-Hall.

—————— , 1980. *Street Level Bureaucracy*. New York: Russell Sage.

Lockard, Duane, 1971. *The Perverted Priorities of American Politics*. New York: Macmillan.

Lockhart, Charles, 1973. *The Efficacy of Threats in International Interaction Strategies*. Beverly Hills, Calif.: Sage.

—————— , 1979. *Bargaining in International Conflicts*. New York: Columbia University Press.

Lucas, Robert, 1978. Unemployment policy. *American Economic Review*, 68 (no. 2): 353–357.

Luce, R. Duncan, and H. Raiffa, 1957. *Games and Decisions*. New York: Wiley.

Lukacs, George, 1923. *History and Class-consciousness*. Cambridge, Mass.: MIT Press.

Lynd, Robert and Helen, 1929. *Middletown*. New York: Harcourt, Brace.

MacBeath, Alexander, 1952. *Experiments in Living*. London: Macmillan.

Machlup, Fritz, 1946. Marginal analysis and economic research. *American Economic Review*, 36: 519–554.

—————— , 1952a. *The Economics of Sellers' Competition*. Baltimore: Johns Hopkins University Press.

—————— , 1952b. *The Political Economy of Monopoly*. Baltimore: Johns Hopkins University Press.

—————— , 1958. Equilibrium and disequilibrium: misplaced concreteness and disguised politics. *Economic Journal*, 68: pp. 1–24. Reprinted in Machlup, 1964, Chapter 5.

————— , 1964. *International Payments, Debts, and Gold: Collected Essays*. New York: Scribner's.

————— , 1967. Theories of the firm: marginalist, behavioral, managerial. *American Economic Review*, 57: 1–33.

————— , 1970. Homo oeconomicus and his classmates. In Maurice Natanson, ed., *Phenomenology and Social Reality*. The Hague: Nijhoff, pp. 122–139.

Mahler, Julie, 1976. Politics and professionalism in a Community Mental Health Center. Unpublished PhD thesis, Department of Political Science, State University of New York at Buffalo.

Mack, Ruth, 1952. Economics of Consumption. In Bernard F. Haley, ed., *A Survey of Contemporary Economics*. Homewood: Irwin.

Malinowski, B., 1922. *Argonauts of the Western Pacific*. London: Routledge.

————— , 1944. *A Scientific Theory of Culture*. Chapel Hill: University of North Carolina Press.

Mandel, Ernest, 1968. *Marxist Economic Theory*. London: Merlin Press.

————— , 1975. *Late Capitalism*. London: New Left Books.

Mannheim, Karl, 1936. *Ideology and Utopia*, tr. L. Wirth and E. Shils. New York: Harcourt, Brace, and World. Harvest Edition.

Mansfield, Edwin, and Harold Wein, 1958. A study of decision-making within the firm. *Quarterly Journal of Economics*, 72: 515–536.

March, James, and Herbert Simon, 1958. *Organizations*. New York: Wiley.

Marcus, Lyn, 1974. *Dialectical Economics*. Lexington, Mass.: D.C. Heath.

Markovic, Mihailo, 1968. *Dialektik der Praxis*, tr. Urban. Frankfurt: Suhrkamp.

Marris, Peter, and Martin Rein, 1967. *Dilemmas of Social Reform*. New York: Atherton.

Marris, Robin, 1968. The truth about corporations. *Public Interest*, (no. 11): 37–46.

Matza, David, 1966. Poverty and disrepute. In Robert Merton and R. Nisbet, eds., *Contemporary Social Problems*. New York: Harcourt, Brace, and World.

Maruyama, Magaroh, 1978. Heterogenistics and morphogenics: toward a new concept of the scientific. *Theory and Society*, 5: 75–96.

Marx, Karl, 1970 (1843). *Critique of Hegel's Philosophy of Right*, tr. O'Malley. Cambridge: Cambridge University Press.

Mayer, Thomas, 1966. The propensity to consume permanent income. *American Economic Review*, 56 (no. 2): 1158–1177.

————— , 1972. *Permanent Income, Wealth, and Consumption*. Berkeley: University of California Press.

————— , ed., 1978. *The Structure of Monetarism*. New York: W.W. Norton.

McPhee, William, 1963. *Formal Theories of Mass Behavior*. New York: Free Press.

————— , and William Glaser, 1962. *Public Opinion and Congressional Elections*. New York: Free Press.

Mead, Margaret, ed., 1955. *Cultural Patterns and Technical Change*. New York: New American Library.

Meade, James E., 1972. *The Controlled Economy*. Albany: State University of New York Press.

Meier, G.M., 1954. Reply to Yeager. *American Economic Review*, 44 (no. 2): 931–936.

Melman, Seymour, 1970. *Pentagon Capitalism*. New York: McGraw-Hill.

————— , 1974. *The Permanent War Economy*. New York: Simon and Schuster.

Merrill, Richard, ed., 1976. *Radical Agriculture*. New York: New York University Press.

Merton, Robert, 1949. *Social Theory and Social Structure*. New York: Free Press.

————— , 1973. *Sociology of Science*. Chicago: University of Chicago Press.

Meyerson, Martin, and E.C. Banfield, 1955. *Politics, Planning, and the Public Interest*. New York: Free Press.

Middlemas, Keith, 1972. *Diplomacy of Illusion*. London: Weidenfeld & Nicholson.

Miliband, Ralph, 1972. *Parliamentary Socialism*. 2d. ed. London: Merlin.

Miller, Arthur H. et al., 1976. A majority party in disarray: policy polarization in the 1972 election. *American Political Science Review*, 70 (no. 3): 753–778.

Millikan, Max, and W.W. Rostow, 1957. *A Proposal: Key to an Effective Foreign Policy*. New York: Harper & Row.

Mills, C.W., 1951. *White Collar*. New York: Oxford University Press.

————— , 1956. *The Power Elite*. New York: Oxford University Press.

Milnor, J., 1954. Games against nature. In Martin Shubik, ed., *Game Theory*. New York: Wiley, 1964.

Minsky, Hyman, 1975. *Keynes*. New York: Columbia University Press.

Mises, Ludwig von, 1960 (1933). *Epistemological Problems of Economics*. Princeton, N.J.: Van Nostrand.

Mishan, E.J., 1975. The folklore of the market. *Journal of Economic Issues*, 9 (no. 4): 681–752.

Mitroff, Ian, 1974. *The Subjective Side of Science*. New York. Elsevier.

————— , and Ralph Kilman, 1978. *Methodological Approaches to Social Science*. San Francisco: Jossey-Bass.

Modigliani, Franco, 1944. Liquidity preference and the theory of interest and money. *Econometrica*, 12: 45–88.

————— , 1977. The monetarist controversy. *American Economic Review*, 67 (no. 2): 1–19.

————— , and R. Brumberg, 1954. Utility analysis and the consumption function. In K. Kurihara, ed. *Post-Keynesian Economics*. New Brunswick, N.J.: Rutgers.

Morgan, Patrick, 1977. *Deterrence*. Beverly Hills, Calif.: Sage.

Moynihan, Daniel P., 1965. *The Negro Family*. Washington, D.C.: Government Printing Office.

————— , 1969. *Maximum Feasible Misunderstanding*. New York: Free Press.

————— , 1973. *The Politics of a Guaranteed Income*. New York: Random House.

Murdock, Clark, 1974. *Defense Policy Formation*. Albany: State University of New York Press.

Mullins, Nicholas, 1973. *Theories and Theory Groups in Contemporary American Sociology*. New York: Harper & Row.

Nardin, Terry, 1968. *Communication and the Effects of Threats in Strategic Interaction*. Peace Research Society Papers, No. 9.

Naroll, Raoul, et al., 1974. *Military Deterrence in History*. Albany: State University of New York Press.

National Resources Committee, 1939. *The Structure of the American Economy*. Washington, D.C.: Government Printing Office.

Needham, Rodney, 1962. *Structure and Sentiment*. Chicago: University of Chicago Press.

Neustadt, Richard, 1960. *Presidential Power*. New York: Wiley.

─────── , 1970. *Alliance Politics*. New York: Columbia University Press.

─────── , 1975. The constraining of the President. In A. Wildavsky, ed., *Perspectives on the Presidency*. Boston: Little, Brown, pp. 431–447.

Niemi, Richard, and H. Weisberg, eds., 1972. *Probability Models of Collective Decision-making*. Columbus, Ohio: Merrill.

Nisbet, Robert, 1966. *The Sociological Tradition*. New York: Basic Books.

Noble, David, 1977. *America By Design*. New York: Knopf.

O'Brien, James, 1978. *American Leninism in the 1970's*. Boston: New England Free Press reprint from *Radical America*.

O'Connor, James, 1973. *The Fiscal Crisis of the State*. New York: St. Martin's.

─────── , 1974. *The Corporations and the State*. New York: Harper & Row.

─────── , 1975. Productive and unproductive labor. *Politics and Society*, 5 (no. 3): 297–336.

Offe, Claus, 1972. *Strukturprobleme des Kapitalistischen Staates*. Frankfurt: Suhrkamp.

Okun, Arthur, 1972. Have fiscal and/or monetary policies failed? *American Economic Review*, 62 (no. 2): 24–30.

Ölander, F., 1975. Search behavior in non-simultaneous choice situations. Satisficing or maximizing? In D. Wendt et al., eds., *Utility, Probability, and Human Decision-making*. Dordrecht, Holland: Reidel.

Olson, Mancur, 1965. *The Logic of Collective Action*. Cambridge, Mass.: Harvard University Press.

─────── , and H. Landsberger, eds., 1973. *The No-Growth Society*. New York: W.W. Norton.

Ong, Walter J., 1974. Agonistic structures in academia: past to present. *Daedalus*, 103 (no. 4): 229–238.

Ophuls, William, 1977. *Ecology and the Politics of Scarcity*. San Francisco: Freeman.

Ordeshook, Peter, ed., 1978. *Game Theory and Political Science*. New York: New York University Press.

Orren, Karen, 1974. *Corporate Power and Social Change*. Baltimore: Johns Hopkins University Press.

─────── , 1976. Standing to sue: interest group conflict in the federal courts. *American Political Science Review*, 70: 723–741.

Osgood, Charles, 1962. *An Alternative to War or Surrender*. Urbana: University of Illinois Press.

Parijs, Phillippe van, 1980. The falling rate of profit: an obituary. *Review of Radical Political Economics*, 12 (no. 1): 1–16.

Parenti, Michael, 1970. Power and pluralism: a view from the bottom. *Journal of Politics*, 32: 501–530.

Parsons, Talcott, 1937. *The Structure of Social Action*. New York: Free Press reprint, 1949.

————, 1940. The motivation of economic activity. *Canadian Journal of Economics and Political Science*, 6: 187–203. Reprinted in *Essays in Sociological Theory*. New York: Free Press, 1949.

————, 1951. *The Social System*. New York: Free Press.

————, 1964. Levels of organization and the mediation of social interaction. *Sociological Inquiry*, 34 (no. 2): 207–220.

————, 1967. *Sociological Theory and Modern Society*. New York: Free Press.

————, 1969a. The academic system: a sociologist's view. In Daniel Bell and I. Kristol, eds., *Confrontation: The Student Rebellion and the Universities*. New York: Basic Books.

————, 1969b. *Politics and Social Structure*. New York: Free Press.

————, R.F. Bales, and E. Shils, 1953. *Working Papers in the Theory of Action*. New York: Free Press.

————, R.F. Bales, et al., 1955. *Family, Socialization and Interaction Process*. New York: Free Press.

————, and Neil Smelser, 1956. *Economy and Society*. New York: Free Press.

Patinkin, Don, 1956. *Money, Interest, and Prices*. Evanston: Row, Peterson.

————, 1972. *Studies in Monetary Economics*. New York: Harper & Row.

Payer, Cheryl, 1974. *The Debt Trap: The International Monetary Fund and the Third World*. New York: Monthly Review Press.

Payne, James L., 1970. *The American Threat*. Chicago: Markham.

Peattie, Lisa, 1968. *The View From the Barrio*. Ann Arbor: University of Michigan Press.

Peterson, Paul, and J.D. Greenstone, 1976. Two competing models of the policy-making process. In Willis Hawley et al., *Theoretical Perspectives on Urban Politics*. Englewood Cliffs, N.J.: Prentice-Hall.

Phelps, Edmund S., et al., 1970. *Micro-economic Foundations of Employment and Inflation Theory*. New York: W.W. Norton.

Phillips, A.W., 1954. Stabilization policy in a closed economy. *Economic Journal*, 64: 290–323.

Phillips, Almarin, 1960. A theory of interfirm organization. *Quarterly Journal of Economics*, 74: 602–613.

Pigou, A.C., 1952. *Keynes's "General Theory", a Retrospective View*. London: Macmillan.

Piven, Frances, and R. Cloward, 1971. *Regulating the Poor*. New York: Random House.

_____, 1979. *Poor People's Movements. Why They Succeed, How They Fail*. New York: Random House.

Polsby, Nelson, 1963. *Community Power and Political Theory*. 2d ed., 1980. New Haven: Yale University Press.

Polsky, Ned, 1967. *Hustlers, Beats, and Others*. Chicago: Aldine.

Popper, Karl, 1945. *The Open Society and Its Enemies*. 5th rev. ed., 1966. Princeton: Princeton University Press.

_____, 1963. *Conjectures and Refutations*. New York: Harper & Row.

_____, 1970. Normal science and its dangers. In Imre Lakatos and A. Musgrave, eds., *Criticism and the Growth of Knowledge*. Cambridge: Cambridge University Press, pp. 51–58.

_____, 1972. *Objective Knowledge*. London: Oxford University Press.

Portes, Alejandro, 1972. Rationality in the slum: an essay in interpretive sociology. *Comparative Studies in Society and History*, 14: 268–286.

Possony, Stefan, 1967. Mao's strategic initiative of 1965 and the U.S. response. *Orbis*, 11 (no. 1): 149–181.

Poulantzas, Nicos, 1973. *Political Power and Social Classes*. London: New Left Books.

Pressman, Jeffrey, and Aaron Wildavsky, 1973. *Implementation* . . . Berkeley: University of California Press.

Prewitt, Kenneth, 1970. *Recruitment of Political Leaders: A Study of Citizen Politics*. Indianapolis: Bobbs-Merrill.

_____, and A. Stone, 1973. *The Ruling Elites*. New York: Harper & Row.

Quade, E.S., ed., 1966. *Analysis For Military Decisions*. Chicago: Rand McNally.

Quandt, Richard, 1956. A probabilistic theory of consumer behavior. *Quarterly Journal of Economics*. 70: 507–536.

Radcliffe-Brown, A.R., 1922. *The Andaman Islanders*. New York: Free Press reprint, 1948.

_____, 1957. *A Natural Science of Society*. New York: Free Press.

Rainwater, Lee, 1967. The Lessons of Pruitt-Igoe. *Public Interest* (no. 8): 116–126.

_____, and W. Yancey, 1966. Black families and the White House. Reprinted in Norman Denzin, ed., 1973. *The Values of Social Science*. New Brunswick, N.J.: Transaction Books.

Rapoport, Amnon, 1967. Optimum policies for the Prisoner's Dilemma. *Psychological Review*, 74: 136–148.

Rapoport, Anatol, 1964. *Strategy and Conscience*. New York: Harper & Row.

_____, and A. Chammah, 1965. *Prisoner's Dilemma*. Ann Arbor: University of Michigan Press.

Rapoport, Roger, and L.J. Kirshbaum, 1969. *Is The Library Burning?* New York: Random House.

Raskin, Marcus, 1974. *Notes on the Old System*. New York: McKay.

Rattinger, Hans, 1974. *Armaments and Tension*. Peace Science Society Papers no. 22.

—————— , 1975. Rüstung in Europa: aufrüstung, wettrüsten, und andere erklärungen. *Österreichische Zeitschrift für Politikwissenschaft*, pp. 231-250.

Ravetz, Jerome, 1971. *Scientific Knowledge and Its Social Problems*. New York: Oxford University Press.

Redfield, Robert, 1960. *The Little Community*. Chicago: University of Chicago Press.

Richardson, G.B., 1959. Equilibrium, expectations, and information. *Economic Journal*, 69: 223-237.

Riesman, David, et al., 1950. *The Lonely Crowd*. New Haven: Yale University Press.

Riker, William, 1962. *The Theory of Political Coalitions*. New Haven: Yale University Press.

—————— , and Peter Ordeshook, 1973. *An Introduction to Positive Political Theory*. Englewood Cliffs, N.J.: Prentice-Hall.

Robbins, Lionel, 1935. *An Essay on the Nature and Significance of Economic Science*. 2d ed. London: Macmillan.

Robertson, D.H., 1951. *Utility and All That*. London: Allen & Unwin.

Robinson, Juan, 1951, *Collected Papers*, Vol. 1. New York: Kelley.

—————— , 1952. *The Rate of Interest and Other Essays*. New York: Macmillan.

—————— , 1953. Imperfect competition revisited. *Economic Journal*, 63. 579-593.

—————— , 1965. *Collected Economic Papers*, Vol. 3. Oxford: Blackwell.

—————— , 1971. *Economic Heresies*. New York: Basic Books.

—————— , 1972. The second crisis of economic theory. *American Economic Review*, 62 (no. 2): 1-10.

Röpke, Wilhelm, 1937. *Economics of the Free Society*, tr. P. Boarman. Chicago: Regnery, 1963.

—————— , 1942. *The Social Crisis of Our Time*. Chicago: University of Chicago Press, 1950.

Rosdolsky, Roman, 1968. *Zur Entstehungsgeschichte des Marx'schen "Kapital"*. Frankfurt: Europäische Verlagsanstalt.

Rose, Arnold, 1967. *The Power Structure*. New York: Oxford University Press.

Rosenbaum, Walter, 1973. *The Politics of Environmental Concern*. New York: Praeger.

Rosenthal, Robert, 1966. *Experimenter Effects in Behavioral Research*. New York: Appleton-Century-Crofts.

Rostow, W.W., 1952. A historian's perspective on modern economic theory. *American Economic Review*, 42 (no. 2): 16-29.

—————— , 1960a. The problem of achieving and maintaining a high rate of economic growth. *American Economic Review*, 50 (no. 2): 106-118.

—————— , 1960b. *The Stages of Economic Growth*. Cambridge: Cambridge University Press.

—————— , 1971. *Politics and the Stages of Growth*. Cambridge: Cambridge University Press.

444   Science and Ideology in the Policy Sciences

_____ , 1977. Balance of power and balance of trade. *Society*, 14 (no. 2): 16–21.
Rothbard, Murray, 1960. Comments. *Quarterly Journal of Economics*, 74: 659–665.
Rothschild, K., 1947. Price theory and oligopoly. *Economic Journal*, 57: 299–320.
Rubington, Earl, and Martin Weinberg, eds., *Deviance: The Interactionist Perspective*. New York: Macmillan.
Rustin, Bayard, 1976. *Strategies For Freedom*. New York: Columbia University Press.
Ryan, William, 1976. *Blaming the Victim*. New York: Random House.
Sale, Kirkpatrick, 1973. *SDS*. New York: Random House.
Samuelson, Paul, 1939. Interactions between the multiplier analysis and the principle of acceleration. *Review of Economics and Statistics*, 21: 75–78.
_____ , 1948. *Economics*. New York: McGraw-Hill.
_____ , 1973a. *Economics*, 9th ed. New York: McGraw-Hill.
_____ , ed., 1973b. *Readings in Economics*. New York: McGraw-Hill.
Sax, Joseph, 1971. *Defending the Environment*. New York: Alfred A. Knopf.
Schattschneider, E.F., 1960. *The Semi-sovereign People*. New York: Holt, Rinehart, & Winston.
Schelling, Thomas, 1960. *The Strategy of Conflict*. Cambridge, Mass.: Harvard University Press.
_____ , 1966. *Arms and Influence*. New Haven: Yale University Press.
Schick, Jack, 1971. *The Berlin Crisis, 1958–1962*. Philadelphia: University of Pennsylvania Press.
Schlesinger, James, and Almarin Phillips, 1959. The ebb tide of capitalism? Schumpeter's prophecy re-examined. *Quarterly Journal of Economics*, 73: 448–465.
Schoeck, Helmut, and James Wiggins, eds., 1960. *Scientism and Values*. Princeton, N.J.: Van Nostrand.
Schon, Donald, 1970. The blindness system. *Public Interest* (18): 25–38.
Schultz, Harry, 1970. *What the Prudent Investor Should Know About Switzerland*. New Rochelle, N.Y.: Arlington House.
Schultz, Klaus, 1962. *Berlin Zwischen Freiheit und Diktatur*. Berlin: Staneck.
Schultz, Theodore W., 1945. *Agriculture in an Unstable Economy*. New York: McGraw-Hill.
_____ , et al., 1953. *Is the U.S. neglecting land reform in its foreign policy?* Chicago: University of Chicago Round Table no. 811.
_____ , 1971. *Investment in Human Capital*. New York: Free Press.
Schumacher, E.F., 1973. *Small Is Beautiful*. New York: Harper & Row.
Schumpeter, Joseph, 1942. *Capitalism, Socialism, and Democracy*. 2d. ed., 1947. New York: Harper & Row.
_____ , 1949. Science and ideology. *American Economic Review*, 39 (no. 2): 345–359.
_____ , 1951 (1919). *Imperialism and Social Classes*. New York: Kelley.
_____ , 1954. *History of Economic Analysis*. New York: Oxford.

Schurmann, Franz, 1974. *The Logic of World Power*. New York: Random House.

Schwartz, Jesse, ed., 1977. *The Subtle Anatomy of Capitalism*. Santa Monica: Goodyear.

Scitovsky, Tibor, 1942. A reconsideration of the theory of tariffs. *Review of Economic Studies*, 9: 89–110.

Scull, Andrew, 1976. The decarceration of the mentally ill: a critical view. *Politics and Society*, 6 (no. 2): 173–212.

Selznick, David, 1950. *TVA and the Grass Roots*. Berkeley: University of California Press.

————, 1957. *Leadership in Administration*. Evanston, Ill.: Row, Peterson.

Senghaas, Dieter, 1972. *Aufrüstung Durch Rüstungskontrolle*. Stuttgart: Kohlhammer.

————, 1973. Rüstungsdynamik als restriktive bedungung. *Österreichische Zeitschrift für Politikwissenschaft*, pp. 5–17.

Shackle, G.L.S., 1955. *Uncertainty in Economics, and Other Reflections*. Cambridge: Cambridge University Press.

————, 1968. *Expectations, Investment, and Income*. Oxford: Oxford University Press.

Shapiro, Nina, 1976. The neoclassical theory of the firm, *Review of Radical Political Economics*, 8 (no. 4): 17–29.

Shefter, Martin, 1976. The emergence of the political machine: an alternative view. In Willis Hawley, et al., *Theoretical Perspectives in Urban Politics*. Englewood Cliffs, N.J.: Prentice-Hall.

————, 1977. New York City's fiscal crisis: the politics of inflation and retrenchment. *Public Interest* (no. 48): 98–127.

Shepherd, W.G., 1970. *Market Power and Economic Welfare*. New York: Random House.

Sherman, Howard, 1976. *Stagflation*. New York: Harper & Row.

————, 1979. A Marxist theory of the business cycle. *Review of Radical Political Economics*, 11 (no. 1): 1–23.

Shibutani, Tamotsu, 1964. The sentimental basis of group solidarity. *Sociological Inquiry*, 34 (no. 2): 144–155.

Shubik, Martin, 1954. Information, risk, ignorance, and indeterminacy. *Quarterly Journal of Economics*, 68: 629–640.

————, 1959. *Strategy and Market Structure*. New York: Wiley.

————, ed., 1964. *Game Theory and Related Approaches to Social Behavior*. New York: Wiley.

Shulman, Marshall, 1963. *Stalin's Foreign Policy Reappraised*. Cambridge, Mass.: Harvard University Press.

Sievers, Allen, 1964. *Revolution, Evolution, and the Economic Order*. Englewood Cliffs, N.J.: Prentice-Hall.

Simon, Herbert, 1947. *Administrative Behavior*. New York: Macmillan.

————, 1957. *Models of Man*. New York: Wiley.

Simons, Henry, 1948. *Economic Policy for a Free Society*. Chicago: University of Chicago Press.

Skinner, B.F., 1935. The generic nature of the concepts of stimulus and response. Reprinted in *Cumulative Record*. New York: Appleton-Century, 1959.

————, 1938. *The Behavior of Organisms*. New York: Appleton-Century.

Slater, Jerome, 1967. *The OAS and United States Foreign Policy*. Columbus: Ohio State University Press.

————, 1970. *Intervention and Negotiation*. New York: Harper & Row.

Smith, David N., 1974. *Who Rules the Universities?* New York: Monthly Review Press.

Smith, Jean E., 1963. *The Defense of Berlin*. Baltimore: Johns Hopkins University Press.

Snyder, Glenn H., 1971. Prisoner's Dilemma and Chicken models in international politics. *International Studies Quarterly*, 15 (no. 1): 66–103.

————, 1972. Crisis bargaining. In Charles Hermann, ed., *International Crises: Insights From Behavioral Research*. New York: Free Press.

————, and P. Diesing, 1977. *Nations in Conflict: Bargaining, Decision-making, and System Structure in International Crises*. Princeton: N.J.: Princeton University Press.

Solow, Robert, 1971. The state of economics: discussion. *American Economic Review*, 61 (no. 2): 63–65.

Speier, Hans, 1961. *Divided Berlin: The Anatomy of Soviet Political Blackmail*. New York: Praeger.

Spinner, Helmut, 1974. *Pluralismus Als Erkenntnismodell*. Frankfurt: Suhrkamp.

Sraffa, Piero, 1926. The law of returns under competitive conditions. *Economic Journal*, 36: 535–550.

Stack, Carol, 1974. *All Our Kin*. New York: Harper & Row.

Stein, Jerome, ed., 1976. *Monetarism*. Amsterdam: North-Holland.

Stigler, George, 1946. *The Theory of Price*. New York: Macmillan.

————, 1959. The politics of political economists. *Quarterly Journal of Economics*, 73: 522–532.

————, 1976. The Xistence of X-efficiency. *American Economic Review*, 66 (no. 1): 522–531.

Stojanovic, S., 1973. *Between Ideals and Reality*. New York: Oxford University Press.

Stoneman, William, 1979. *A History of the Economic Analysis of the Great Depression in America*. New York: Garland.

Stretton, Hugh, 1969. *The Political Sciences*. New York: Basic Books.

Sudman, Seymour, and Norman Bradburn, 1974. *Response Effects in Surveys*. Chicago: Aldine.

Suttles, Gerald, 1968. *The Social Order of the Slum*. Chicago: University of Chicago Press.

Sztompka, Piotr, 1974. *System and Function*. New York: Academic Press.

Tanter, Raymond, 1974. *Modelling and Managing International Conflicts: The Berlin Crises*. Beverly Hills, Calif.: Sage.

Tarshis, Lorie, 1967. *Modern Economics*. New York: Houghton Mifflin.

Thompson, James Clay, 1980. *Rolling Thunder: Understanding Policy and Program Failure*. Chapel Hill: University of North Carolina Press.

Thurow, Lester, 1970. *Investment in Human Capital*. Los Angeles: Wadsworth.

————, 1980. *The Zero-Sum Society*. New York: Basic books.

Tobin, James, 1952. Asset holdings and spending decisions. *American Economic Review*, 42: 109–123.

————, 1958. Liquidity preference as behavior toward risk. *Review of Economic Studies*, 25: 65–86. Reprinted in R. Thorne, ed., *Monetary Theory and Policy*. New York: Random House; and in Tobin, 1971.

————, 1961. Money, capital, and other stores of value. *American Economic Review*, 51 (no. 2): 26–37. Reprinted in Tobin, 1971.

————, 1965. The monetary interpretation of history. *American Economic Review*, 55 (no. 3): 464–485. Reprinted in Tobin, 1971.

————, 1971. *Essays in Economics*, Vol. 1. Chicago: Markham.

————, 1972a. Inflation and unemployment. *American Economic Review*, 65 (no. 2): 1–16.

————, 1972b. Friedman's theoretical framework. *Journal of Political Economy*, 80: 852–863.

————, 1975. Keynesian models of recession and depression. *American Economic Review*, 65 (no. 2): 195–202.

————, and Willem Buiter, 1974. *Long-run Effects of Fiscal and Monetary Policy on Aggregate Demand*. Cowles Paper no. 384. Reprinted in Stein, 1976.

Tobin, Richard, 1979. *The Social Gamble*. Lexington, Mass · Lexington Books.

Triffin, Robert, 1940. *Monopolistic Competition and General Equilibrium Theory*. Cambridge, Mass.: Harvard University Press.

Truman, David, 1951. *The Governmental Process*. New York: Alfred A. Knopf.

Tsiang, S.C., 1957. Liquidity preference and loanable funds theories, multiplier and velocity analysis: a synthesis. *American Economic Review*, 46 (no. 2): 539–564.

Tucker, Robert C., 1967. The deradicalization of Marxist movements. *American Political Science Review*, 61: 343–358.

Tullock, Gordon, 1967. *Toward a Mathematics of Politics*. Ann Arbor, Mich.: University of Michigan Press.

Turgeon, Lynn, 1980. *The Advanced Capitalist System*. White Plains, N.Y.: M.E. Sharpe.

Tustin, Arnold, 1953. *The Mechanism of Economic Systems*. Cambridge, Mass.: Harvard University Press.

Ulam, Adam, 1968. *Expansion and Coexistence: The History of Soviet Foreign Policy, 1917–1967*. New York: Praeger.

Vidich, Arthur, and J. Bensman, 1958. *Small Town in Mass Society*. Princeton: Princeton University Press.

Vinacke, W.E., 1959. Sex roles in a three-person game. *Sociometry*, 22: 343–360.

Viner, Jacob, 1937. Mr. Keynes on the causes of unemployment. *Quarterly Journal of Economics*, 51: 147–167.

Voegelin, Eric, 1952. *The New Science of Politics*. Chicago: University of Chicago Press.

Wachter, Michael, 1976. Some problems in wage stabilization. *American Economic* Review, 66 (no. 2): 65–71.

Wallerstein, Immanuel, 1979. *The Capitalist World-economy*. New York: Cambridge University Press.

Walton, Richard, and R. McKersie, 1965. *A Behavioral Theory of Labor Negotiations*. New York: McGraw-Hill.

Wax, Rosalie, 1975. Review of Wuebben, et al., *The Experiment as a Social Occasion. Society*, 13 (no. 1): 88.

Weidenbaum, Murray, and Linda Rockwood, 1977. Corporate planning vs. government planning. *Public Interest* (no. 46): 59–72.

Weil, R.L., 1966. The n-person Prisoner's Dilemma. *Behavioral Science*, 11: 227–233.

Weinstein, James, 1968. *The Corporate Ideal in the Liberal State, 1900–1918*. Boston: Beacon Press.

Weintraub, Sidney, et al., 1977. *Keynes, Keynesians, and Monetarists*. Philadelphia: University of Pennsylvania Press.

Welch, William, 1971. Soviet expansionism and its assessment. *Journal of Conflict Resolution*, 15 (no. 3): 317–328.

Wenders, John T., 1972. What is profit maximization? *Journal of Economic Issues*, 6 (no. 2): 61–66.

Wilber, Charles K., 1979. Empirical verifiction and theory selection: the Keynesian-monetarist debate. *Journal of Economic Issues*, 13 (no. 4): 973–982.

Wildavsky, Aaron, 1964. *Leadership in a Small Town*. Totowa, N.J.: Bedminster.

————, 1967. The political economy of efficiency. *Public Interest* (no. 8): 30–44.

————, 1975a. The richest boy in Poltava. *Society* (Nov. 1975): 49–56.

————, 1975b, ed. *Perspectives on the Presidency*. Boston: Little, Brown.

Wilensky, Harold, 1967. *Organizational Intelligence*. New York: Basic Books.

————, 1975. *The Welfare State and Equality*. Berkeley: University of California Press.

Williams, Philip, 1976. *Crisis Management*. New York: Wiley.

Williamson, Oliver, 1970. *Corporate Control and Business Behavior*. Englewood Cliffs, N.J.: Prentice-Hall.

Wilson, J.Q., 1969. The mayors vs. the cities. *Public Interest* (no. 16): 25–40.

————, 1975. *Thinking About Crime*. New York: Basic Books.

————— , 1977. Thinking about thinking about crime. *Society*, 14 (no. 3): 10ff.

Wirt, Fred, 1974. *Power in the City*. Berkeley: University of California Press.

Wittfogel, Karl, 1957. *Oriental Despotism*. New Haven: Yale University Press.

Wohlstetter, Albert, 1959. The delicate balance of terror. *Foreign Affairs*. Reprinted in Charles Hitch and Roland McKean, eds., 1965. *The Economics of Defense in the Nuclear Age*. Cambridge, Mass.: Harvard University Press, pp. 333–357.

————— , 1974. Is there a strategic arms race? *Foreign Policy* (no. 15): 3–20; (no. 16): 48–81.

Wolfe, Alan, 1973. *The Seamy Side of Democracy*. New York: McKay.

————— , 1977. *The Limits of Legitimacy*. New York: Free Press.

Wright, Erik Olin, 1978. *Class, Crisis, and the State*. London: New Left Books, verso edition.

Wuebben, Paul, et al., 1974. *The Experiment as a Social Occasion*. Berkeley: Glendessary Press.

Yeager, Leland B., 1954. Some questions about growth economics. *American Economic Review*, 44 (no. 1): 53–66.

Zeitlin, Maurice, 1970. *Revolutionary Politics and the Cuban Working Class*. 2d. ed. New York: Harper & Row.

Zeuthen, Fred, 1930. *Problems of Monopoly and Economic Warfare*. London: Routledge and Kegan Paul.

Zinn, Howard, 1965. *SNCC: The New Abolitionists*. Boston: Beacon Press.

Index

450